MORRIS E BODRICK
P.O. BOX 87535
HOUGHTON 2041
SOUTH AFRICA

The Roots of
Black South Africa

David Hammond-Tooke

The Roots of
Black South Africa

Jonathan Ball Publishers
Johannesburg

For
Graeme, Rick, Jill, Jan
and the
Grandchildren

All rights reserved. No part of this publication may be reproduced,
stored in a retrieval system, or transmitted in any form or by any means, electronic,
mechanical, photocopying, or otherwise, without the prior permission of the publisher.

© W.D. Hammond-Tooke, 1993
Illustrations – Please refer to Acknowledgements page

Published in 1993 by
Jonathan Ball Publishers (Pty) Ltd
P O Box 2105
Parklands 2121

ISBN 1 86842 002 7

Endpapers The dance of the Xhosa *abakwetha* is watched by an appreciative crowd of kin and neighbours. This is the one occasion on which the initiates appear formally in public. (Alice Martens)

Frontispiece A Xhosa initiate during a pause in his galvanic, stamping dance. His skirt, made of palm leaves, is about six metres long and wound in layers around the waist. (Alice Martens)

Design by Michael Barnett, Johannesburg
Typesetting and reproduction by Book Productions, Pretoria
Printed and bound by Colorcraft, Hong Kong

Contents

	Preface	7
	Transformations on a Theme	11
Chapter 1	Origins and Classification	23
Chapter 2	Land, Cattle and Settlement	45
Chapter 3	Chiefs, Councillors and Commoners	65
Chapter 4	The Settlement of Disputes	89
Chapter 5	The Importance of Kin	101
Chapter 6	The Centrality of Marriage	117
Chapter 7	Growing Up	131
Chapter 8	In the Shadow of the Ancestors	149
Chapter 9	Witchcraft, Sorcery and Pollution	169
Chapter 10	The Search for Health	185
Chapter 11	Material Culture	199
	Epilogue	215
	References	220
	Suggestions for Further Reading	222
	Index	223

ACKNOWLEDGEMENTS

GRATEFUL acknowledgement is made to the following publishers for permission to make use of longish quotations from works published by them: C. Hurst & Co., for A. I. Berglund, *Zulu Thought-patterns and Symbolism*. London: 1976, on p. 154; David Philip, for R.R. Inskeep, *The Peopling of Southern Africa*. Cape Town: 1978, on p. 27; J. L. van Schaik, for H.O. Mönnig, *The Pedi*. Pretoria: 1967, on p. 57 and 190; The Government Printer, for N.J. van Warmelo and W.D.M. Phophi, *Venda Law*: part 1. Pretoria: 1948, on pp. 89 and 159 (permission granted under Government Printer's Copyright Authority 9612 dated 6 May 1993); Oxford University Press, for J.D. and E.J. Krige, *The Realm of a Rain-queen*. London: 1943, on pp. 60–61 and 129; for M. Hunter, *Reaction to Conquest*. London 1936, on pp. 114, 124 and 189; and for I. Schapera, *Praise Poems of Tswana Chiefs*. London: 1965, on p. 73; Penguin Books, for R. Oliver and J.D. Fage, *A Short History of Africa*. London: 1962, on p. 24; Routledge and Kegan Paul, for W.D. Hammond-Tooke, ed., *The Bantu-speaking Peoples of Southern Africa*. London: 1974, on pp. 69 (Van Warmelo), 50 (Sansom), 125 and 133 (Van der Vliet), and 205 and 209 (Shaw); and for A. Kuper, *Wives for Cattle*. London: 1982, on p. 127; University of Natal Press, for A. Delegorgue (translated by Fleur Webb, Introduction by S.J. Alexander and C. de B. Webb), *Travels in Southern Africa (Voyage dans l'Afrique Australe*, 1848). Pietermaritzburg: 1990, on p. 84; Witwatersrand University Press, for E.J. Krige, 'A Lovedu prayer', *African Studies* 33, 1974, on p. 167; and for H. Kuckertz, 'Symbol and authority in Mpondo ancestor religion', *African Studies* 42, 1983, on p. 164; A.C. Watts for I. Schapera, *Government and Politics in Tribal Society*. London: 1956, on p. 70.

Grateful thanks are also due to the following for permission to reproduce illustrations: A. Martens and J. Broster, *African Elegance* (Purnell, 1978), endpapers, frontispiece, pp. 179, 183; Africana Library, pp. 11, 15, 47, 50, 53, 54, 64, 67, 69, 75, 82, 83, 84, 86, 88, 99, 100, 103, 109, 122, 125, 128, 139, 187, 200, 202, 206; H. Kuckertz, pp. 17, 44, 92, 93, 148, 157; Anitra Nettleton, pp. 18, 40, 77, 138, 144, 145, 156; Horst Röntsch, pp. 80, 135; Greg Marinovich, pp. 81, 130, 142, 143, 156; A.G. Schutte, pp. 146, 147; J. Morris and B. Levitan, *South African Tribal Life Today* (College Press, 1986), pp. 20, 26/7, 60, 76/7, 112, 168, 183, 195; South African Museum, pp. 23, 160/1, 176/7; Department of Archaeology, University of the Witwatersrand, pp. 25, 29, 30, 31, 33, 34, 35, 37; Department of Art History, University of the Witwatersrand, pp. 28, 132, 136; McGregor Museum, Kimberley, pp. 49, 185; H. Oppenheimer (Brenthurst Collection) as published in *Art and Ambiguity* (Johannesburg Art Gallery), pp. 52, 198, 199, 203, 205, 208, 209; Patricia Davison, *Lobedu Material Culture*, Annals of the South African Museum vol. 92, 1984, pp. 58, 90, 204, 206, 212; H. Ashton, *The Basuto* (Oxford University Press, 1952) pp. 62, 96, 133, 134, 137; E.M. Shaw and N.J. van Warmelo, *The Material Culture of the Cape Nguni* part 4, Annnals of the South African Museum vol. 58, 1988, pp. 66, 71, 99, 127, 210; Barbara Tyrell, *The Tribal Peoples of Southern Africa* (Books of Africa, 1968), pp. 68, 85, 120/1, 128; N.J. van Warmelo and W.M.D. Phophi, *Venda Law* parts 1–4 (Government Printer, 1948–9) (reproduced under Government Printer Copyright Authority 9612 dated 6 May 1993), pp. 94, 111, 113, 115, 191, 204; W.D. Hammond-Tooke, *Bhaca Society* (Oxford University Press, 1962), p. 116, *Boundaries and Belief* (Witwatersrand University Press, 1981), pp. 141, 147, 150; Aubrey Elliott, *Sons of Zulu* (Collins, 1978), pp. 123, 214; Rhoda Levinsohn, *Art and Craft in Southern Africa* (Delta, 1984), pp. 145, 189, 206, 207; Johannesburg Art Gallery, p. 200; A. Kuper, *Wives for Cattle* (Routledge and Kegan Paul, 1982), p. 57.

Although every effort has been made to trace copyright holders, this has not always been possible. Should any infringement have occurred, the author and publisher apologise and undertake to amend these omissions in the event of a reprint.

I should like to express my more personal thanks to the following persons who were involved in the book's production: Jonathan Ball, for talking me into writing the book in the first place, and who suggested the title; Francine Blum, production manager, who expertly guided its production, Frances Perryer, who was a supportive and meticulous editor, and, certainly not least, Michael Barnett. The book, as a physical object, is testimony to his artistry and designing skills. Naomi Musiker did the index.

Finally, two valued collegues at the University of the Witwatersrand, Noel Garson and Carolyn Hamilton, read parts of the manuscript and made useful suggestions.

I thank them all
David Hammond-Tooke

PREFACE

IN 1895 the great missionary ethnographer of the Tsonga-speaking peoples, Henri Alexandre Junod, was visited by Lord Bryce, Regius Professor of Civil Law at Oxford University, then gathering material for his *Impressions of South Africa* (1897). The scene was Lourenço Marques, where Junod, head of the Swiss Romande Mission, had his headquarters. Bryce had become intrigued by the life of the indigenous peoples he had met on his travels and had made pleas for what he, as a typical product of the nineteenth century, described as the 'scientific' study of their cultures. A remark by Bryce during one of the two men's many conversations made such an impression on Junod that he recorded it in the Introduction to his monumental study of the Tsonga, *The Life of a South African Tribe*: 'How thankful should we be,' said Bryce, 'we men of the nineteenth century, if a Roman had taken the trouble fully to investigate the habits of our Celtic forefathers! This work has not been done, and we shall always remain ignorant of things which would have interested us so much!'

This comment resulted directly in Junod's switch from his 'favourite pastime' of entomology to ethnography and his subsequent fame as a pioneer of South African anthropology. The fortuitous (and unfortunate) conjunction between natural science and the study of culture was typical of late nineteenth century thought. The great advances made by science in general, but particularly its contribution to what was universally conceived of as evolution-driven 'progress', made its inductivist and positivist approach to knowledge the only acceptable one. From this point of view, the study of man and his works could only be advanced by the same methods as were applied to the phenomena of nature. This 'scientific' approach to cultures had potentially unfortunate consequences. People tended to be treated as dehumanised objects, rather like butterflies pinned on a display board, and their cultures and behaviour patterns forced into often highly speculative classificatory systems with strong determinist implications. As far as Junod himself was concerned, however, the warmth, humour and obvious intelligence of his Tsonga informants steered him clear, for much of the time, of these excesses. He describes the Tsonga with sympathy and compassion, and his monograph remains a celebration of a way of life that has since changed fundamentally in many ways. Unlike Bryce's Celts, the Tsonga had found their Roman!

What has also changed fundamentally since Junod's time is the approach of anthropology, although there is much progress still to be made. No longer do anthropologists believe in the possibility of a value-free, distanced, relationship between themselves and those whom they study. Observer and observed share a common humanity, and a common mental equipment. What is sought now is *understanding* – and this, in essence, derives from insights into the *meanings* that people give to their actions. It is in this spirit that *The Roots of Black South Africa* is written.

The time would seem right for a book that attempts to record for future generations the life-ways of the ancestors of the great majority of present-day South Africans. Elsewhere in Africa interest in cultural roots has been prominent, especially in Francophone Africa where the powerful concept of *négritude* flourished in the 1940s and 50s. Both here and in the United States there has been a great deal of interest in roots, as Haley's book attests. This interest has not been so evident in the ex-colonies of the British Empire, and there is perhaps a good reason for this. France conceived of her colonies as integral parts of the mother country, and actively encouraged the assimilation by her colonial subjects of French language and culture. Not so in the British colonies. Here the emphasis was on the Dual Mandate and the guiding of the colonies to some unspecified (but far off) goal of independence. District officers were expected to use the local vernacular and there was no official policy of absorption, indeed a rigid segregation was universal in the Empire.

How much more is this true of South Africa, where the official apartheid policy rigidly separated not only black and white but also ethnic group from ethnic group. The politically motivated emphasis on cultural differences, coupled with the refusal to admit blacks to the full benefits of western civilisation, lay at the very heart of the system. It is no wonder that ethnicity was rejected by most contemporary black political movements, and with it an interest in traditional cultures.

It is to be hoped that the ending of legalised apartheid and the full participation of all South Africa's people in the New South Africa will result, on the part of black South Africans, in a more relaxed and self-confident interest in and understanding of the black South African past, of the two thousand years during which their forebears gained control over the often harsh southern landscapes through the design of cultures that, however poor in material possessions and sophisticated technology, yet were built firmly on principles of order, morality and human decency. This book aims to present and explain the customs of the past, especially the logic underpinning those customs which seem on the surface to be strange or irrational, thus demystifying them. Behind the differences lies our common humanity. The book also seeks to show that, despite important differences in detail, a common culture was possessed by the indigenous Bantu-speaking communities, which itself should work towards healing the wounds caused by the (often artificially created) present ethnic divisions. It is thus dedicated to the youth of the townships and countryside, in the spirit that activated Lord Bryce's plea to Henri Junod, especially to those who realise that self-confidence in the present stems from a sense of personal worth that is rooted in the full acceptance of the past.

NOTE ON HISTORY

This book is not a history, in the sense of a narrative that traces change through time. It seeks, rather, to describe a way of life at a particular point in history – defined as 'pre-contact' or 'pre-colonial'. This poses problems, as 'history' depends essentially on *written* accounts of eye-witnesses and other contemporaries of the period, documentation that is obviously lacking for pre-contact South Africa. An attempt is made to overcome this dilemma by conceiving the period broadly as that between 1750 and 1850 and utilising the writings and drawings of travellers, missionaries and others who recorded a way of life then comparatively unchanged by western influences. Such men as Le Vaillant, Barrow, Burchell, Campbell, Livingstone and Moffat have left invaluable eye-witness accounts of the period after about 1795. The earliest writers were privileged to observe the traditional cultures untouched by western civilisation. Extracts from their writings are quoted frequently in these pages. They give a vivid picture of a way of life which is past and their comments are worth pondering, even though they were creatures of their time and place, influenced by philosophical and other preoccupations, even prejudices.

Finally, there are the writings of anthropologists. These all date from the early twentieth century to the present and refer to societies that have been strongly influenced by the west for periods sometimes going back a hundred and fifty years or more. Great changes have occurred and it is obvious that one cannot take contemporary rural societies and cultures as being identical to those of these same societies before contact. Yet it is true that *some* customs, values, attitudes and ways of life have persisted to the present, and it is argued that these can be used to throw light on the past, provided that they are used with extreme caution. In this account recourse is sometimes had to this type of evidence.

In addition, some objects of material culture have survived for us today: in such cases use has been made of modern anthropological research and museum specimens to fill the gaps and shed light. The same is true for the illustrations, all of which are *ipso facto* post-contact. This is done in full awareness of the dangers of extrapolating back from a later period to an earlier one: one works within the limits of one's material.

For readers interested in the vital question of the impact of colonialism on these societies, and on changes in the centuries before 1800, there is a rich and rapidly expanding literature, much of which is in scholarly journals. There are, however, a few broad syntheses, notably those of Wilson and Thompson, *The Oxford History of South Africa*, two vols, Oxford, 1964 and 1971, and P. Maylem, *A History of the African People of South Africa: From the Early Iron Age to the 1970s*, Cape Town, 1986. Other accessible references are: the Reader's Digest *Illustrated History of Southern Africa* (1989); Cameron and Spies (eds) *An Illustrated History of South Africa* (Johannesburg, 1986) and J.D. Omer-Cooper, *The Zulu Aftermath* (London, 1966). Jeff Peires's *The Dead Will Arise: Nongqawuse and the great Xhosa Cattle-killing of 1856–7* (Johannesburg, 1989) is a particularly distinguished study of a major episode in South Nguni history.

THE ROOTS OF BLACK SOUTH AFRICA

Transformations on a Theme

THIS BOOK seeks to present what is known of the societies and cultures of the ancestors of black South Africans during the centuries immediately before the arrival of white settlers. It has been written, firstly, because of the intrinsic interest of the subject. A reconstruction of the indigenous past surely leads to a greater appreciation of the present, in the same way as the record of the life of classical or medieval times enriches our knowledge and understanding of contemporary Europe. It may be true that 'The past is another country. They do things differently there,' but this is not the whole story. Things may have been done differently, but there is a sense in which the worldview of present-day Europe resonates with echoes of the past. Western culture is still informed by the critical cast of Greek thought, the logical categories of Roman law and the moral and religious teachings of the fathers of medieval and sixteenth century Christendom. Anyone who has read the letters and meditations of classical authors must be struck by the essential *modernity* of their thought and expression, in the same way as western observers at an African court case recognise the forensic skills of the interlocutors and the search for the 'reasonable man'. Here there has undoubtedly been continuity in the fundamentals of our common humanity, and it is important, for South Africans in particular, to recognise the essential identity of all men, past and present, despite the often differing premises on which they base their thinking. Some of the beliefs we shall meet in this book are remarkably similar to those held in Europe a mere three hundred years ago.

Secondly, the book was written to try to demonstrate the essential unity of the Southern Bantu congeries of peoples. Despite the efforts of succeeding white governments to stress differences between the various groups, there is a sense in which all these peoples had a common culture. The differences, which were undoubtedly there (and which add to the richness of the tradition) were, in fact, transformations on a theme. By the end of the first millennium the movement onto the highveld of certain groups set in motion the series of modifications which resulted in the broad cultural division between the Nguni, Tsonga, Sotho and Venda, members of the four large language groups to which present-day black South Africans belong. Essentially the causes of these divergencies (it will be argued) were environmental, in the broadest sense. This is not, of course, to deny the importance of historical factors, for the Southern Bantu past was not a static one and there was a continual movement of groups throughout the region that, with its resulting conflicts, subjugations and cultural borrowings, makes the detailed unravelling of cultural influences extremely difficult. There was probably never a 'Golden Age' of

Tswana dwellings, 1834, by C.D. Bell. Note the extension of the roof to form a shady veranda, a response to the heat of the western Transvaal summer, and the reed-fenced courtyard. (Reed fencing subsequently almost everywhere gave way to clay walls.) (Africana Library)

peace and prosperity in southern Africa – any more than this existed anywhere else in the world.

As we shall see in Chapter 1, the origins of Southern Bantu culture lay in the first centuries after the beginning of the Christian era, with the movement into the area south of the Limpopo of iron-working communities who farmed with crops and cattle and, presumably, spoke dialects of the same language. For most of the first thousand years they were confined to the hot savannah bushveld of the northern and eastern Transvaal, where malaria and tsetse fly limited the raising of cattle. One group, however, the early Nguni, managed to move south, probably along the eastern foothills of the Drakensberg, into the present-day Natal, Zululand and, ultimately, the eastern Cape. Here the rich pastures allowed for the great proliferation of cattle-keeping, almost to the detriment of agriculture, that is the most striking feature of Nguni culture. Milk became the staple, and the symbolic importance of cattle permeated every aspect of their society, from marriage to the ancestor cult. Here they also came into contact with San (Bushman) hunters and, in the south, with Khoikhoi (Hottentot) pastoralists, adopting, among other things, the click consonants that characterised the Khoisan languages. Here also they adapted to the more variegated ecology of the east by spreading over the country in scattered settlements. The country they inhabited was devoid of iron or copper deposits and these metals had to be traded from the north, and were highly prized for this reason.

Another group was settled along the coast north and south of the present Maputo. These were the Tsonga, also living in scattered homesteads, tilling their fields, but prevented by the tsetse fly from keeping many cattle. They turned rather to hunting and, especially, fishing, and were the only southern African peoples to eat fish and develop the boat. The rich bushveld environment allowed them a far more varied diet than those further inland. After the establishment of a Portuguese trading settlement at Delagoa Bay in the fifteenth century, the Tsonga acted as middlemen in the ivory trade between the whites and the Zulu to the south of them.

By the end of the first millennium the northern and eastern Transvaal was the home of numerous small chiefdoms all speaking dialects of what was to become the Sotho language family. They, too, had cattle, more than the Tsonga but fewer than the Nguni. They also seem to have placed more emphasis on agriculture and on hunting, and many were actively involved in mining and metal-working. It was the Sotho who scaled the ramparts of the Drakensberg in the early years of the second millennium and established themselves on the plains of the highveld plateau, adapting themselves to the rigours of the cold continental winters. Some of them learned to build in stone (because of the lack of suitable building timber). They also had problems of defence, situated as they were on the rolling grasslands and bushveld flats that stretched out endlessly to the north and west and afforded little in the way of military strongpoints. Exceptions were the Hananwa, on their eyrie in the Blouberg, which rises precipitously from the Pietersberg plain, and the Lovedu on their cycad-covered mountain. The reaction of the Sotho was to build their settlements close together, as is seen in the complex of stone-walled ruins that stretch for kilometres along the foothills of the Magaliesberg and in the catchment area of the Vaal River.

Finally, in about the fourteenth or fifteenth century, certain Shona groups crossed the Limpopo and established themselves over the Sotho populations, such as Ngona and Mbedzi, in the northern Transvaal, centring their domination in the fertile ranges of the Soutpansberg. They called themselves Venda and managed to

Aerial view of part of Mochudi (a Tswana capital) in 1967. Note the compact settlement and the groups of contiguous homesteads, each typically inhabited by sons of a common father. The actual composition of one of these groups in 1934 may be found on page 57.

insulate their chiefdoms from attack, or indeed outside interference. They also extended their influence southwards, over the Sotho chiefdoms they found occupying the lowveld enclave below the Drakensberg, giving rise to the Sotho-Venda group of Lovedu, Kgaga, Thabina, Sekôrôrô and Narene. The Venda language is a mixture of Shona and Sotho; the language and culture of the Sotho-Venda, a mixture of Venda and Sotho. The Venda domination of the original inhabitants led to their unique political arrangements, with non-royals existing as 'tenants' on land owned by the chiefly lines.

The more extreme social and cultural variations that accompanied this geographical separation presumably developed over the five or six hundred years before the colonial era, that is, from about 1100 to 1400. But evidence is lacking for this remote period and we have perforce to work with evidence from the eighteenth and nineteenth centuries in guiding our discussion.

It is the thesis of this book that these variations were caused essentially by adaptations to different environments and that they were logical developments of the possibilities inherent in the original Iron Age culture. This is undoubtedly a gross oversimplification of an extremely complex historical process, and I wish to avoid any naive environmental determinism, but I am persuaded that the approach has a certain plausibility. I have also adopted a 'bird's-eye' view and looked for broad patterns: it has been impossible, within the scope and nature of this work, to examine in detail the historical and cultural minutiae that would demonstrate (or refute) the conclusions arrived at.

Southern African language and political groupings, c. 1900–1950

A South Nguni
B North Nguni
C Swazi
D Tsonga
E Venda
F North Sotho
G Tswana (West Sotho)
H South Sotho
I Ndebele (Zimbabwe)
J Shona
K Konde
L Ndebele (Transvaal)

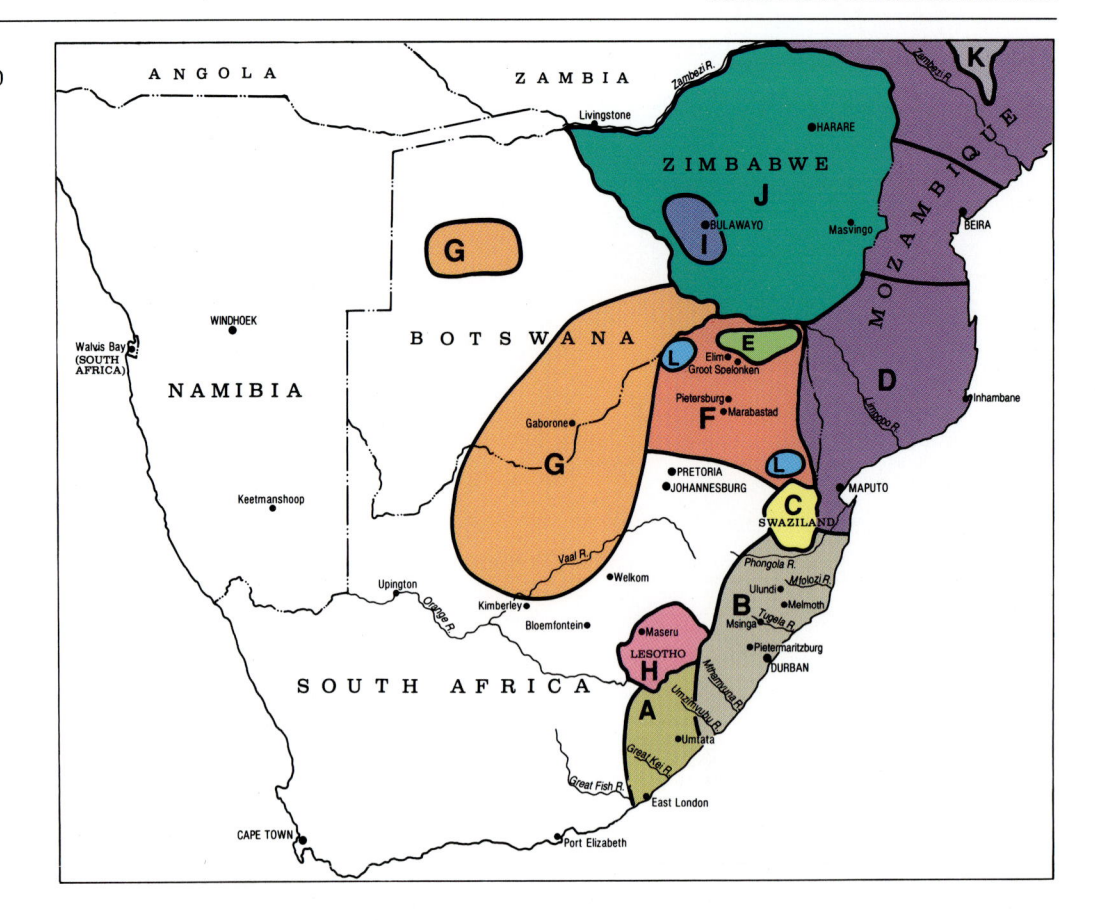

The four major groupings into which present-day Bantu-speaking populations are divided, Nguni, Sotho, Tsonga and Venda (see map), can be squarely located in four major geographical and ecological regions. These, in turn, can be grouped into two wider regions, what Sansom (1974) terms the East and the West, defined essentially as the coastal strip (sometimes very wide indeed) and the central plateau. Thus the Sotho and Venda were associated with the central plateau and the Nguni and Tsonga with the Indian Ocean littoral. The crucial difference here, as we shall see in Chapter 2, was the configuration of soil and vegetation types in these two areas – the variegated possibilities of these resources in the East as opposed to their more uniform distribution in the West. Let us examine briefly the implications of this East-West ecological division for the development of the cultures associated with these specific areas: these matters will be discussed in greater detail in Chapter 2.

The most basic effect was on settlement patterns. Here the essential point to note is that the presence, in the east, of localised areas containing varied arable soils, interspersed with grazing and enjoying abundant water, made it possible for a local community to be fairly self-sufficient. Contrasted with this were the vast stretches of uniform soil-type on the highveld with little variation in vegetation and a notable shortage of surface water. It seems that scattered homesteads, on the one hand, and nucleated settlements, on the other, were 'forced' on the Southern Bantu through differential access to agricultural and pastoral resources, the availability of water supplies and, particularly on the highveld plateau, the need for defence. The implications of this were fundamental.

Concentration in large settlements meant, firstly, that the chief and other political authorities could keep a direct control over their people. Instead of decentralising local administration to outlying areas under sub-chiefs and headmen, as the Nguni did, Sotho and Venda central authorities could exercise close watch on political activities, a possible reason for their more autocratic governments when compared with the more 'democratic' Nguni, especially the Xhosa-speaking South Nguni. Decision-making was centralised and major matters affecting the chiefdom were aired at the typical Sotho institution of the *pitso*, or general assembly; the Nguni did have occasional meetings on a chiefdom scale, but not nearly as frequently (Chapter 3).

The converse of this was that the Nguni had problems relating to the political integration of their far-flung membership. There was always the possibility that district chiefs would break away, especially as their administrative areas were comparatively self-sufficient. It was perhaps the need to provide strong political links to the centre that explains the greater ritualisation and militarisation of the first-fruits ceremonies among, especially, the Zulu and Swazi, at which the chief was symbolically strengthened against his enemies in the presence of his regiments and the populace at large. The close-knit political clique among Sotho and Venda made it logical (as well as practical) for the chief's closest advisors to be members of the royal family, whereas among Nguni, councillors were more often commoners. Political systems were basically similar; the differences flowed from differences of settlement.

Centralisation also affected the details of initiation rituals. These important rites were organised chiefdom-wide by Sotho and Venda, but locally among Nguni (Chapter 7). The gathering of all the young men and women of more or less the same age at the capital for the 'second' initiation schools of the *bogwêra* and *byale*, among Sotho, and the *domba* and *vhusha*, among Venda, coupled with the lifelong

G.F. Angas's painting of a Zulu homestead near Umlazi, occupied by a polygamous family. Note its isolation from other homesteads, typical of the scattered Zulu settlement pattern, and the typically Nguni beehive structure of the dwellings. The reed screens in the centre are designed for the comfort of the homestead head and his friends. (Africana Library)

Climate, topography and distribution of the main cultural groups in the eighteenth century, showing the Escarpment, dividing the East from the West, and the limits of the summer rainfall area.

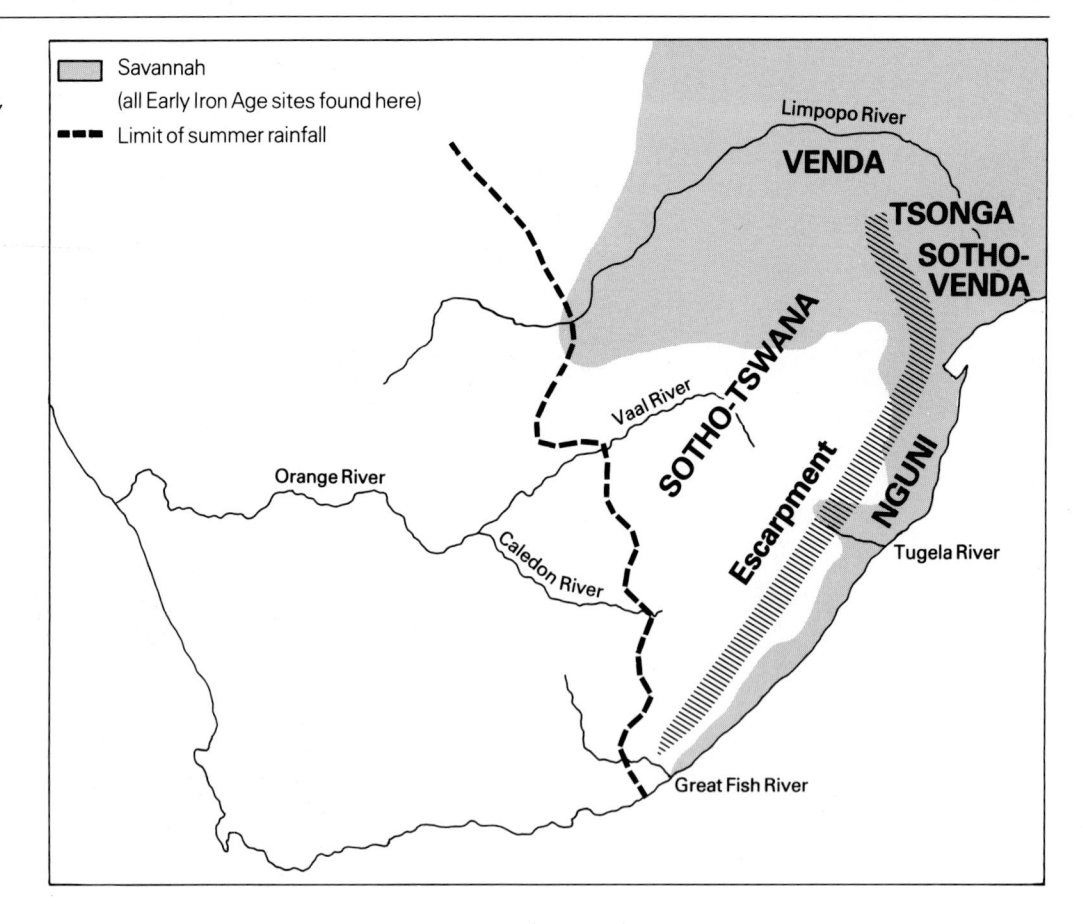

sense of camaraderie and mutual interest that went with the traumatic experiences of the initiation rituals, made possible the institution of age regiments among these peoples. Once formed, they could be used both as units in the army and to provide civil labour for the chief in times of peace. (Among South Nguni the army was mobilised on a territorial basis, warriors mustering first at the great place of their headman and then proceeding, under his command, to the district chief, and thence to the capital.) The adoption, in the early nineteenth century, of the regimental system by the Zulu under Shaka, and its extension to other North Nguni offshoots, such as the Swazi, can perhaps be explained by the necessity, in an expanding Nguni state, of developing a stronger integrating mechanism than heretofore to bind together the emerging nation. Something had to be done to offset the problems of decentralised local government, and membership of age regiments cut across the (divisive) membership of families. And yet, at a more fundamental level, the essentials of initiation were the same for all Southern Bantu. In addition to the fact that the terms used for the complex of rites (*ubukhwetha* and *bogwêra*) were the same, some of the actual ritual was identical. To take one example, present-day Mpondomise (South Nguni) initiates in the Transkei, returning from washing off the white clay of seclusion at the river, cover their faces with their hands in reverence to the observing ancestors: I witnessed exactly the same symbolic gesture among Kgaga (Sotho) initiates in the lowveld in 1966.

But the implications of closer settlement can perhaps be traced further, although the link is admittedly now becoming more tenuous. One of the most striking differences between Nguni and Sotho lay (and lies) in the area of marriage rules (Chapter 6). While all Nguni and Tsonga strictly prohibit marriage between kin, all Sotho and Venda encourage such marriage, especially with a cross-cousin. It is

A section of a headman's ward in coastal Pondoland. (H. Kuckertz)

tempting to associate this with differences in settlement pattern. As we have seen, one of the problems faced by Nguni and Tsonga was how to integrate the scattered homesteads firmly into the tribal polity. Among these peoples the homestead was an essentially autonomous unit, almost completely self-sufficient. In such a society the rule insisting on 'marrying out' would have the effect of spreading bonds of marriage alliance far beyond the homestead, linking it to other homesteads, perhaps in other parts of the chiefdom, thus exerting a powerful force for integration. This mechanism was not necessary among Sotho and Venda, who were effectively held together through proximity to the capital.

Transformations can also be seen in variations in the institution of bridewealth, as Adam Kuper has elegantly shown in his pioneering work (1982). Cattle were exchanged for wives in all Southern Bantu communities, and the same set of ideas underlined the transactions everywhere. Yet, as Kuper writes, 'the organization of these transactions varies, local bridewealth systems adapting to local circumstances . . . The process by which modifications develop is regular and rule-bound . . . In consequence the various local institutions represent highly constrained transformations of each other' (A. Kuper 1982: 157).

Kuper sees three sets of factors as being responsible for variations in local bridewealth systems: (a) the relative importance of pastoralism as opposed to agriculture, (b) the marriage rules, especially different forms of cross-cousin marriage, and (c) the influence of social stratification. It seems that, where agriculture was the main subsistence activity, as among South Sotho, Sotho-Venda (those lowveld North Sotho people influenced by the Venda), Tsonga and Venda, bridewealth payments were high, but where agriculture was less significant, as among Tswana and Nguni, payments were low. In the first group the comparatively few cattle tended to be reserved the bridewealth payments, while in cattle-rich communities, bridewealth 'formed a minor element in the flow of cattle'.

Of the four types of marriage system identified among Southern Bantu by Kuper, namely, (a) the ruling families marrying close paternal kin; (b) preferential cross-cousin marriage with the mother's brother's daughter; (c) second and third cousin marriage; and (d) non-kin marriage, (a) is found among Sotho-Tswana aristocrats, (b) is common among all Sotho commoners and Venda, (c) refers to (uncommon) Swazi and Tsonga practice, and (c) is the Nguni option. Despite these apparent differences all systems were 'linked to the same bridewealth ideology. Specifically, all invoke a debt a brother is felt to owe to his cattle-linked sister or to his father' (see Chapter 6).

As regards the influence of social stratification (which occured among the ethnically mixed Tswana and Venda and among Zulu and Swazi; see Chapter 3), Kuper was unable to find a clear pattern, except that there seemed to be a connection between strong centralisation and marriage with the mother's brother's daughter, which has to do with the (highly technical) matter of the relative status of wife-givers and wife-receivers, a subject it would be inappropriate to discuss in detail here.

Even differences in cosmological systems can be traced to the pervasive influence of the settlement pattern. Although all Southern Bantu were strongly patrilineal, this emphasis was far stronger among Nguni than among others. This can be seen in their attempt to retain the memory of the paternal line only, as far back into the past as possible, and their possession of clans and lineages as 'pure' descent categories (Chapters 5 and 8). A possible reason for this preoccupation with

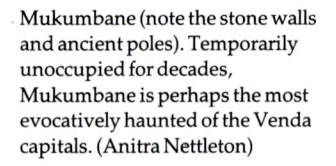

Mukumbane (note the stone walls and ancient poles). Temporarily unoccupied for decades, Mukumbane is perhaps the most evocatively haunted of the Venda capitals. (Anitra Nettleton)

descent may lie in the important sociological effect of descent group exogamy, spreading bonds of marriage alliance in an attempt to achieve wider social integration in a 'scattered' society, as suggested above. In such a marriage system the calculation of descent becomes vitally important and could have led to a strong emphasis on descent-based groupings. This, in turn, goes some way in explaining the characteristic features of Nguni ancestor religion, with its exclusive patrilineal emphasis when compared with the bilateral nature of Sotho, Venda and Tsonga worshipping groups, who were concerned with ancestors only as far back as grandparents, on both the mother's and the father's side. The extreme Nguni emphasis on cattle might also explain why the typical Nguni sacrifice involved the spilling of the blood of a head of cattle or small stock, whereas a libation of beer was the accepted 'gift' in the other, more agriculturally orientated, groups (Chapter 8).

The Nguni fear of witchcraft (as opposed to the Sotho fear of sorcery) can perhaps also be related to settlement patterns. As we shall see (Chapter 9), witchcraft among them was typically associated with women and sorcery with men. This might be due to the more 'extrovert' nature of sorcery, where medicines had to be obtained from herbalists, involving the fear of detection. Men, with their greater individual freedom of movement and activity, could 'cover' such purchases on the pretext of obtaining medicines for crops and protection; it would be strange for a woman to do this. Witchcraft, on the other hand, was inherited and intensely personal, and thus a more 'feminine' occupation. Could it be that the greater social visibility of women in Nguni society (after all, they lived in isolated homesteads so that their activities could be satisfactorily monitored by male in-laws) made them far less likely to be seen as sorcerers and more likely to be suspected of witchcraft? We shall see that Nguni women were at risk of being cast in the role of 'witch' precisely because of their status as strangers in the homestead – a status deriving from the rules enjoining non-kin marriage.

Finally, ideas of ritual pollution seem also to have been affected by environmental factors. Among Sotho pollution was conceived of as 'heat', which had to be countered by the performance of cooling rituals, while among Nguni it was thought of as 'dirt' or 'darkness', to be eliminated by emetics and laxatives. But there was another difference. It appears that the Sotho were much more preoccupied with pollution beliefs than were the other groups. Why was this so?

The choice of metaphor through which to think about and manipulate pollution beliefs can be explained, in the Sotho case, by shortage of water and, in the Nguni case, by the system of scattered homesteads. One of the crucial problems faced by the originators of Sotho culture was that of uncertainty of water supply. Since at least the end of the eighteenth century precipitation on the inland plateau had declined dramatically towards the west until it prevented settlement on the marches of the Kalahari desert. The concept of heat as a metaphor for ritual danger was almost certainly derived from the overriding importance of rain. If rain – or its associated quality of 'coolness' – was though to 'stand for' a state of health, prosperity and social harmony, it was logical that the converse of these qualities should be symbolised by its opposite, heat. Heat was typically caused by contact with death, or by contact with a woman who was menstruating or who had experienced an abortion. Twins were also 'hot'.

Sotho rituals to nullify pollution were all based on the idea of coolness or cooling. The four dominant cooling substances were water, chyme, ash and soot (or charcoal). Water could be substituted by other liquids (beer, gruel, saliva and urine) and these liquids could be drunk in infusions, used to wash with, poured onto

South Sotho dwellings in the Maluti highlands. Note the stone construction and the projecting porch, a response to the severe Drakensberg winters, with their heavy snowfalls. (Morris and Levitan 1986)

shrines, or boiled and their fumes inhaled. Twins, and an aborted foetus, were buried in damp earth to prevent the country being struck by drought. Chyme (the green stomach contents of an animal) was seen as green and 'cool' and was associated with the ancestors, while ash and soot were in a sense the 'opposite' of fire, and therefore of heat.

The Nguni, especially Zulu, conception of pollution in terms of 'darkness' or 'dirt', which came either from the environment, from medicines left around by sorcerers or by contact with persons in a state of pollution, particularly by death, was strikingly different. The blackness caused by the death of a homestead head was removed by the ceremony of the 'washing of the spears' at a ritual hunt, so that the emphasis was on cleansing, not 'cooling'. Appropriately, the main technique used by Zulu to expel the evil of pollution was the use of enemas and vomiting, to get rid of the intrusive contagion.

The origin of this metaphor would seem to lie in Nguni perceptions of their society. The isolation and comparative autonomy of the Nguni homestead was striking. As Bryant (1949: 74) put it: 'Each [homestead] is in itself a tiny city-state, a private village, self-complete, building itself, feeding itself, clothing itself, and, for the most part, governing itself ... [Each] was a detached residence situated within its own grounds, always alone, a dot on the landscape, far away from the nearest neighbour'. It seems that the image Zulu had of their society was that of a body that was continually being threatened by pollution that came from without. Like the human body, Zulu society itself had boundaries whose integrity was constantly being threatened with invasion from without, and this image was derived from the very nature of Nguni settlement.

As already mentioned, Sotho were apparently less preoccupied with witchcraft than were the Nguni. Perhaps this difference, too, was associated with settlement patterns. In all Southern Bantu societies witchcraft was a sign of strained social relations. The image of the witch expressed this and allowed the conflict to be handled by eliminating the offender in a public execution. Witchcraft accusations, then, were indices of competition and jealousies between kin and neighbours.

Although comparative figures are not available, it would seem that the effect of witchcraft accusations within the closed, claustrophobic Sotho communities would have been much more devastating than in the more 'open' Nguni society. The Kriges state that among Lovedu 'only a very small proportion of cases of witchcraft lead to an open accusation' and that there was a tendency to ignore a suspected witch, and Sansom recorded a similar state of affairs among the (North Sotho) Pedi. We shall see in Chapter 9 that it is precisely in close-knit communities that witchcraft accusations tend to arise. I argue here, however, that although witchcraft accusations were *potentially* more common in Sotho society, the results would have been so socially disruptive that they had to be avoided at all costs. An *impersonal* causal agent of ritual pollution would be preferable as an explanation of illness (Hammond-Tooke 1981).

It would seem, then, that there was indeed a broad connection between the environment in which the early Bantu-speakers found themselves and the ways in which they modified their cultures in an effort to achieve successful adaptation to them. A contributory factor seems to have been the need for defence, itself dictated partly by the environment. Once the settlement pattern was in place a certain logic was imposed on people, which did not *determine* the way they had to go (people always have choices), but at least allows us to attempt explanations, in retrospect, of the decisions they took. We can do this with some confidence because of the universal characteristics of the human mind.

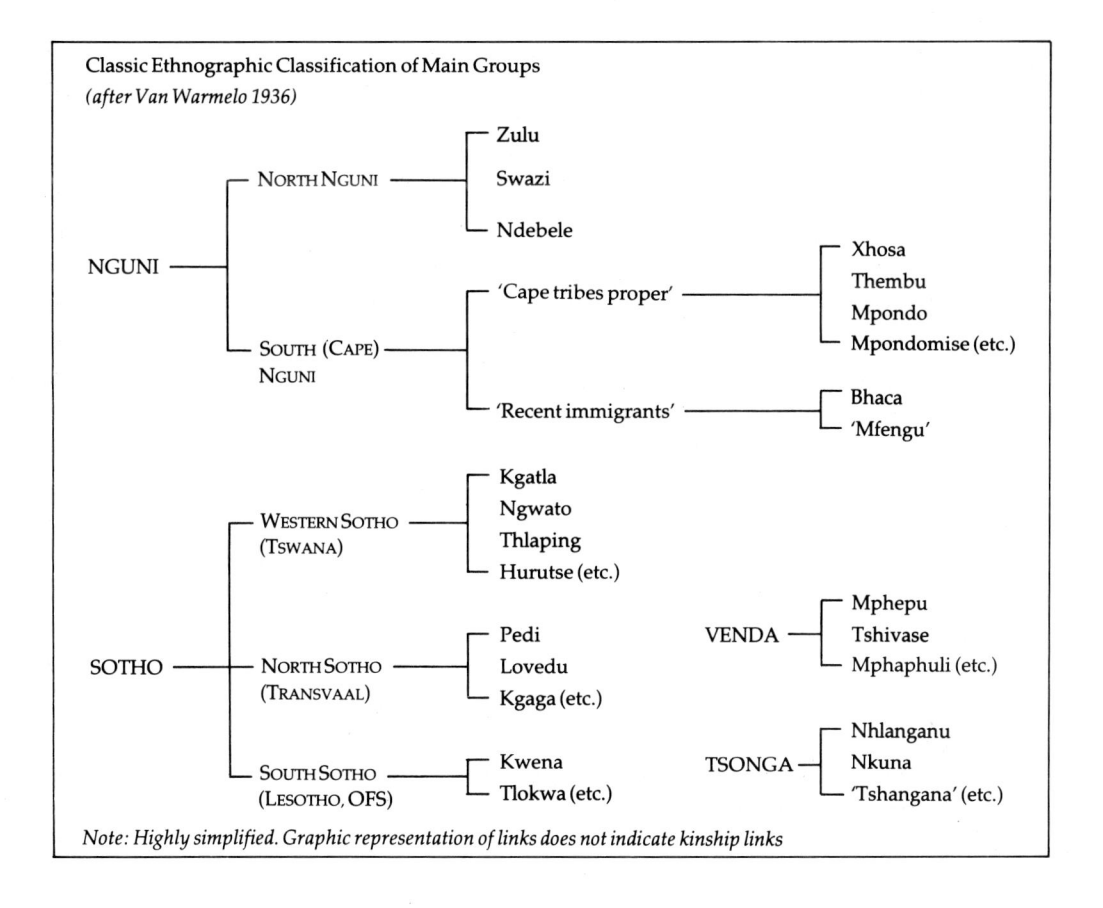

Classic Ethnographic Classification of Main Groups
(after Van Warmelo 1936)

NGUNI
- NORTH NGUNI
  - Zulu
  - Swazi
  - Ndebele
- SOUTH (CAPE) NGUNI
  - 'Cape tribes proper'
    - Xhosa
    - Thembu
    - Mpondo
    - Mpondomise (etc.)
  - 'Recent immigrants'
    - Bhaca
    - 'Mfengu'

SOTHO
- WESTERN SOTHO (TSWANA)
  - Kgatla
  - Ngwato
  - Thlaping
  - Hurutse (etc.)
- NORTH SOTHO (TRANSVAAL)
  - Pedi
  - Lovedu
  - Kgaga (etc.)
- SOUTH SOTHO (LESOTHO, OFS)
  - Kwena
  - Tlokwa (etc.)

VENDA
- Mphepu
- Tshivase
- Mphaphuli (etc.)

TSONGA
- Nhlanganu
- Nkuna
- 'Tshangana' (etc.)

Note: Highly simplified. Graphic representation of links does not indicate kinship links

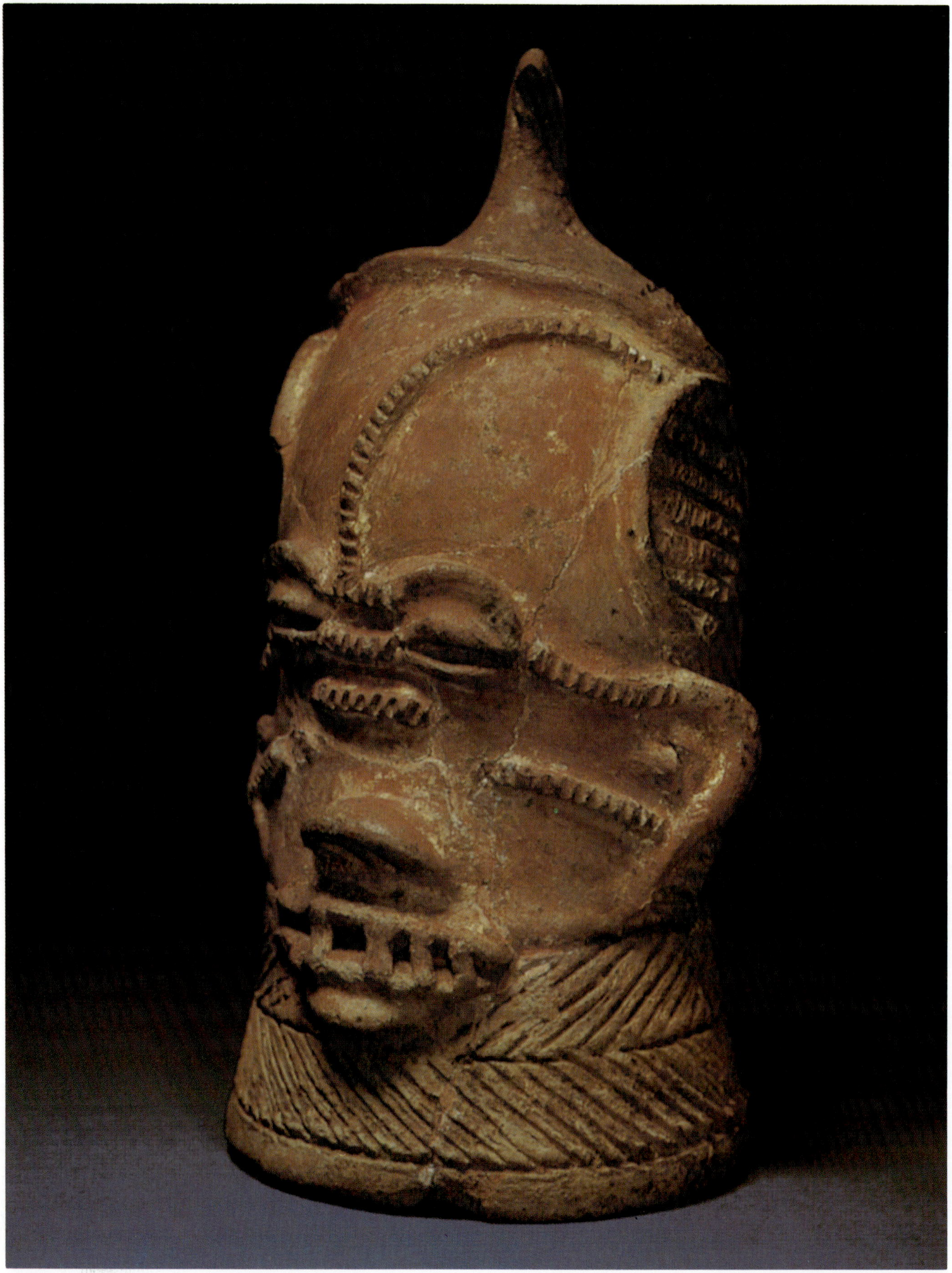

CHAPTER 1

ORIGINS AND CLASSIFICATION

THE ROOTS of black South Africans lie, of course, in black Africa. Since at least classical times, this vast land mass has been a place of mystery to outsiders, a 'dark continent', defined by an enigmatic coastline (mangrove swamps, inhospitable desert), haunted by dangerous fauna and with a population supposedly oppressed by superstition and the heavy weight of witchcraft. In a very definite sense it has represented the 'opposite' of the west, the epitome of the 'Other'. For some, indeed, Africa's otherness symbolised the dark underside of the human psyche – the Jungian shadow. To a great extent these responses were based on ignorance. The reasons for this lack of knowledge were mainly geographical. Cut off from the Mediterranean north by the expanse of the Sahara Desert, with a regular, unindented coastline with rivers seldom navigable far from their mouths, and with a daunting range of tropical diseases, the continent was for millennia effectively insulated from outside contact.

And yet, Africa was the cradle of mankind. Modern research has established that the emergence of the forerunner of *Homo sapiens* from ape-like pre-human forms took place in East Africa, some five or six million years ago. This was *Homo habilis*, with a brain between 600 and 800 cc (modern man, 1 345 cc) and making the earliest flaked stone tools. By 1.5 to .5 million years ago *Homo habilis* had evolved into the bigger-brained (935 cc) *Homo erectus*. *H. erectus* seems to have spread beyond the African continent, for his remains have been found also in Java and China. He had acquired the secret of making fire and his stone tools were made to a clearly identifiable pattern. By 10 000 years ago all the modern forms of man were in existence and had spread over most of the globe. Physical anthropologists distinguish four main races of *Homo sapiens* – the Caucasoid (or 'Indo-European'), Negroid, Mongoloid ('Asiatic', including the American Indians and Polynesians) and Australoid (Australian Aborigines).

In the long history of mankind true man is therefore a comparatively recent newcomer, and the marked physical differences between the four races indicate a fairly rapid divergence in physical type, presumably due to environmental factors and to isolation.

By six or seven thousand years ago Africa was inhabited by the ancestors of the four main racial types regarded as indigenous to the continent. These were the Khoisan ('Bushmen' and 'Hottentots'), the Pygmies of the equatorial forest, the Caucasoid 'Hamites' and the Negroes. The 'Hamites' almost certainly entered Africa from the north-east in Late Stone Age times (their languages are distantly related to the Semitic languages) but the other three evolved out of older African

One of seven Early Iron Age earthenware heads (c. AD 500) excavated near Lydenberg in the eastern Transvaal. Too small to be a mask (210 mm), they were probably attached atop a pole from which a grass costume hung, and used in initiation ceremonies. It has not been possible to relate their makers to present-day Bantu-speaking groups, whose forebears entered South Africa in the second millenium AD. (South African Museum)

stock. Recent research indicates that the Khoisan and Pygmies are in fact derived from Negroid stock and are merely evolutionary adaptations to different environments – open grasslands, in the one case, and equatorial forests, in the other.

It seems that the Negro physical type arose in the narrow savannah belt north of the equatorial forest at a time when the southern Sahara enjoyed about a third again as much rain as it receives today. They appear to have been a people of the forest margins and essentially fish-eaters, a fact that allowed them to form settled communities while still following a hunter-gatherer style of life. In the second millennium BC, however, they came under the influence of the Neolithic Revolution, associated with the domestication of plants (especially wheat and barley) and animals, and, later, the emergence of towns and cities, that had occurred in the Middle East and Egypt in the fourth millennium. They adopted the cultivation of crops, but of indigenous species, especially *Sorghum* (guinea corn or great millet), *Pennisetum* (bulrush or pearl millet) and *Eleusine corocana* (finger millet), all native to sub-Saharan Africa, especially the light woodland savannah from Senegal to the upper Nile. Movement south into the tropical forest itself by some Negro groups resulted in problems of food production, as the environment was not suitable for these cereals. Strangely, practically none of the food crops of the forests were domesticated by them and for two or three thousand years (until the introduction of maize and cassava from the Americas in the sixteenth and seventeenth centuries AD) the forest food-crops grown in Africa were mainly of South-East Asian origin – the banana, yam and coco-yam.

As far as language is concerned, the Negro communities spoke dialects belonging to two main ancient language groups, the Eastern Sudanic languages spoken to the north of the equatorial forest, from the Nile to Lake Chad, and the Western Sudanic, spoken west of the lake. As Oliver and Fage comment:

> In sharp contrast to these ancient groupings, however, the Bantu languages spoken today by the Negroes over most of Africa south of the equator are so closely related to each other that they are generally agreed to be very much younger. As little as two thousand years ago Bantu may have been a single language spoken in an area much smaller than that occupied today by its descendants, and it is further likely that the relationship of this original Bantu language was towards the Western Sudanic rather than the Eastern Sudanic group. (Oliver and Fage 1962: 24).

The origin, then, of the Bantu-speaking peoples, as a distinct category, was comparatively late, and occurred probably in the centuries immediately before the beginning of the Christian era. It was associated strongly with the coming of the Iron Age and seems to have occurred south of the equatorial forests, probably in the savannah highlands of Katanga (in present-day Zambia) and the region of the Great Lakes. A series of changes, still not completely understood, resulted in a tremendous population explosion that drove Bantu-speakers east, south and west, to the limits of the 500 mm (20 inch) isohyet, in effect, the summer rainfall area. By the first centuries of the Christian era they had reached the Limpopo River and entered what is today South Africa.

The story of the two millennia since then is still very patchy. During most of this enormously long period there were, of course, no written records and our knowledge of it has had to be painstakingly pieced together from the researches of archaeologists, linguists, physical anthropologists and even biologists. The societies and cultures of the past are no longer with us so we shall never know the really

A modern San encampment, possibly similar to the hunter-gatherer settlements of the Late Stone Age. (Department of Archaeology, University of the Witwatersrand)

KHOISAN AND BANTU-SPEAKERS

When they arrived south of the Limpopo the Bantu-speaking peoples of the Iron Age found the country sparsely inhabited by groups of small, yellow-skinned hunter-gatherers, all speaking languages characterised by the presence of the so-called 'click consonants'. Some of these languages differed from one another to such a degree that they were mutually unintelligible. These people were organised into bands that fluctuated in size through the seasons, and some were artists of distinction, especially those living in the foothills of the Drakensberg and in the folded mountain ranges of the western Cape. They were called Thwa by the Bantu-speakers and Bosjesmans (Bushmen) by the early white settlers. ☐ Along the coastal strip, from the Kunene River in the west to the Sundays River in the east, there were also groups of nomadic pastoralists, of the same physical type as the Bushmen, who worked copper and grazed their herds on the fynbos and karroo bush of the western Cape and its hinterland. They were organised into patrilineal clans, under chiefs, and called themselves by 'tribal' names such as Inqua, Gonaqua, Outeniqua and Namaqua. They also spoke a click language, which scholars believe had developed, far back in the past, from a Central Bushman language. These pastoralists referred to themselves as 'Khoikhoi', meaning 'men of men', and called Bushmen, contemptuously, 'San'. The Khoikhoi, in their turn, were dubbed 'Hottentots' by the settlers. (Present terminology uses 'San' for the people and their culture, and 'Bushman' for their language.) ☐ Because they were separated by the arid Karroo from the summer rainfall area, contact between Khoikhoi and most Bantu-speakers seems to have been limited, except in the area of the present Ciskei, where much intermarriage took place and one tribe, the Gonaqua, became absorbed by Xhosa-speakers as the amaGqunukhwebe. Physical anthropologists, using genetic markers, have shown that the South Nguni generally have a greater percentage of Khoisan genes in their blood than do groups further north and it is to this close contact that one must look for an explanation for the click consonants that are such a striking feature of Xhosa and, to a lesser extent, Zulu. Interaction between Bantu-speakers and San was not so close, and there is evidence of frequent disputes over stock raiding. Yet the South Nguni often employed San as rain-makers, and many elements of their religious and healing systems have been borrowed from them. Thus, the Xhosa term for diviner (**igqira**) and the divination dance (**xhentsa**) are of pure Bushman provenance.

interesting aspects of their social and religious life – the precise languages they spoke, their marriage rules, the nature of their politics, their hopes and fears. All that they have left to us are pieces of pottery (pottery is practically indestructible), beads, the foundations of hut floors and other evidence of settlement pattern, and, if we are lucky, traces of rusted iron implements. There are also the bones of the animals they ate and (very rarely) their own bones, usually in graves.

This is not the kind of evidence that speaks for itself. It has to be interpreted, using sophisticated dating methods, theoretical models and comparison of sites from over a wide area. Interpretation involves forming a hypothesis, a suggestion of how the facts fit together; facts subsequently collected then either confirm or refute the theory, in which case a new theory is sought. With so few facts at their disposal it is not surprising that archaeologists have come up with sometimes conflicting theories and explanations, which have to be critically assessed. Yet, over the last few decades, a general consensus as to the broad lines of Southern Bantu origins has begun to emerge.

All the evidence points to a revolution taking place in southern Africa in the early centuries of the first millennium AD. Before this time the country south of the Limpopo was inhabited by hunter-gatherers, using Late Stone Age tools and spread fairly uniformly over the entire sub-continent. Some of these Stone Age communities, particularly in the western Cape, also kept sheep; generally, however, they were hunters and foragers.

Suddenly, in the general area of the Transvaal lowveld and bushveld, and always

A Tsonga village nestling in its maize gardens. The Tsonga migrants from Mozambique tended to occupy the river valleys and humid flats of the lowveld. Most social life took place in the open air. (Morris and Levitan 1986)

at lower, warmer altitudes, there emerged settled communities, engaged in agriculture, working (and sometimes smithing and smelting) metal and with a distinctive type of pottery. The archaeologist Ray Inskeep sums up the position:

> What is clear is that South Africa's first farming communities were established at least by the end of the third century. They were cultivating *Pennisetum* [millet] and in all probability a variety of other plants. By the fifth century populations were established in large villages of pole and thatch houses with plastered walls and floors. Their technology included the smelting and smithing of iron and copper, the manufacture of elaborate pottery, the carving of shallow bowls and dishes from soapstone, and the carving of bone and ivory. Salt was extracted from alkaline mineral springs by evaporation in soapstone dishes. The localized nature of such industry combined with the importance of the product almost certainly resulted in its being traded. Some form of trading contacts with the east coast is suggested by the occasional Indian Ocean sea-shells that turn up in many sites. (Inskeep 1978: 131)

It is certain that most Early Iron Age communities had at least some cattle (despite the prevalence of tsetse fly), herded in central cattle byres, for dung deposits have been found associated with some of them, and also that, from at least AD 800, they were under the control of chiefs. This is deduced from a number of sites in Botswana, the northern Transvaal and south-western Zimbabwe in which there is a hierarchy of settlement size, large cattle byres and sometimes an adjacent court, all

> ## Henry Francis Fynn's Description of Tsonga around Delagoa Bay in 1800
>
> 'Of the four Tribes inhabiting the borders of Delagoa Bay, Mapoota is the largest. Each has a King or ruling Chief, whose authority appears to be paramount both in war and peace. The population of each tribe is divided into Villages, each governed by a chief [headman] who is generally a relative of the King's ... The Villages generally consist of from 15 to 30 Huts which are placed in a Circular form, each Village having in its centre a large Tree on the branches and round the Trunk of which they hang the heads of all wild beasts killed by the Inhabitants near the Village. The Huts are of a round or bee-hive construction with upright walls about 4 feet high. The roof which rises into a narrow point at the top projects over the Walls 2 or 3 feet. The whole is constructed of rushes stitched to a wooden frame work and neatly plastered with clay, and is kept very clean. Cultivation is performed entirely by the Women. They use only one implement resembling an American Hoe with the addition of a pick at the back of the handle. It is about 3 foot long. They dig the soil to the depth of 5 inches and keep the Earth always loose round their sweet Potatoes.
>
> A Tsonga dwelling, Transvaal. (Department of Art History, University of the Witwatersrand)
>
> ☐ Their hair is dressed carefully ... in which the Chiefs place a bunch of red feathers and two or three Gall bladders blown ... Round their Necks they wear Necklaces of beads, round pieces of Wood with the thorns that grow on them, and frequently the back bones of a Snake, each of which they place in a number of fancyful forms. From their wrists to above their elbows they wear brass rings which fit their arms so exceedingly close as to cause the flesh frequently to grow up between ... they wear a mat of plaited grass round their middle from four inches to sometimes 2 feet in length. On their ankles they tie pieces of hide and bones. This King wears only a piece of Green Baize trimmed with yellow, and the chiefs either a Blanket or a piece of Gurrahs thrown loosely round the body. The Women wear beads round their wrists and waists and a piece of Gurrahs about 6 inches square. Another ornament indispensible to the Women ... is a string of Iron beads.' (Theal 1898: 481 ff)

pointing to a firmly institutionalised central government. These Early Iron Age people were undoubtedly Bantu-speakers, although there is no direct evidence of this, nor do we know to which modern language group their language(s) belonged. The few excavated Early Iron Age skeletons are all of Negroid type, whereas remains from the Later Stone Age are usually Khoisan. As Huffman writes: 'The different racial identity of the previous inhabitants, the widespread distribution of the Early Iron Age skeletal samples, and their different ceramic associations demonstrate that the Early Iron Age was introduced by a Negro people' (1982: 138).

At about AD 1200–1300 there is an apparent hiatus in the archaeological record, signalled by changes in pottery types. Some archaeologists have identified a widespread early pottery tradition, which they term 'Western Stream', emanating from the region of northern Angola and moving through Botswana into the Transvaal and, later, into Natal and the eastern Cape. This tradition has been associated with the Early Iron Age. This Western Stream was subsequently overlain by an 'Eastern Stream' that first appeared in East Africa in about AD 200 and moved down the east

Venda stone walling at Mukumbane, showing Zimbabwe influence. (Department of Archaeology, University of the Witwatersrand)

coast into Mozambique and Natal in the second half of the first millennium. It is this Eastern tradition that is believed to be ancestral to historical Southern Bantu cultures. (There was also a 'Central Stream' that had little impact on South Africa.) The pottery of these two streams is very different, although there were undoubted broad similarities in other aspects of culture. The ceramic differences between the Early Iron Age sites and sites later than about AD 1200 would seem to indicate that another wave of Bantu-speakers entered the bushveld at this time. Their origin is uncertain, but oral traditions, as well as their 'Eastern' pottery, seem to point to an East African origin. These were the ancestors of present-day Nguni, Sotho and Tsonga. The Early Iron Age populations were either dispersed or, more likely, absorbed by these newcomers.

The Later Iron Age also saw a movement of communities speaking dialects of what was to become the Sotho language, from the tropical savannah bushveld westward onto the interior plateau. Here they prospered, probably because of the interconnected factors of population growth and an increase in the number of cattle owned. Soil on the highveld was not as fertile (and thus less suitable for agriculture) as that in the lowlands, but the grasslands were ideal for cattle-keeping. The new environment, as we shall see in Chapter 2, also provided limits and new directions for social organisation, and it is here, from perhaps about the thirteenth century, that the original Early Iron Age culture gradually began to diverge into those of nineteenth century South African chiefdoms.

It is difficult, at this stage of our knowledge, to trace the early history of the speakers of the four main languages, Nguni, Sotho, Venda and Tsonga, back to this early period, for oral traditions only go back a few hundred years at the most. What is clear is that the move onto the highveld, with its relative lack of trees, led to extensive building in stone, especially in the area of what is now the Free State and the southern and western Transvaal. Areas near the Magaliesberg and the catchment area of the Vaal River are covered with stone ruins, with stone hut foundations, byres, enclosing walls and corbelled stone huts, that extend for

An ancient copper mine at Olifantspoort, Transvaal. The earliest copper mine has been dated to the eighth century AD. The most important copper deposits were at Phalaborwa and Messina and the present-day Phalaborwa are direct descendants of the miners. (Department of Archaeology, University of Witwatersrand)

kilometres, and, significantly, settlement is closer the further west one goes. This would seem to indicate continuity with the present-day Tswana peoples (belonging to the Sotho group), noted for their large towns on the fringes of the Kalahari. When Moffat visited the Tswana in 1835 he saw the stone walls of 'towns of former generations' said to have been built by the Hurutshe:

> Innumerable vestiges remain of towns, and some very large ones. Some are miles in circumference, which must have cost immense labour, being entirely built of stones, that is the fences and folds; also the lower part of the houses, the upper part of which there are but few vestiges, having been built with clay mixed with cow dung.
>
> [And further on:] The country was formerly thickly inhabited with many tribes of Bakueans [Kwena] and innumerable ruins are scattered under all the mountains and on every hill. They build their fences with stone. (Moffat 1945)

The extent of these settlements bespeaks a greatly increased population. It has been suggested that this was caused by the greater consumption of milk and its by-products made possible by freedom from tsetse and the availability of extensive pasturage. Inskeep has stated that, given favourable conditions, herds in Africa can show an annual increase of from four to ten per cent, a rate greater than that of their owners. With larger herds came the need for new land and this would explain in part the rapid movement of chiefdoms onto the highveld. It is also tempting to suggest that it is from the advent of the Later Iron Age that the extreme elaboration of what has been called the 'cattle complex' – the incorporation of cattle into almost every aspect of social life, from marriage to religion – can be dated. That an ecological explanation is not the only possible one is shown by the fact that the

Nguni, who did not inhabit the highveld, were even more cattle-orientated than were the Sotho. This is partly, no doubt, due to their cultural links with the East African cattle area (their pottery belongs to the 'Eastern Stream' that is cognate with ceramics found in Kenya), but also because their portion of the eastern seaboard lay in a more temperate, tsetse-free area, in which rolling grasslands on the higher areas coexisted with temperate thornveld (see Chapter 2).

Population increase, in itself, does not *necessarily* involve changes in social organisation but there is a sense in which it poses problems of the ordering of social life which demand adjustments and thus social change. Perhaps the most fundamental problem faced by all societies is that of control over their members, so that the rapid dispersion of the Southern Bantu in the thirteenth century and later necessitated the development of more complex systems of local government. As we shall see, the dispersed nature of Nguni settlement demanded handling in quite a different way than did the nucleated settlements of the Sotho that emerged later, and changes in political structure tended to go hand in hand with other changes, especially in marriage and religion. The evidence is that it was in the eighteenth century that the final separation of the four major cultural traditions from the undifferentiated Early Iron Age tradition took place.

The processes of cultural diversification, however, were not entirely internal. There were two other (external) factors that influenced the trajectory of cultural development, namely the emergence of the Zimbabwe Empire in about AD 1020 and the introduction of external trade. The two are related.

Huffman has shown that the Zimbabwe Culture was not the same as the Bantu Cattle Culture south of the Limpopo. The former's origins can be traced to the Leopard's Kopje site of K2, dated to about AD 980, in the elephant haunted mopane

The site of Mapungubwe, in the extreme north-western Transvaal, close to the Zimbabwe and Botswana borders. It was abandoned, probably because of prolonged drought, and succeeded by the establishment of Great Zimbabwe. (Department of Archaeology, University of the Witwatersrand)

The Mfecane

Although chiefdoms in precolonial times were typically fairly isolated, and warfare was limited to raids and skirmishes between neighbouring chiefdoms or migrating groups, this comparatively peaceful scene was shattered in the early nineteenth century by successive waves of violent population movement that shook southern Africa to its core. This 'time of troubles' is referred to by Nguni as Mfecane ('The Crushing') and by Sotho as Difaqane ('the Hammering'). ☐ The causes of this development are still unclear. Scholarly theories have ranged from an analysis of Shaka's personality through environmental changes to population pressures. Recently Julian Cobbing has sought an explanation in terms of the external forces of a colonial 'pincer movement', especially those emanating from the Mozambican slave trade, based on Delagoa Bay, and attempts to acquire forced labour in the north-eastern Cape colony. Be this as it may, the expansion of Zulu power caused a chain reaction that was to have repercussions far beyond the borders of the Zulu kingdom.

☐ The Mfecane was occasioned by the rise to power of the small Zulu chiefdom under its chief Shaka. As explained in Chapter 3, conflicts developed between certain northern Natal chiefdoms, exerting pressure on those lying to the south of them. One of these, the Mthethwa under Dingiswayo, grew rapidly, particularly after Dingiswayo initiated a number of changes, notably the establishment of age-regiments (amabutho) into which the young men of approximately the same age were drafted. This standing army allowed him to embark on an expansionist policy. The Mthethwa system was adopted by Shaka, who had served in Dingiswayo's army. By 1820 Shaka had gained control over the whole of Natal north of the Thukela River, incorporating the northern chiefdoms into a unitary state surrounded by large tracts of depopulated country. Within his domain Shaka reigned as an absolute monarch, ruthlessly stamping out opposition with his regiments armed with the short-hafted stabbing spear and based on strategically placed military barracks. ☐ The effective beginning of the Mfecane was the breakaway of the Ndwandwe chiefs, Soshangane and Zwangendaba, after their defeat by Shaka. They moved separately, first into southern Mozambique (1821). In 1828 Soshangane was again attacked by Shaka's regiments and moved across the Zambezi to settle eventually in the Songea district of modern Tanzania. Here he founded the kingdom of Gaza. Zwangendaba, after being defeated by Soshangane, led his followers westward, defeated the Rozwi rulers of the later Zimbabwe Empire, and too crossed the Zambezi on 19 November 1825 (dated from a solar eclipse), to establish the Ngoni kingdom between Lakes Tanganyika and Nyasa. 1834 the land south of the Zulu kingdom between the Thukela and the Mzimkhulu rivers was devastated. The Thembu fled southwards and ravaged southern Natal and even attacked the Mpondo chief Faku. Annual Zulu raiding expeditions swept through southern Natal, capturing cattle and destroying crops. In 1824 the Mpondo were attacked again and Faku (temporarily) pledged fealty to Shaka. Other Natal groups fled southwards into the area of the South Nguni. Such were the Bhaca, under their chief Madikane, and a group of chiefdom fragments, mainly Hlubi, Zizi and Bhele, who settled among the Xhosa and were called by them amaMfengu (from ukufenguza, 'to wander about seeking shelter').

☐ But the greatest effect of the Mfecane was on the highveld. The process was begun by the dislodgement of two Nguni peoples in the Natal midlands, below the Drakensberg. These were the Ngwane, under Matiwane, and the Hlubi. Forced to flee, the Ngwane fell upon the Hlubi, defeated their chief and were eventually practically destroyed by colonial forces under Henry Somerset when they attacked the Thembu near Umtata (1828). The Hlubi, under Mpangazitha, also crossed the Drakensberg and, equipped with the short stabbing spear, laid waste the highveld Sotho south of the Vaal River. ☐ The first South Sotho chiefdoms to take the brunt were the Tlokwa and Sia, living near the Drakensberg passes. The Tlokwa were led by MaNthatisi, regent for her minor son, Sekonyela. Her reputation was such that the name 'Mantatees' was incorrectly applied to all marauding bands during this period. Raiding and pillage stretched as far west as the Tswana. Early visitors describe scenes of devastation on the highveld. The landscape in places was littered with human bones, stone walling was destroyed, and refugees were forced to live as hunter-gatherers, in extreme cases resorting to cannibalism. It took the genius of the South Sotho chief, Moshweshwe, to gather up some of these scattered groups, thus laying the foundations for the present BaSotho nation. ☐ For further details, and an insight into the contemporary debate, the following two books are essential: J.D. Omer-Cooper, The Zulu Aftermath (1966) and Carolyn Hamilton (ed) The Mfecane Aftermath (1993).

A view of Mapungubwe from the Iron Age site Bambandanyelo. (Department of Archaeology, University of the Witwatersrand)

woodland near the confluence of the Shashi and Limpopo rivers, whose inhabitants were engaged in ivory (and possibly gold) trade with the east coast, obtaining vast quantities of glass beads in return. Huffman argues that control of this trade, in addition to a great increase in cattle and the separation of the tribal court from the central byre, marked a fundamental change from what went before and laid the foundations of a powerful state, the first in southern Africa. K2 was later abandoned and the settlement moved to Mapungubwe Hill, one kilometre away. On this sheer-faced promontory a capital was established that dominated the surrounding countryside. Trade, wealth and power increased enormously. Cloth was imported from the east coast, and gold objects appeared for the first time in southern Africa. The famous gold sceptre and rhinoceros were found in a cemetery on the hill-top. By 1220 Mapungubwe was the capital of a state with several district centres and its influence spread as far as Great Zimbabwe 200 kilometres away. Mapungubwe was abandoned about 1270, possibly because of prolonged drought, and the centre of power then shifted to Great Zimbabwe.

The relevance of this excursion into history north of the Limpopo to the theme of this book is the connection of Zimbabwe with the Venda. By the fourteenth century the influence of the Zimbabwe Empire stretched from the Zambezi in the north to the lowveld enclave formed by the Drakensberg and the Olifants River in the south and there is evidence that Venda was at one time an outlying province of that Empire. Many of the unique features of Venda culture can be attributed to this fact.

Soon after the beginning of the eighteenth century a further development occurred among the Sotho of the highveld. They began to aggregate into closer communities, usually centred on rivers or permanent water points. This process of

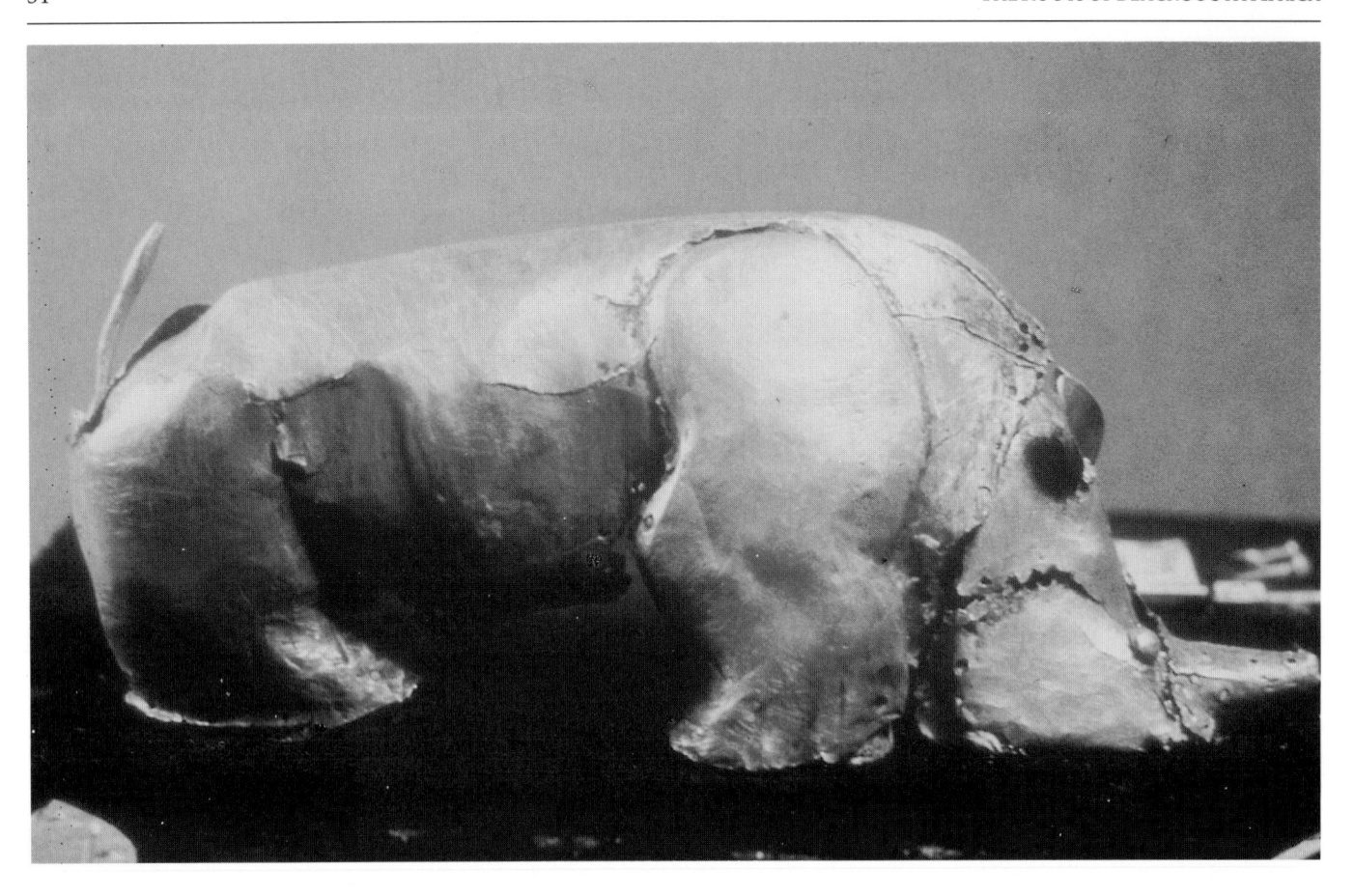

The gold rhinoceros of Mapungubwe. This famous statuette is one of the most beautiful objects to have been produced by Iron Age peoples. It was found with other smaller gold artefacts on Mapungubwe hill. Gold and copper were probably carried by traders to foreigners from Arabia and India who were present along the east coast as far south as Zanzibar from at least the first century AD. (Department of Archaeology, University of the Witwatersrand)

aggregation, which is traceable in the archaeological record (Huffman 1986), continued throughout the eighteenth and nineteenth centuries until, in the twentieth, some Tswana settlements were very large indeed, the whole chiefdom, in some cases, being accommodated in one enormous town.

This was indeed a major departure from the scattered settlements that appear to have characterised what went before. Huffman explains this aggregation in terms of the need for defence in an increasingly turbulent environment resulting from the expansion of settlers from the Cape Colony, the activities of Griqua bands and, especially, the disruption caused by the *mfecane*, the 'Time of Troubles' caused by the expansion of the Zulu kingdom under Shaka. But the process was undoubtedly also influenced by environmental factors. The nature of the highveld terrain, with its endless plains and lack of dense bush, exposed these little communities to attack to a much greater degree than were those groups living in the bushveld or in the broken country of the coastal strip. It is also significant that the size of settlement tended to increase the further west it was situated; that is, with decreasing rainfall. The need for perennial water supplies, then, joins with the need for defence to explain the Sotho move to aggregated settlements. As always, causes are multiple.

But there is a problem here. If the dating of Sotho closer settlement is correct, as it seems to be, it means that at least some of the range of cultural differences that distinguished nineteenth century Nguni and Sotho (to be discussed below) developed over an extremely short period of time (between about 1700 and 1800) and are of comparatively recent origin. This runs counter to conventional wisdom, and is indeed counterintuitive – unless we revise our theories as to the rate of cultural change in African societies.

To sum up, the differences between the four major groupings (Nguni, Sotho,

Aggregated settlement (possibly pre-Tswana) at Vlakfontein, Transvaal. Note the central assembly area. The resemblance between its layout and that of the larger Tswana towns of the eighteenth century is striking. (Department of Archaeology, University of the Witwatersrand)

Venda and Tsonga) appear to have been generated by a combination of (a) two very early traditions, going back to the Early Iron Age, (b) environmental influences stemming from Later Iron Age dispersal onto the highveld plateau from about the fourteenth century, and (c) the post-seventeenth century elaboration of cultural differences between the four groups, especially the establishment, among highveld Sotho, of aggregated settlements.

We have absolute certainty of this direct link with the past as far as the Sotho are concerned. This is particularly so of the Tswana. As Inskeep points out: 'The architectural details and grouping arrangements of these sites are so similar to those described from the early nineteenth-century Tlhaping capital of Dithakong and later (1820) Kuruman, and to the modern Tswana villages with their wards, that there can be no hesitation in identifying them as Tswana settlements.' At least one of the sites was occupied between 1470 and 1650, indicating that the Tswana had reached the southernmost limits of their expansion by the fifteenth century. Dating is not so certain for the Nguni, because of the relative absence of discovered Iron Age sites in Natal and the Transkei. Historical documents show, however, that Nguni-speakers were settled south of the Mthatha River well before the end of the sixteenth century, while oral traditions suggest that they were in the foothills of the Drakensberg as early as AD 1300.

CLASSIFICATION

In the Preface to this book, I hinted at the dangers of the classification of peoples in a pseudo-scientific way – the subtle shift of attitude that can arise when people are studied 'scientifically' and 'objectively' ('like butterflies pinned on a display board'). This is particularly evident in the work of physical anthropologists, with their aim of placing man within the biological kingdom: perhaps they have no choice in the matter.

But caution is needed when studying social and cultural phenomena. Cultures are products of the human mind and, to a great extent, are independent of biology. Any human being, whatever his or her genetic origin, is perfectly capable of learning any culture. Cultures change through time, as adaptations are required of them. Human beings also have choices. They can change their behaviour, make new rules, new interpretations, and, most importantly, can join any group that will have them. They are not determined by their culture, or group membership, nor, as animals are (to a very great extent), by their genes. Human groups, then, are not absolutes. They are constructs. They are also unstable, can disappear, or be absorbed into larger groups.

The main problem with classification in the world of men is that it can be abused politically. It can be used, on the one hand, to establish a particular group as superior, thus justifying political power and privilege, or, on the other hand, to

THOMPSON'S DESCRIPTION OF 'NEW LATTAKOO' (KURUMAN) IN 1823

'New Lattakoo' was established in 1817 by the Tlaping (Tswana) chief Mothibi after 'Old Lattakoo' (Dithakong) was abandoned. It lay at Maruping, 10 miles north-west of Kuruman, the London Missionary Society mission station under Robert Moffat. ☐ 'After breakfast I went out, accompanied by Mr Moffat, to survey the town, which is very extensive, containing from eight to ten thousand inhabitants. Though built without any plan or attention to regularity, it has a very lively and agreeable appearance. Everything is kept so neat and clean, that one cannot but feel pleased with the inhabitants, in wandering through the streets and lanes. The houses are all of circular form and of a very pleasant and convenient fashion, considering the climate and the circumstances of the people. The roof is raised upon a circle of wooden pillars, including an area of from twenty to thirty feet in diameter. About two yards within these pillars is raised a wall of clay, or of wattle and plaster, which is not generally carried quite up to the roof, but a space is left above for the free admission of air. In the centre or back part of the hut is constructed a small apartment where they keep their most valuable effects. Between the wall and the wooden pillars the people generally recline under the shade during the sultry hours. Each of these houses is enclosed within a close-wattled fence about seven or eight feet high, which is carried round it at the distance of six, eight, or ten yards, thus forming a private yard, within which are placed the owner's corn jars, and other bulky property. Each of these yards has a small gate, and all the houses are built exactly in the same style, and nearly of the same dimensions, except the king's, which is almost double the size of the rest. The king's house, and those of the principal chiefs, are each erected near a large camel-thorn tree, which is left there as a sign of rank. The streets are kept perfectly clean; neither bushes, rubbish, bones, or any other nuisance, are allowed to be thrown upon them. The best idea I can convey of a Bechuana town is to compare its appearance, from a little distance, to a immense barn-yard; the huts, with their conical thatched roofs, resemble very much so many stacks of corn. ☐ At a short distance from the main-town is a considerable suburb or village, containing about five hundred souls.' (Thompson 1827 (1967): 84)

The traveller Burchell's first view of Dithakong, in 1812.

debar a group from these resources. The relevance of this here is that ethnic classifications were used by colonial authorities to divide and rule. The problem of governing large black rural comunities, incorporated into South Africa by a succession of annexations, led administrators to adopt a policy of direct rule. But limitations on finance and manpower made it necessary to depend, at the local level, on the traditional authorities. The need to define the limits of their jurisdiction necesitated the defining of the margins of administrative units with precision, and this was done by importing the concept of 'tribe'.

The word 'tribe' comes from the Latin *tribus*, and is found in a number of European languages. It originally referred to the three founding political groupings in Rome (the Tities, the Ramnes and the Lucares), which were probably based on clans, but the term was later extended to the clan-based Germanic peoples, under chiefs, living beyond the borders of the Roman Empire. In Africa, 'tribe' was applied typically to chiefdoms, but was also used for larger groupings and categories, such as clusters of related chiefdoms, groups under headmen, and even such broad categories as Nguni- and Sotho-speakers. The term was thus extremely

Stone-walled ruins at Dithakong. Although adjacent to the eighteenth century Tswana town, it is not certain who the original builders were. They are thought to have been Khoikhoi. (Department of Archaeology, University of the Witwatersrand)

vague, and also subtly derogatory. Tribes were what other, less advanced people had: the West had 'nations' or 'ethnic groups'. These considerations have led anthropologists, historians and others to stop using the term, in favour of the more precise description of social units. The imposition of cultural ('ethnic') classification (based ultimately on the work of anthropologists and linguists) has been particularly pernicious in South Africa. It formed the basis of the system of Bantu Authorities introduced in the 1950s, and of the so-called 'homelands'. The obverse of the coin is that ethnic classification can be used for sectional interests, as in the claims, in some quarters, to an inalienable primordial group existence.

Be this as it may, some form of classification is necessary to help us conceptualise the complexities of the Southern Bantu past. But it is important to understand the nature of anthropological classifications. They do not necessarily refer to *groups* 'on the ground', but rather to broad categories based on linguistic, cultural and, often, historical criteria.

As we have seen, although they all shared a basically common way of life, described by Huffman (1982) as the 'Bantu Cattle Culture', Southern Bantu societies

---

THE SURVIVORS OF THE *SANTO ALBERTO* MEET THE XHOSA-SPEAKERS IN 1593

The Portuguese ship Santo Alberto *was wrecked on 24 March 1595, 'at the Rock of the Fountains, where the Land of Natal commences', probably the promontory to the west of the Bushman's River mouth. The survivors were greeted with great kindness by a chief, Lupance, 'with about sixty negroes'. The situation would seem to indicate that these people were the most western representatives of the Xhosa, probably of the mixed Xhosa-Khoi group of Gqunukhwebe, judging from the description of their huts. Lupance was probably a petty chief, and does not appear on 'official' genealogies. Here is the description of the people by the Portuguese recorder of the wreck, the pilot, João Baptista Lavanha, chief cosmographer to the King of Portugal:* ☐ 'The dress of these Kaffirs is a mantle of ox-hide, with the hair outwards, which they rub with grease to make it soft. They are shod with two or three soles of raw leather fastened together in a round shape, and secured to the feet with straps; in these they run with great lightness. In their hands they carry the tail of an ape or a fox [jackal] fastened to a thin piece of wood, with which they clean themselves and shade their eyes when observing. This dress is used by almost all the negroes of Kaffraria, and their kings and chiefs wear, hanging to the left ear, a copper ornament made after their own fashion. ☐ These and all other Kaffirs are herdsmen and cultivators of the ground, by which means they subsist. They cultivate millet, which is white and the size of a peppercorn; it is the fruit of a plant of the size and appearance of a reed. Of this millet, ground between two stones or in wooden mortars, they make flour, and of this they make cakes, which they cook among embers. Of the same grain they make wine, mixing it with a quantity of water which, when it has fermented in a vessel of clay and has cooled and turned sour, they drink with great enjoyment. ☐ Their cattle are very fat, tender, well-flavoured, and large, the pastures being very rich. Most of them are hornless, and the greater number are cows, in the abundance of which their riches consist. They use milk and the butter which they make from it. ☐ They live in small villages, in huts made of reed mats, which do not keep out the rain. These huts are round and low, and if any person dies in one of them, the others take it down with all the rest of the village, and remove to another spot, thinking that in a place where their neighbour or relation died everything will be unlucky [a reference to witchcraft beliefs]. And so, to save this trouble, if anyone is ill they carry him into the thicket that if he is to die it may be out of the houses. They surround the huts with a hedge, within which they keep the cattle ... ☐ ... Most of the inhabitants of this land, from latitude 29° and downwards, are circumcised ... They obey chiefs whom they call Inkosis. The language is the same in nearly all Kaffraria, the difference being only like that between the different dialects of Italy and the ordinary dialects of Spain. The people never go far from their villages, and thus they know nothing except that which concerns their immediate neighbours ... ☐ They value the most necessary metals, as iron and copper, and for very small pieces of either they will barter cattle, which is what they esteem most, and with which they trade, exchanging them for other treasures.' (Theal 1898: 293–4)

have been subdivided by scholars into four main categories: Nguni, Sotho, Venda and Tsonga. Briefly, the Nguni were strongly cattle-orientated, spoke a language containing the so-called 'click' consonants (derived from Khoisan sources) and lived in scattered settlements, the Sotho occupied the central interior plateau and parts of the Transvaal bushveld, the Venda the well-watered mountain ranges of the Soutpansberg and the Tsonga the hot flatlands of the Transvaal lowveld and Mozambique.

By the late eighteenth century these major groupings had themselves become differentiated culturally. The Nguni chiefdoms south of the Umzimkulu River all spoke related dialects of a language which had changed somewhat from that spoken north of the river. The southernmost dialect of these peoples, that of the group of chiefdoms that called themselves 'Xhosa' (Gcaleka, Ngqika, Rarabe, Gasela), was the first to be reduced to writing by the missionaries, thus giving its name to the whole dialect group, including those variations spoken by Thembu, Bhaca, Mpondo and Mpondomise. The Nguni dialects north of the Umzimkulu, similarly related (although some scholars distinguish linguistic sub-groups), were

Junod observed this Venda iron smelting furnace in the Soutpansberg, built into a termite mound. Note the skin bellows and the tuyere of antelope horn. The mining and smelting of iron and copper was confined to Sotho and Venda, in whose country deposits occurred. Nguni smiths were adept at working the metal obtained from the north. Fuel was dung, charcoal or leadwood and a stone hammer was used.

In the courtyard of a Venda chief. (Anitra Nettleton)

accorded the general label 'Zulu', from the dominant state in the area. Similar linguistic divergence occurred in the Sotho and Tsonga groups. The dialects spoken by western Sotho, Sotho in the north and central Transvaal, and those in the eastern Free State and Lesotho, were sufficiently different to allow them to be classified as Tswana, North Sotho and South Sotho respectively, while Junod distinguished five Tsonga 'sub-dialects' (actually languages – Ronga, Hlanganu, Djonga, Bila and Hlengwe). Certain cultural differences were added to those of dialect in making these classifications.

The Sotho peoples were in some respects less homogeneous than the others. As we have seen, this was because of the strong influence on some of them of the Venda. Although the Venda themselves preferred the fertile valleys of the Soutpansberg, their influence spread southwards into the lowveld bay lying beneath the escarpment, strongly influencing the cultures of the Sotho communities they found there. Such were the Lovedu, Kgaga, Thabina and Sekôrôrô, whose cultures began to differ quite strongly from those Sotho situated on the plateau. The main cultural differences seem to have been: a greater ritualisation of the chiefship, with elements of divine kingship; a greater interaction with nature, for instance the annual 'biting' (*loma*) of the termites (see Chapter 3); the presence of a drum cult;

the centrality of the fabulous 'Beast' in the initiation ceremonies (see Chapter 7); cross-cousin marriage with the mother's brother's daughter only; an apparent greater freedom of women than was the case among other Sotho (with the possibility of female chiefs) and the ritual prominence of the father's sister in the ancestor rituals. Finally, the lowveld environment meant far fewer cattle and the relative absence of blood sacrifice. In the light of the above it seems useful to make a distinction between Sotho-Tswana, including all those on the highveld (Tswana, Pedi, South Sotho) and Sotho-Venda (the lowveld chiefdoms just described).

The major cultural groups of the nineteenth century, then, were:

NGUNI — (a) South Nguni (Xhosa-speakers)
(b) North Nguni (Zulu-speakers, Swazi)
SOTHO — (a) Sotho-Tswana (Tswana, South Sotho, North Sotho of the highveld)
(b) Sotho-Venda (North Sotho-speakers of the Lowveld,
e.g. Lovedu, Kgaga, Thabina, Sekôrôrô)
VENDA
TSONGA

Of these groups the Nguni and Sotho were by far the most numerous. Population figures are obviously unavailable, but the Venda were always confined to their mountains in the far north and the Tsonga, settled for centuries in Mozambique, seem to have been fairly recent arrivals in South Africa, in the second half of the nineteenth century. Despite the differences between them, it is possible to collapse these groups into two broad categories or culture complexes – the Nguni and Tsonga, on the one hand, and the Sotho and Venda, on the other. This division coincides with geography. Nguni and Tsonga inhabited the eastern area between the Drakensberg escarpment and the Indian Ocean. Sotho and Venda, on the other hand, were western central plateau people, with the exception of the Sotho-Venda of the lowveld, an interstitial group, as we have seen. The main associated cultural elements were as follows:

EAST — NGUNI/TSONGA	WEST — SOTHO/VENDA
ecology diverse	ecology uniform
scattered settlement	nucleated settlement
decentralised administration	centralised administration
local initiation	centralised initiation
exogamous marriage	endogamous marriage
territorial army	age regiments
strong patriliny	bilateral emphasis
clan ancestors	bilateral ancestors
witchcraft feared	sorcery feared
pollution by 'dirt'	pollution by 'heat'

It is a major theme of this book that the differences between Nguni and Sotho are the result of transformations that have occurred as a response to adaptations made to these two very different environments. The genius of the Southern Bantu as innovative social engineers is apparent here in a way that dispels the picture, so often presented, of 'primitive', static, peoples, the passive victims of chance.

Despite these classificatory attempts it is important to recognise the essential unity of the Southern Bantu culture area. This is clearly seen in the languages spoken. They all belong to the vast language family that stretches south from a line drawn across the continent from about Gabon, in the west, to Kenya, in the east,

Dampier's Description of Natal in the Seventeenth Century

'The country of Natal lies open to the Indian sea on the East, but how far it runs back to the West is not yet known. Great part of the country which respects the sea is plain, champion, and woody; but within it appears more uneven by reason of many hills which rise in unequal heights above each other. Yet it is interlaced with pleasant valleys and large plains, and 'tis checked with natural groves and savannahs. Neither is there any want of water, for every hill affords little brooks, which glide down several ways [into the rivers] ... ☐ The natives of this country are but of middle stature, yet have very good limbs. The colour of their skins is black; their hair crisped. They are oval visaged, their noses neither flat nor high, but well proportioned ... Their chief employment is husbandry. They have a great many bulls and cows, which they carefully look after, for every man knows his own, though they all run promiscuously together in their savannahs, yet they have pens near their own houses, where they make them gentle and bring them to the pail. They also plant corn, and fence in their fields. They have guinea-corn [millet], which is their bread; and a small grain [sorghum], which is their drink. ☐ Here are no arts or trade, but every one makes for himself such necessaries as need or ornament requires, the men keeping to their employment, and the women to theirs. ☐ The men build, plant, hunt, and do what is to be done abroad. The women milk [incorrect], cook etc. Their houses are not great or richly furnished, but are made close and well-thatched ... They wear but few clothes, and those extraordinary mean. The men go in a manner naked, their common garb being only a piece of cloth, of silk-grass, as an apron. At the upper corner it has two straps around the waist; and the lower is fringed with the same, and hangs down to their knees. They have caps made of beef-tallow, 9 or 10 inches. They are a great while making these caps, for the tallow must be very pure ... It would be ridiculous for a man to be seen without a cap, but boys are not allowed to wear any. [This is a reference to the Zulu headring.] ☐ The women have only short petticoats which reach to the knee. The common subsistence of these people is bread made of guinea-corn, beef, milk, fish [?], eggs, ducks, hens & c. They drink milk often to quench their thirst, and this sometimes when it is sweet, but commonly sour. ☐ Besides milk, they make a bitter sort of drink from grain purposely to make merry with; and when they meet on such occasions, the men make themselves extraordinary fine with feathers stuck in their caps very thick ... ☐ Every man may have as many wives as he pleases; and without buying none are to be had; neither is there any other commodity to be bought or sold but women. Young virgins are disposed of by fathers and brothers: the price according to beauty. ☐ They have no money in the country, but give cows for wives, and therefore the richest man is he that hath most daughters or sisters. They make merry when they take their wives, but the bride cries all her wedding day. ☐ They live together in small villages, and the oldest man governs the rest, for all that live together are of kin, and therefore they submit to his government. They are very just and civil to strangers. (Bird 1888: 56–9)

A Swazi man making fire in the traditional way by twirling a hard stick in a block of softer wood. His headring of beeswax denotes a married man.

characterised by a unique grammatical feature called the 'alliterative concord' which governs the form of all elements in the sentence according to the prefix of the main noun, thus imparting an alliterative beauty to expression, and a precision that equals that of Latin or Greek. A (Zulu) example must suffice:

Izinkomo zikabhabha zonke zaluka entabeni.
Cattle of my father all graze on the mountain.

Abantwana bakabhabha bonke badlala entabeni.
Children of my father all play on the mountain.

There are slight differences in grammmatical structure between the main language families but many of the differences in vocabulary are due to phonetic variations that go far back into the past and are governed by sound shifts of a type similar to that occurring in Germanic languages according to the rules of the so-called Grimm's Law (whereby, for instance, *th* becomes *d*, as in English 'thank' becoming German 'dank'). The main sound shifts between Nguni and Sotho are as follows:

Nguni	nk	becomes	Sotho	kg
	th			r
	nd			t
	ng			k

Applying these rules (Meinhof's Law) it is possible to explain why the Zulu word *thenga* (to buy) becomes *reka* in Sotho, *thanda* (to love) becomes *rata* and *inkosi* (chief) becomes *kgosi*. It is often possible to guess at the meaning of a word by applying the rule changes: doing so can also reveal otherwise unsuspected connections, as that between the name for the boys' initiation school among Sotho *(bogwêra)* and the rather different Xhosa circumcision rite *(ubukhwetha)*. They are identical terms, despite their seeming difference. Even the clicks in Nguni (especially in Xhosa) are fairly superficial substitutions of Khoi or Bushman consonants for normal Bantu ones, although a number of terms, especially those to do with divining and ritual, were taken over by the Xhosa-speakers from San. Venda is the odd man out here, as in many other respects. In grammar it is related to the Shona of Zimbabwe but its vocabulary is strongly influenced by Sotho, reflecting the Shona domination of the original Sotho stratum. Some Tsonga, especially those subjected to Zulu domination in the nineteenth century (such as the so-called 'Shangaans') and those who acted as middlemen in trade between Zululand and Lourenço Marques, possess a striking linguistic phenomenon in that the women speak Tsonga in the home while the men speak Zulu. David Webster (1991) has shown how this is linked to strategies of situational survival. Today migrant Tembe-Thonga men in the Kosi Bay area use Zulu in order to find employment in the outside world, and in regional politics, while Tsonga women use Tsonga when they wish to assert their authority within the homestead, for the Tsonga gave much more status to women than did the rather chauvinistic Zulu.

These, then, are the peoples with whom this book deals. The following pages take up different aspects of their societies and cultures in more detail, seeing these institutions in terms of the problems that faced the Southern Bantu in the distant past, and the often elegant solutions they designed to meet them. Cultures are, after all, structures intended to achieve security, happiness, and, above all, meaning, for those who practise them.

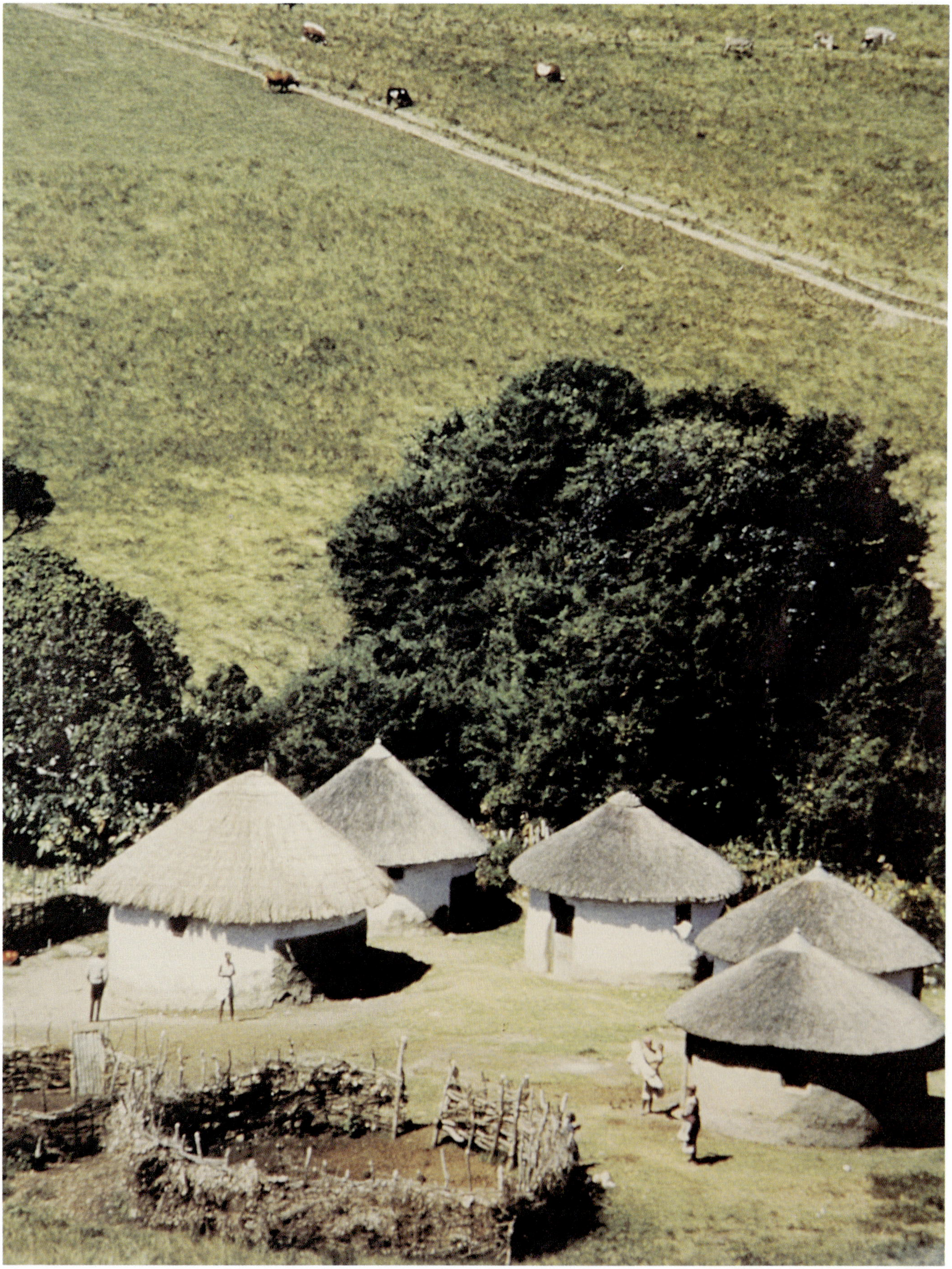

CHAPTER 2

LAND, CATTLE AND SETTLEMENT

THE SOCIETIES described in the last chapter were all faced with the same basic challenge – the efficient exploitation of the natural environment to ensure the basic subsistence requirements of their peoples. Agropastoralism demanded suitable soils for raising crops and for pasturage, the latter free from tsetse fly. There were also other prerequisites: clay for the potters, thatching grass, wood for fuel, building material and utensils and, where possible, iron and copper ore for smelting and the fashioning of weapons. Proper management of these resources was such an important matter that its control was a crucial responsibility of the political authorities. And here ecological factors came to the fore, imposing differing strategies on the rulers.

These strategies have been clearly spelt out by Sansom (1974). Broadly speaking, a distinction can be made between the hot, deciduous savannah of the low-lying bushveld, situated between the Drakensberg escarpment and the coast (the favoured area of Early Iron Age settlement), and the rolling grasslands of the central plateau that were progressively occupied by Later Iron Age peoples after about AD 1000. Bushveld-type environment commences, in fact, in the region of the Great Fish River, in what is now the eastern Cape, and continues north along the Indian Ocean coastal strip as dense coastal bush and patches of evergreen forest as far as northern Natal, where it merges into the characteristic subtropical lowveld. This stretches like a sea from the escarpment of the Berg, through today's Kruger National Park, across southern Mozambique to the coast. From this seemingly endless plain rise isolated koppies and ranges of low hills, many the defensive centres of small chiefdoms.

The bushveld vegetation varies somewhat from south to north. The savannah of Natal and the eastern Cape (known technically as temperate thornveld), is dominated by a single type of tree, *Acacia karroo*, mixed with species of *Maytenus* (mainly pendoring) and *Rhus* (kareeboom), and enjoys a rainfall of 600–900 mm a year. The country away from the coast is undulating and bisected by many rivers and streams, the more favoured areas being covered by the nutritious and 'sweet' *rooigras*, excellent for livestock. Much of the area, however, is sour grassveld in which the grasses lose their palatability in winter. The Transvaal lowveld is far hotter, summer temperatures often soaring into the 40s. The bush is much denser and contains a wide variety of deciduous trees, such as species of *Acacia* thorn (e.g. knobthorn), *Combretum* (e.g. leadwood), marula and bushwillow, with mopane in the north. Beneath the canopy of bushveld trees there is a thick cover of tall grasses which supported the herbivore fauna for which the area is still famous and the

A typical Mpondo homestead in the rugged coastal strip. Note the close link with the cattle byre. (H. Kuckertz)

small herds of cattle owned by the Early Iron Age communities. Rivers are few and surface water is not as abundant as in the south. This rich vegetation provided a varied diet for both man and beast. The Kriges, working among lowveld Sotho (the Lovedu) in the 1930s, published a list of over 500 plants which they collected ('a small proportion of the flora') many of which were used as relishes or as medicines. The marula nut, in particular, when made into beer, has strong antiscorbutic properties. The sophistication of recipes this rich floral resource makes possible contrasted strongly with the comparative blandness of diet among peoples of the plateau and the uplands of the eastern seaboard.

As we have seen, it was not until the emergence of the Later Iron Age (about AD 1000) that Bantu-speaking communities moved up over the escarpment onto the rolling grasslands of the central plateau. Here they met a vastly different ecological reality. Especially in the south of the area (the present Free State and the southern Transvaal) the mild winters gave way to extremely dry winters with severe frosts between May and September and trees effectively disappeared, apart from small patches of trees and bushes in protected places, such as river beds and rocky outcrops. For the first few centuries the country appears to have been fairly well watered, but by the seventeenth century there had been a marked change in climate and drought was an ever-present threat. A stage was reached when annual rainfall dropped steadily the further west one moved until the crucial threshold of 500 mm (20 inches) per year was reached. Beyond this point the staple crops of millet, sorghum and later maize could not be grown and grassland for cattle gave way to semi-desert.

Conditions to the north of the central plateau were not as extreme. From the watershed of the Witwatersrand the plateau drops steadily towards the Limpopo River, temperatures rise and the vast plains are covered in plateau bushveld, a habitat dominated by sweet-thorn (*Acacia karroo*). This vegetation type occurs when there is an annual rainfall of 500 mm (20 inches) or a little more, so the area was in fact marginal for traditional settlement. The tree crowns do not touch (as in the lowveld) and the country has a parklike appearance, often merging into grassveld. The grass layer is made up of more or less tufted species, including *rooigras* on which cattle thrive, but because of the long dry winters large concentrations of stock may be difficult to maintain in a small area throughout the year.

These two broad ecological zones, which Sansom calls the East and the West, had a marked effect on both the subsistence economy and the system of local administration of the communities inhabiting them. There is also evidence that this influence went even further, impinging on such aspects as kinship, marriage, religion and even attitudes to witchcraft, sorcery and ritual pollution. Certainly, the natural environment affected material culture, art and symbolism in general. Here we are concerned with its effect on economic life.

Sansom has suggested that the main difference between the cultures of lowveld and highveld, East and West, were caused by differences in terrain. In the East the relatively high rainfall, broken country and variations in altitude resulted in considerable diversity of soils and vegetation within a relatively small area. Particularly in Natal and the eastern Cape, 'the terrain undulates in a sequence of lozenge-like formations, bounded by brooks, streams or rivers' in which grassy hills and slopes provide cattle pasture, the alluvial bottoms of streams yield rich arable soil for crops, and clay and thatching grass, although patchily distributed, are at least within fairly easy access. Sansom describes it as 'a country of small-scale repetitive configurations that contained a variety of natural resources'. The West was quite different. Here, on the central plateau, one is often confronted with large expanses of relatively uniform country. To find different soil types, vegetation cover and, especially, water means travelling long distances. The implications of this are clear. In the East it was at least possible for the population to be scattered fairly uniformly over their territory, for each little community could be self-sufficient in the raw materials necessary for subsistence. In the West, on the other hand, this was more difficult. Merely possessing large areas of grazing only, or of arable soil, was not enough: these resources had to come in a package in which each element was present, something not found in the West. Thus different exploitation strategies were forced on the communities of East and West – leading to the contrasting settlement patterns of the Nguni and Tsonga, on the one hand, and the Sotho and Venda, on the other, as well as different emphases in social organisation and worldview.

In the well-watered East, occupied by Nguni and Tsonga, it was possible for people to spread out over the country in a fairly uniform manner. Each homestead had its own fields and cattle byre and homesteads were scattered at varying distances from one another, from a few hundred yards to several miles. The Nguni tended to build residential sites along the spurs and hills that characterise Natal and the Transkei. These were often intersected by deep, bush-filled valleys, which provided fuel, building material and the all-important medicinal plants; fields were usually sited along the ridges or, preferably, on the rich soil of a stream or river bank. Higher ground, typically grass-covered, served as pasturage, so that cattle were never far away and were herded nightly in the byres that formed the symbolic centre of each homestead. Occasionally a more extensive grazing range

A view of Dingane's capital, Mgungundlovu, by Allen Gardiner. Built in 1829, on a slope near the grave of Zulu, founder of the clan, it contained, at the top, the seraglio where Dingane's wives lived while the regiments occupied numerous grass huts grouped around the enormous parade ground. The capitals of the Zulu kings were unique in South Africa for their size, and were basically military barracks. (Africana Library)

was felt to be necessary and cattle posts, manned for months at a time by herdboys, were established in the mountains and highlands.

Among Tsonga, on the other hand, settlement was typically in the lowveld bush, relatively flat country with less surface water. Even when, in the nineteenth century, many Tsonga groups moved westward and settled among Sotho and Venda, they tended to occupy the lower-lying areas, either from preference or because forced to do so by more powerful neighbours. The Kriges describe the Lovedu (Sotho) situation in the 1930s: 'The people of the royal group, the nucleus of the tribe, live mostly in the mountains; the valleys and flats are occupied by Shangana-Tsonga, recent-comers who are despised by the Sotho.' The Tsonga headmen, who with their followers formed part of some eastern Venda chiefdoms, occupied areas that the Venda themselves found impossibly hot.

This ecological variation made it possible for Eastern political officers to delegate local authority on a wide territorial basis. Areas of larger chiefdoms, lying at a distance from the capital, were placed under a hierarchy of control by which the chiefdom was divided into large districts under sub-chiefs. These, in turn, were subdivided into wards (called 'locations' by white administrators after annexation) under headmen who were responsible for the welfare of the members of homesteads within their area. Each smaller area 'nested' within the next larger, producing a four-tiered hierarchy of estates of administration. The whole chiefdom was thus subdivided into a series of increasingly large estates, each of which contained all the resources needed for economic life. At each level the political authority (chief, sub-chief, headman) was responsible for allocating residential sites and land for agriculture or grazing, as well as for regulating the agricultural cycle. The whole system was ordered through a series of courts, culminating in the court of the chief, to settle disputes arising from conflicting interests – typically encroachment on lands and damage to crops and stock. This model was particularly characteristic of Nguni. Tsonga chiefdoms tended to be much smaller, with the chief assisted by ward headmen, so that the full hierarchy was not necessary.

The situation in the West (Sotho and, to some extent, Venda), at least in the eighteenth century, was very different. The entire chiefdom had to be handled as a whole so that the scattered resources could be deployed to the advantage of all its subjects. This was achieved by the concentration of the people into villages, under

---

XHOSA TERMS FOR CATTLE

The importance accorded to cattle is reflected in the complex terminology used to describe them. Special terms are used to describe shape of horns and colour. The following is a selection from a list of such terms given by J.H. Soga in his book The Ama-Xosa: Life and Customs (1931): ☐ HORNS ☐ empikwane ('wings') – growing backwards towards the neck ☐ equtu – turned inwards towards forehead ☐ exaka – hanging down on each side of jaws ☐ enqhukuva – without horns (polled) ☐ entsasaule – upstanding horns ☐ enxele (left-handed) – pointing in opposite directions ☐ emanqindi ('fists') – horns blunted to prevent damage ☐ COLOURS ☐ ebadi ('springbok') – red or black with small white spots ☐ elubelu – cream coloured ☐ ebomvu – red. Any shade except light ☐ emdaka – dun coloured ☐ emfusa – dark brown, nearly black ☐ egwangqa – light bay or light red ☐ emhlope – white ☐ elunga – white with black patches ☐ emnyama – black ☐ epemvu – black and red with white face ☐ empofu ('eland') – yellowish ☐ enala – irregular white marks on forelegs of red or black ox ☐ enco – red and white patches ☐ engqombo – yellow or cream, with dark brown on flanks and muzzle ☐ engwevu – grey, with red or black background ☐ enkone – white along backbone ☐ (There are nine other terms for colour.)

Aggregated settlement: part of the Ngwato (Tswana) capital of Serowe, in 1934. The pattern is similar to that of Mochudi (p. 13). (McGregor Museum, Kimberley)

the direct control of the chief. Originally each chiefdom probably occupied a single village. As population grew, however, satellite villages would arise, always strongly orientated towards the capital. This tendency towards nucleated settlement was strengthened as surface water decreased, reaching its apogee among Tswana in the western Transvaal, especially on the marches of the Kalahari desert, where large towns sometime contained the whole chiefdom. The position of the various sections of Venda was similar, but strongly modified by the forested ranges of the Soutpansberg mountains on the southern flanks of which the chiefs built their impressive stone-walled capitals *(musando)* modelled on the Zimbabwe complex to the north.

It is obvious that these large concentrations of population created certain problems. Fields and, to a certain extent, cattle could not be accommodated close to homesteads. The Tswana, therefore, were forced to establish their fields some distance from the town, in areas of good soil. This led to a form of transhumance. For part of the year (from planting to harvest) some family members resided in small temporary settlements close to the fields to tend them and keep birds away. Cattle, too, were herded at permanent cattle posts situated in the grazing; milk had thus to be transported daily from these outlying areas back to the capital. In contrast Nguni herds were dairy herds and Nguni thus enjoyed milk as an important staple. It is tempting to suggest that this led to a de-emphasis on agriculture among Nguni: there is some evidence that Nguni fields were smaller than those of the Sotho and that Sotho (and Venda?) men were more willing to work with their womenfolk in tillage than were Nguni. Among Tsonga, tsetse fly in large areas of their subtropical bushveld limited the cattle population, thus contrasting strongly with Nguni affluence.

To sum up the main administrative difference between East and West, especially from the eighteenth century onwards: the eastern chiefdoms decentralised economic control to lesser political officers, while western chiefs administered the total chiefdom from their capitals as an integral unit. As Sansom comments

> The Sotho economy turned men outward. Each man surveyed the tribal territory from the town, seeing in it a wide ambit for personal opportunity ... This contrasts with the inwardness of the Nguni whose complement of resources comes in a neat package. The Nguni overlooks a neighbourhood from his family kraal, and that neighbourhood contains ... the best part of the resources to which he has access. (1974: 145)

It is clear from the archaeological record that South Africa's first farming communities were established at least by the end of the third century and that they were cultivating millet *(Pennisetum)* and probably other plants. By the seventeenth century we find the full range of millet, sorghum (*Holcus sorghum*), maize, several varieties of bean, pumpkins, melons, tobacco and dagga (*Cannabis sativa*) in existence. Maize was a late arrival: it is thought to have reached Africa, at the mouth of the Congo, in 1560 from America and to have spread rapidly thereafter, probably becoming the predominant crop (in certain areas) in the mid-twentieth century.

The adoption of agriculture, wherever it first occurred in Africa, transformed not only the diet (leading to population increase) but also the very nature of these societies. The hunter-gatherer strategies of the Late Stone Age, which imposed continual movement over a territory, gave way to fairly permanent settlement and

---

XHOSA LOVE OF CATTLE

'*The Kaffirs live principally by cattle-breeding. For the well-being of the family, a sufficient number of cattle are required, whose attendance and treatment is the sole responsibility of the father of the family, in which he is assisted by his sons. The Kaffir's cattle is the foremost and practically the only subject of his care and occupation, in the possession of which he finds complete happiness. He sees to their grazing, and in the evening they return to the stable, constructed of a jumble of thorny branches, and which adjoins his hut. He also attends to the milking of the cows and generally to everything requiring attention in cattle raising. The bellowing or mooing of a cow is so pleasing to the ear of a Kaffir that it can enchant it to the point where he will pay greatly in excess of its worth, and cannot rest until he has acquired it. Frequently one sees the horns of these cows and oxen, which reach an unusual length, and which are bent in various directions and figures in accordance with the fancy of the owner. At times they surround the back of the head and come together below the throat. In the case of another pair of horns, only one has this downward direction, and the other stands upright; others are bent in a similar way to that of one or other kind of antelope, and for choice one sees an imitation of the spiral-shaped antlers of the antelope known in the Colony under the name of Eland. (Alberti 1815: 54)

A Zulu homestead painted by G.F. Angas. (Africana Library)

a sedentary way of life. It also raised urgent problems of the division of labour between men and women, the ownership of land and crops, inheritance and the handling of trespass and crop damage, all of which demanded the formulation of rules to manage them. Control of these matters necessitated the appointment of officials who had the authority to adjudicate between competing interests and the establishment of amounts of compensation for infraction of the rules.

The growing of crops also necessitated methods of storage, ways of protecting the crops from birds and drought and recipes for food preparation – and here the importance of beer, in both social and ritual life, began to loom large. Environment even influenced cosmological ideas. Strong medicines and elaborate rituals were developed to ensure rain, control insect pests and ensure the fertility of the fields.

As we have seen, land was ultimately under the control of the political authorities. This, in effect, meant the ward or village headman, who was responsible for seeing that each homestead head in his area of jurisdiction was allocated a piece of land for each of his wives. This was always done in consultation with all ward members to ensure that the rights of others were not infringed. Field boundaries were roughly indicated where population density was low and there was an abundance of land, but precisely demarcated in areas where arable land was in short supply or where population pressures increased. Clear boundaries, usually consisting of narrow strips of unworked land left between the fields or a furrow or ditch dug in the presence of both parties, came into being. There was a tendency for members of the same descent group to occupy a certain piece of territory, and here the headman attempted to allocate lands together, but the patchy nature of soil type distribution and rainfall also made it advisable to spread the risk by not having all a homestead's fields in the same area.

Theoretically all land belonged to the chief, and could not be alienated. Yet, once a man had been allocated a field, he enjoyed the perpetual right to use it against all comers, provided that he (or his wife) continued to cultivate it. He thus had rights of usufruct. Perhaps more importantly, the produce of the fields was his, and his alone – although, as we shall see, in actual fact produce belonged to the 'house' of the wife whose field it was. It was she who owned the produce and her approval had to be obtained before her husband could dispose of it. Rights in fields lapsed temporarily after harvest, when they were opened up to the cattle of the entire community for stubble-grazing. It was deemed the height of anti-social behaviour to prevent this.

Southern Bantu cultivators were well aware of the qualities of the various soils. The Pedi, for instance, recognised seven different types of soil. Except among Nguni, the main agricultural implement was the hoe, consisting of an iron blade attached to a wooden haft. The size and shape of the blade differed between groups. The Tsonga used a short-handled diamond-shaped hoe-blade while South Sotho and Tswana hoes had large oval-shaped heads with a horizontal curve, mounted on long handles. Hoe-heads were made by smiths from locally mined iron and were so valuable that, among Venda, they frequently took the place of cattle in the bridewealth exchanges. Nguni, on the other hand, used wooden digging sticks for cultivation, possibly because of the scarcity of iron in their area.

Work in the fields was the responsibility of women, although the heavy work of clearing virgin ground and breaking the soil was done by men. Work parties were organised whereby neighbours were invited to assist at the crucial period of weeding and harvesting, recompensed by convivial beer-drinks. Storage among Nguni and Venda tended to be in grain pits dug in the cattle byre and covered with a flat stone, sealed with cow dung. All Sotho stored grain in enormous woven baskets or (especially in the extreme west) in granaries specially constructed to discourage termites. One Nguni-speaking group, the Hlubi of the Natal uplands, also used Sotho-type grain baskets: it is interesting that these people have traditions that link them to the legendary period when Nguni and Sotho cultures separated from each other.

Agriculture may have been the earliest element in the Iron Age revolution and the principal source of subsistence, but cattle, particularly by the end of the first millennium, loomed far larger in the thoughts of men. Even in the lowland bushveld cattle were kept if at all possible; among Nguni and Sotho-Tswana they were a major preoccupation. Not only were they a source of food (especially milk), but their skins and horns were used for clothing and utensils – and even their dung was an important source of fuel and plaster. In many groups oxen were used as beasts of burden and cattle racing was a popular pastime among Nguni. All the Bantu languages have words describing cattle in terms of sex, age, coloration and shape of horns, while favourite oxen had praise names and were trained to re-

ALBERTI'S DESCRIPTION OF A XHOSA LION HUNT IN 1807

To kill Lions or Tigers [leopards], the hunters form a closed ring round the animal by filing close up to one another, when all are equipped with shields. One throws javelins at the hemmed-in animal, and if it leaps at one or other of the other hunters, he throws himself to the ground and covers himself with his shield, when others instantly rush up and stab it. In this kind of hunt, the hunters are not infrequently wounded and sometimes killed. ☐ Although in other respects the killing of a Lion is regarded as very creditable, it is nevertheless connected with moral impurity; in general such a feat is usually followed by a special festivity. When the hunting party has returned to the neighbourhood of the village, the one who inflicted the first wound on the Lion that was killed, is hidden from view by shields held in front of him. At the same time one of the hunters leaves the troop and praises the courage of the slayer with a screaming voice, accompanied by a variety of leaps, and then returns again, when another one repeats the performance, during which the others incessantly shout hi! hi! hi! and beat their shields with knobkirries at the same time. This is continued until they have reached the village. Now a rough hut is constructed not far from it, in which the Lion slayer has to remain for four days, separated from any association with the rest of the horde, because he is impure. Here he colours his whole body with white ochre, and youths who have not yet been circumcised, and who moreover are in the same position of moral impurity [see Chapter 7], bring him a calf for his sustenance ... When the four days have passed, the impure person washes himself, covers himself again as usual with red ochre, and is conducted back to the horde by an official of the chief. Finally a second calf is slaughtered, which everyone may eat with him, as the impurity no longer exists. (Alberti 1815: 76–7)

A Tswana lion hunt in 1837, recorded by Cornwallis Harris. Each man carried two or three assegais and a six foot stick topped by a plume of ostrich feathers that was planted in the ground to distract the lion, much like a matador's cape. (Brenthurst Library)

spond to whistled commands. The Bomvana of the Transkei even had a sacred herd held by the chief in trust for his people. Cattle raiding, to swell the chief's herd, was one of the most important duties of young Nguni warriors and often led to war with other chiefdoms. Cattle were slaughtered only with reluctance, and usually only as part of the worship of the ancestors. They were the principal medium of exchange, especially in contracting a marriage; their passage from the groom's family to the bride's family legitimised the children, and possession of many cattle allowed a man to acquire many wives (and thus fields), thus increasing his wealth and ensuring him the resources to dispense all-important hospitality. Johnny Clegg, well-known musician and Zulu expert, in a personal communication, has described the almost total identification of a homestead head and his bull among present-day Zulu. It is crucial that the head rises and passes water each morning before his bull does if he wishes to retain his authority over his homestead. There is indeed a very definite mystical relationship between the family herd, in its central cattle byre, and the human family itself, and their fortunes are interlinked. This link was further stressed among all Nguni among whom sour milk (*amasi*, the main article of diet) could only be drunk with members of the same clan. It thus served as a metaphor for kinship and appears as such in one class of Zulu folktales in which the refusal of twins to share *amasi* is undoubtedly a concealed reference to a desire for incest on their part (Hammond-Tooke 1992).

Hunting was practised by all groups, but was secondary to agropastoralism. It was undertaken mainly for food – except among the Zulu, who much preferred beef (Maclean 1992: 82) – and clothing, and as an exciting pastime. The most effective method was by drives that herded game into V-shaped fences leading to pitfalls or, for single large game such as elephant and hippopotamus, covered pits

Hurutshe (Tswana) women preparing grain for storage. Note the enormous wicker baskets, typical of Sotho, in which the grain is placed. The only Nguni who used such baskets were the Hlubi, whose origins seem to show close Sotho contact. (Africana Library)

Drawing of a Tswana game drive, by A.A. Anderson. Note the elaborate system of game pits into which the animals were driven – a unique piece of evidence of past ingenuity and collective effort. (Africana Library)

set with sharp-pointed wooden stakes. A variety of traps was also used for smaller animals and birds. Shaw states that 'The Venda alone stretched nets across valleys; they were loosely fixed so that they collapsed on the animals that walked into them' (Shaw 1974: 97). Spears and axes were used: only the Venda had the bow and arrow. Hunting was set about with ritual. Hunters and their dogs were doctored, and hunters purified after killing dangerous animals. South Nguni subjected antelope killed to a special ritual, performed by a young pre-pubertal girl in the cattle byre, before this 'wild' meat could be appropriated for domestic use. Monica Wilson believes that the Sotho depended more on hunting than did other groups, based on their use of animal names, such as Crocodile, Wild Pig, Buffalo and Ape, for their wider patrilineal lines of descent (see Chapter 5). As she writes (1969:162) 'One can hardly escape the conclusion that the ancient Sotho rituals reflect the life of a people for whom hunting was more important than cattle-keeping, and some of whom, in the distant past, recognized the smelting of iron as their major resource.' This last comment refers to the Rolong (Tswana) who 'danced' (*bina*) in honour of the hammer and of iron.

Fishing was not a part of Southern Bantu economic life except among the Tsonga, who used wicker basket traps in the rivers and fish weirs on the coast. They were the only peoples to have canoes, square-sterned and made of boards laced together. These were manned by two men, one rowing with two paddles and one baling, and could accommodate twelve persons, but were only used on rivers.

THE CENTRALITY OF THE HOMESTEAD

Whether the population was scattered, or concentrated into villages or towns, the basic unit of settlement among all Southern Bantu was the homestead. Indeed, Kuckertz (1990) has described the Mpondo homestead as a universe in microcosm. It was in the confines of the homestead that the whole pageant of life and death was played out – children born and socialised, food prepared, clothing and utensils manufactured and the warm (but sometimes tense) relationships of the family group experienced. Each homestead was to a degree a self-contained economic and

The homestead of a Swazi chief's wife. As with the Zulu, chief's wives, with their retainers, were often situated at strategic points within the chiefdom to provide surveillance over the local population.

legal unit, with its own cattle and crops, so that, in a very definite sense, the homestead and the chieftainship were, in their different ways, the two essential pillars on which society was built. In fact the homestead head was a little king within his domain, with powers of life and death over all who lived in it. As we shall see in the next chapter, in all chiefdoms there were local administrative officers over the various territorial subdivisions, as there were wider groups based on kinship, but in a sense these were secondary to the primordial relationship between homestead head and chief.

In all groups the homestead consisted of a group of dwelling huts and store huts arranged in a traditional pattern. Among Nguni and Tsonga these were always also associated with a cattle byre, but this was not always true of Sotho and Venda villages, where cattle had perforce to be herded at distant cattle posts. Both the spatial arrangements of homesteads *vis-à-vis* each other and the use of space within each dwelling hut carried a symbolic message. The Southern Bantu were polygynous, that is, a man could have more than one wife, although not all men, by any means, availed themselves of this possibility. Wives were ranked, typically in order of marriage, each wife with her children constituting a 'house' (Nguni *indlu*; Sotho, *lapa*), and this fundamental fact had to be given visible social expression, for the ranking had major legal implications, especially for inheritance. The number of wives a man had, then, affected the spatial layout of his homestead.

The exception to the ranking of wives by order of marriage was found among the Nguni. Among South Nguni there were two main divisions, termed the 'great house' (*indlunkulu*) and the 'righthand house' (*esukuneni*) (and sometimes, a third house 'of the grandparents'), and all wives were allocated as 'rafters' (*amaqadi*), or auxiliary houses, to these major divisions. Among other Nguni, the great house was that of the homestead head, with wives allocated as righthand and lefthand to it. This arrangement governed inheritance. If there was no heir in the great house, its property passed down to the first rafter of that division, and so on, until the last rafter inherited the whole divisional estate. The same was true of the righthand division. Normally the children of one division could not inherit from the other: this had implications for succession to the chieftainship (see Chapter 3). Often the establishment of the two divisions and the allocation of supporting wives was only done fairly late in a man's life, one reason for the succession disputes that bedevilled Nguni family life. Among non-Nguni groups the great wife was the first wife married, with subsequent wives ranking accordingly.

This system meant that, in the past, homesteads tended to be large and complex in structure, although it is almost certain that some polygynists preferred to establish separate homesteads for their different wives, sometimes at some distance away. Detailed information on this matter is lacking, but the practice was still common in the twentieth century.

We are indebted to Adam Kuper (1982) for our understanding of the spatial symbolism of homestead layout. He has demonstrated that, despite differences in detail, there was an underlying organisational pattern, based on two underlying plans, one concentric and one diametric. In the concentric representation the centre was opposed to the periphery, and the inner was contrasted with the outer. In the diametric representation there was opposition between 'right' and 'left', and between east (or 'up') and west (or 'down').

Among Nguni the important elements in the homestead were the orientation of the cattle byre to the dwelling huts, and the relative siting of the huts of wives of the two great divisions to each other. The relationship of the byre to the great hut was perhaps the most crucial, for it symbolised the opposition between the patrilineal principle, in the person of the husband, on the one hand, and the affinal (marriage) relationships, associated with the wives (who, through the exogamy rules, were always strangers) on the other. A great gulf existed between these two principles. Wives and cattle were, in a sense, symbolically equated in the bridewealth exchanges and (paradoxically) had to be kept separate from one another. No wife, during the age of childbearing, could enter the byre, nor might she have anything to do with the cattle. The sour milk of the Nguni herd, as we

MPONDO ELEPHANT HUNT 1824

'After the messenger had been dispatched, I was presented with a cow by the chief of the amaNtusi tribe, Manyaba. This tribe was part of the amaMpondo nation ... On the following morning we were awakened by the noise of the inmates of the kraal. They were getting ready to hunt some elephants that were near at hand. We accompanied the party. Each man carried as much as six or 12 assegais. Presently, they and their dogs approached the elephants. The dogs, by constant barking, so attracted the elephants' attention as to afford the hunters an opportunity of coming close enough to throw their assegais. The first that was flung struck one of the animals' left shoulder. This hit, in accordance with custom, entitled the thrower to claim the tusks. The rest of the party then threw a shower of assegais. This process was repeated until the elephant became so exhausted as to become an easier target to its assailants, who, creeping closer, whilst the dogs continued to keep the animal at bay, threw their assegais at it with greater force than before. When, at length, the elephant's strength failed he fell, crushing the bushes under him, and then died in a few minutes. The hunters now withdrew their assegais, almost as numerous as the quills of a porcupine. Another elephant was then attacked and dispatched in like manner, except that it did not suffer its fate quite so tamely, for it twice chased the hunters during the assault ...'

☐ This hunt was observed by Henry Francis Fynn in the Lusikisiki district of Eastern Pondoland in 1824, and recorded in his diary. (Stuart and Malcolm 1969: 104)

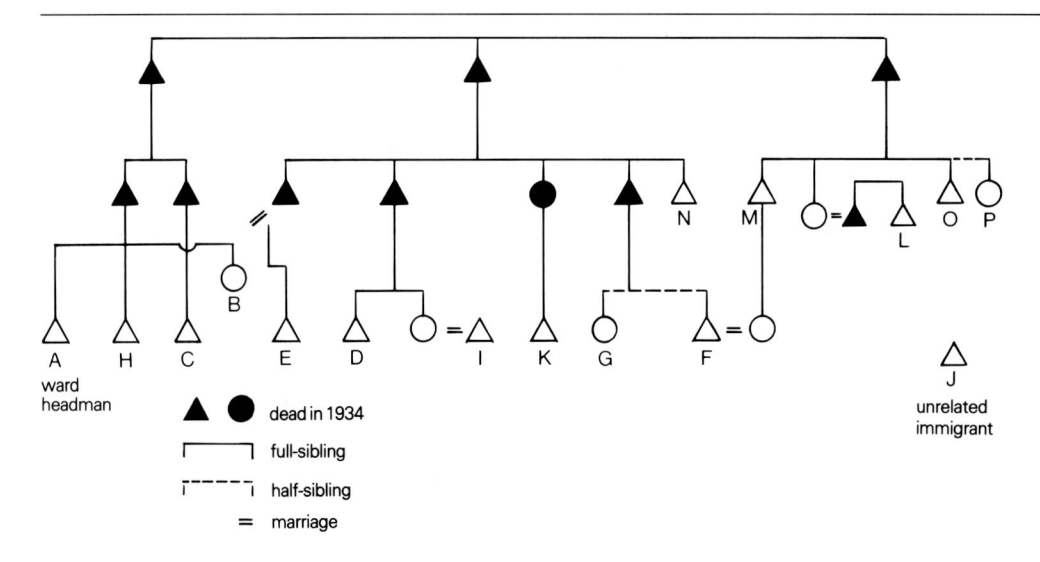

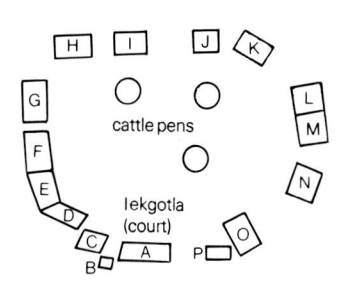

The structure of a Tswana ward, showing genealogical relationships between household heads. Rampedi ward, Mochudi, 1934 (after Schapera).

have seen, could only be consumed by patrilineally related members of the homestead: a newly married wife, as a stranger, was not allowed to drink it – until a special sacrifice of a goat was made to allow her to 'drink the milk'. The cattle byre was also sacred to the patrilineal ancestors: the sacrificial offering to them was slaughtered within its confines and the corn stored in pits dug beneath the thick covering of dung. The first thing the homestead head should see on awakening each morning was the horns of his beloved cattle silhouetted against the dawn. In Kuper's terms the axis between the houses of the homestead and the cattle byre was one of up/down (homesteads were frequently built on a slope with the huts looking downhill towards the byre).

The symbolic expression of the ranking of the wives lay at right angles to this, and involved a right–left axis. Here there was much variation among Nguni. The entrance to the cattle byre could be placed facing, or opposite, the wives' dwellings; the placement of junior wives could vary, and the absolute positioning of 'right' and 'left' was not fixed (it could depend, for instance, on whether one was looking towards or away from the byre). Thus the Bomvana (South Nguni) and Zulu reversed each others' orientation of the right and left sections, but had the same organisation of more junior wives; the Swazi arranged wives in the same way as the Mpondo, but reversed the orientations toward the byre, and so on (see Kuper 1982: 140ff).

Kuper considers that the Sotho-Tswana had a similar pattern, although overlaid by the conditions of village living. He quotes Mönnig (1967: 212–3):

> Ideally the Pedi consider that a polygamist should build the homesteads of his wives in a specified order according to rank. A man should build the *lapa* of his second wife on the left of that of the first wife, and immediately adjoining it, so that one outside wall serves for both homesteads. The third wife's *lapa* is then built on the right of the superior homestead. Subsequent wives then have their homestead alternately to the left and the right. This has the effect, due to the building pattern, of the homesteads forming a semi-circle, with the superior homesteads in the middle.

It appears that in the distant past Nguni homesteads (which were not fenced) frequently also included the dwellings of married sons. Wilson (1969: 116) states that in the early nineteenth century three generations living in one homestead was the

Variations in homestead layout. Note the positioning of the entrance to the byre (after A. Kuper).

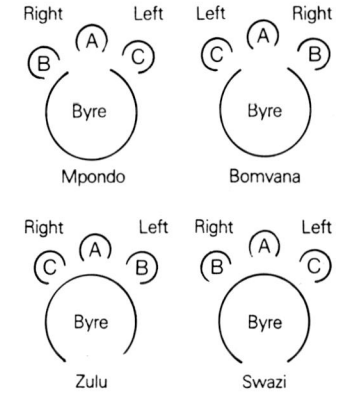

The letters A, B, C indicate the order of seniority of the women

widespread pattern and quotes 'elderly Mpondo men', in 1931, saying that it was not unusual to find twenty married men in one household, although small homesteads of only two huts also occurred. A similar tendency characterised the Sotho, among whom the homesteads of brothers tended to be contiguous, occupying a specific part of the village or town.

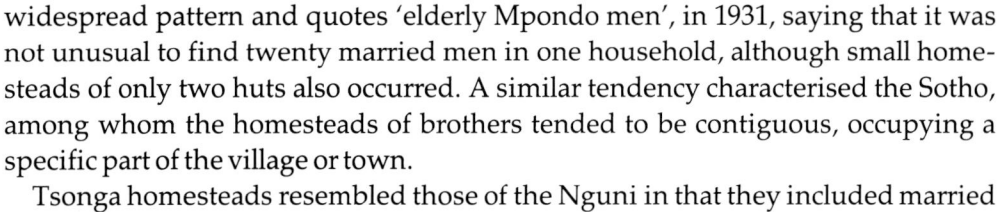

Tsonga homesteads resembled those of the Nguni in that they included married sons and their families and were often very large and built in a complete circle. According to Junod they were invariably fenced, not for defence but as a protection against witchcraft, and tended to be situated in patches of bush which served not only as a protection against winds and prying eyes, but also the functions of a privy. Each homestead also had a central byre, and a special tree, 'the mystical stem of the village [homestead]', that served as the family altar. Unlike Nguni and Sotho, Tsonga did not divide property by houses. While the homestead head was alive, all homestead property belonged to him and he could do what he liked with it. Succession was also very different. Instead of going from father to son, as elsewhere, it went from eldest brother to the next eldest, only then reverting to the son of the eldest (delphic succession).

Venda, like Sotho and Tsonga, lived in large, stockaded villages, each ruled by a chief or petty-chief, usually built in almost inaccessible positions on a mountain slope or other elevation, linked by winding footpaths through the bush. Within the village each family lived in its own walled homestead in which the dwelling huts and store huts were arranged around a mud-paved courtyard. Wives were ranked, but there was no visible clue to this, as in other groups, in the spatial disposition of the houses (Van Warmelo and Phophi 1948: 345), although the rank order was of course known to the family elders. The status of chief wife depended on her being married by cattle especially denoted by the family council as *dzekiso* cattle: even a cross-cousin (the preferred marriage mate) would not be accorded great wife status if she was not a *dzekiso* wife.

The symbolic expression of the ranking of wives in the homestead (the right/left or inner/outer axis) was intimately connected with the important matter of inheritance and the conservation of household property. The rules regulating this have been termed the 'house-property complex', perhaps the most distinctive aspect of Southern Bantu domestic life.

Each house, associated with its respective wife, formed an independent economic unit with its own dwelling huts, fields, kitchen and granary. Livestock, especially cattle among the Nguni, could be attached by the homestead head to a house, their issue becoming house property in the full sense. Once allocated, house property was inviolable and could only be used for the benefit of the children born to it. Perhaps most importantly, cattle coming into a house could be used to enable a son to marry and to this end brothers and sisters were linked together. A Kgaga (Sotho) homestead head told me in 1966: 'this homestead belongs to my sister. She provided the cattle for my wife', and this is probably the reason why, among Venda and Sotho-Venda, the father's sister (*rakgadi*) is the appropriate ritual officiant in the ancestor cult (see Chapter 8). Should the homestead head wish to use cattle to obtain a wife for a son in another house, he had to first get the consent of the wife concerned. It is clear that this principle of the independence of houses put wives in an extremely strong position in the homestead.

There were, of course, also debits to the polygynous account. Although a man was expected to treat all his wives with scrupulous impartiality, jealousy between co-wives was proverbial, especially over the fortunes of their sons, and this was

Lovedu grain pit. Below the opening is a bell-shaped cavity. The entrance is sealed with a stone and covered with earth and dung. Similar grain pits were used by South Nguni. (Davison 1984)

exacerbated by the frequent custom of leaving the formal announcement of ranking to later in marriage. Witchcraft accusations between co-wives were endemic. Sons of chiefs were particularly at risk (there was so much to gain or lose) and they were typically sent away to be brought up with maternal relatives to avoid assassination. Yet perhaps, on balance, the influence of polygyny was benign, in terms of the enhanced status and power it gave to women in the domestic sphere. Relationships within this sphere of the homestead, and beyond, will be further discussed in Chapters 5 and 6.

Scattered settlement: a Zulu homestead near Lake St Lucia. Note its isolation from other homesteads and the central cattle byre.

THE SPATIAL DISTRIBUTION OF HOMESTEADS: THE WARD

Although the homestead was the most basic social unit, enjoying almost complete social and economic autonomy, a single homestead could not be entirely self-sufficient. Three things forced it to look outside its confines to other homesteads for its very existence. Firstly, marriage. Even those societies, like those of Sotho and Venda, that permitted marriage with close kin, forbade it between brothers and sisters, so that wives for homestead sons had to be obtained from other homesteads. Secondly, certain seasonal economic tasks demanded intensive labour over a limited time span – labour beyond the resources of the homestead, such as bush-clearing, weeding, harvest – and the assistance of others was indispensable. Thirdly, there was the need for defence against both human and animal attack. Single, isolated, homesteads were just not socially viable. Even among Nguni, the scattering of homesteads was never uniform over the whole tribal territory and settlement tended to cluster in certain areas. These areas were always under the control of local governmental officers, called 'headmen' in the literature, the areas

Everyday Life; The Evening Meal

Although it is impossible to depict with any authenticity the daily life lived in precolonial South Africa, there are still today rural pockets where the daily rhythm has continued comparatively unchanged. Here is an extract from The Realm of a Rain-Queen, the beautifully written study of the Lovedu by the distinguished anthropologist, Eileen Krige, and her husband, Jack Krige. It describes their impressions when they began fieldwork in Duiwelskoof in 1928. ☐ 'The sun has sunk low in the western horizon when you wend your way back to the village. The herdboys, with whistles and cries, are bringing home the cattle, goats, and donkeys. Two of them, one on an ox, one on a donkey, are having a race on the last level piece of ground near home. Others carry bundles of wood under their arms for the khoro [courtyard] fire... ☐ Everyone is converging homewards. Some women are coming with... pots of water on their heads... Those coming from the fields bring with them baskets of pumpkins and green mealies for the evening meal. One woman, carrying a bundle of sugar-cane, is being tormented by two men who, despite her obvious unwillingness to give them any of it, are helping themselves; for people are thought to have a sort of right to picked sugar-cane, which is not a food, but like sweets among ourselves, something pleasing to the palate, to be shared with others. Last of all, panting heavily, come the young girls who went to fetch wood, each with a heavy load on the head. ☐ In the village some of the fires are already lit. One woman is cooking pumpkins for the evening meal. She cuts them into convenient pieces, removes the pips but not the outer skin, then packs them one above the other in a large pot, at the bottom of which is a little water. A second pot, wide-mouthed and shallow, is inverted over the top, smeared down with a little of the red substance covering the seeds, and the whole allowed to steam over the fire... Another woman is preparing some relish to eat with porridge from the morning. It grows darker and darker. The fires, some in the courtyard, some in the huts, but each the centre of a little family group, become a deep crimson, their cheerful flickering giving one a sense of homeliness and quiet joy. At the courtyard fire where you are sitting, a small girl is cooking her tin of "food", consisting of five treasured grasshoppers mixed with tomato, which she found growing in the kraal hedge. Every now and then she stirs this brew with a stick. The others are roasting mealies and nuts. A herdboy comes in and lays down beside his grandmother a bird he has killed. She is pleased with the gift, thanks him warmly and praises him with the praise of his name... Boys are always told by their grandmothers to bring them birds; this they like doing, for there are so many ways in which grandmothers can return the gesture – boiled njugo beans, monkey nuts, or sugar-cane being always welcome. ☐ In the khoro, the three men of the village are sitting by their fire; the herd-boys sit at another... A boy, who has just been called for supper, comes back with a cake of porridge and some relish in his hands to eat it in male company in the khoro. Another goes home to eat, but returns later on. The conversation has veered round to the hunting of cane rats with wooden traps, the prevalent sport for this time of year, when one of the boys comes with some monkey nuts which he has begged from an old woman. These are roasted in their shells in the fire and eaten by the company... "Let's ask riddles", intervenes Khiebe. "Here is

LAND, CATTLE AND SETTLEMENT

Venda (far left) and Thembu (above) women stamping maize; (left) Mpondomise girl carrying wood (H. Röntsch); (right) Xhosa women at beerdrink (Morris and Levitan 1986)

one: riddle-me-riddle-me-ree (thaiii), the witches are dancing on the thorns". "Stupid", scornfully rejoins Mudumi. "We all know that one. Hailstones, of course, for they bounce as they fall on the grass". After pondering a moment he challenges: "Thaiii, the ox of my father has entered the pool, I remain holding its tail". Roars of derision issue from the rest, "A porridge-twirler", they answer almost all together. The spiked head of a twirler is like the horns of an ox; it is thrust into the pot of water, while one holds it by the handle ... It is impossible to capture the poetry of these riddles; you cannot render their alliteration or play upon words in English ... ☐ The men have retired to their huts, whence they will not reappear. The women have eaten the evening meal informally round the fires and are just chatting. In a hut three girls are sitting by candlelight, one of them, who has been to school, is writing a love-letter for her friend to her lover in town. "Why are you throwing me over?" she asks. "Why don't you write? Please send me a nice cloth and blanket, but not one like that which you gave your wife!" In another hut some children have persuaded Mamujaji, an elderly woman, to tell them tales. She begins,

"Ngano-Ngano (a story, a story)". They reply, "Ngano". Once upon a time" she continues, but before she gets further they again interject, "Ngano". Then she goes on, "there lived a boy who had sores all over his body". "Ngano", they repeat whenever the speaker hesitates or takes a breath. "One day when the girls went to fetch grass ..." this is the beginning of a story about a bird who gives away the girls who kill the boy. A marked characteristic is the frequent occurrence of a song and refrain, during the telling of a tale, in this case, "Phogu, Phogu ya burwa", & c ("bird, bird of the south"), so that what with the interjections and singing of the chorus of the refrain, the listeners appear to take as active a part as the narrator herself ... ☐ By eight o'clock most of the people have already retired. The bigger boys ... stay up latest; but soon all is quiet. On moonlight nights, however, the boys and girls dance and play in the khoro or outside the village until a late hour. Similarly, if there is beer in the village, there will be noise well into the night and very often quarrels and fights as well. When the spirit of a possessed woman comes upon her, there may be drumming and singing for her to dance all night; then no one gets much sleep.' (J.D. and E.J. Krige 1943: 27–8)

they controlled being termed 'wards'. Among Sotho and Venda, wards were contiguous and formed parts of the main village or town; among Nguni, they were largish areas of country, perhaps a hundred square kilometres in extent, into which the chiefdom territory was divided for administrative purposes. Some variation occurred between and within groups: here two examples will be discussed – Zulu (Holleman 1986) and Tswana (Schapera 1935), representing the two broad classifications. It is, of course, impossible to know for certain the exact composition of pre-contact wards, for they were never recorded. These examples date from the 1930s, but refer to areas relatively untouched (at least in this regard) by change; they can thus be tentatively used to reconstruct the past.

Among Zulu, a ward (*isigodi*) came into existence with the movement of population into a new area, either because of the expansion of power of a particular chief, overpopulation at the centre, or because of illness or misfortune in the original home area. In all cases, the establishment of a new ward needed the approval of the chief, in fact it was usually instigated by him and organised around one of his wives. She and the sons of her house, with their families, would be settled in the area. Invariably they were accompanied by a number of unrelated families, and these founder families, royal and commoner, were together termed *abadabuka* ('those who broke away'). Subsequently other unrelated families, either singly or in groups, submitted themselves under the *khonza* rule (see Chapter 3) as subjects of the ward headman. They were known as *izikhonzi*: without *izikhonzi* there could not be an administrative area. Each ward thus had a dominant lineage, usually of the royal clan, the head of which was the formally appointed headman. This domination, although basically political, tended also to be numerical, for royal wealth in cattle allowed for the acquisition of wives, and such lineages burgeoned.

As time passed the ward area filled up, both with descendants of the original *abadabuka* families and by the accretion of more *izikhonzi*. At this point there was a tendency for the more powerful of these families to demand more space for expansion, leading the *induna* – with the approval of the chief – to allocate them new areas of settlement within the general ward area. These areas were not intended to be merely parcels of lineage land on which wealthy extended families could settle and multiply. The settlements were, rather, the nuclei around which, over the years, foreign elements (individuals or family units, belonging to different clans) would range themselves. In this way there developed, within the ward, separate homestead clusters (almost like villages), each constituting a distinct territorial unit or sub-ward (*isiqinti*). Each had its dominant lineage, whose head was recognised by the *izikhonzi* who subsequently settled in the area. This 'sub-headman' oversaw his little area and represented its members at the headman's court. A picture emerges of a settlement pattern in which the individual homestead was surrounded by others to which it stood in a variety of different relations. Some were homesteads of members of the same extended family, others were unrelated neighbours, but all were members of the same little community, united under the sub-headman and ward head. The ward was thus the point of articulation of homesteads into the political system.

The pattern of related homesteads tending to be established in a particular area seems to have been a basic one among Southern Bantu and is even more clearly demonstrated among Sotho. Among them village life made it impossible for every homestead to have its own cattle byre, and limited space forced people to settle close together. Among Tswana, for instance, a village or town was built up from small groups of related homesteads, arranged in a circular plan with the com-

Threshing maize in a private courtyard. Note the typical South Sotho porch. (Ashton 1952)

Construction of a Zulu hut. The method of interlacing the saplings is typically North Nguni. South Nguni bent the saplings inward and joined them at the apex, like the spokes of an umbrella.

ponent homesteads distributed in a ring facing towards a central open space, the meeting place *(kgôtla)* of the men. It also contained one or more cattle byres and a shelter against the elements. Schapera refers to such a unit as a 'hamlet'. Bigger villages were made up of several, or many, of such hamlets, clearly separated from one another by lanes or roads of varying widths; the pattern can still be discerned in the ruins of Later Iron Age settlements in the Transvaal.

The important point for us to note is that the inhabitants of each hamlet formed a distinct social grouping, each with its own *kgôtla* where members met to discuss their affairs. The homesteads in the circle were frequently joined by a common outside wall and were the dwellings of a group of men descended from a common grandfather or great grandfather in the male line. Schapera (1935) recorded the exact composition of such a hamlet in the Kgatla capital of Mochudi in 1934 (it also had the status of a full ward): a plan of its layout, with the genealogical relationships between its homestead heads, will be found on p 57. Twelve of the sixteen homestead heads in Rampedi belonged to segments of a single family tree. Of the remaining four homestead heads, one had been adopted by a ward member, two were married to ward women and one was a 'stranger'.

What is clear is that, in all groups, homesteads of close patrilineal kinsmen tended to cluster together for mutual support. To this extent, descent was an important factor in social life. The question as to whether or not there were, in addition, wider-ranging groups based on the descent principle (so-called 'clans', 'lineages' or 'totem groups') will be discussed in Chapter 5.

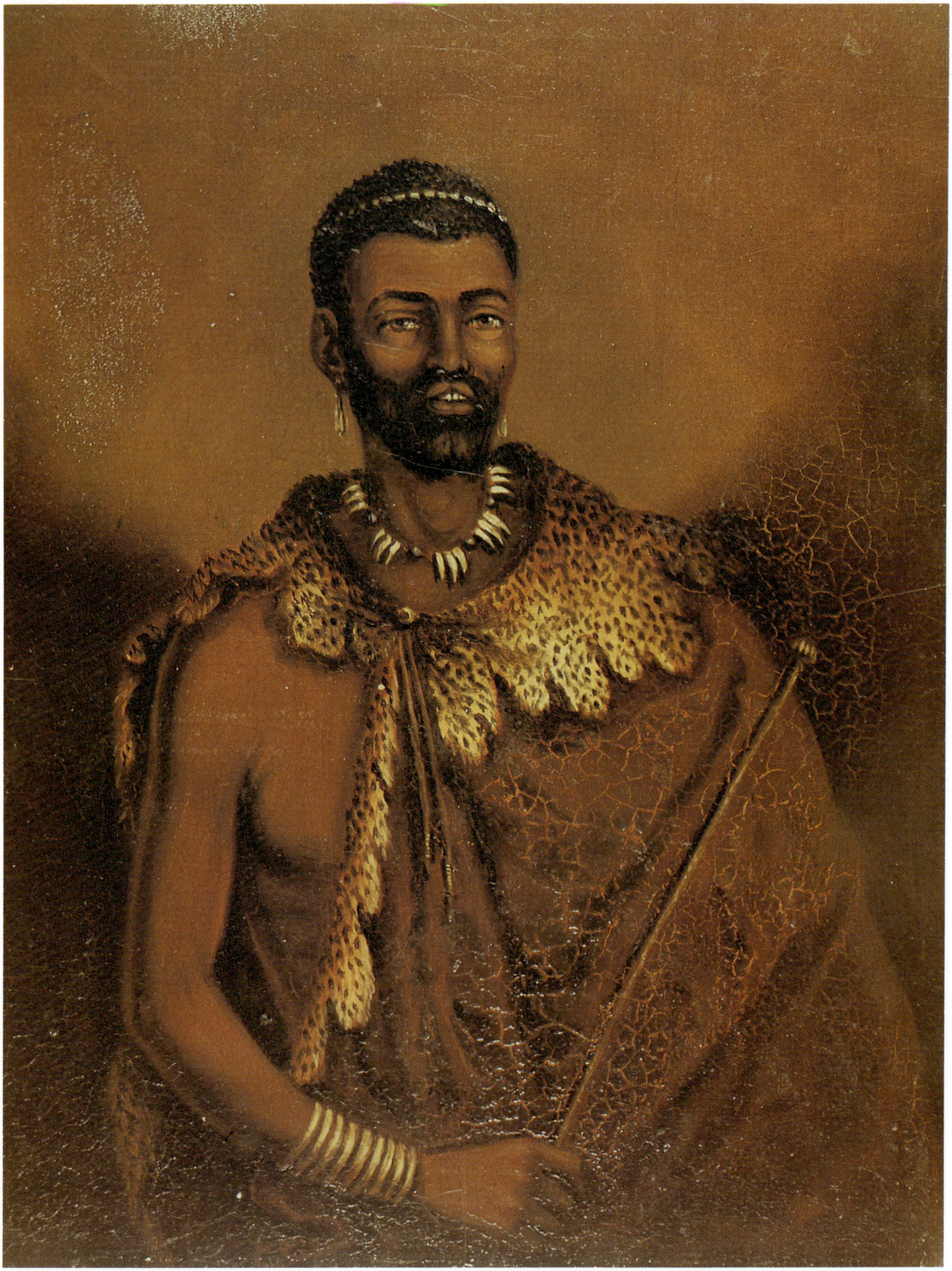

CHAPTER 3

CHIEFS, COUNCILLORS AND COMMONERS

THE SOUTHERN Bantu have been living under chiefs since at least AD 800. We do not know precisely how this major change in social organisation took place. Certain scholars believe that it developed from a previous system of independent, territorially based descent groups (clans and lineages) whereby a numerically dominant clan gained control over others, its head becoming chief. Despite the plausibility of the theory this is not the only way in which the move to chiefs could have occurred. In some other parts of Africa chiefs and headmen attained power through sheer force of personality and natural leadership qualities, founding villages and attracting around them a group of followers, usually patrilineal kin but also matrilineal, as well as non-relatives. Unlike the Clan Model, in which the new political unit was essentially kin-based, and patrilineal at that, the Big Man Model stresses the fundamental fact that political groups always include unrelated peoples. This is their defining quality. But all this is speculation. We shall probably never know for sure how Southern Bantu chiefdoms developed.

The Ngqika chief Sandile, by F.I'Ons. (Africana Library)

What we do know is that the coming of chieftainship transformed the essential nature of these societies. Now, for the first time, certain individuals were accorded the authority to make decisions on behalf of the group as a whole, and also to settle disputes between its members. Non-state societies tend to be egalitarian, political authority, where it exists, being based on age (as, for instance, among some East African societies); acceding authority to one man was a major step that presumably was taken only with hesitancy and circumspection. The main problem, then, was to ensure that this authority stuck. The only way to achieve this was by ritual, by clothing the chieftainship in mystical sanctions to ensure, as far as possible, compliance with this new political (or governmental) authority.

This was achieved, firstly, by developing the concept of 'royal blood' ('blood' being a metaphor for descent). The chieftainship reposed in a royal family and succession to the office depended on the claimant being in the correct relationship to the previous chief. A division thus developed between royalty and commoners. Secondly, the chief was deemed sacred. This vague term denotes a mystical link between the person of the chief and the chiefdom as a whole. In its extreme form this meant that the health and strength of the ruler could influence the weather, crops and general wellbeing of man and beast. In southern Africa this sacredness reached its highest point with the Venda (possibly due to the origin of their rulers in the Zimbabwe Empire) and with the Lovedu (of the Sotho-Venda division) whose queen, Mudjadji, was expected to commit ritual suicide – and thus achieve divine status – after the fourth initiation school of her reign. This extreme elaboration of divine kingship was not typical, though, and Southern Bantu chiefs, although accorded great respect, were generally closer to their subjects. Thirdly, chiefly status had to be protected by strong medicines to ward off witchcraft, sorcery, assassination and attack from other, antagonistic, chiefdoms. Finally, the integrity of the chiefship was ensured by the sacra, the sacred heirlooms and medicines that symbolised chiefly authority, possession of which was the ultimate legitimation of the ruler – as in the sacred grass ring, impregnated with the body dirt of previous chiefs, known as *inkatha* among Nguni.

THE POLITICAL UNIT

However it came into being, once in place the Southern Bantu political unit was essentially based on territory. It was never a purely kin-based group, for the authority of the chief extended over all who lived within his domain, whatever their origin. This was accompanied by a new concept, that of fealty to a political functionary. The Nguni word for this was *khonza*, the act of granting allegiance to a political superior in return for land and protection. Here we stand before a new type of relationship, something not found in those societies that anthropologists term 'stateless', in which the only authority exercised is authority over kinsmen. And here it is important to stress that the anthropological use of the term 'state' differs significantly from that used in marxist analyses, a fact that has caused much misunderstanding among Africanist historians among whom 'state' is used to describe polities of some complexity in which social classes can be clearly distinguished. Southern Bantu chiefdoms were states, in the anthropological sense, precisely because they had institutionalised political authority.

As we shall see, some chiefdoms created wider, more complex, structures that dominated certain areas and that came to be called kingdoms, confederations or paramountcies. Such were the Zulu kingdom under Shaka, the South Sotho kingdom under Moshweshwe, the Swazi kingdom, the Pedi confederacy and (perhaps) the nineteenth century Xhosa state. All were later developments, however, of the basic chiefdom that, for 1500 years, formed the pattern of Southern Bantu government.

Government involves two types of activity, political and administrative. M.G. Smith (1956) has drawn a clear distinction between power and authority. The exercise of power, which is essentially political, is always between equals and always attempts to influence the course of events. If this attempt is successful it can be said that power has been exercised, *ex post facto*. Administrative authority, on the other hand, which is always associated with a hierarchy of office (as in a bureaucracy), is regarded as legitimate and is delegated. Thus, an electoral candidate during an election (even a member of parliament), stands in a political relationship to his constituency. He has no authority over them and must seek to influence their votes by promises and cajolery. Only when elected, and especially as a member of the cabinet, does he achieve authority over all in his government department. Both administration and politics occurred in Southern Bantu chiefdoms, but they operated at very different levels.

The government of these chiefdoms faced two main problems, namely the maintenance of the integrity of the state, and the administration of areas lying outside the capital. It also had two major tasks – the making of decisions relating to public life and the settlement of disputes between its subjects.

The Bhaca sacred grass ring *(inkatha)*. The inkatha symbolised the chieftainship and the unity of the chiefdom. It consisted of a thick grass coil about 80 cm in diameter, to which was added the body dirt of kings and their closest relatives, and other matter touched by royalty. It was believed to protect the king and the chiefdom from misfortune. (N. J. van Warmelo)

South Sotho war dance, 1825, by C.D. Bell. (Africana Library)

The integrity of the chiefdom was constantly threatened both by the possibility of external attack and by schisms emanating from the political process itself. The first typically took the form of raids for cattle or clashes over grazing and, as such, was comparatively minor, but chiefdoms were on occasion threatened by the large-scale expansion of rival chiefdoms under ambitious rulers. Such were the raids and population movements of the early nineteenth century, commencing with the expansion of Zulu power under Shaka, that sent shock-waves over the highveld and eastern Cape. There were others: the Tlôkwa under MaNthathisi, the Ngwane under Mathiwane and the Ndebele under Mzilikazi, for example. Schism, on the other hand, came essentially from internal succession disputes. These were frequently caused by lack of clarity as to the correct heir, due to uncertainty about the identity of the great wife, the legitimacy of her eldest son, and so on. Sometimes a regent, appointed during the minority of the heir and typically a younger brother of the late chief, was tempted to usurp the chieftainship.

We shall discuss the methods used to govern the chiefdom, both from a secular and from a mystical point of view, in more detail below. Here must be recorded a striking feature of these polities – their tendency to split. The history of all groups is characterised by the constant hiving off of sections, always under a member of the royal family, to form new chiefdoms – a tendency repeated today in the constant proliferation of separatist churches and herbalist associations. The reasons for this were to be found in the dynamics of royal family life, especially in the house system and the ranking of wives discussed in Chapter 2. Although the formal rules of succession were clearly laid down (the heir was the eldest son of the chief's great wife) there was frequently doubt about who precisely this chief wife was. Among Nguni and Venda the allocation of this status was either left until late in a reign

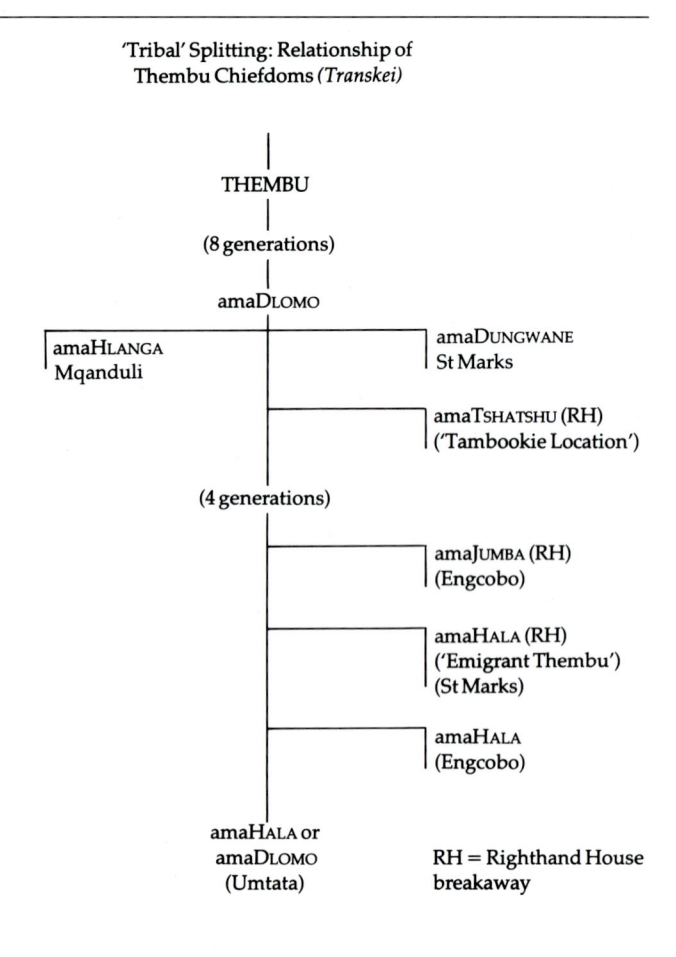

Ntwana warrior, with breastplate of genet skin and headpiece of wildebeest horns, together with a diviner wearing dancing rattles and carrying a cowtail switch, a typical insignia of her craft. (Barbara Tyrell)

'Tribal' Splitting: Relationship of Thembu Chiefdoms *(Transkei)*

```
THEMBU
(8 generations)
amaDLOMO
├── amaHLANGA         ├── amaDUNGWANE
│   Mqanduli          │   St Marks
│                     ├── amaTSHATSHU (RH)
│                     │   ('Tambookie Location')
│                     (4 generations)
│                     ├── amaJUMBA (RH)
│                     │   (Engcobo)
│                     ├── amaHALA (RH)
│                     │   ('Emigrant Thembu')
│                     │   (St Marks)
│                     ├── amaHALA
│                     │   (Engcobo)
amaHALA or
amaDLOMO              RH = Righthand House
(Umtata)              breakaway
```

(the chief indeed sometimes dying before a declaration was made) or kept secret from the people. Wives themselves were intensely ambitious for their sons and intrigue and politicking were rife. Disputes as to the rightful heir are a leitmotif running through the oral histories. Antagonism between brothers within a house, and between houses, was endemic and proverbial, and these disputes either led to usurpation or to the secession of one of the sons. The great majority of existing chiefdoms are said to have originated in this manner, so that the reigning chiefs of many can trace their descent to a common ancestor. The seceding son was accompanied by some of his brothers and other close relatives but the bulk of his supporters were commoners, often personal retainers or, as among Tswana, members of his age-regiment. Thus, among Tswana, the Ngwaketse and Ngwato broke away separately from the Kwena early in the eighteenth century, and the Tswana subsequently seceded from the Ngwato (in about 1795); the Rolong broke up in about 1780 into four separate chiefdoms and, as recently as 1884, the Tlôkwa divided into four sections under the sons of Chief Matlapeng.

Among Nguni this splitting acquired the status of an institution. Indeed, there seems to have been a built-in expectation that the chiefdom would split along the lines of great and righthand houses every generation, the righthand heir establishing a separate chiefdom. As informants state, 'The chieftainship is like the horns of a bull.' Whether or not this fission actually occurred depended on circumstances, but from the end of the seventeenth century the original Xhosa chiefdom split into ten separate chiefdoms over six generations. Four of these divisions originated in the secession of the righthand house: among the South Nguni as a whole there were fifteen cases of the righthand house seceding. Among Venda 'the chiefs of most tribes are genealogically related through descent from Ndyambeu, under whose sons the hitherto united tribe began to break apart early in the eighteenth century' (Schapera 1956: 27).

The two infallible indications of political subordination were (a) the payment of tribute to the chief and (b) the sending of cases on appeal to a superior's court. This has relevance for an understanding of the nature of South Nguni political arrangements in the eighteenth and nineteenth centuries, more especially in the light of Peires's claim that the independent Xhosa chiefdoms mentioned above were in fact component parts of an expanding unitary Xhosa state. In fact these related chiefdoms (Gcaleka, Ngqika, Ndlambe, Jingqi, Dange and Mbalu) sent no tribute or appeals to the court of the Gcaleka chief, styled 'Paramount Chief' by colonial administrators. The so-called paramount, as senior member of the Xhosa royal family, was consulted by the other chiefs on family matters, such as royal marriages and ancestor rituals, and was accorded precedence in the performance of the first-fruits rituals, but he had no *political* control over them. (The Gcaleka chief Hintsa lost his life through the action of troops under Sir Harry Smith in 1835 because he was mistakenly held responsible by the latter for their raids against the Colony.) Peires claims that all the sons of a chief were *ipso facto* chiefs, but this is based on a misconception. They were indeed all given the honorific title 'chief', but they did not hold chiefly office, with all its politico-religious implications

Apart from the broad distinction between royalty and commoners, it is difficult to discern classes, in the marxist sense of an exploitative category of the population. As we have seen, each homestead was an independent unit, providing subsistence and the necessary material goods for its members. Some men were wealthier than others, and there is no doubt that members close to the royal family or to the ward headman stood a better chance of obtaining fields in more favourable areas than those not so situated. The attempts by some scholars to cast homestead heads in the role of exploiters of their sons (thereby 'finding' a vestigial class system in these traditional societies) do not bear close scrutiny. All members of a homestead were personally concerned in the fortunes of the family herd and sons owed their very marriages to house cattle which, in any event, they would inherit.

The nearest approximation to classes occurred among Venda, some Western Tswana and the Ndebele of Zimbabwe, all of which resulted from the conquest of peoples of differing ethnic or cultural origins. The ancestors of Venda nobility invaded the Soutpansberg and subjugated the apparently more primitive peoples living there, such as the Ngona and Mbedzi. They made themselves masters of the country and, in fact, owned the country, the common people being merely 'tenants paying their dues', as Van Warmelo expresses it, a system quite unlike that found elsewhere 'where people and land were one'. As Van Warmelo comments:

> Not so here. In Venda, it is royalty and the land that are one. The people, the commoners, are dwellers on that land. They do not and would not dare to say, 'This is our land'. This notion would not occur to commoners, for only royalty exercises dominion over land. Royalty chased off its land becomes like the rest of the populace, landless and subject to the local rulers ... The whole of Venda at one time consisted of these mutually independent kingdoms, polarized around a few powerful dynasties. (Van Warmelo 1974: 79)

When the Western Tswana peoples entered what is now Botswana from the Transvaal in the early eighteenth century they found the country occupied by scattered groups of San, Kgalagadi, Tswapong, Yeei and others, who usually sub-

A South Sotho war chief, by C.D. Bell. Note the shape of the shield, very different from the oval shields of the Nguni, and the V-shaped breastplate of cowhide. The ostrich feather plume was much used by Sotho warriors, whereas widow bird and crane feathers were favoured by Nguni. (Africana Library)

mitted to their rule without resistance. The areas where they lived were divided into districts under the control of an 'overseer' (*modisa*), either a senior noble or a trusted retainer of the chief. These annexed peoples became serfs *(malata)* of the local overseer, who made them herd his cattle, cultivate his fields and perform menial tasks at his home. He could appropriate whatever property they acquired, especially the spoils of the chase. Serfs remained permanently attached to their master's family and were inherited by his children, but apparently were seldom bought or sold. They lacked civil rights, could not own livestock and had no access to the courts (Schapera 1956: 128).

A similar system was established by the Ndebele under Mzilikazi when they occupied parts of southern Zimbabwe in 1832. At the height of its power Mzilikazi's kingdom consisted of three distinct social classes: *abazansi*, descendants of Mzilikazi's original Zulu following; *abenhla*, descendants of Sotho and other peoples absorbed into the group during its sojourn in the Transvaal; and *amahole*, local Shona groups captured in raids. The latter were a servile class with whom no intermarriage was permitted. They did all the menial work, were drafted into the army and paid tribute to the Ndebele. These developments were, however, due to special historical circumstances and were aberrations from the typical Southern Bantu pattern.

The chief was the epicentre around which the entire life of the chiefdom was organised, indeed he can be thought of as its human embodiment. He enjoyed absolute *authority*, in M.G. Smith's terms. As Schapera puts it:

> ... he is entitled to obedience and service from his subjects ... He may send people where and on what errands he wishes, summon them to attend court cases or tribal meetings, mobilize them for public works or for war, move them from their homes and settle them where he pleases, and order them to do anything else in the public interest. He may also call upon them to build or repair his own huts and cattle-kraals, clear land for, and work in, his wives' fields, and supply them with timber, thatching grass and water. (Schapera 1956: 96)

Only the chief could convene national assemblies, arrange the ceremonies of rain-making and crop protection, create new age-regiments, declare war or impose the death penalty or banishment.

SHAKA'S PRAISE POET

'On mustering sufficient courage to look about me, my attention and that of my shipmates was arrested by a strange and ludicrous object, which at first sight appeared to be a complete nondescript. It was a kind of wild animal in an erect posture, and proved in reality to be a human being enveloped from head to foot in the skin of a tiger [leopard], so fitted on him that the skin of the hind legs served as pantaloons and that of the fore did duty as sleeves for the upper garment. Thus he was in reality the only individual in the assembly, except ourselves, that could be said to have any clothing. The skin of the tiger's head being drawn over his face served as a covering for the head, on which was mounted a pair of huge horns belonging to some animal of the deer tribe. These were decorated with several bunches of different coloured feathers, presenting altogether a most extraordinary and ludicrous appearance. ☐ We were at a loss to conceive what this monster was intended for, and what duty he had to perform as an appendage to his Majesty's establishment. We could hardly consider him as an ornament, and were not a little surprised on being informed that he was an imbongi dedicated to the worship of the Nkosi Kakhulu (Great King). It was certainly a novel idea of Shaka's, when he assumed the attributes and power of a deity, to clothe his priests in the garb of wild beasts of prey ...'
From The Natal Papers of John Ross (Maclean 1992: 121–2)

This administrative authority was given sybolic expression. At the annual first-fruits ritual the chief and his family had to 'bite' (*luma*) the newly ripened crops before anyone else could taste them: this prerogative was so jealously guarded that its breach constituted treason. The status of chief was also expressed by insignia of office such as a leopardskin cloak, ivory or copper arm-rings and special bead necklaces, but these were usually only worn on special occasions. Normally chiefs dressed much as did their subjects and early travellers, particularly to the South Nguni, comment with surprise at their unpretentious garb. When the youthful 'John Ross' first met Shaka in 1825 the Zulu king was sitting before his council quite naked (the normal state for men at the time) and anointing his body with grease, admittedly before donning his 'royal war dress' (Maclean 1992: 121). Chiefs were addressed by their title, or by the name of their chiefdom, clan or totem group and special praise singers hymned them in praises full of recondite allusions and delivered in a characteristic staccato style. Among Zulu and Tsonga there was a taboo on using any word that contained a syllable also occurring in the chief's name (*hlonipha*), while among Venda the chief and whatever pertained to him were sometimes described in a special vocabulary known only to the habitués of the capital; thus 'His door or hut is called the "crocodile", his beer-pot is the "shade", his salt is "sand", his dogs are "messengers"; if he is asleep he is "breathing", and if he is eating he "works"' (Stayt 1931: 202).

But, despite all this, the authority of the Southern Bantu chief was not absolute. There existed among all his subjects a clear perception of fairness and justice, a concept of how a 'reasonable' chief should behave – and a chief exceeded these bounds at his peril. The ultimate sanction was rebellion, or the moving away of a section of the population under one of his brothers. With the exception of the Venda – who, as we have seen, were unique in this respect – there was a clear idea that chief and people were complementary, expressed in the oft-quoted aphorism: 'A chief is chief because of his people.' This ideal could obviously not be left to the vagaries of personality and the political arrangements included a series of checks and balances to limit chiefly tyranny and to provide for wider participation in the decision-making process. In all groups, then, the chief governed in association with a council of advirsors and, on occasion, called meetings of all his subjects to discuss cases of importance to the chiefdom as a whole.

These advisors were an informal body consisting of men who enjoyed the trust of the chief and whom he consulted privately on all matters of importance. The group was a fluctuating one and different men would be consulted according to their expertise on the question at issue. Among Tswana they numbered from about six to ten. In addition chiefs had a more formal council that met fairly regularly as a body to discuss matters concerning the general administration of the chiefdom. This also involved the settlement of disputes, so that the council also acted as a court of law. Typically it included the headmen of the various wards into which the chiefdom was divided, each headman representing the interests of those living in his area of jurisdiction. It also included prominent individuals who, because of their personal qualities of probity and eloquence, were natural 'committee men'. Many of the latter lived permanently at the capital, or spent long periods there, forming a core of experience. A headman was usually accompanied by one or more of his subjects, especially by the sub-headmen appointed by him as 'eyes' overseeing local areas within his ward. Among Tswana and Venda the proceedings of the council were private but, among South Nguni, they were open to all adult men who wished to attend and take part in the deliberations. Among

The crane-wing headdress of a Xhosa warrior. (Shaw and Van Warmelo 1988)

this group, too, the chief's advisors (*amaphakathi*, 'those inside') were ideally commoners. It was felt that royal brothers were too close to the chieftainship themselves to be completely impartial in their advice. Tswana, on the other hand, favoured close kin (brothers and uncles) as confidants while, among Venda, the affairs of the chiefdom were managed by the royal family council *(khoro ya muti)* itself in an entirely authoritarian way.

Of all groups it would appear that the South Nguni Xhosa-speakers were the most democratic. Chiefs were extremely cautious about making decisions that might be unpopular. As a Mpondomise ex-regent explained to me in the 1960s:

> Even strong chiefs like Mhlontlo never made laws that went against the wishes of the people. A chief always had his councillors. These men were his advisers on matters of law and order. A chief would have to listen to their advice on what action to take: they would refuse to sanction tactics which they regarded as dangerous.
>
> In making a new law a chief had to discuss the intended law with them. Then a meeting of the whole tribe would be called and the matter laid before them. Influential men would have the chance of airing their views and, after thorough discussion, the chief and his advisors would have the feeling of the meeting. Opponents of the plan were encouraged to speak out because the people should not be a stream that flows in one direction only. After full discussion, the chief and his councillors would withdraw so that the advisors could voice their opinion as to whether they felt that the majority was in favour of the matter or not, and whether modifications should not perhaps be made.

Sometimes further precautions were taken to protect the chief from criticism. Once a decision had been taken it was the chief *induna* who pronounced it, not the chief. As the five Ngqika councillors who gave evidence before the 1883 Cape Native Laws and Customs Commission explained, 'A chief can do wrong, and it often happens that when a chief does wrong he would be interfered with, and punished, by having his favourite councillor, or prime minister, eaten up [i.e. have his stock confiscated] ... The prime minister is the chief's mouthpiece, and the other councillors say, as a reason for eating him up, that it must have been by his advice that the chief did wrong.'

This is an important comment. The South Nguni seem to have gone to extraordinary lengths to protect the chief both from the danger of autocratic rule and from carrying the blame for wrong decisions taken. Since all decision-making involves the possibility of error, they made their chiefs constitutional monarchs, above the hurly-burly of politics. It is perhaps because they did not 'rule', in the sense of making executive decisions, but rather 'reigned', that South Nguni did not need to have the institutionalised criticism of the chief that appears to have been the case among Zulu and Swazi. The same process characterised decision-making in the courts. Cases were discussed by those present and the function of the chief was merely to pronounce the verdict. In fact it was not strictly necessary for the chief to be present personally during the proceedings.

This extreme form of democracy was not universal. It may have existed among Tsonga, but there is much evidence that Sotho (especially Tswana) chiefs acted, on occasion, in an authoritarian manner, and Venda chiefs were outright autocrats. The special case of authoritarian dictatorship, that of Shaka and Dingane, will be alluded to below when the (few) cases of the development of indigenous 'nation states' are considered.

PRAISES OF A TSWANA CHIEF

Praises were characterised by a special, staccato method of delivery and by certain stylistic qualities. The poem was broken up into short phrases, each of which appeared to be uttered with one breath, and emphasis fell periodically on the penultimate syllables of certain words, each of which would be followed by a perceptible pause. Stylistically, much use was made of parallelism, whereby, in each pair of lines, the first halves were identical in wording, and the second were basically alike in meaning, as in □ They were in the kraal of his maternal kin/they were in the kraal of Tshukudu □ or chiasmus/(the first half of one line corresponds to the second half of the other, and vice versa), as in Carry them in a calf baby-sling/in a calf baby-sling, people-carrier □ Much value was attached to (often obscure) historical allusions. □ The following is a praise of Chief Mmakgotso of the Kgatla (c. 1790–5) and refers to his victorious battle against the Fokeng chief, Moseletsane.

Lightnings of the southern clouds;
the lightnings flash all over the bushveld, Kuate,
Kuate, son of Mathudi the Baboon.
   Young men in the south, turn back,
come that you may gnaw the bones,
the bones of cattle lifted from others,
taken from Moseletsane the extortionate.
   You who milk the cows of Ntseanyane the Kwena,
when milking put some by for the Milk-lord,
the milker of sorrows, son of Kgafêla.
   The steenbok is cut into shields,
the duiker is made into leggings,
the hare is cut into tassels,
at the home of the Obstructor, Pheto's son.

Kgadima tsamaru aborwa;
kgadima ditlêtse merokwa, Kuate,
Kuate wagaMathudi a Tshwêneng.
   makau aakwaborwa hularang,
letlê gophura marapô,
marapô akgômo diamogwa batho,
ditsêêtswe kgagapa Moseletsane.
   Lona legamang tsôôNtseanyane aMokwêna,
legamê lesiêlê Magamêlli,
magama-dibotlhoko wagaKgafêla.
   Phuduhudu masêgwa thêbê,
photi entshiwa manaila,
mmutla osêgwa meja-mebyane,
kwagabôRramathibêdi aPhetô.

Notes □ Kuate was Mmakgotso's second name. □ Mathudi, his mother, was a Kwena woman (totem, the baboon). □ 'Lightnings of the southern clouds' refers to the battle against the Fokeng (who lived south of the Kgatla). □ 'Milk-lord': praise-name of Mmakgotso. □ Kgafêla was the first chief of this branch of the Kgatla. □ 'The Obstructor' refers to Mmakgotso's elder brother. (Schapera 1965: 47–8)

Except among Sotho, the council was the main organ of government, and its decisions were binding. But among Sotho, and especially Tswana, almost all matters of public interest were discussed finally at a popular assembly *(pitsô)*, with adult men expected to attend, at which matters were presented and the chief gave his decision.

The question is often raised as to whether or not these traditional systems of government were 'democratic'. This term is a proverbially slippery one, and one that, with its different meanings, has been used with very different emphases and nuances, from 'liberal democracy', through 'peoples' democracy' to 'participatory democracy'. It is clear from the above discussion that it is impossible to generalise for all the Southern Bantu, but it does seem that only the South Nguni conformed (to some extent) to the usually accepted idea of popular participation. Behind all these systems was the extraordinary prestige of the chief and his local political officers, which placed enormous constraints on freedom of speech. This was exacer-

Henry Francis Fynn's Description of Shaka, 1824

'On arriving within a mile of the king's residence, we were directed to wait under a large tree till the arrival of the messengers ... ☐ The kraal was nearly two miles in circumference. At the time of our entering the gates, the kraal was surrounded by about 12 000 men in their war attire ... ☐ After exhibiting their cattle for two hours, they drew together in a circle, and sang and danced to the war-whoop. Then the people returned to the cattle, again exhibiting them as before, and at intervals dancing and singing. The women now entered the kraal, each having a long thin stick in the right hand, and moving it in time to the song. They had not been dancing many minutes when they had to make way for the ladies of the seraglio, besides about 150, distinguished by the appellation of 'sisters'. These danced in parties of eight, each party wearing different coloured beads, which were crossed from the shoulders to the knees. Each wore a headdress of black feathers, and four brass collars fitting close to the neck. The king joining in the dance was accompanied by the men. The dance lasted half an hour. The king then made a long speech. He desired to know from us if ever we had seen such order in any other state, assured us that he was the greatest king in existence, that his people were as numerous as the stars, and his cattle innumerable. The people now dispersed, and he directed a chief to lead us to a kraal, where we could pitch our tents ...

☐ On the following morning we were requested to mount our horses and ride to the king's kraal. On our arrival we found him sitting under a tree, in the act of decorating himself. He was surrounded by about 200 people, a servant standing at his side, and holding a shield over him to keep the glare of the sun from him. Round his forehead he wore a turban of otter-skin, with a feather of a crane erect in front, full two feet long. Earrings of dried sugar-cane, carved round the edge, with white ends, and an inch in diameter, were let into the lobes of his ears, which had been cut to admit them. From shoulder to shoulder he wore bunches, three inches in length, of the skins of monkeys and genets, twisted like the tails of these animals, and hanging half down the body. Round the ring on the head ... were a dozen bunches of the red feathers of the loorie, tastefully tied to thorns which were stuck into the hair. Round his arms were white ox-tails, cut down the middle so as to allow the hairs to hang about the arm, to the number of four for each. Round the waist a petticoat, resembling the highland plaid, made of skins of monkeys and genets, and twisted as before described, having small tassels round the top, the petticoat reaching to the knees, below which were ox-tails to fit round the legs, so as to hang to the ankles. He had a white shield with a single black spot, and an assegai.'
(Stuart and Malcolm 1969: 73–5)

bated by the rule of respect to seniors that permeated these societies. It was extremely difficult for commoners to be seen to be opposing a chief, even among Xhosa-speakers. In the light of this, every attempt was made to achieve consensus, the illusion of unanimity. In particular, there was no concept of an institutionalised opposition, charged with the responsibility of acting as a watch-dog against misgovernment. Perhaps this was unnecessary as, although these societies *were* changing, the pace of change was slow and the issues before the people were not fundamental, in the sense that there were no differing philosophies of 'good government', nor any idea of the necessity of planned change. The political system was uncritically accepted as given, as being in the nature of things: the governmental system was good; only particular chiefs were bad.

Administration and decision-making were generally entirely in the hands of men, but there were significant exceptions. Among the Venda and those Sotho-Venda peoples influenced by them, and among the Swazi, certain women were accorded important roles in government.

Despite his sacred status (in middle age a chief would have the *phembela* rite performed for him, transforming him into a (living) ancestral spirit), the Venda chief was not an absolute monarch. The appointment of a new chief was in the hands of his father's sister (*makhadzi*) and his father's brother (*khotsimunene*). When these two persons indicated the heir they simultaneously appointed one of his sisters as the *khadzi* and one of his brothers as the *ndumi*. It was these two persons who, on the death of their brother, assumed the positions of *makhadzi* and *khotsimunene* to his son. Stayt (1931: 196) explains the logic behind this. The chief did not hold his position primarily because of military prowess, nor even because he was the most suitable man for the post. He did (and does) so as the sacred representative of the royal family. The *makhadzi* was usually the late chief's eldest sister by a different mother. She received a portion of the taxes, all important matters of state had to be referred to her and the chief was expected to follow her judgement. She lived at the capital and was treated with all the respect due to a chief. She had to marry within the royal family or make a diplomatic marriage with the son of a neighbouring chief. The *khotsimunene* also received taxes and the army commander was directly responsible to him in time of war. Even today, when matters of public import, especially succession, are discussed by the Venda government, the question is asked at the start: 'Are the *makhadzi* and *khotsimunene* present?' and proceedings are postponed until they are.

An analogous complexity in the office of chieftainship was (and is still) found among the Swazi. Here the dominating figure was the Queen Mother, the 'She-Elephant' (*Indlovukati*) to her son's *Ingwenyama* (Lion). She and her son ruled in tandem, presiding over the highest courts, controlling the age-regiments and allocating land, and were the central figures in the great national ritual of *incwala*. Hilda Kuper (1947: 55) comments that 'Between the *Ingwenyama* and the *Indlovukati* there is a delicate balance of power, legal, economic and ritual.' The Queen Mother was in charge of the second highest court, her home was a place of sanctuary and although the king took the leading role in the national ceremonies, she was the custodian of the sacred objects of the nation. 'In all activities they should assist and advise each other, for he is *Inkosi* [chief] and she is also *Inkosi*.' They are often spoken of as twins. Confict between the two rulers was a threat to the wellbeing of the whole nation.

But the extreme example of female political authority occurred among the Sotho-Venda of the lowveld, particularly the Lovedu and, to a much lesser extent, the

Bangazitha, son of Mpondo chief Faku, by A.G. Bain. (Africana Library)

Young Swazi girls at the *umhlanga* (reed dance) ceremony. They are moving forward to present the best reeds to the King, so that the Queen Mother's residence can be repaired. The beadwork, coloured cloth and tassels are, of course, modern. (Morris and Levitan 1986)

Kgaga (who were influenced by them). The Lovedu, under their mysterious Rain Queen, Mudjadji, have captured the imagination of South Africa. She and her successors (all bearing the dynastic title 'Mudjadji') were renowned far and wide as the great rain-makers of southern Africa and even Shaka is reputed to have sent a delegation to her to supplicate for rain. She lived in seclusion from outsiders, and her legendary reputation formed the basis of Rider Haggard's African romance, *She*.

Mudjadji represents the most advanced example of a divine kingship in southern Africa. In two centuries there have only been four queens. Lovedu say that the queen must have no physical defects and must poison herself, not when

CHIEFS, COUNCILLORS AND COMMONERS

she is old, but at the end of the fourth initiation *(bodiga)* of her reign. Dirt from her body was used as an important ingredient in the rain medicines. Apparently her death was not linked with her state of health or the wellbeing of the country: the suicide conferred divinity on her.

Perhaps because of her gender, Mudjadji did not depend, as other chiefs did, on the army to maintain peace and the political integration of her chiefdom. This was effected, rather, by her ritual position as rain-maker and also by marriage ties. As we shall see in Chapter 6, it was possible among Southern Bantu for women to marry wives, employing close male kinsmen to impregnate them (the bridewealth-paying woman being termed 'father' by the offspring). The Lovedu employed this

A carved female figure at the entrance to the Lovedu queen Mudjadji's living quarters. It is uncertain whether it has any symbolic significance: it is more likely to have signalled the threshold of royal privacy. (Anitra Nettleton)

strategy extensively. Every headman sent a daughter to be a wife of the queen, while she reciprocated by marrying off some of these wives to important subjects, thus establishing relationships of both wife-giver and wife-receiver to the most influential persons in her realm. By this means the silken ties of marriage replaced the sinews of war in the political process.

There are other instances of the appointment of female chiefs, for example among the Kgaga, Mmamaila, Letswalo and Makgoba, but in none of these cases did it become institutionalised, as among Lovedu. It is significant that all these peoples are Sotho-Venda and were influenced in this matter by the dominant position of Mudjadji in the area.

It is probable that the earliest chiefdoms were fairly small and most settlement was within easy distance of the chief's great place. But soon, in both East and West, rapidly expanding population made some form of delegation of administrative authority imperative. This was particularly necessary among Nguni, with their penchant for scattered settlement. Here there developed a hierarchy of local government based on the subdivision of the chiefdom into manageable areas each

Nomkhubulwana, the Princess of Heaven

The Zulu seem to have been unique in their belief in Nomkhubulwana or Nkosazana yeZulu (literally, the Princess of Heaven). Henry Callaway was the first to record it in his The Religious System of the AmaZulu (1868–70). This is his informant's account: ☐ 'The account of the Inkosazana who came out on the same day that men came out of the earth. ☐ She is not commonly seen. We hear it said the primitive men knew her. She is said to be a very little animal, as large as a polecat, and is marked with little white and black stripes; on the one side there grows a bed of reeds, a forest, and grass; the other side is that of a man. Such is her form. ☐ If she meet with a man she conceals herself and speaks with him without his seeing her; he hears only a voice saying to him, "Turn your back; do not look at me, for I am naked". Saying thus because her buttocks are red like fire. And so the man no longer looks in that direction, but believes that it is indeed the Inkosazana about whom he has heard; and turns his back from fear, because it is said that if a man look on her face to face, he will be ill and very soon die.

☐ Nomkhubulwana was thought to be a virgin and some believed that she was the daughter of the Sky God. She was thus especially associated with young girls, who performed an annual festival in her honour. She was closely linked to the morning mists that herald the coming of spring and also with the rainbow. She had the power to bring about steady and frequent rains, and was thus associated with fertility of man and beast. ☐ The rituals connected with Nomkhubulwana were organised on a local basis. When the first mists appeared, special millet beer was brewed and, while it was fermenting, the girls borrowed their brothers' everyday wear, dancing shields and sticks. Thus dressed, they would enter their father's cattle byre and drive out one or two beasts to be herded by all the girls on the hill slopes. One of the beasts should be a heifer and the other a milch-cow. At the pastures the cows would be left under the care of two of the girls, while the rest would carry a calabash containing the special beer further up the mountain. Seeds of maize, pumpkin, millet and beans were also carried. These would all be placed as offerings on a large prominent rock

and a song was sung, inviting Nomkhubulwana to come and partake. Some of these songs contained explicit references to sexual matters, and any men and boys coming across the gathering were chased away with stones.
☐ Girls told Berglund in the 1950s that they performed the rites in order that 'things may go well during the coming year. We wish to marry but do not know whether our lovers will remain faithful. So we do the work of our sister... She will bless the fields so that they give a good harvest.'
☐ Dressing in garments of the opposite sex, and herding cattle (normally taboo to women), is a classic example of the role reversal that is so often used in ritual, worldwide, to express, in vivid symbol, the sacredness of an occasion. Some writers have noted the resemblance between the Nomkhubulwana rite and certain elements of the first-fruits ceremony. In both, subordinate groups (girls in the one case and commoners – who may insult the king with impunity – in the other) act in a contrary way: it has been suggested that, by doing so, they are helped to accept their subordinate role in society.

Carved pole figures at the gateway to the Lovedu royal precinct. (Anitra Nettleton)

under an administrative officer. Among Zulu, for instance, the chiefdom *(umhlaba)* was divided into districts *(izifunda)*, themselves divided in turn into wards *(izigodi)* and sub-wards *(iziqinti)*. The areas nested in each other in a increasingly inclusive way. Zulu wards were under *izinduna* and districts under sub-chiefs. Generally speaking, among Southern Bantu there were two levels of local government – sub-chiefs in charge of major divisions such as districts (or large villages among Tswana) and under them headmen in charge of smaller units such as sub-districts (Nguni and Tsonga), villages (Venda and many Sotho) or wards (Tswana and some North Sotho). The grading of these hierarchies depended on the size and complexity of the chiefdom. Schapera compared the Tlôkwa of Botswana, where all lived in one village divided into five wards, with the Ngwaketse who had five sub-chiefs and 133 headmen. Each of these administrative areas was administered like a chiefdom in miniature, the head being the chief's local representative. Each had a court, in which local cases were heard, with appeal to the court of the chief.

Decision-making must be translated into action. All chiefs had executive functionaries whose task it was to ensure that decisions were carried out. One of these officers, often called 'chief *induna*', was a kind of lord lieutenant, the chief intermediary between the chief and his subjects. He was the chief's mouthpiece and could himself act as judge in addition to supervising the running of the royal household. There was also the important post of chief's messenger. Among South Nguni his official title was *umsila* (tail) from the leopard's tail he carried as a badge of office. To obstruct a chief's messenger was a treasonable offence. Also important were the tribal herbalists who were employed by the chief to protect his person, doctor the army and assist him at the rain-making and first-fruits festivals.

Ultimately political power relied on force and the army was under chiefly control as the ultimate sanction for laws being carried out. Everywhere, except among South Sotho and Nguni, it was based on age-sets or 'regiments' into which all adult members of the chiefdom were grouped at initiation. New regiments, for men and women, were created every five years or so and given distinctive names. Regiments fought as separate units in the army, but were also used for public tasks such as cultivating the chief's official fields. Among South Sotho and Xhosa-

A Swazi man dressed for the *incwala* (first fruits) festival.

The Compleat Imbongi

Hoye ka Soxalase, imbongi (praise-singer) of the Zulu chief Solomon ka Dinizulu, discussed his craft with James Stuart on 14 September 1921:
☐ 'When bongaing for the king takes place, say after some work for the king has been done – viz. cutting trees and branches, building cattle kraals or huts – and after the king has given cattle to kill, the king comes into the assembly, and seats himself, with the princes and the big, elderly izinduna [officials] also seated. When the imbongi is about to begin, all the company except the king and princes and izinduna rise and remain standing, each holding a stick in his hand. The stick is held upwards. They stand on being ordered to do so by an induna, who may say, "Rise, and let the king's food be praised!" ☐ In [King] Solomon's presence, now I, as imbongi, begin with him. On finishing his eulogies, I go straight on to those of Nzibe ka Senzangakhona, for his praises are regarded as the proper introduction to those of the other kings. Nzibe was a royal warrior and a leader in battle. No sooner are his praises ended than I go at once to the beginning of those chiefs or kings known to me, viz.

A Xhosa *imbongi* (praise singer), photographed by Horst Röntsch in the 1950s.

Jama [father of Senzangakhona and grandfather of Shaka], for I do not as yet know Ndaba or Punga [earlier chiefs], etc. I say as I begin a king, "I now start on —", then bonga straight to the end, then say, "That, then, was —". Then, "I now start on —", i.e. the following king, and go to the end, repeating the same words at the end, and so in chronological order, except that Mnkabayi [sister of Senzangakhona and Shaka's aunt], being a woman, comes right at the end. If I knew Nandi's [Shaka's mother's] eulogies, she would come in at the end too ... ☐ Not a word is uttered by any of the assembly when I am bongaing. Were anyone to say a word or cough, he would be turned out, perhaps beaten, and sent away, as well as rebuked. Nor is any response of any kind, by whistling or otherwise, made during the recitations of the eulogies. It may be done at the end, however. ☐ If the imbongi has gone on a very long time, the king may call on some well-known warrior to come forward and giya [perform a solo war-dance]. This is done to allow the imbongi to break off. Were this giyaing to take place, that would be the signal for me that there would be no more bongaing that day ☐ The sticks stand on the ground whilst held, or are held upwards. When I have reached the end of all the eulogies, I will give the salutation, "Bayede!" The whole company then raise their sticks up in the air, whilst the izinduna and princes stand up too, and all exclaim, "Bayede!" together.
(Webb and Wright 1976: 168)

---

speakers the army was organised on a local basis. The men of each district, regardless of age, constituted a separate division of the army: on mobilisation they gathered at their headman's great place and then marched to that of the district chief, and so on to the capital. The regimental system was introduced by Shaka to the North Nguni only at the beginning of the nineteenth century.

The mystical nature of the chieftaincy and the uncertainties of life in southern Africa united in the creation of communal rituals to protect the chiefdom and ensure its continued wellbeing. Perhaps the most obvious threat was the failure of the rains. All these societies occupied the summer rainfall area which, in good years, provided excellent grazing and agricultural possibilities, but droughts were common. The notorious Madlathule drought of the early nineteenth century was so devastating as to cause changes to the social structure in Natal. Things were worse on the interior plateau. Schapera records for the Kgatla of Mochudi that, in one series of nine consecutive seasons, in only three was there sufficient rainfall to produce a satisfactory harvest, and it is salutary to realise that a three-week drought could ruin the crops. Even in Venda, where the southern slopes of the Soutpansberg are well-watered, a large area north of the mountains is dry and arid.

The rain rituals were generally directed towards the royal ancestors. Even among Venda and Pedi, who thought that the supreme being ultimately controlled the weather, sacrifices were made to the chief's ancestors in times of extreme drought. Among both Tsonga and South Nguni (e.g. Mpondo), royal ancestors were upbraided at their graves for withholding rain and the Tsonga beat the royal graves with sticks to express their displeasure. The rain rite everywhere involved the killing of a black bull (whose colour expressed the darkness of the rain clouds) and the use of potent rain medicines, containing human remains as an essential component. Among Pedi and Lovedu (North Sotho), for instance, the chief ingredient was skin of the deceased chief and prominent councillors. Among North Sotho, in particular, a special chiefdom-wide rain-hunt was organised: the Mamabola and Letswalo used the entrails and blood of the klipspringer antelope and guineafowl as an important ingredient in the rain medicines. The Mudjadji, the rain-maker *par excellence*, worked alone with her medicines, but other chiefs were typically assisted by specialist rain doctors. Mpondomise chiefs relied for rain-making on certain San families who lived among them and who subsisted on charity in recognition of their services.

The boundaries of the country had to be doctored annually against hail, lightning and pests. Among Zulu special 'heaven-herds' ran out with their weapons and rain-shields, shouting at the lightning to move away (as if herding cattle), but among all groups the country was doctored by herbalists using pegs hammered into the ground and smeared with the chief's medicines. Among Nguni the crops were protected against maize blight by a ceremony in which young girls ran through the fields clad in bead aprons. Among Zulu alone this was associated with Nomkhubulwana, the mystical 'Princess of Heaven', a beautiful maiden who combined within herself aspects of nature.

The special relationship between chief and vegetation was expressed through two other ceremonies that formed perhaps the most important episodes in the annual ritual cycle. These were the doctoring of the seed to ensure a fertile crop, and the first-fruits ritual that celebrated the successful harvest while controlling access to the new crops.

The doctoring of the crops took a similar form among all Southern Bantu. Seeds from the harvest were set aside for the next planting. On instructions from the chief young girls, before the age of puberty, moved through the country collecting some of this seed from each homestead in the chiefdom and travelling with it to the capital. Here all the seed was mixed with the seed from the chief's fields in a great pot with strong medicines – and was then redistributed down through the administrative hierarchy of district, ward and sub-ward, back to the individual homestead, thus ensuring that each man's crops would be infused with the fructifying power of the chieftaincy.

Of all these ceremonies, that of the first-fruits was by far the most important. It was believed that people should be protected against the power of the new growth and that they themselves had to be purified lest they 'spoil' the crops. It is important to remember that even in a normal year there was a severe dearth of food through spring and the early summer months of August, September, October, and even later. During the whole of this period children as well as adults had usually to be content with one meal a day. To obtain even this they had often to fall back on veld herbs and insects. The forces at work at this crucial conjunction of society and

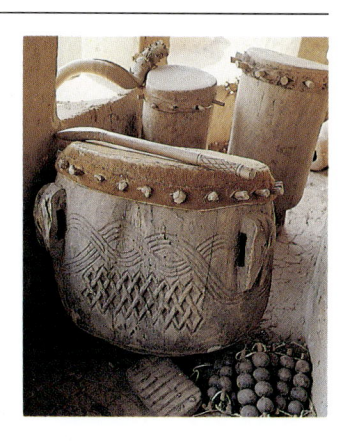

The Lovedu sacred drums. They were played at important public ceremonies such as the first fruits and the annual festival of the 'biting' *(loma)* of the emerging termites. (Greg Marinovich)

A Xhosa impi crossing a stream, by F. I'Ons. (Africana Library)

nature were so powerful that they could only be managed by the chief and, in fact, the initiation of the rites was the most potent expression of political authority. For a sub-chief or headman to give permission for a local ceremony before it had been performed at the capital was a treasonable offence.

First-fruits rituals were universal in southern Africa. Among Sotho and Tsonga they were called *loma* ('to bite' – from the ritual act of 'biting' the new millet, sweet reed and pumpkin), the Venda ritual was *thevula* and the Nguni *ulibo* (or *shwama*). Among one Nguni group, the Zulu, the traditional agricultural rite was added to, in the late eighteenth century, by a specific strengthening of the chieftainship and doctoring of the army, in an annual ceremony of great drama and complex ritual. The Zulu named this rite *umkhosi* (either from the word for 'chief' or that for 'ancestral spirit') and it was adopted by various Natal chiefdoms and Zulu offshoots such as the Swazi, where it was called *incwala* (and is still performed today), Bhaca (*ingcubhe*), Ndebele and Ngoni. There is also evidence that the Mpondo had a similar link between the agricultural ceremony and army doctoring (*ingxwala*), probably adopted from Zulu practice. In other groups army doctoring took place immediately before going into battle and not on an annual basis.

First-fruits festivals, in the strict sense, essentially involved the prohibition on eating (or 'tasting') the new crops until this had been formally done by the chief in a ritual involving special medicines. To do so was deemed not only treasonable, but a sin against the tribal ancestors. The effect of this was to place control of the harvest squarely in the hands of the central political authority and to make an unambiguous statement of relative political status between chiefs of related tribes and between chiefs and their local administrative officers. Most Tswana tribes trace a common origin in the Hurutshe: David Livingstone wrote that he found evidence 'of very ancient partition ... The other tribes will not begin to eat the early pumpkins of the new crop until they hear that the Bahurutse have "bitten" it'. Gluckman has suggested another function. He points out that the appearance of the new crops often leads to quarrelling (over theft from the fields of those whose crops ripen first) and to waste (it must be remembered that the crops ripen in a period of dearth). By means of the *luma* [Zulu spelling] rite the harvest season was not spoilt by jealousies. As Gluckman says: '... the effect of the taboo on the early eating of the crops is that no such source of friction can possibly arise to spoil the good fellowship of the harvest, since by the time that the individual is allowed to reap, after the chief's and the sub-chief's ceremonies, it is possible that most headmen will have ripe crops' (Gluckman 1938: 35). Among North Sotho, especially, there was also a *loma* of the termites, when they emerged after the first spring rains.

The integration of the first-fruits with the doctoring of chief and army was developed by the Zulu and their offshoots on quite another scale. Shooter wrote in 1857 that 'Tshaka added to it [the *ulibo*] certain military rites, and gave it much more the aspect of a war-feast.' The *umkhosi* was divided into two parts, separated by a month. The 'little' *umkhosi* was explicitly a 'stepping into the new year' and was designed to protect the Zulu king from the dangers that might result in his coming into contact with those who might have partaken of the new season's crops without purification. Prominent men and certain selected regiments assembled at the capital and took part in a great hunt for the fiercest wild animals of the veld. Messengers were sent to fetch *uselwa* (gourds), in particular a bitter-tasting one especially associated with the ritual, and seawater from the coast, as well as riper crops stolen from neighbouring chiefdoms. In some tribes, e.g. Bhaca, the skull and body parts were an important element. The centre of the ritual was the strangling of a black bull, bare-handed, by one of the regiments, its flesh being burnt with medicines. At dawn, on rising ground facing east, the King licked this 'black' medicine from his fingers and squirted it towards the sun, to confuse his enemies. At the same time the chiefdom's herd was driven to the graves of the deceased kings. The completion of the little *umkhosi* usually signalled permission to eat the crops.

During the period before the Great Festival the king was continually doctored, while 'the whole nation poured into the capital, for attendance is compulsory on pain of death. A vast camp of grass huts springs up on all sides'.

> The next day the people gather at the great place. Chanting, striking their shields, stabbing with their assegais, they call on the King to come out. He emerges clad from head to toe in a costume made of long, thin, green rushes, to which may be added herbs, corn leaves and Kafir corn, and stalks of sweet sorghum. He dances before his warriors, struts about and brandishes his war-shield and sceptre. He shouts and gesticulates as he goes, to the roaring plaudits of the crowd. (Gluckman 1938: 27)

Umkhosi was without doubt the most impressive ceremony devised in southern Africa. It has elicited great theoretical interest among anthropologists, particularly the apparent criticism of the king by his warriors that led Gluckman to typify it as a 'ritual of rebellion'.

KINGDOMS AND FEDERATIONS: WIDER POLITICAL STRUCTURES

Although the chiefdom was the 'protype of polity', throughout precolonial southern Africa there were instances of larger political structures, bearing testimony to the organisational abilities of the Southern Bantu. The first of these, as

Mgedi, a Xesibe sub-chief, by A.G. Bain. The Xesibe were a small South Nguni chiefdom living in the Mount Ayliff district of the Transkei. Note the long-tailed widow-bird feathers in his elaborate hairstyle. (Africana Library)

Delegorgue's Description of Mpande's Umkhosi, 4 December 1841

'By almost eight o'clock in the morning I was seated on the ground at the right hand of Panda, who was enthroned on an enormous wooden armchair, carved all of a piece. He was completely engrossed in the prospect of the festivities and in the expectation of seeing his warriors parade before him. His conversation was only of them, their costume, their dance, their songs. He was waiting to receive the salute of the regiments of the abafanas [young men] …

☐ Then suddenly, from 1500 paces away, an immense cry arose … Our eyes were drawn to the place from whence it came, to the slopes of the opposite hill, and we became aware of great black masses of abafanas, 6000 of them divided into six groups. They were preparing to advance, each regiment leading off in turn. Some minutes elapsed and then, suddenly they were before us, only 2000 paces off, each regiment arranged in ranks of 100 men, ten ranks deep. Another great cry arose, accompanied this time by shrill whistling. The cry was sustained as they charged in a confused mêlée of men and shields, which surged forward like a great wave, and finally crashed at our feet as a breaker crashes on the shore. It was a fine disorder such as I could not have imagined, which suddenly resolved itself once more into the most perfect order. ☐ As the first battle-cry rang out, the dancers lept up and, repeating the cry, they began to dance, a rhythmical, leaping dance which stirred the spirit to combat; then they proceeded with slow stamping, until the earth rang beneath their feet, and trembled under their weight. From time to time, several abafanas would emerge from the ranks to salute the prince by leaping in the air and striking their shields with both feet at once.

☐ This display of gymnastics made a fine show, and I began to appreciate its qualities of grace and orginality. Suddenly, without warning, the dancers all spun about, and converged upon us as they had previously done; then, coming to a sudden halt within twenty paces of us they formed themselves into a snake, which wound its way before Panda. Each man went past at a slow trot, contorting his features and acknowledging the king in tones of seeming anger, gesticulating with the tonga [stick] in a threatening manner, until all had past in salutes and the next regiment heralded

A Zulu warrior, by C.D. Bell. (Africana Library)

its approach with a ringing call …

☐ [Next day] twenty-five regiments passed in salute before the king, following the same procedures as on the previous day. The celebrations had taken on a more impressive character; each regiment was distinguished by its shield which stood four feet six inches high and were made of ox-hide of various colours; some were white, some black, others red, blue or yellow, or white with red or black markings; the colours were uniform for each regiment. The elite regiments were distinguished by the symba [insimba], a sort of kilt which hung from the waist to the knees and which was made of 300 to 400 strips of genet fur; these tassels parted gracefully and closed again to allow the free movement of the body. The head was encircled with a padded strip of otter fur from which there arose a long Numidian crane feather. ☐ Several hours later, when all the regiments had passed in salute before the king, the massed warriors formed a circle and began chanting warlike songs with such perfect comprehension of musical sound, such faultless precision, such accuracy of note, that I was greatly astonished … At a given signal the crowd … squatted on the ground … the distinguished orators came forward from the ranks and, taking up a position fifteen paces before the king, they improvised speeches … ☐ [Later] Panda had made his appearance. He seemed much altered. He was beautiful, superb, magnificent, imposing; his bearing had become that of a warrior and he wore his insignia with a martial grace … In his left hand he held four light assegais, artfully fashioned, and a great white shield patterned in black … while in his right hand a tip of an iron assegai protruded from a band of monkey tails … His brow was adorned with a circlet of otter fur from which square lappets of purple silk plush descended to his shoulders. A feather, two or three feet long, was attached at the top of the head in front and swayed gracefully in the air. From high up at the back of the head … rose a tuft of two touraco feathers (Corythaix porphyreolopha) the upper one of which was red and the lower blue. ☐ Suspended from his neck, front and back, were tassels of red and green wool which were overlaid upon oxtails dyed red, and thrown into relief by an under-layer of monkey tails, admirably arranged …'
(Delegorgue 1847 (1990): 196–201)

Swazi warriors in *incwala* regalia. The spectacular headdress and the collar of teased-out tails of cattle are 'full dress'. (Barbara Tyrell)

we have seen in Chapter 1, was the embryo kingdom of Mapungubwe and its development into the extensive Zimbabwe empire. Here trade with the east coast appears to have been a major determinant.

South of the Limpopo such endogenous developments seem to have occurred twice. Both examples were characterised by the imposition of an overarching unity on collections of formerly independent chiefdoms, although the extent of such unity differed considerably. These examples were the Zulu kingdom under Shaka and the Pedi federation under Thulare and subsequent chiefs. The South Sotho kingdom established by the great African statesman, Moshweshwe, was not an indigenous development in the same sense but rather a response to the sweeping social changes of the later nineteenth century. The Swazi kingdom can best be seen as being built on a modified Zulu pattern, though the custom of preferred cross-cousin marriage and the special position of the queen mother show considerable Sotho, and especially Venda, influence.

Until the eighteenth century all Nguni were organised into relatively small chiefdoms based on the general pattern discussed above. However, by the latter half of the century certain forces were at work among North Nguni that led to fundamental changes in the concentration of power in certain chiefdoms. First, the northernmost chiefdom, the Ngwane, came under pressure from the Tembe-Thonga, the dominant power in the Delagoa Bay hinterland, and expanded south, conquering and subjugating those groups adjacent to them. Still further south the Ndwandwe, who dominated trade between the coast and the highlands of the interior, also expanded their influence. Similar expansion of territory and influence occurred among the most southerly chiefdoms of Qwabe and Mthethwa, especially the latter under the chief Dingiswayo. Under Dingiswayo Mthethwa power grew rapidly, particularly after he had contracted a commercial alliance with the Tsonga kingdom of Maputo at Delagoa Bay. Tensions increased between these four power blocs and Dingiswayo was killed by the Ndwandwe. His death opened the way for Shaka to seize power. The son of Senzangakhona, head of the small Zulu chiefdom, Shaka had served in the Mthethwa army. When Senzangakhona died in 1816, Shaka killed the heir, his half-brother, and assumed the Zulu chieftaincy.

There followed a period of expansion in which Shaka's impis subjugated the whole of northern Natal, so that at the height of his power Shaka could claim to hold sway over a vast area bounded by the Indian Ocean, the Phongolo in the north, the Drakensberg, and the Thukela in the south. This was made possible by drastically restructuring Zulu society, with social control imposed by strongly disciplined army regiments, concentrated in military barracks and equipped with the short-shafted stabbing assegai. The name 'Zulu' was extended to all within the kingdom, whatever their origin.

Details of the Zulu kingdom under Shaka are well known. It was an extreme example of the despotic rule of one man, who imposed his will on the entire kingdom. The Zulu nation, made up of conquered chiefdoms and other groups, was contained within what Sansom calls a *'cordon sanitaire*, a great expanse of waste land that separated the Zulu people from other, lesser tribal polities'. Within the nation control was absolute and secession virtually impossible, although there were cases of groups breaking away. Such were the Ndebele under Mzilikazi (who founded the Ndebele state in Zimbabwe), the Bhaca under Madzikane and the Ngwane under Mathiwane. The checks and balances contained in the Southern Bantu system of councils and advisors disappeared, male initiation was abolished

Tswana and Ndebele warriors, by G. Baxter. The artist contrasts the style of weaponry of Sotho-Tswana with that of Ndebele warriors of the great chief Mzilikazi. The Ndebele were an offshoot of the Zulu, using both the oval shield and the stabbing assegai. (Africana Library)

and, as we have seen, the great ceremonies were militarised and men attended them in regiments. Loyalty to descent groups and local neighbourhoods was played down in favour of loyalty to regiment and king. Basic to the whole system was the exercise by Shaka of naked terror as a principle of public policy. People were put to death at the king's whim and this terror was maintained by the apparently arbitrary selection of victims for execution. Walter (1969) has argued that the very arbitrary nature of this power ensured its success as an instrument of government. It is clear that the Shakan tyranny was entirely foreign to Southern Bantu ideas of 'good government' and, indeed, Shaka's reign only lasted seven years (1821–8) before he was assassinated by his brother Dingane.

The Pedi federation (1824–79) represents quite a different approach to the problem of creating wider political structures on the building block of the chiefdom. In the latter half of the eighteenth century, during a period of increasing conflict between various chiefs in the general area of what is now Sekhukhuneland, one of these chiefdoms, the Maroteng, extended their control over the region and succeeded in bringing the most powerful chiefdoms, among them the Masemola and Tau, under their paramountcy. Two strategies were employed, one ritual, the other social.

The Maroteng declared that they were the ritual superiors of all the chiefs of the federation. All the rituals of chiefship discussed above could only be performed by constituent chiefs with the consent of the paramount; in particular they had to supplicate annually for permission to commence the performance of the first-fruits ceremonies in their areas. At intervals of four to six years they sought permission to 'castrate their bulls', that is, to hold circumcision schools. They were also forced to pay tribute of clay, thatching grass and spoils of the chase to the paramount. The paramount could withhold permission for harvest and thus endanger the well-being of the subordinate chiefdoms; he could also show political displeasure by postponing initiation.

Perhaps even more importantly, the Maroteng established themselves as wife-givers to all subordinate chiefs. A great wife had always to be the daughter of the Pedi paramount and her important political role was ritually expressed by a ceremony in which her hearth-fire was dowsed and then rekindled with new fire carried by runners from the capital. 'By supplying brides, the paramount gave recognition to the successors of chiefs and he could create new chiefs, incorporating new groups into the federation or recognising the division of one chiefdom into several new political groupings' (Sansom 1974: 270). Like the Lovedu, the Pedi paramounts utilised bonds of marriage alliance as instruments of political integration.

Finally, the Pedi paramount had the option of force to maintain the federation. As he did not have a large army at his disposal, he relied on alliances with subordinate chiefs by which he formed 'punishment commandos' to bring dissidents into line. Sansom sums up the nature of Pedi polity:

> Thus the Pedi federation was a loosely bound collectivity of chiefdoms whose paramount enjoyed limited federal powers. His federal discriminations were expressed in the idiom of rank and ritual and could only be backed by force if he could sponsor an alliance of chiefs against a victim chiefdom. (Sansom 1974: 271)

But these developments were atypical. Throughout the thousand years of rule by chiefs it was the independent chiefdom that characterised the essentials of Southern Bantu government and that placed its stamp on the nature of civil society.

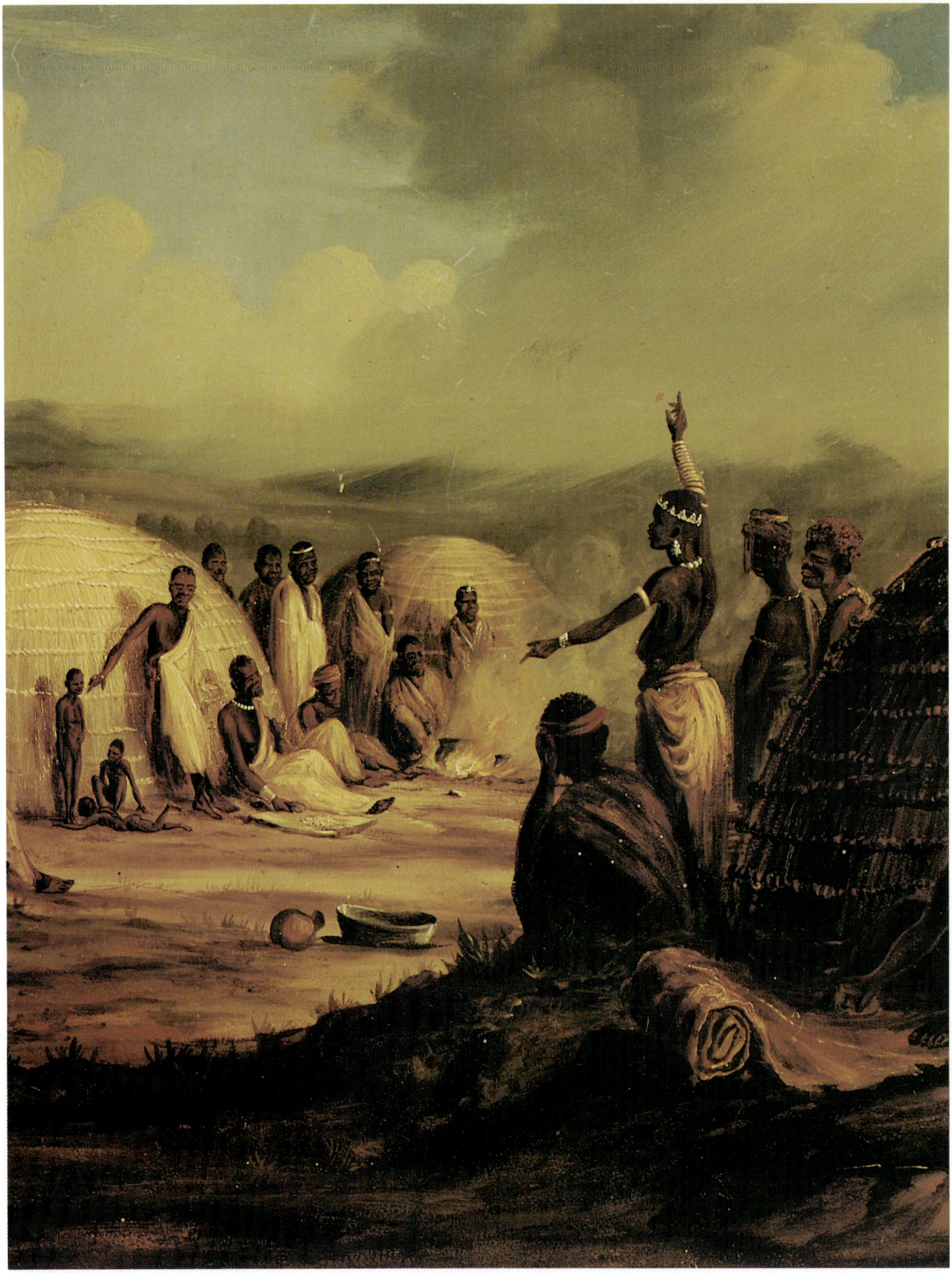

Chapter 4

The Settlement of Disputes

IN APPROACHING the nature of traditional law and the process of dispute settlement in pre-colonial South Africa it is necessary to make an imaginative leap and try to visualise the circumstances under which these institutions operated. Van Warmelo's evocative sketch of Venda life may help us to do so:

> In those days the Zoutpansberg mountains were covered from end to end with dense bush and high rain forest, threaded only by narrow footpaths along which danger lurked at every turn. The tiny gardens, which had to be guarded against wild animals all through the summer, supported a small population broken up into tribes which fought one another at intervals in a desultory way. The stockaded and fortified villages, crammed with people (nobody dared to live alone), lay carefully concealed in dense bush. At sunset the single narrow entrance was barred and hedged with thorn branches, and the men would lie down to sleep with their arms at hand, never certain of what the night would bring. Not only was there no security without, there was also very little within. Inside the village, even within one's own family, there might be envy, jealousy, hatred and witchcraft, besides the universal enemies: famine, sickness and death. Struggling man, beset by so many perils and hostile forces, sought security in social organization, first in the primordial unit of the bloodgroup, then in the community of groups forming a tribal unit. If anyone was to be trusted it was the brother, the sister, the close kinsman, and so we find that the family and kinship are the basic facts of Venda life. (Van Warmelo and Phophi 1948: 10–11)

Van Warmelo comments that, in such a situation, Venda law and custom constituted a system designed to guarantee not individual rights, but rather the rights of, firstly, the family and, secondly, the chiefdom itself. This led to a great stress on the *obligations* of an individual as compared with his *rights,* especially to his or her descent group, as we shall see in the next chapter. One of the great contrasts between these societies and those of the west was a relative absence of the individualism so characteristic of the latter. There was a poignant realisation that man cannot stand alone but is ultimately dependent for his very existence on the wider community. Even today there is a marked reluctance to dominate and impose one's will on others, especially if there is no relationship of kinship seniority. This also means that a court would not normally support an individual against his own group.

Another important factor was the relative smallness of these societies. Particularly among Sotho and Venda, with their intimate village life, quarrels and disputes could be extremely disruptive. What was crucial was not abstract justice, but

A Mfengu homestead near Fort Beaufort, painted in 1848 by Thomas Baines, who described the scene as follows: 'The majority (of the inmates) came out as they had slept, dragging their sole covering behind them, and arranging it in decent folds as soon as they had room to stand upright ... a female orator delivered a long and energetic harangue ... to the individuals of the softer sex, who, on its conclusion, departed to fetch wood and water, while ... their lords and masters ... carefully disposed their limbs so as to enjoy, with the least possible inconvenience to themselves, the luxury of the warm sun and their tobacco pipes. An aged female ... sat at the door of one of the huts with a dish of grease beside her, rubbing a bullock's hide with a large stone to render it sufficiently pliant to be used for an article of dress ...' (Africana Library)

The central *khoro* (meeting place) at Mudjadji's capital. The densely packed Sotho nucleated settlements, with their intricate alleys and cul de sacs, must have had all the lively complexity of a bustling medieval Italian town. (Davison 1984)

the urgent patching up of the rift. Unlike the case in the west, where large urban concentrations give a certain anonymity, and where it is possible for disputants to move away from each other, disputes in these little communities could be devastating. Individuals were locked together in many-stranded relationships. A man might, at the same time, be related to another as a mother's brother, a father-in-law, a fellow member of an age-regiment, a member of a co-operative work party and a co-member of the chief's council of advisers, and breach of trust in one relationship could spill over and affect all his other relationships. The main task of the courts, then, was not to decide an issue in terms of legal abstrations (as in the west) but to ensure that reconciliation took place. Judicial decisions were based on precedent, but legal niceties were never allowed to stand in the way of reconciliation.

These factors also affected the composition of the courts. It is clear that disputes were seldom purely between individuals *per se*, but between groups, and fractured relationships could quickly get out of hand, spreading along lines of cleavage between groups. As Van Warmelo puts it, each dispute was in effect a 'national' emergency. Its resolution, therefore, was placed squarely in the hands of the administrative authorities. Courts were not separate from the decision-making bodies that assisted chiefs and headmen in the running of their wards and chiefdoms; there was no separation between the administration and the judiciary. The same body of men who met regularly to run the affairs of the group also sat as a court of law, although they always made it perfectly clear when they did so, using different terminology. Among South Nguni, for example, the council of men was called *ibandla*; when it converted itself into a court it became an *inkundla*.

In the light of this the question arises as to whether the Southern Bantu had laws at all. Were they not merely governed by custom?

In societies where chiefs and other political functionaries do not exist (the 'stateless' societies of the anthropologist) this is indeed a difficult question to answer, and a number of elegant attempts have been made to define 'law' in cases where there is no mechanism for enforcing the carrying out of decisions. Among the Southern Bantu, though, this problem was absent. Administrative authority was always enforceable by official sanction, essentially physical. Among South Nguni, as we have seen, there was the special office of chief's messenger. If, for instance, the court imposed a fine of cattle on a man the *umsila* would proceed to his homestead and place his leopard's tail against the wall of the cattle byre. Within a stipulated number of days the culprit had to drive the cattle to the capital: if he failed to do so an armed posse was despatched to attach them.

The Southern Bantu made a clear distinction between 'custom' (Nguni: *amasiko*) and laws applied by the court (*imithetho;* Sotho: *milau*). Custom (and precedent) formed, as it were, a reservoir of rules and expectations that were *potentially* available for a court to apply in any particular case. Once this had been done, that particular custom attained the status of 'law', and could be quoted as such in later court cases. The law was thus continually being added to in the process of judicial decision-making (though, in the absence of writing, it depended on the memories of men). It could also, apparently, be formally created by legislation. There are many recorded cases of a chief and his council 'making' law – especially among Sotho – but these mainly refer to the post-contact period and, in societies that were changing only slowly, the necessity for such legislation was probably slight.

THE JUDICIAL PROCESS

The formal handling of disputes was the work of the hierarchy of courts associated with the administrative areas into which the chiefdom was divided, starting with that of the ward headman and ending with that of the chief at the capital. Here the chief was assisted by a small panel of 'remembrancers' who had the special task of advising him on points of law and were expected to attend all sessions to supply continuity of experience. Otherwise the court itself was the same body that made administrative decisions.

Before discussing the work of the courts more fully, reference must be made to less formal bodies also charged with the settlement of disputes. The most important of these was the 'court' of the local descent group. We have already noted the extreme importance of the Venda *khoro ya muti*, dominated by father's brothers and father's sisters (*khotsimunene* and *makhadzi*), and something similar was common among all groups. Matters concerning the immediate family, and also the wider descent group, were discussed initially within these bodies, under the chairmanship of the genealogically senior man – for family matters were secret and dirty linen should not be displayed in public. The type of issue discussed at this level was essentially domestic – quarrels between husband and wife and the non-fulfilment of kinship obligations – and this 'family court' had the power to fine members and impose damages. But it had no power to enforce these decisions and had to rely ultimately on the threat of a ritual curse by the senior man. It was, in fact, a court of arbitration: if it failed to achieve reconciliation the matter would have to be placed before the headman's court, which then acted as a court of first instance, hearing evidence *de novo*. That the family court was considered im-

An Mpondo sub-chief conducts an assembly of the men of his ward at his homestead to discuss administrative matters. (H. Kuckertz)

portant is shown by the fact that in cases between kinsmen they would always be asked by the court, 'Has the matter been discussed by the family court?' – and, if not, the case would be sent back to them until it had. In addition, some Sotho had regimental courts which dealt with offences committed in connection with the initiation schools or regimental duties, and special women's courts (associated with the female age-regiments – see Chapter 7).

The process of bringing a case to court was simple and logical. If a man felt that his rights had been violated – if, for instance, his crops had been trampled by a neighbour's cattle – he would report the matter to his sub-headman, or go with this official to the headman of the defendant's ward (if they lived in different wards) to report the matter. A date was set, as soon as possible, for the hearing and the defendant and the other men of his group were instructed to attend, bringing any witnesses they might have. There were no fixed sessions and courts only met when there was a case to be settled.

The case was heard in the men's meeting place, which was a prominent feature of the homestead of chief or headman (usually adjacent to the cattle byre and preferably under a large shade tree). The judge, with his assessors and close relatives, sat facing the rest of the people (in effect the male members of the ward), who were free to take part fully in the proceedings. Women were not permitted to be present unless they were personally involved in the case. The two parties involved usually sat in the front, towards the middle, backed by a semi-circle of the general public. Witnesses were not kept separate from the proceedings and, presumably, could modify their evidence in the light of the developing drama.

The proceedings commenced with the judge briefly outlining the circumstances that had brought the case to his attention and then the plaintiff was called upon to

A case being heard at a sub-chief's court in Pondoland. The chief sits in the centre, bare-headed, while the litigants – a widow on the extreme left, and a young man (foreground, striped jersey) – face him and the jury. (H. Kuckertz)

state his grievance. Great latitude was allowed here: he could be as discursive as he wished and could not be interrupted or called to order. The defendant was then called upon to reply, under the same rules. Both parties were then cross-examined, both by the judge and his assessors and by any of those present, and, if there were witnesses, they were requested to make their contribution. When all had had their say the matter was thrown open for general discussion, and here again speakers were given much latitude to range widely and probe deeply. The criterion used by the court was the universal one; that of the 'reasonable man'. What the judges did in trying to establish accountability was to compare the behaviour of the defendant against a generalised conception as to how a reasonable father, kinsman, neighbour would have behaved in the particular circumstances of the case – and the defendant, of course, was at pains to convince them that he *had* behaved reasonably. The assessors then gave their opinions, speaking strictly in ascending order of seniority. Finally, the judge summed up the evidence (and the various points of view that had been expressed) and, if possible, quoted precedent to guide the court. His judgement should reflect, not his own views, but those of the majority.

The process of judgement was sophisticated: impassioned rhetoric and penetrating forensic questioning were the order of the day. Eye-witness accounts and material evidence formed the basis of discussion, and the impression made on the court by disputants (as well as knowledge of their characters) all played a part. Circumstantial evidence was sometimes deemed acceptable (being discovered at night in a woman's hut was *prima facie* evidence of adultery, unless there were other factors), but hearsay evidence was treated with caution. Tswana and Venda punished flagrant cases of false witnessing. But running like a thread through all

The court of a Venda chief in session in the 1930s. Note the extensive stone walling. The royal residence extends up the terraced steep slope behind the *khoro*, for Venda capitals were built against the southern slopes of the Soutpansberg mountains. The chief's private dwelling was secluded at the top, its elevation symbolising political pre-eminence. (N.J. van Warmelo. Reproduced under Government Printer's Copyright Authority 9612 dated 6 May 1993)

these proceedings was a concerted effort, not only to establish blame, but to ensure that the loser accepted the decision with good grace. In these small-scale societies the dispute just had to be settled amicably, to prevent the breach in relations from festering and causing disturbance in the future. Great efforts were made by judges to bring the guilty party to a realisation that he had acted wrongly ('unreasonably') – and to exert pressure on his accuser to forgive the injury. As Gluckman records for the Barotse of Zambia (themselves a Sotho offshoot), 'The comments of the judges read like sermons', for they are not only concerned that people should behave reasonably, but also that they should behave *generously*. Here law and morality came together. As Gluckman puts it: 'The law demands right and reasonable action: morality asks for right and generous action. A man should not insist on the letter of his rights, and he should be prodigal in meeting his obligations' (Gluckman 1963: 192).

THE CATEGORIES OF LAW

Although the rules applied by the courts were not codified and, as we have seen, were less clearly defined than in the west, it is possible to distinguish between two categories of rules that, although not identical, correspond broadly with the western concepts of civil law and criminal law. Civil law concerned the private rights of people in regard to personal status, property and contracts, while criminal law defined various actions as offences against the society as a whole. Civil law provided for redress, in the form of restitution or compensation, while criminal offenses carried the penalty of punishment through fines or death. One of the main differences between civil and criminal offences was in the action taken and, in this respect, practice was similar to that of the west. If a civil wrong was committed it lay with the injured party to decide whether or not action should be taken. A criminal wrong, on the other hand, had to be reported to the authorities. As Schapera writes:

> The principal remedies open to the victim of a civil wrong are restitution and compensation. The former aims at cancelling the wrongful act, as far as that is possible. A trespasser will be removed, borrowed or stolen property will be restored, an unfulfilled contract will be carried out, a disputed right will be upheld. Compensation is paid, usually in livestock, for a wrong which cannot be undone, such as seduction, damage to property, and defamation ... Another remedy sometimes exercised is vengeance or self-help, where the victim 'takes the law into his own hands' and forcibly exacts what satisfaction he can. The general tendency in Bantu law has been to limit self-help as far as possible, and it is condoned only in exceptional instances, such as the killing or the assaulting of an adulterer, homicide, or thief caught red-handed. (Schapera 1936: 200)

XHOSA COURT PROCEDURE 1850

The following is an extract from the Revd William Holden's The Past and Future of the Kaffir Races (1866), quoting from a report by the Revd Henry Dugmore, made in the 1850s. It gives a vivid description of the atmosphere in a headman's court: □ 'There is nothing in which their [the Xhosa's] mental power is so fully developed, as in conducting their law cases, which afford ample space for all their forensic skill, and supply no questionable proofs of their decided ability. I will quote a part of one of those processes, as given by Mr. Dugmore:– □ "Then comes the tug of war. The ground is disputed inch by inch; every assertion is contested, every proof attempted to be invalidated; objection meets objection, and question is opposed by counter question, each disputant endeavouring, with surprising adroitness, to throw the burden of answering on his opponent. The Socratic method of debate appears in all its perfection, both parties being equally versed in it. The rival advocates warm as they proceed, sharpening each other's intellect, and kindling each other's ardour, till, from the passions that seem enlisted in the contest, a stranger might suppose the interests of the nation to be at stake, and dependent upon the decision. □ "When these combatants have spent their strength, or one of them is overcome in argument, others step in to the rescue. The battle is fought over again on different ground, some point, either of law or evidence, being now brought forward, and perhaps the entire aspect of the case changed. The whole of the second day is frequently taken up with this intellectual gladiatorship, and it closes without any other result than an exhibition of the relative strength of the opposing parties. The plaintiff's company retire again, and the defendant and his friends review their position. Should they feel that they have been worsted, and that the case is one that cannot be successfully defended, they attempt to bring the matter to a conclusion, by an offer of the smallest satisfaction that the law allows. This is usually refused, in an expectation of an advance in the offer, which takes place generally in proportion to the defendant's anxiety to prevent an appeal. Should the plaintiff accede to the proposed terms, they are fulfilled; and the case is ended by a formal declaration of acquiescence. □ "If, however, as it frequently happens, the case involves a number of intricate questions that afford room for quibble, the debates are renewed day after day, till the plaintiff determines to appeal to the umpakati, who has charge of the neighbouring district. He proceeds with his array of advocates to his kraal, and the case is restated in his presence. The defendant confronts him, and the whole affair is gone into again on an enlarged scale of investigation. The history of the case, the history of the events which led to it, collateral circumstances, journeys, visits, conversations, bargains, exchanges, gifts, promises, threatenings, births, marriages, deaths, that were taken, paid, made, given, or occurred in connexion with either of the contending parties, or their associates, or their relatives of the present or past generations, all come under review; and before the 'Court of Appeal' has done with the affair, the history, external and internal, of a dozen families for the past ten years is made the subject of conflicting discussion." ' (Holden 1866: 177–8)

Among Tswana and North Sotho only, corporal punishment was frequently imposed: the Tswana were also exceptional in that they occasionally permitted self-help, something not countenanced in other groups.

Civil wrongs seem to have arisen mainly from illicit sexual relations. As wives and daughters were perpetual minors, it was the husband/father who was deemed to have been wronged, especially as the marriageable value of the woman had been reduced. Seduction was thus a major offence and was actionable among Nguni whether or not pregnancy occurred, although all other groups reserved this for cases of the latter. Nguni (again uniquely) went to court for each subsequent seduction. Although adultery of a wife was not usually grounds for divorce, a husband could claim damages from her lover. The onus of proof, however, was on the husband, but he could assault the culprit, even kill him, if the couple was caught *in flagrante delicto*.

Damage to property was probably the next most common civil wrong. Trespass on gardens was met by forcible removal by the court messenger and if cattle strayed onto the unfenced fields while crops were growing compensation was demanded. (We have already seen that fields, after harvesting, were open to all the cattle of the community.) Damage to other forms of property entitled the owner to restitution or compensation. Theft, on the other hand, was not a crime and was treated as a civil offence. Usually the thief had to restore the stolen property or its equivalent, but, in addition, had to pay an amount, of equal value, to the victim. Stock theft was taken very seriously, as it still is in South Africa. Among Tswana a man caught rustling cattle could be justifiably killed or have his hands cut off.

Schapera states that defamation was not regarded as an actionable wrong, except among Nguni among whom accusations of witchcraft were a 'most serious charge', actionable in the courts.

In addition to these mechanisms seeking to redress damages to persons, the Southern Bantu had a well-developed concept of contract. Perhaps the most important of these was marriage, which will be discussed in a later chapter, but there were others, usually associated with property or service. Contracts had to be concluded before witnesses and the property to be lent or alienated, or the service to be rendered, had to be clearly specified. Failure to fulfil a contract could lead to a court action and the award of compensation. Women and children were debarred from entering into a contract without the consent of their guardian.

The most widespread form of contract was the custom of *ukusisa*, a form of patron-client relationship, whereby a wealthy man would place one or more of his cattle in the keeping of another. The client was entitled to the milk, and should treat the cattle as his own, but he could not sell or slaughter them. All deaths had to be reported to the owner. The contract stated that the cattle must be returned if and when required, and when this happened the client might be given a heifer for his trouble. Chiefs and headmen frequently used *ukusisa* as a political weapon. By lending out stock in this way they created a network of clients totally dependent on them for their wellbeing and who could be ruined by the sudden withdrawal of their stock by the chief. Through the operation of this essentially economic relationship the total loyalty of these men was assured in a way unobtainable through the rather abstract loyalties of kinship and *khonza*

Other main contracts were the maintenance fee (Nguni, *isondlo*; Sotho, *dikotlô*), usually of one beast, paid to people for looking after non-related children, and fees paid to herbalists for doctoring illnesses.

As far as criminal law was concerned the main offences were homicide, grievous

A South Sotho court member questions witnesses. (Ashton 1952)

assault, rape, crimes against the chiefdom's authorities and witchcraft/sorcery. Incest was so heinous an offence that its punishment was either immediate death or to be left to the supernatural sanction of the wrath of the ancestors. As far as homicide was concerned there were some differences between the various groups. Among Nguni any injury to the person of any member of a chiefdom, whether male or female, was looked upon as an injury to the chief, to whom, and to whom alone, reparation was due. This meant that no reparation or damages could be claimed by the bereaved family; it was the chief who had been wronged, and only he should be compensated, although he could, if he so wished, pass on a portion of the fine to them. As Schapera puts it: '... the Chief in such cases acts in his official position as head of the tribe. Homicides and assault are therefore not wrongs against him as a private person, but wrongs against the tribe of which he is the public representative.' A homicide was punished by seizure of all the culprit's property. The Venda handled homicide in much the same way as the Nguni, but the North Sotho and Tsonga insisted that the relatives of the executed murderer pay cattle to the victim's family so that they might acquire a woman to raise up seed for their dead kinsman.

Assaults involving maiming or serious injury also came before the chief's court. Among Nguni, Tsonga and Tswana the usual penalty was a fine (of which some part might be passed on to the family) while among Venda the fine was a beast killed and eaten by the court, but among both South Sotho and North Sotho such assault was treated more as a civil offence. The reason for these differences is unclear.

Disobedience of any order given by the chief was punished by a fine and, in serious cases of extreme insubordination, resulted in the culprit being 'eaten up', i.e. having all or most of his stock seized. Rebellion against the chief was another matter, and was regarded as one of the greatest crimes that could be committed. The offender was killed, often secretly, and his property confiscated: he had threatened the very basis of society.

THE PILLARS OF MORALITY

The work of the courts involved questions of accountability and right behaviour. Ultimately it was based on ideas of morality.

How should morality be defined? How does it differ (if at all) from religion? Although in practice religion supports and gives sacred backing to moral codes, religion and morality are not the same: it is possible for a religious man to be immoral and atheists can be models of moral rectitude. Yet a useful distinction between the two must be attempted. 'Religious' behaviour may be defined broadly as that involving right behaviour between man and the supernatural; 'moral' behaviour as right behaviour between man and his fellow man. Also, moral norms must apply universally. What is good for one is good for all, irrespective of status and condition. Moral norms seem to have a 'given' quality: they are intuitively 'right' and therefore do not have to be bolstered up by threats and sanctions (as religious behaviour so often has to be). They are founded on a people's conception of the very nature of things and we should therefore expect that moral codes reflect the absolutely basic values of social life, without which the society would cease to be what it is. Moral behaviour is, then, essentially concerned with 'good' actions.

How did the Southern Bantu conceive of the 'good' man? Firstly, the good man was one who did not disturb the delicate balance between society and nature. It was believed that there was a complex relationship between harmonious social life and the wellbeing of man, beast and crops. As we shall see in Chapter 9, illness and misfortune were almost inevitably interpreted in human terms. A failure in health or fortune was typically caused by some failure in social relations, either with the ancestors or with one's kin or neighbours. The worlds of nature and society were not distinct. Rather did they form one moral universe in which actions and attitudes in one sphere affected the other. A premium was thus placed on good social behaviour, for failure here could have drastic consequences for the whole of life.

What were the basic values of the Southern Bantu? All these societies were patrilineal, with strong emphasis on male authority, and all were stratified into both kinship and political hierarchies (see Chapters 3 and 5). This gave rise to three basic principles of social life – patrilineal decent, rank and generation – and, as we should expect, the fundamental nature of these factors was reflected in the moral code.

Perhaps the most fundamental moral injunction was to show respect (Nguni: *intlonipho*) to seniors, especially those of one's descent group. This respect was inculcated from the earliest years. Children were taught absolute obedience to parents: they should always use formal modes of address to them, could not interrupt while grown-ups were talking, nor shout across to them. People whose children failed to behave well were said to feel shame. Younger brothers had to respect older brothers and members of a descent group its head. But respect was expected towards all seniors, whether related or not. At beer-drinks or feasts there was no intermingling of individuals who belonged to different age groups. Each group sat by itself and young men did not eat from the same dish as older men. Seating arrangements reinforced this. A junior could not sit on something that made his head appear higher than a senior's. The same applied to women, who had always to respect men. It was 'wrong' for a woman to join a man's group unless specifically invited to do so and young wives, in particular, were not permitted to attend beer-drinks without their husbands. They had to be particularly respectful towards their in-laws.

This emphasis on respect ran through all the kinship groups, from family to clan, and was associated with the emphasis on loyalty and mutual assistance to kin. The importance of safeguarding the interests of the kinship group meant that truth-telling, as a moral absolute, was absent. It was morally acceptable to lie if to tell the truth would threaten the safety of the group – and here one should bear in mind the insecurity of life in the past, described by Van Warmelo.

As far as sexual morality was concerned, this again bore the imprint of the special conditions of precolonial life. Here the great preoccupation was with fertility. It was essential that the community reproduce itself and sex, in its procreative aspect, was conceived of as a mystical force that had to be treated with circumspection and was hedged around with prohibitions. But mere love-making was morally neutral, indeed good, and a young person who had no lover was ridiculed. There were special techniques of limited intercourse and premarital sex was conducted specifically to avoid pregnancy. As it did not involve the basic value of fertility, this type of sex had no moral implications. Seduction, on the other hand, was wrong and punishable in the courts and by the ridicule of age-mates. Adultery was wrong for women and here, as in seduction, there operated a double standard, reflecting male dominance.

The importance of the solidarity of the descent group (see Chapter 5) was reflected in the husband-wife relationship. It was somehow thought wrong for a man to be too closely involved with his wife, as this could conflict with his loyalty to his paternal kinsmen. Husband and wife did not spend their leisure time together (men and women were segregated at beer-drinks and other functions) and a man who walked beside his spouse or showed her too much affection in public was suspected of being bewitched by her.

But the 'good' man was not only he who respected seniors and was loyal to his kin group. He was also a good neighbour. This meant co-operation with non-related members of his sub-ward or ward, indeed it was said that it was from neighbours, rather than from kin (who could possibly be conspiring over household property) that a man could expect disinterested assistance in time of trouble. Neighbours assisted one another in working in the fields, bringing home the harvest and in times of sickness. The good man was also he who was generous – with his time, his concerned involvement with others' troubles, and with his worldly goods. Generosity was the chiefly virtue *par excellence* and every man strove to act like a chief. Here again there were sanctions to ensure compliance. People assisted one another not only because it was the morally right thing to do, or because of the glow of self-satisfaction that came from knowing that one had behaved correctly. They did so because, if they did not, they themselves could be refused assistance later. The sense of neighbourhood, of belonging to a particular area, gave rise to strong local loyalties. But living close together also raised problems. There was always the possibility of jealousies arising from differential success in agriculture, and in life in general. The neighbourhood was the area of witchcraft accusations, reflecting these tensions, as we shall see later. A good man was one who was a good neighbour, untainted by the least suspicion of witchcraft.

An Mfengu headman painted by F. I'Ons, c. 1850. (Africana Library)

This importance of moral behaviour between neighbours was given expression in the work of the courts. As the Kriges say of the Lovedu court: 'All the procedures aim, not at settling legal issues, but at effecting compromises and reconciliation. The *khoro* ... relies, not on force, but on friendly adjustments.' Important here was the Lovedu custom of *hu khumelwa* ('to beg pardon of one another'), by which reconciliation was reached through an emissary who intervened between the two parties, usually with the slaughtering of a goat. This granting of pardon stopped court procedures and the Kriges estimate that, in the 1930s, about eighty per cent of disputes were solved in this way without ever coming to court.

The widest area in which morality operated was the chiefdom, and here loyalty to the chief and his political officers was a supreme good. The good man was he who was prepared to die for his chief. Connected to this was the prohibition against manslaughter, for this involved the killing of the chief's man.

The virtues of the good man were, then, respect for seniors, loyalty to kinsmen, assistance to neighbours, freedom from the suspicion of witchcraft, generosity, meticulous observance of custom, loyalty to the chief and political officers, kindness and forbearance. Most writers on the Southern Bantu maintain that morality tended to be confined to within kin groups. We have seen that it was wider than this and that it included all those who were thought of as members of the community, whether it be homestead, neighbourhood, district or chiefdom. It does seem as if there was a tendency for the moral community to end with the chiefdom, and that loyalty, truth-telling and so on were only expected within it, but against this there is the hospitality universally enjoined towards strangers, captured in the Xhosa proverb *Unyawo alunompumlo* ('The foot has no nose'). Strangers, being isolated from their kin, and thus defenceless, were particularly under the protection of the chief and were accorded special privileges.

THE ROOTS OF BLACK SOUTH AFRICA

CHAPTER 5

THE IMPORTANCE OF KIN

IN THE conditions of precontact South Africa people could not stand alone. Although the homestead was to a great extent self-sufficient, it was necessary, as we saw in Chapter 2, for it to be associated with other homesteads so that larger tasks, including the all-important one of defence, could be adequately carried out. Principles on which wider associations could be based were necessary. Neighbourhood was obviously one of these principles, but one of fairly limited application. Some wider-ranging principle of association was required and kinship was an obvious choice, for it provided a ready-made structure based on the fundamental reality of biological descent. The mere fact that people were related to one another (or believed themselves to be so related) provided a moral basis on which relationships could be structured and on which wider social groupings could be built. In these Southern Bantu societies kinship was without doubt the most important organising principle of social life.

Right at the start a distinction must be drawn between 'kinship' and 'descent', for, although they are part of the same wider system, they are not synonymous. 'Kinship' is the wider term, and includes 'descent'. It refers to the linking of people through both biological descent and marriage, the descent aspect involving relationships on both the father's and the mother's side of the family. In this sense all people, everywhere, have kin. It is part of the human condition. Each one of us stands, as it were, in the centre of a fan of kin that radiates out, linking us with our total heritage. Descent, on the other hand, refers to an emphasis, for social purposes, on one or other of the two aspects of biological kinship – the paternal side or the maternal side. Some societies in Africa (but not in southern Africa) trace descent through the mother's side, and are thus termed 'matrilineal'. Among them inheritance of status and property passes from the mother's brother to his sister's son, for even in matrilineal societies men have the power and status. (The 'opposite' of a mother's brother is, of course, his sister's son).

All Southern Bantu were patrilineal, with inheritance and group membership passing from father to son (except the Tsonga, among whom the estate was first passed from brother to brother before reverting to the next generation).

The importance of descent is that it allows both for clear rules of inheritance and for the formation of larger social groupings, what have been called 'clans' and 'lineages' by anthropologists. We shall have to consider later to what extent Southern Bantu had descent groups.

But, even in societies with patrilineal descent, there remain the kin on the mother's side, who continue to play a most important role in the lives of their

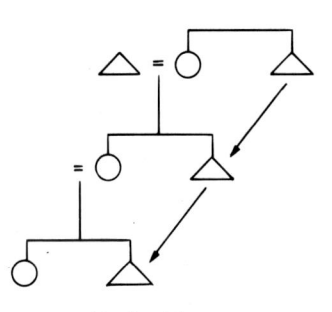

Xhosa woman, by F. I'Ons. (Africana Library)

Patrilineal descent

Matrilineal descent

The Basic Kinship Diagram

It is ironic that kinship, so basic to human beings (who learn to use their own terms and behaviour patterns effortlessly), should present so many difficulties, and appear so daunting, when approached from the outside. This is, of course, because of the extreme difficulty of visualising both the complexities of the compound terms – such as mother's brother's daughter or father's father's brother – and the relationships between them. One needs a simple model, or key, to anchor one's thoughts and guide one through the maze which, indeed, can get extremely complex. One should always have paper and pencil handy when thinking about kinship: it is virtually impossible to practise mental (kinship) arithmetic! ☐ In actual fact classificatory systems all have as their raison d'être the need to simplify the potentially large variety of kin into a few broad categories. The principles on which the basic classifications are made are remarkably few. They are: descent, generation, age and gender, combined in different ways. Thus a primary distinction is always made between father's people and mother's people; between kin of one's own generation (siblings and cousins) and those of parents (uncles and aunts) and between grandparents and grandchildren; between male and female kin; and, often, between older and younger. The terms, and their associated behaviour, can be logically extended outwards to take in more distant relatives, but, for most purposes, the really significant close kin are those depicted in the diagram (a). ☐ The most basic principle underlying these systems is known as 'the social equivalence of siblings'. This means that, for social purposes, brothers and sisters tend to be considered as identical. This explains why a FB is classified as 'F'; they are the 'same' – and this also goes for the MZ, who is a kind of mother. ☐ The relaxed relationship between a man and his MB is similarly explained. The MB is a kind of mother (equivalence of siblings) and one thus expects from him the warmth associated with mothers. But, he is also a male of the generation above one (that of your father) all members of which you must respect. In a sense he is both a mother and a father, and this is why, in South Africa, he is called by a term meaning 'male mother' (malume). This clash between warmth and respect, in the same relationship, may be the reason for the ritual joking so often found between mother's brother and sister's son (as among, for instance, the Tsonga). The relationship is so 'strange', and the emotions involved so complex, that a 'joke' is made about it to achieve catharsis. ☐ The same explanation holds for the father's sister – but here the relationship is the 'opposite' of that with the mother's brother. As we shall see, father's sisters are treated with very great respect and, among Venda and Sotho-Venda, act as officiators in the ancestor cult. A father's sister is, in a sense, 'the same as' a father (equivalence of siblings), and must thus be treated with the respect due to a father. But she is of the opposite sex (to a male Ego) and gender difference imposes a widened social distance between them. The FZ is referred to as rakgadi in Sotho, that is, 'female father'. ☐ The children of these two relatives (MB and FZ) are one's cross-cousins and, in South Africa, are called by a special term (abazala/batswala). They are never called 'brother' and 'sister', as parallel cousins (children of FB and MZ) are. They always belong to a descent line different from Ego, and this makes it possible for them to become preferred marriage partners, as among Sotho and Venda (diagram b).

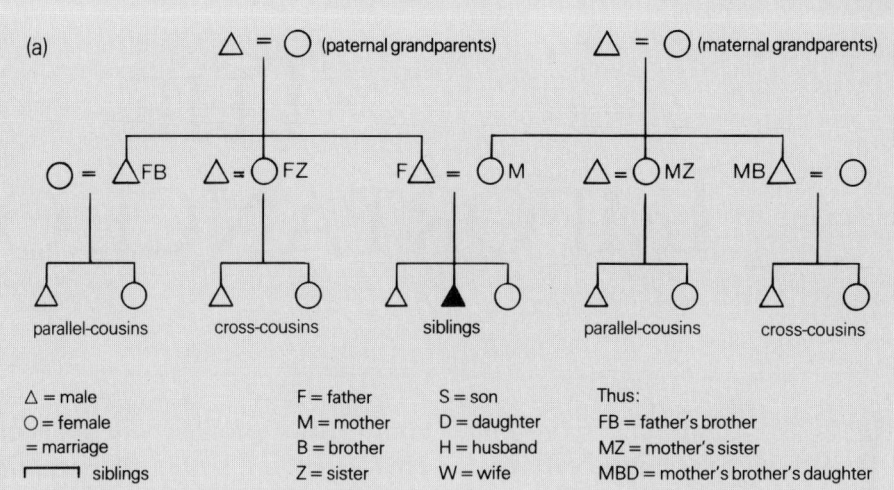

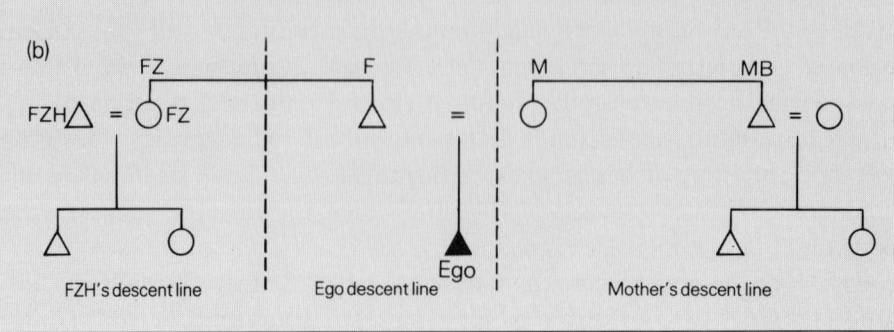

descendants. It is important, therefore, to distinguish between three types of kin: patrilineal (called *agnates* by anthropologists), maternal (*uterine* kin) and kin by marriage (*affines*). These three categories all had their important part to play in traditional social life, as we shall see.

The other thing to be stressed is that kinship, although based on the concept of biological connection (expressed in the metaphor of being 'of the same blood'), is a social fact – not, essentially, a biological one. People consider themselves kin because their society says they are, even in cases where there may not be any real biological connection between them. Thus, as we shall see, some cousins (but not others) may be considered 'the same as' brothers and sisters; some uncles are thought of and treated as fathers (and others not), and non-related children may be adopted in a fictitious kin relationship. In the Christian church the relationship between godparents and godchildren is of this type: in the past they could not marry. We have already noted the Lovedu queen's standing as a 'father' to her 'children'.

The basis of all kinship systems is the nuclear family of father, mother and children, and it is from the family that all kinship systems derive their structure. The basic relationships involved here are husband/wife, father/son, father/daughter, mother/son, mother/daughter and brother/sister (the Old English term 'sibling' is conveniently used for both brother and sister). These are the 'real' kin, and the importance of the relationships between them is underlined by the prohibition against sexual relations between them, that is, the incest taboo. Incest is almost universally considered a sin, possibly because it threatens so fundamentally the harmony of the crucially important family group. In the terminologies of the west the close-knit group of family members is clearly marked off from other kin (family terms, such as 'father', 'mother', 'brother' and 'sister', are *never* used for aunts, uncles and cousins). In most non-western societies, however, this is not the case. The family is merged with the wider group of kin and the family terms are applied much more widely. This way of ordering kin is termed a 'classificatory system of kinship terminology', and is of extreme social importance.

A newly married Bhaca girl. (W.D. Hammond-Tooke)

THE CLASSIFICATION OF KIN

The main types of classificatory system found world-wide are all based on the term a man uses to refer to three significant relatives – his father, his father's brother and his mother's brother. There are four possibilities here. He can use a separate term for all three; he can reserve the term 'father' for his real father and lump the other two together under one term (as with the western term 'uncle') that includes both father's brother and mother's brother; he can call all three 'father' or he can classify father and father's brother together as 'father' and use a separate term for the mother's brother. This last option is known to anthropologists as the Iroquois system (after the well-known North American Indian tribe who also classify in this way) and is found among all the Southern Bantu except the Tsonga. The Tsonga have a variant of the Iroquois system, called the Omaha, which differs from it in the way cousins are termed. There is a further variation (not found in Southern Africa) that brings the main types of classificatory system to six.

Systems of kinship terminology work with precise logic. If you call a man 'father' (even if he is in reality your father's brother) you will call his children (your parallel cousins) 'brother' and 'sister', and will be prohibited from marrying them. You will also treat him with the respect due to a father. It is obvious that such a system

The spacious interior of a Zulu hut, by G.F. Angas. Note the sleeping mats against the wall and dried sorghum and implements hanging from the cross beams. A headrest is on the left and maize porridge is cooking on the central fireplace, covered with a pot to contain the steam. The calabashes against the wall probably stored sour milk. (Africana Library)

means that an individual can have many 'fathers' and 'mothers', something which has caused some confusion (and cynical comment) on the part of white employers in South Africa, when an employee repeatedly asks for time off to bury his 'mother'!

Among the Southern Bantu the operation of the Iroquois system meant that an individual called his father's brother 'father', usually with a suffix indicating whether he was an elder or junior brother (for relative age was also important), and treated him with great respect. It will be noted that this terminology stressed the importance of the patrilineal principle in these societies, for all father's male kin were regarded as essentially belonging to the same group. The father's brother's wife was called (logically) 'mother' and his children (one's parallel cousins) 'brother' and 'sister'. Equally logically, no marriage was permitted with them. Even among Tswana, among whom marriage with the father's brother's daughter was uniquely permitted, this was only common among royalty.

The mother's brother, on the other hand, was not called 'father', but addressed by quite a different term, one meaning 'male mother' *(malume)*. Quite unlike the father-like father's brother, the *malume* was a warm, indulgent figure who was expected to have a special interest in his nephews and nieces. After all, he had no ulterior motives. Belonging to a different descent line (that of one's mother), he could never be a competitor for family property or status, nor could his son displace oneself (as a father's brother's son could in certain circumstances). As Kgaga informants explained to me: 'The *malume* is just a friend to us. You can tell him anything. But he is also the relative first told of an impending marriage, for which his advice is always sought. Fathers have nothing to do with marriage [they should not take an interest in the sex life of their daughters], nor do mother's sisters.' The

Tsonga mother's brother is famous in anthropological literature for the 'joking relationship' that existed between him and his sister's son. Among these people the nephew could joke with his maternal uncle, take his food, and snatch the meat at an ancestral sacrifice. The children of the maternal uncle were not styled 'brother' and 'sister' (as were the children of the father's brother) but referred to by a separate term (Nguni, *mzala*; Sotho, *motswala*) which can perhaps best be translated 'cross-cousin'. Among Sotho and Venda, the mother's brother's daughter was the preferred marriage-mate and, if this marriage was accomplished, was usually accorded the status of senior wife, but Nguni and Tsonga prohibited marriage with all cousins, of whatever type.

As far as aunts were concerned, a similar difference existed between the mother's sister and the father's sister as did between mother's brother and father's brother. The mother's sister was called 'mother' and her children 'brothers' and 'sisters', but the father's sister was quite a different sort of person. Called 'female father' (*rakgadi*; Venda, *makhadzi*), she was accorded extreme respect and, among the Venda and Sotho-Venda especially, was the family priest, charged with approaching the ancestors on its behalf. Among Venda she was the most prominent member of the family council, as we have seen.

We have been discussing how the system of kinship terminology classified kin at the level of the parent's generation and that of their children. There remain the relationships between alternate generations – grandparents and their grandchildren. Here different terms were used, usually containing the suffix 'great' or 'big' (*khulu, golo*) for the grandparents, as in the Tswana *rrêmogolo* and *mmêmogolo*. Relations between grandparents and grandchildren, on both sides of the family, were typically relaxed, as seems to be the case all over the world. It is almost as if there is a universal 'law' that, when two adjacent generations (always characterised by respect) are brought together (father-son, father-son), the respect and social distance between them is cancelled out and the relationship becomes a relaxed one of equality. It is as if it is the grandchildren, and not their fathers, who 'take over' from the grandparents, in a cycle that reflects the fact that, at any one time, three generations are 'in occupation' in normal social life. Despite this, the aged were greatly respected. As long as his father lived, a man was under his authority, and this continued even after death, when the father became an ancestor. Grandmothers were important members of the homestead, and were the story-tellers *par excellence*.

If generation differences were important in these systems, so too were those of age. Age difference was frequently stressed in the terminology. This was particularly true of siblings. Among Nguni a clear terminological distinction was made between elder brother and younger brother, and this was reflected, in the father's generation, in the different terms for *father's* elder and younger brother. In Xhosa, for example, an individual referred to his elder brother as *mkhuluwa* (*khulu* =big) and the younger brother as *umninawe*, but age was not used to distinguish sisters, who were all called *dadewethu*. This was reflected in the father's generation. Here the father's elder brother was referred to as *bawomkhulu*, and father's younger brother as *bawomcane*, literally 'big father' and 'little father', although a man addressed them both as 'father'. The Sotho did things slightly differently. Among them, a man called his elder brother *mogolo* (*golo* = *khulu* = big) and his younger brother *moratho*, and, as among Nguni, this age characterisation did not extend to his sisters, all of whom were called *kgaitsadi*. But among Sotho the terms were applied differently if a woman was speaking. A woman used the same terms

An Mpondo baby being washed. The mother takes a mouthful of water which she squirts on the infant.

The Oral Tradition

In the absence of writing, all literature was oral and transmitted by word of mouth. Its freedom and versatility make it difficult to impose rigid categories, but the following is an attempt to identify the main types. It will be noted that the categories presented here are mixed, an indication of the provisional nature of the scheme. A particular form can, in fact, be classified in more than one way: folktales, mainly divertive, could also be didactic or, indeed, 'mythic'; riddles could be both divertive and didactic, and be in prose or verse. Expression often reached pure poetry, especially in the praise poems.

PROSE
narrative   myths, legends
                 histories
didactic   proverbs
divertive   riddles
                 folktales

VERSE
discriminatory   initiation formula
lyric-based   songs
eulogistic   praise poems

☐ myths – *sacred narratives purporting to describe the creation of the world, men and animals; the origin of evil and of death.* ☐ legends – *tales claiming to be historical, but containing larger-than-life heroes and improbable, often magical, events.* ☐ histories – *narratives of tribal migrations and successions to chieftainship. In reality, often texts justifying contemporary political alignments.* ☐ proverbs – *pithy statements of folk wisdom, ranging from truisms to profound insights.* ☐ riddles – *brainteasers with conventional meanings.* ☐ folktales – *told by grandmothers to children, and often involving tricksters, talking animals, cannibals and monsters. Make much use of set refrains.* ☐ initiation formulae – *versicles and responses taught to initiates, to be perfectly memorised as future proof of initiation.* ☐ songs – *simple, often repetitive, lyrics, usually on personal or local themes, such as war, courting, marriage, harvesting, and so on.* ☐ praise poems – *eulogising chiefs, in often recondite images, often functioning also as legitimation of political authority and the establishment of group identity. Regarded by the people themselves as the highest form of literary art.*

(*mogolo* and *moratho*) for her elder and younger sisters respectively, and *kgaitsadi* for her brothers. *Kgaitsadi* is thus difficult to translate into English. It carries no gender implications and seems to mean 'sibling of the opposite sex'. These terms for siblings were used in exactly the same way for parallel cousins.

This age ranking of siblings and parallel cousins was confined to these relatives. They were, it will be noted, all patrilineal kin, with an interest in the family property and thus in their exact relationship to one another. Cross-cousins, on the other hand, who belong to different descent lines, were not ranked in this way, nor did they need to be, for they were not involved in competition over descent group property. They were all lumped together under one term (Nguni, *mzala*; Sotho, *motswala*), which ignored both age and gender.

It is important to remember that this system could be greatly extended on the paternal side to include more distant kin, such as father's father's brother's son's son, who was, of course, called 'brother' (see diagram). Kinship systems were nothing if not logical.

Patrilineal Kin and the Nature of Descent Groups

The strong patrilineal emphasis of the Southern Bantu left its mark on every aspect of social life, from settlement patterns to religion. As we have seen, there was the tendency for brothers (and therefore paternal uncles) to settle close together, often in the same homestead; patrilineal inheritance gave paternal kin a keen interest in the family herds while loyalty to patrikin was a major moral injunction; kinsmen supported each other when called before the courts; and, especially among Nguni, they worshipped deceased paternal kinsmen as the most important of their ancestral spirits. But they went further. They used the patrilineal principle to establish larger social groups that had an existence over and above that of the family, groups that extended over time and space and played an extremely important role in a person's life. These groups are called 'clans' and 'lineages'.

Definitions are required here. A lineage is defined as a group of people who form a distinct social group and who can actually trace their descent to one another on a common family tree. The emphasis here is on *demonstrated* relationship. Clans, on the other hand, are groups of people who *believe themselves* to be related, although they are unable to demonstrate this genealogically. The reason that they believe themselves related is because of the possession of a common clan name which is used in addition to the personal name. Typically, fellow clansmen cannot marry, for, in a metaphorical sense, they think of themselves as 'brothers' and are therefore subject to the incest taboo. Clans are exogamous. It is as if all the Smiths in the world believed themselves to be related and were debarred from marrying each other because of this fact. Clansmen are also expected to treat one another with consideration and hospitality.

In those societies without chiefs, political officers or courts, there is a strong tendency for clansmen to live together in the same stretch of territory, defending it against all comers. Where this happens one can perhaps speak of the clan as a 'group' – a collection of people who are potentially in face-to-face relationships with each other, think of themselves as a group and who, together, control an estate of land and cattle. But this is unusual in societies, like those of the Southern Bantu, that *also* have formal government.

A moment's reflection will show why this vagueness about the 'groupishness' of clans exists. The origins of clans are always located far back in the past, and this

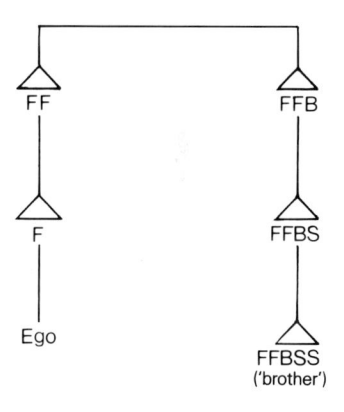

> ## Umdlubu and the Toad: A Zulu Folktale
>
> A king marries the daughter of another king. She becomes his favourite wife and attracts the jealousy of his other wives. She gives birth to a girl, Umdlubu. Umdlubu grows into a beautiful child and the other wives plot against her. They all go to gather grass for mat-making and the child is taken with them. The mother inadvertently leaves her in the fields and the king is desolate. ☐ An old woman of the royal household of another chiefdom goes to fetch water and hears the child playing. She calls the chief wife of her king, who takes Umdlubu home, bathes and suckles her. Umdlubu grows up as a sister to the king's son. Later the king's councillors advise the boy to marry Umdlubu. He answers in dismay, 'Oh, what is the meaning of this? Is she not my sister?' They reply, 'No, she was found in a valley.' He denies this, saying, 'No, she is my sister.' He is greatly troubled. On another occasion the old woman informs Umdlubu that she is to marry her 'brother'. She, too, remonstrates with her and is greatly troubled. ☐ Umdlubu takes a pot and goes to the river to draw water, crying all the while. A great toad comes out of the pool and she tells him her troubles. He tells her to fetch all her favourite possessions. She does so and the toad swallows them all, and Umdlubu as well. He sets out for her home.
> ☐ On the way the toad meets, first a file of young men, then a file of adult men, some herdboys and, finally, Umdlubu's own true brother. Each group tries to kill him, but each time he sings the refrain: I am but a toad; I will not be killed. I am taking Umdlubu to her own country, *and they let him pass*. When he arrives at her home he hides in a thicket, vomits up Umdlubu, cleanses her with caster oil plant, and tells her to put on her ornaments. She takes a brass rod, enters her father's cattle byre and then her mother's hut. Her mother does not recognise her at first. Umdlubu accuses her of losing her because of lack of love. At this, recognition dawns, the news is broadcast and there is great rejoicing. A messenger is sent to the king her father. ☐ Umdlubu's father enquires as to how she has returned. The toad is feasted and told to ask what he wants for a reward. He asks for cattle and people. He establishes himself as a great chief with a great town and people flock to join him.

is the reason why genealogical connection is *assumed*, not *demonstrated*. Without written records there was just no way in which the links between all the members of a Southern Bantu clan could be demonstrated, any more than those between all the Smiths could be. With the passage of generations, clans also expanded 'on the ground' and members became scattered over wide areas, often in other chiefdoms. It is clear that clans were not 'groups', in any sociological sense, but *categories* of people, most of whom never met, nor were even aware of the existence of most of the other members. But clans did provide 'catchment areas' from which actual social groups could be recruited.

Lineages form parts, or segments, of clans. In stateless societies, where they are of extreme importance, lineages tend to be localised social groups; in societies with formal governmental organs, they tend to be dispersed. Although they can actually trace their relationship if they meet, members of the lineage do not necessarily form a social group. In state-type societies lineages therefore also tend to be categories (or 'descent constructs'). Yet they play an important social role. The mere fact that you *know* you are related to someone else, and can show the precise connection on a family tree, places moral obligations upon you to treat him or her in a certain way.

It is, of course, impossible to know for certain the precise nature of descent groups among Southern Bantu in precolonial times. This kind of data can only be gleaned from detailed investigations, done on the spot, in contemporary society – collecting genealogies from informants, plotting the spatial distribution of kin in a specific area, attending meetings and rituals and recording precisely who attends, and their relationship to the others present. People can tell you, in rather vague terms, who *should* be present at a ritual, but this is not nearly enough. For the purpose of describing descent groups in the past, one has perforce to work backwards from the present state of affairs and make informed guesses. There are obvious dangers in this, as fundamental changes have occurred since the colonial era, but it is the only method we have. The following discussion must be seen in this light.

From recent research it is clear that, at least today, the important descent groups (as distinct from social categories) are not the lineages themselves so much as that part of the lineage which occupies a local area. It is obvious that, to form a group, people must be in physical contact with one another, at least part of the time, so that they can interact meaningfully. The only Southern Bantu peoples who might have had clans and lineages in the past were the Nguni but, even among them, the only group that today functions in this way is that consisting of homestead heads descended from a common grandfather or great grandfather and who occupy a section of a sub-ward. This is the group termed the 'agnatic cluster'. Even today Nguni can produce family trees that go back five or six generations and contain the name of scores of homestead heads, but it is seldom if ever that all these people live together, or even come into meaningful contact with one another. They all belong to one 'lineage' (i.e. descent category), but they do not form a *group*. Our most detailed evidence comes from studies from the Mpondomise and Mpondo. Among these South Nguni, agnatic clusters vary in size from twenty related homesteads to clusters of one and two. These small numbers are obviously due to the vast social changes that have taken place over the last two centuries and it is likely that they were much larger in the past.

The head of the agnatic cluster was the most senior man genealogically – the eldest son of an eldest son. He acted as 'chairman' of the cluster council and had to

Women brewing beer in a Zulu homestead, by G.F. Angas. The brewing of beer was a major activity, for hospitality was a factor in the social status of a household. Beer also played a major role in the ancestor cult. (Africana Library)

be present at all rituals for the ancestors held by the constituent homestead heads. The agnatic cluster council met to solve disputes among its members and discuss family matters, but the head had no authority to impose his will on them and relied on the respect due to seniors or, ultimately, on the threat of a curse. He also acted as a ritual elder, especially in times of illness, when he had to 'present' the afflicted person to the shades. He had to be present when a newly married man was established 'in the seat of kraalhead', at marriage negotiations and at initiation ceremonies which, among Nguni, were always performed on a local basis. As a Mpondomise informant told me: 'The job of the *inkulu* [cluster head] is heavy. It gives one work that is unpaid. The *imilowo* [agnatic cluster members], especially widows, expect you to help them. You must be present when the go-betweens arrive for marriage negotiations. There are always disputes.'

Nguni clans, as we have seen, were widely dispersed and membership was indicated by a special name, usually that of the founder. Their dispersed nature seems to be reflected in the Xhosa word for clan name, *isiduko*, from *duka*, 'to wander among strangers, to be lost to view'. The Zulu term for it was *isibongo*, from the word to 'praise', referring to the praise songs and other verbal formulae that were associated with the clan name and used on special occasions. Clan members had no mutual economic responsibilities, nor did they consult one another. If, however, a traveller happened to call at the homestead of one of his own clan he would be specially well received. Otherwise the main relevance of clans, as we shall see in a later chapter, was in the ancestor cult. The clan ancestors brooded over all clan members, wherever they might be, and were invoked by the recitation of the clan praises.

Among South Nguni certain clans had special functions. Thus, among the Mpondomise (whose royal clan name was Majola) the Tyeni had the task of burying the chiefs, the Zumbe ritually roasted the meat at the river burial of the chiefs of the Ngwanya dynasty, the Cesana were responsible for negotiating for rain with the local San who acted as rain-makers, while the Bhukwane supplied the tribal herbalist and the Nqana formed the vanguard of the army. But clans as such were not involved, merely locally based individuals or families who were appointed to these tasks because of their possession of the right clan name.

These 'pure' descent groupings of the Nguni were not found among Sotho, Venda or Tsonga, except perhaps in the royal families among whom tracing descent far back into the past was important for their claims to royalty. In these three groups the patrilineal principle was fundamental as a way of ordering kin, but among them the 'lineage' was either very shallow in depth (the Tsonga only traced back three generations) or the wider 'descent' group also contained other kin, such as maternal kin and affines, thus 'contaminating' the exclusively patrilineal descent. Here we seem to be in the presence of a continuum which ranged from the strongly patrilineal Nguni system to a less patrilineal one. The range extended, by way of the (still strongly patrilineal) Sotho-Tswana, through the bilaterally organised Sotho-Venda, to the Venda and Tsonga. It also indicated a move from a strongly unilateral emphasis towards a bilateral system in which increasing emphasis was placed on both the father's and the mother's side of the family.

Among Sotho-Tswana several different households, living side by side and acknowledging a common elder, constituted what Schapera calls a 'family group'. It consisted basically of families whose men were all descended agnatically from a common grandfather or great-grandfather, by whose name the group was known. The family group thus looked, on the surface, remarkably like the Nguni agnatic

A Venda village scene at Tshakuma. Note the hut form and large wooden stamping block made from a tree from the heavily forested Soutpansberg. (N.J. van Warmelo. Reproduced under Government Printer's Copyright Authority 9612 dated 6 May 1993)

cluster. But there was an important difference. The group could also include other relatives, such as affines or maternal kin, or even families of unrelated dependants. It was thus not a pure descent group. The family group was a closely knit unit, whose members co-operated in such tasks as building and thatching, agricultural labour, assisting each other with gifts and loans. It dealt with such matters as 'betrothal and marriage, the organization of feasts, the settlement of estates, and the future of widows, all of which [were] held to concern not one household alone but the group as a whole' (Schapera). As in the case of the agnatic cluster, it also met, under the elder, to arbitrate over internal disputes.

As far as Sotho kinship terminology was concerned there was a collective term for all kin, including affines. This was *lesika* or *leloko*, and some scholars refer to the category so formed as a 'kindred'. Within this category two sub-categories were distinguished, namely patrilineal kin and close agnates of a person's mother. Patrilineal kin were referred to as *kgotla* (which also referred to homestead, sub-ward and ward) or as *ba ga etsho*, 'our people', or 'the people of our place'. Kin on the mother's side were *ba ga etsho mogolo* or, alternatively, 'mother's brothers'. It seems that paternal kin living outside a man's ward were merged with his maternal kin as a single undifferentiated kindred with no special functions. They were, however, expected to attend important rituals in his life, such as birth, initiation, marriage and death. The members of the family group itself were commonly referred to as *lesika*, stressing its broad kinship (rather than descent) nature, but it was more generally spoken of as *lekgotlana* (the diminutive form of *lekgotla*, 'ward'). This is significant. Adam Kuper has suggested that the Sotho-Tswana emphasis was not on descent as such (although the core of the family group were patrilineal kin) but

A Venda mother *phehla's* maize meal and water in the first stage of making porridge for her children. (Morris and Levitan 1986).

on the group's integration into the administrative system of the chiefdom. This would seem to be connected with the centralised nature of Sotho settlement which, as we have seen, differed so markedly from Nguni practice. This 'confusion' between patrilineal and matrilineal kin was also linked to marriage arrangements. Among Sotho, the preferred marriage partner was a mother's brother's daughter or a father's sister's son. This meant that a child, tracing descent through either the father's or the mother's line, would find these lines connected through the generations.

Among the Sotho-Venda of the lowveld (Lovedu, Kgaga) the balance had moved towards a more bilateral emphasis. As the Kriges say of the mother's side of the family among Lovedu: 'Nothing of interest or importance takes place without their presence; even at the annual harvest beer offerings, given to the gods on the father's side, relatives on the mother's side, who are not concerned with the religious aspect of the ceremony, would be present for the beer and social amenities.' The father's sister was undoubtedly the most important figure, especially the one linked to the father through the marriage cattle (see Chapter 6), but, unlike the position elsewhere, there was not the relaxed relationship with the mother's brother. Among Lovedu this relative had to be treated with the greatest respect, for one day he might be your father-in-law. As we shall see when discussing the ancestor cult, the ancestors of both sides of the family were important among all Sotho-Venda.

This emphasis on both sides of the family appears to have reached an even more definite form among Venda. Stayt maintains that a person belonged to both a patrilineage and a matrilineage, but this is incorrect if he means descent groups similar to those of the Nguni. He is obviously referring to a bilateral system, like that of the Sotho-Venda. Generally speaking, Venda kinship terminology was similar to Sotho.

The Tsonga, with their Omaha system of kinship terminology, also lacked lineages and clans. All that they had was a patrilineally inherited common name *(shibongo)* and a prohibition against marrying a girl with the same name. In this respect they were closer to the Nguni than to other Southern Bantu, possibly due to the direct historical influence of the Nguni on them. But in other ways they represent an extreme form of bilaterality. The Tsonga mother's brother had the responsibility of sacrificing to his nephew's mother's ancestors, while the boy's

---

Some Tsonga Proverbs and Riddles

PROVERBS

☐ *Ndlopfu a yi fi hi rimbambu rinwe.* An elephant does not die of one (broken) rib. (A strong man does not lose heart over a single misfortune.)

☐ *L'a ndzi fambisaka ni vusiku, ndzi ta nwi nkhensa loko ri xile.* He who led me in the night, him will I thank at day-break. (A man should say that he is safe only when he has reached home. 'Call no man happy till he dies' (Solon 630–555 BC).)

☐ *Kutsongo-kutsongo ku yiwa kule.* Little by little one goes far. (Slowly does it.)

☐ *U nga fayi tandza, swihlangi swi langutile.* Do not break an egg while children are looking on. (Secrets should not be discussed in public.)

RIDDLES

☐ *Nkuwa wa le kaya, manavetana?* Makwenu. The figtree of home, source of eager desire? A. Your sister.

☐ *Lexi, loko xi halakile, xi nga rholeriwiki, n'xini?* I mati. What is the thing which, once poured out, cannot be gathered again? A. Water.

☐ *Maxaka ya mina ya tele?* Tinyeleti. My relatives are numerous? A. Stars.

☐ *Entsungeni a va pfalangi?* I tinhomphu. They did not close (the hut) on the hill? A. The nostrils.

A general view of a Venda village in the 1930s. (N.J. van Warmelo. Reproduced under Government Printer's Copyright Authority 9612 dated 6 May 1993)

father did the same for those on the paternal side. In addition, all his life a man had a special responsibility for his wife's father, reminiscent of the bride service found in matrilineal societies north of the Zambezi.

Sotho and Venda did have wider 'groupings' that were analogous to the Nguni clan, except that these were not exogamous, nor did they carry the name of a human founder. Instead they were known by the name of some animal, plant or object. Anthropologists refer to them, rather vaguely, as 'totem groups', despite the fact that, like the Nguni clans, they were not really groups at all, but categories. Junod, who lived among the (North Sotho) Kgaga between 1899 and 1907, states that the term used by them to express the relationship between men and their totem was *go bina*, 'to dance', as in the expression *'Ke bina phuthi'* ('I dance the duiker'). But at that time there were no such dances, and all attempts to get his informants to demonstrate what they had been like in the past drew a blank. It seems that this 'totemic' system was more complex in the distant past but we shall never know its details. We do know that the totem animal was never eaten or killed for fear of calling down sickness upon oneself. It seems clear that the totem group's main function, like that of the Nguni clan, was to provide wide-ranging contacts that crossed chiefdom boundaries and a safe refuge for travellers in a hostile environment. Monica Wilson believes that this totemic emphasis derived from the firm basing of Sotho economy on hunting, cultivation and iron-working, rather than on cattle.

THE ROLE OF MATERNAL KIN

In these strongly patrilineal societies the role of the mother's kin was secondary. Among the exogamous Nguni and Tsonga, wives always came from a stranger group, often situated some distance away or even from another chiefdom, although this could not have been common in precolonial conditions. Their people were therefore treated with distant respect and often with some suspicion. Among Sotho and Venda things were rather different. Among them a wife was frequently a relative, and from a family well-known and trusted. Although, even here, the legal implications of patrilineal descent tended to relegate her people to a slightly lesser role, this role was emotionally a most important one. The very absence of formal authority (and competition over descent group property) ensured that the relationship was one of warm nurturance and trust, all qualities associated with the role of mother.

Among Nguni, although it was common to send a first-born to be brought up with the mother's people, a child was not normally in intimate daily contact with his mother's brother and his children. There were no special economic obligations between mother's father (or brother) and daughter's (or sister's) son. A boy did not inherit anything from his mother's people, nor were they expected to assist him with bridewealth cattle.

Affinal kin, those linked by marriage, shaded into maternal kin (depending on whether the relationship was looked at from the point of view of son or father), and more will be said of these matters in the chapter on marriage.

KIN AND NEIGHBOURS

Although there was a strong tendency for kin to live near one another, they were also always in close contact with neighbours. This was due to the existence of the territorial division of the chiefdom by the political authorities, with its emphasis on citizenship. We have already seen how the establishment of a Zulu ward by a section of the royal lineage always included *izikhonzi*, non-related supporters of the dominant group.

Neighbourliness was a much-lauded quality and it was expected that neighbours, whether kin or not, should help one another. In some circumstances

---

GOOD NEIGHBOURLINESS

'*But kinship is not the only basis of grouping in the Pondo social system. Imizi [homesteads] are often close to one another, and neighbours who are not necessarily related see a great deal of one another. Women are constantly dropping in to neighbouring imizi to gossip, to borrow a stamping-block, or beg tobacco. If they happen to arrive when women of the umzi [sing.] are eating they are invited to share in the dish. Their fields are usually in the same valley, and when one makes a work party her neighbours try to attend it. When one umzi is grinding beer neighbours come to help; when an animal is killed they help to draw wood and water and cut up the carcass. At big feasts they sit together sharing a portion given in the name of their petty headman. When a man has a case, or is going to consult a diviner, he very often summons neighbours to advise and accompany him. Always between neighbouring imizi there are paths, well worn, and full of shadow-holding hollows, made by bare toes in the dust.*' (Hunter 1936: 59)

Zulu woman with hoe, from a drawing by G.F. Angas.

neighbours were more important than kin, especially in emergencies such as when a hut caught fire or a homestead was attacked. Neighbours assisted in times of illness and bereavement and, at childbirth, women from adjacent homesteads would assist in the delivery and cook for the family until the mother was strong enough to take over.

It was in agriculture that neighbours came into their own. At hoeing, weeding and reaping, work parties were organised, the cores of which were made up of kinsmen from the family group or agnatic cluster, but often strengthened with additional, non-kin, labour, without which the work could not have been completed. Payment was made in the form of a feast or beer-drink, held at midday in the fields.

So neighbourliness had great social value and was sanctioned by reciprocity. Among South Nguni, for instance, non-related neighbours who had sons of about the same age co-operated in having them circumcised together and secluded in the same lodge. Relations between non-kin were essentially unstructured and egalitarian. Unlike those of kinsmen and political officers, neighbours' interactions were governed more by friendship and mutual assistance than by considerations of structured hierarchy or authority. Neighbours co-operated, not because of the jural constraints of kinship and descent, but because it was the moral thing to do, a morality guided, perhaps, by the anticipation of reciprocal assistance when their time came to need it. As we shall see, however, this close involvement with one another in a small, restricted area could have a negative side. Claustrophobic conditions could generate rivalries and envy of another's good fortune, and accusations of witchcraft were common between members of the neighbourhood.

A Venda homestead clinging to a forested mountainside – a contrast to the savannah bushveld and grasslands of the Sotho and Nguni. (N.J. van Warmelo. Reproduced under Government Printer's Copyright Authority 9612 dated 6 May 1993)

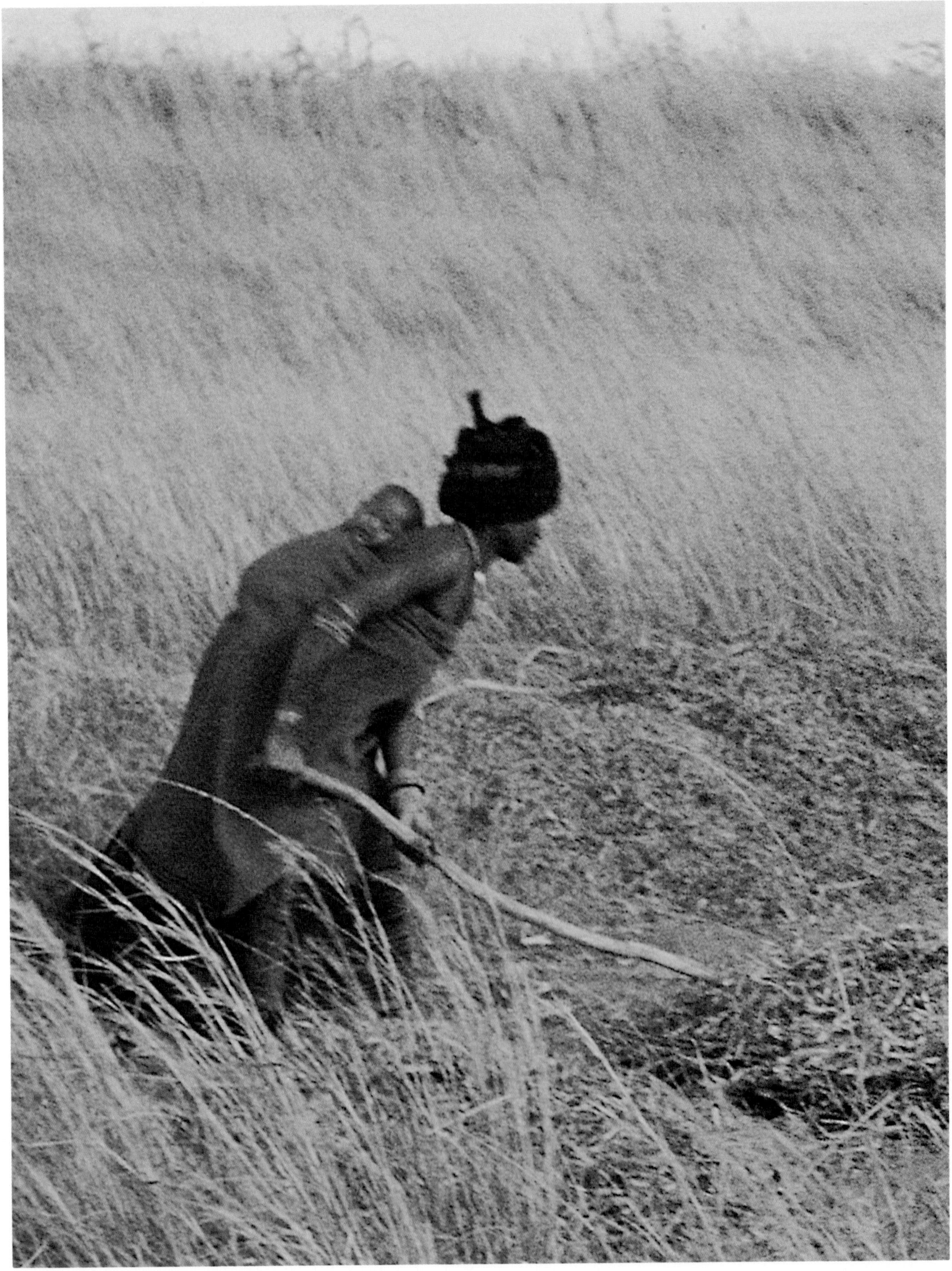

Chapter 6

The Centrality of Marriage

MARRIAGE IS the institution around which the whole social structure is locked. It can be likened to the keystone of an arch, holding biology in tension with society. Its primary biological function is to produce children, new members of society, and to ensure that the human needs of sexuality, intimacy and psychological and physical comfort are met. The complementarity of the sexes (the most fundamental example of the division of labour) provides its basis, but this fact is so important that all societies reinforce this mutual interdependence by allocating certain tasks specifically on the basis of gender. In a very definite sense, the fact that some tasks can only be performed by women, and others by men, makes it incumbent on people to marry. From the social viewpoint, marriage lies at the very basis of society. The practically universal incest taboo can be looked upon as a rule that forces individual families to create bonds of marriage alliance that are the first steps in linking them into a wider social system.

As we shall see, different types of marriage rule have rather different effects on this social integration. Then, too, marriage legitimises children and, in so doing, provides mechanisms for the transference of group membership and property. It is a necessary condition for the establishment of families, with their vital role of nurturing and socialising children. It is no accident that the chapter on marriage stands at the very centre of this book!

Marriage among the Southern Bantu was indeed an important institution. Eleanor Preston-Whyte comments that, despite some differences in the manner in which marriages were arranged, there were three basic marriage rules: (a) while a woman might have only one spouse, a man might have more than one wife at a time if he so wished, (b) a woman should join her husband after marriage, and (c) marriage could only be effected by the transfer of bridewealth. This latter aspect was so fundamental to – and characteristic of – indigenous South African marriage that reference to it forms the title of Adam Kuper's definitive book on the subject (*Wives for Cattle*, 1982).

Although polygyny was the ideal, it is very unlikely that, in the past, every man had more than one wife. Differences in wealth undoubtedly existed and this was linked to the ability to acquire further wives.

When the missionary explorer, David Livingstone, first encountered the Tswana he recorded that no more then thirty per cent of men were polygynists. Southern Bantu chiefs, on the other hand, had numerous wives, sometimes as many as a hundred.

Mpondomise woman threshing. (W.D. Hammond-Tooke)

> ## POLYGYNY: SOME EARLY NINETEENTH CENTURY STATISTICS
>
> A unique piece of evidence as to the earlier incidence of polygyny comes from a survey of an area in southern Natal made in the 1840s or 50s by a Mr Perrin: ☐ 'In the district whose boundaries are, in the north and north-east, the Ifafa river, west and south-west, the Umzumbe, east and south-east, the Indian Ocean, and a line drawn from the Umzumbe to the Ifafa, about ten miles inland, there are 180 kraals, containing 797 huts; giving an average of nearly 4½ huts to a kraal. Classified, they average thus:— 6 kraals contain 1 hut each; 21 kraals contain 2 huts each; 48 kraals contain 3 huts each; 34 kraals contain 4 huts each; 28 kraals contain 5 huts each; 17 kraals contain 6 huts each; 10 kraals contain 7 huts each; 4 kraals contain 8 huts each; 4 kraals contain 9 huts each; 6 kraals contain 10 huts each; 1 kraal contains 14 huts each; 1 kraal contains 15 huts each. ☐ 'One hundred of these kraals (containing 454 huts) have a population of 1,689, averaging 17 per kraal, and nearly 4 per hut. ☐ 'Of 201 married men belonging to these kraals, and taken fairly one with another, — 52 men have 1 wife each; 54 men have 2 wives each; 33 men have 3 wives each; 23 men have 4 wives each; 16 men have 5 wives each; 9 men have 6 wives each; 6 men have 7 wives each; 5 men have 8 wives each; 2 men have 10 wives each; 1 man has 13 wives. 201 men have 600 wives. This gives an average of nearly 3 wives to a man. ☐ 'Although 52 have only 1 wife each, yet these are chiefly young men, who in the course of time will have as many wives as their means will allow'. (Holden 1866: 138–9)

THE CHOICE OF MARRIAGE PARTNER

The decision of whom to marry depended, of course, on personal factors such as physical attraction, personality and the status of the girl's family, but there were also rules and expectations which, as it were, directed a young man's attention in certain directions.

Among Nguni, with their strict rules of clan exogamy, any girl with the same clan name as oneself was *ipso facto* excluded from consideration, as was one from the mother's and father's mother's clan. This meant that many, but by no means all, of the young women in one's immediate environment were not available as marriage mates and one's bride tended to come from some distance away, probably from the next ward. Agnatic clusters were undoubtedly larger in the past than they are today and many of one's immediate neighbours were brothers and patrilineal cousins of one's father (and their daughters). Yet their homesteads were interspersed with those of unrelated neighbours, whose daughters were part of the local youth group, easily available sweethearts to be protected at all costs from the unwelcome attentions of young men from other wards. But, whoever one married, she was a stranger, in the sense that she came from a different descent group. This had a fundamental effect on the position of an Nguni wife in her husband's home, as we shall see, and made her a favourite target for accusations of witchcraft (see Chapter 9).

Among Sotho and Venda things were very different. In all these groups there was the expectation that a young man would marry a cousin, either a cross-cousin (mother's brother's daughter or father's sister's daughter) or a parallel cousin (father's brother's daughter). A bride, therefore, was not a stranger, but a girl one had known since childhood, and this was bound to have an effect on the marriage relationship. We have seen that a parallel cousin was a member of a man's agnatic kin group and termed 'sister' in the kinship terminology. The implications here of incest make father's brother's daughter marriages distinctly unusual in world ethnography: the Sotho-Tswana, who practised it above all other forms of cousin marriage, were therefore, with the Bedouin, unique in Africa in this respect. Marrying a parallel cousin meant that no bonds of alliance were formed with strangers (as among Nguni), nor was it strictly necessary to transfer bridewealth, although this was always done. As the Tswana put it, in justifying their preference, marrying a father's brother's daughter 'keeps the *bogadi* (bridewealth) in the family'. Tswana lacked, therefore, the socially integrating effects of widespread marriage bonds, and it is tempting to connect this with their concentrated settlements, which made such bonds unnecessary. Parallel cousin marriage among Tswana was particularly favoured by members of the nobility, interested in conserving their elite status.

The effects of a cross-cousin marriage were rather different. Cross-cousins always belong to a descent group different from one's own. A mother's brother's daughter is a member of your mother's family, while a father's sister's daughter belongs to the family of the man who marries her. Here, then, there was no implication of incest. In societies where a person *must* marry a cross-cousin (there are none in Africa), marriage with the mother's brother's daughter means that, over generations, a family *always* takes its brides from a specific other family, so that there is a permanent marriage relationship between the two groups. Group A gets its wives from Group B, who, in turn, gets brides from Group C, and so on. Ultimately, of course, the last group in the chain has to marry a girl from Group A, so forming a 'marriage ring'. The number of families involved in such a ring varies – but it is obvious that such a system allows for the linking together of a number of families by marriage.

Although they did not *insist* on mother's brother's daughter marriage, the Sotho-Venda (such as Lovedu and Kgaga) had elements of this 'prescriptive' system. It

The interior of a South Nguni hut. Note the central fireplace and the rough headrest made from a forked branch.

Xhosa Marriage in the Nineteenth Century

The following is an extract from a report entitled *Kaffir Laws and Customs, Compiled by Direction of Colonel M'Lean, Chief Commissioner of British Kaffraria*, and dated c. 1858. Its main contributors were the Wesleyan missionary, the Rev. H.H. Dugmore; J.C. Warner, the Tambookie [Thembu] Agent; Charles Brownlee, Ngqika Commissioner, and John Ayliff, missionary among the Mfengu (Fingo):

☐ 'The younger sons of a family are not competent to marry while their elder brother remains single. The order of seniority is not, however, observed any farther. The firstborn once "settled for life", the rest may follow, as inclination and circumstances lead. The origin of this custom is probably to be found in the priority of claim which the eldest son, in virtue of his primogeniture, is deemed to have upon his father's aid in providing a dowry. ☐ The business of negotiation in matrimonial affairs differs accordingly as the proposal comes from representatives of the bride, or from those of the bridegroom. A man sometimes fixes his desire upon a young woman, and at once proposes to her guardians that she shall be sent to his residence in the ordinary manner. ☐ It sometimes *occurs that the entreaties of the daughter prevail over the avarice of the father; but such cases, the Kaffir admit, are rare. Kaffir fathers have for the most part their full share of those principles of human nature which in more enlightened countries lead parents to sacrifice the "foolish" inclinations of their children at a golden shrine; and accordingly the highest bidder usually gains the prize. ☐ In the mean time the dowry negotiation is going forwards between the representatives of the two parties; the demands of the one, and the statement of difficulties of the other, occupying a considerable time. At length the men of the bridal party are summoned to the cattle kraal. An ox is caught in their presence. They look on in silence and retire. The animal is slaughtered, and the meat sent to them. This is the ratification of the contract, and the signal for the marriage festivities to commence. The presents of the father of the bride to his son-in-law are produced. These are, one head of cattle for a kaross, another, the hair of the tail of which is to be worn round his neck as a charm, and, if the bride be a person of rank, a number of cows, to furnish the milk-sack and its contents for his sustenance. The number of the latter varies from two or three to ten, according to the wealth or ostentation of the party who sends them. The neighbours are invited to*

Xhosa married women. Before contact, Xhosa and Thembu women wore skin caps, preferably of blue duiker skin. The use of cloth turbans dates from about 1827. (Barbara Tyrrell)

The Centrality of Marriage

the wedding, and the dancing and feasting begin. ☐ *These festivities usually last three days among the "commonality". When a chief of rank is married, they continue eight or ten days. On the last day, when the sun is declining, the ox races are held. While the youth and the more fiery of the elder guests are absent at this sport, the* ukutshata *takes place. This is the great ceremonial of the occasion ... The bride, and two of her companions as supporters, walk in procession. Their only clothing consists of the skins of the oribie, tied round the loins. Their heads are bare, and their bodies coloured with light red ochre, which presents the more remarkable appearance from the bright yellow of the oribie skins. They proceed arm in arm, "with solemn steps and slow", towards the gate of the cattle kraal, the bride carrying in her hand a single assegai. Their air is that of victims about to be offered in sacrifice, for which they would certainly be taken by any one ignorant of the customs of the country.* ☐ *As they proceed on their way, one of the male attendants removes any sticks or stones that may by chance lie in the path. On reaching the kraal gate, the bride throws the assegai within it, and leaves it there. The procession then moves towards where the men are assembled, the women of the place preceding the bride, and imitating in dumb show her future duties, such as carrying the wood and water, and cultivating the ground. On reaching the assembly of the men, the procession halts, and the bride is lectured on her future conduct by any one of them who chooses. There is no deficiency of coarse brutality of remark in this part of the ceremony, which continues as long as the lecturers please, the bride standing before them in perfect silence, It is, however, the* finale *of the ceremony. On receiving permission to retire, the procession returns to the place from which it set out, the guests depart, the bride takes possession of a new hut that has been erected for her, and assumes her assigned position in the domestic establishment of her "lord and master".* ☐ *The number of guests present at these festivities is sometimes very great. At the marriage of chiefs of high rank, they amount to thousands. On such occasions the greater portion of the tribe assembles, and all the other chiefs within one or two days' journey are expected either to attend in person, or send their racing oxen. To neglect to do either would be considered an affront. The bridegroom and his friends provide the slaughter cattle for the feast; but the guests bring their own milch cows and milk-sacks. From four or five to fifty head of cattle are slaughtered, according to the wealth and rank of the parties.* ☐ *Such is the marriage ceremonial in the "respectable circle" of Kaffir society. There is also an abridged form, in which the* umtshata *and the ox racing are omitted, and the feasting and dancing much curtailed. This, however, is considered a discreditable mode of getting married, and is therefore chiefly confined to the poorest of people.'*

A wood engraving of Zulu household utensils. (Africana Library)

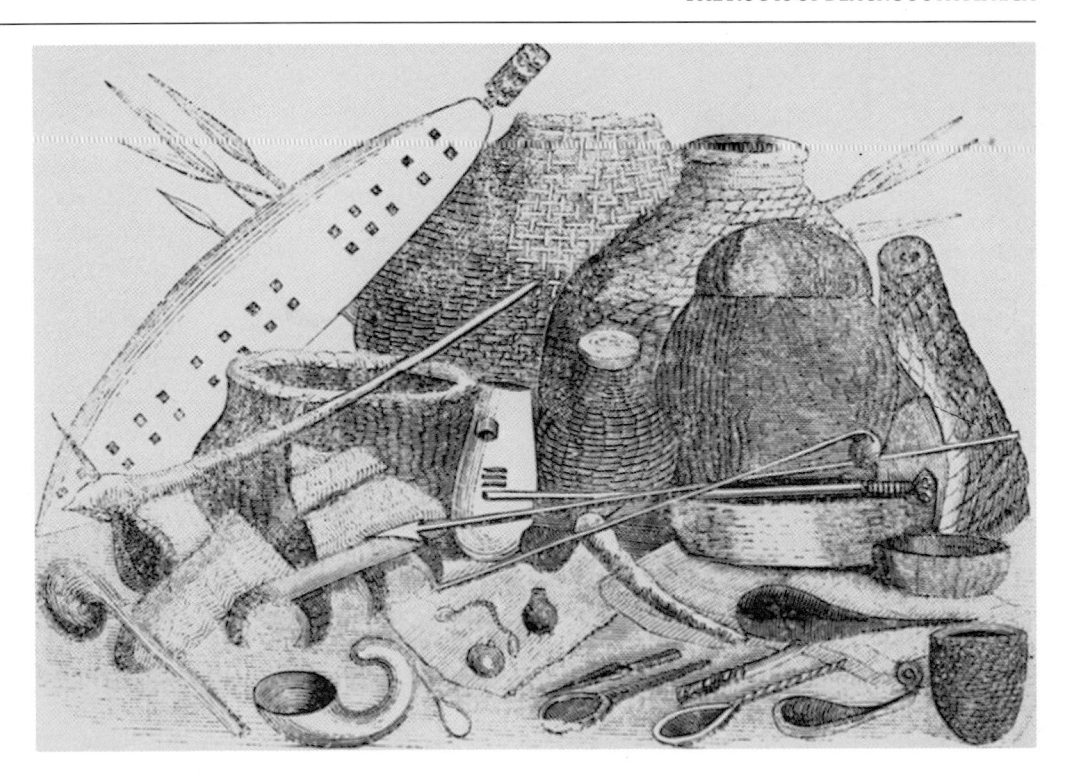

was expressed in the strong linking of a brother and a sister, such that the bridewealth obtained from the girl's marriage was used in order to obtain a wife for her brother. This is why my Kgaga informant, mentioned in Chapter 5, told me that his homestead 'really' belonged to his sister: she had provided the bridewealth for him to marry and so establish it. The strong link between brother and sister among Lovedu in effect meant that the two were regarded as complementary and equal. Thus the eldest brother succeeded his father as head of the extended family, while his (linked) elder sister took over from her father's sister (*rakgadi*) as the religious head of the family, responsible for important sacrifices (see Chapter 8). The link also gave a sister considerable control over the house established with her bridewealth and a legal right to one of its daughters to become her daughter-in-law. The repetition of such marriages by brother-sister linkage in each successive generation resulted in the emergence of clearly marked wife-giving and wife-receiving groups (*vamakhulu* and *vaduhulu*). This marriage system was only found among Sotho-Venda, and was associated with a relative scarcity of cattle, for the same cattle were passed along the chains of the bridewealth ring. What cattle there were were almost exclusively used for bridewealth payments.

The Sotho-Tswana, like Nguni, were relatively rich in cattle, and thus did not need the cattle-linking of brother and sister to the extent that the Sotho-Venda did. They, in fact, had a wide choice of what type of cousin marriage to follow. Also, cousin marriage blurs the distinction between agnates, mother's kin and affines (relatives by marriage), for an uncle can also be one's father-in-law. This wide choice of mate allowed for the development of marriage strategies, ways of using marriage for economic and political advantage. Schapera has shown how competition was rife in Sotho-Tswana societies, possibly because of the lack of strong patrilineal descent groups. This competition was typically 'between brothers, father and son, uncle and nephew and other relatives and revolve[d] around property and inheritance, seniority and status, rights and duties in respect of position, such as guardianship of women and children' and was particularly evident between

THE CENTRALITY OF MARRIAGE

A Zulu wedding: ritualised opposition to losing the bride to her husband's people is expressed in a sham fight between the girls of the bride's age and boys of the groom's. (Elliott 1978)

members of the royal family among whom the fruits of office were most rewarding. In such a situation, marrying maternal kin provided one with allies, trustworthy because they were excluded by birth from being in competition with one. Whereas among Sotho-Venda a man's mother and sister had rights in the marriage and could exert pressure on the couple, marriage among Sotho-Tswana (except perhaps the Pedi) was by free choice and was not prescribed.

There is little direct evidence of the Venda marriage rules of the past, but what there is seems to indicate a system very like that of the Sotho-Venda, including the great importance in the family of the father's sister. The Tsonga neither had exogamous descent groups like the Nguni nor preferred cousin marriage like the Sotho; their one rule was to avoid marrying the descendant of a common grandfather, including first cousins of all kinds.

A Zulu man dressed for a wedding. The small shield is ornamental. Nguni men dressed much more elaborately than those of other groups for special occasions, especially for courting, partly because their marriage rules freed them to seek brides from non-related families.

BRIDEWEALTH

The logic behind the payment of bridewealth, the passing of cattle from the family of the groom to that of the bride, flows from the incest prohibition referred to earlier. This taboo states that a wife cannot come from within the family, but has to be obtained from some other family; it divides a man's perception of the opposite sex into sexually acceptable women (potential wives) and those not acceptable (sisters). But some compensation is required, to restore the gap left by the departing daughter. How is this to be arranged?

One way, found in some societies (but, in fact, extremely rarely) was for a group of brothers to exchange sisters – in other words, the exchange of a sister for a wife. Obviously much would depend on the availability of suitable sisters, and most peoples substituted some other form of compensation – either service performed by the groom for his father-in-law (as in the biblical story of Laban's daughters) or, more commonly, some form of material benefit.

Among Southern Bantu, it was the passing of bridewealth in the form of cattle that was the essential act in legalising a new union. It had the effect of transposing certain rights over a girl, up to now vested in her father or guardian, to her husband and his family. The emphasis was on the linking of two groups, rather than of the two individuals concerned, and several important consequences flowed from this. One of these was that, if the woman was barren, certain institutions came into play to deal with the matter, for marriage was a contract in which the acquisition of a child-bearer was the most important consideration. Especially among Nguni, but also among Tswana and some other Sotho, this could take the form of a sister being sent to 'to put a child in the womb' of the barren woman, in a custom called the sororate. No further bridewealth was paid and the children referred to the barren woman as 'mother'. Similarly, in the case of a wife dying without giving birth, a substitute could be sent to 'raise up the house that has fallen'.

Relations with In-laws: An Mpondo Husband's First Formal Visit

Among Mpondo a man's relations with his wife's family were restrained and formal. Where there was a betrothal period, it was short, and the groom did not visit the bride's home during that time. Bridewealth arrangements were conducted by go-betweens. After marriage the groom paid a formal visit to his wife's people. Michael Geza, Monica Wilson's assistant in her fieldwork among the Mpondo in the early 1930s, describes this first visit. ☐ 'Before paying a visit to his wife's people (abakhwe) the son-in-law (umkhwenyana) first makes preparations. He takes his best blankets, grinds snuff, and fills his snuff-pot, and also takes some money with him. He is also told by his parents not to do things that are not customary. Off he starts. When he arrives he is given a mat to sit upon. After he has sat, all come one after another to shake hands with the umkhwenyana, except his wife's mother (umkhwekazi) who will not shake hands until she has been given money by him. The people of the umzi [homestead] show all the kindness due to him, ask after his health, ask for his relatives at home, and his wife. Then one by one they ask for snuff, which he is always supposed to possess, even though he does not take it himself. If the wife's mother asks for snuff she will have to send somebody to take it for her. Also, if the wife's mother wishes that they should touch each other, she will say, 'Mkhwenyana, you are my child as you have married my child, I do not like that you should keep off me, I like that we should touch each other'. Then the umkhwenyana gives her money and she gives the umkhwenyana money so that they begin to touch each other. ☐ On learning that the son-in-law has paid a visit, the wife's father (usomfazi) asks his wife what the umkhwenyana will eat. Of course, the mother has nothing to say, but the father selects a goat to be killed. Then at sunset the goat is shown to the umkhwenyana. The goat is caught, led to the hut where the umkhwenyana is, and it is there that these words are said: "Mkhwenyana, as you have married our daughter, you have caused union between two families; know that henceforth you are our child, as you are the child of your parents. From this day forwards, look upon this home as yours and have the same qualities at this home as our daughter your wife has (i.e. be a real son in this house). We give you this kid so that you may eat food and drink water at your will". Thus speaks the old man. After that the goat is led outside to be killed. When all is prepared the chest and entrails of the goat are eaten and all the people go to sleep. The umkhwenyana goes to sleep in a store-hut with his wife's brothers and sisters. The remaining meat is then cooked overnight. Early the next morning the meat is all eaten. The wife's father takes the gall-bladder, blows it up, and gives it to the umkhwenyana, who puts it on his head as a public sign that he has been killed for. He then bids farewell to all the people and goes home.' ☐ Professor Wilson comments: 'As is indicated in this description of the first visit, there is mutual respect and avoidance between mother-in-law and son-in-law. Neither may mention the other's name, the mother-in-law is careful to cover her head and breasts in the presence of her son-in-law. She cannot cross to the men's side of the hut in an umzi to which he belongs. He in turn avoids the women's side of her hut ... and also the back of the hut where the milk sacks, spears and other objects connected with the ancestral spirits of the umzi are kept ... Mother-in-law and son-in-law cannot eat of the meat of ritual killings made for one another, and cannot touch one another ... or take a dish of food directly, until gifts have been exchanged ... Note that the avoidance and respect is mutual and gifts are given by both parties.' (Hunter 1936: 49)

An Mfengu homestead scene in the Transkei, 1848, by Thomas Baines. (Africana Library)

The rights that were transferred to the husband's group were complex. Van der Vliet puts them succinctly:

> The rights over a woman which are transferred to her husband and his agnatic group include rights in her both as a wife (rights *in uxorem*) and as a mother (rights *in genetricem*). Into the first category fall rights of sexual access and to her labour, both domestic and in the fields. Her husband can claim reparation for adultery or any other injury which impairs the fulfilment of these duties. Rights *in uxorem* are, of course, matched by the duties on the part of the groom and his agnates to provide the woman with a 'house' – living quarters, fields and lifelong security. The second set of rights transferred on marriage relates to the procreative powers of the woman. Rights *in genetricem* acquire for the husband and his lineage legal control over all children born to a woman unless and until the marriage is dissolved by divorce, which may entail the return of bridewealth. The importance of this aspect of marriage is expressed in the saying found in many of these societies: 'Cattle beget children'. (Van der Vliet 1974: 187–8)

The above reference to the reciprocal duties of a husband towards his wife brings us to a consideration of the levirate. In all groups, except Xhosa, Thembu and, possibly, the South Sotho, should a man die an approved relative would be allocated to assume responsibility for the widow and children. In some cases the levir undertook full domestic and marital duties, in others he visited and supplied economic support for the widow, but his primary duty was to beget children in the name of the dead man. This was not a new marriage, and the children born of the arrangement continued to call the deceased man 'father'. All Southern Bantu made a clear distinction between physical fatherhood and social fatherhood. The 'real' (social) father was the man who had given bridewealth for their mother, no matter who the genitor might be. It was this principle which made possible woman-to-woman marriage, as found for instance in the case of the Lovedu queen, who married the daughters of her district headmen (Chapter 3). Woman-to-woman marriage was also found among Venda and Pedi.

The amount of bridewealth and the way it was decided upon differed somewhat among the groups. Among Nguni the amount was the subject of considerable bargaining, and the bridewealth was frequently paid off over the years in instalments, but among some Sotho (especially the Pedi, and certain Tswana) the total amount was transferred before marriage, and bargaining (and instalments) were unthinkable, except, apparently, among South Sotho. The husband's people offered what they thought fair, or could afford.

Marriage negotiations could be opened by the parents of either the boy or the girl. While it was most common for the boy's family to take the first step, both methods could be found side by side. Among Xhosa the girl's family frequently took the initiative, and among Zulu it was usual for members of royal families to approach a suitable man on behalf of their daughters. The North Nguni, indeed, had the custom of *ukubaleka* whereby a girl, at the instigation of her lover or her father (or indeed without the knowledge of either) could present herself at the homestead of the man she wished to marry.

Wedding Ceremonies

If it was possible to delay the passage of all the bridewealth, when precisely did a marriage came into existence? In effect this was the actual physical movement of the bride from her father's home to that of her new husband. It was important that this change in status be given full social visibility, and the marriage was celebrated by elaborate wedding ceremonies. Adam Kuper has provided valuable insights

---

Status of Xhosa Women in 1807

'Although the supremacy of the male generally expresses itself decidedly and clearly, the woman is nevertheless in possession of a certain gentle authority which she exercises over the men, and by means of which she obtains influence and standing. This power is undoubtedly based upon respect. The women are completely excluded from deliberations which deal with the general welfare of the tribe, so that their presence is in fact not tolerated ... Moreover, the women are completely separated on such and similar occasions from the males and keep themselves apart at some distance. On the other hand, the influence of the woman in domestic affairs is very conspicuous. She participates in the right of disposal of the common means and not infrequently guides the mind of the man who never disposes of the meanest trifle without having assured himself of her consent. Also when, on several occasions I have wanted to exchange a small milk-basket or something of the sort with a Kaffir, he came back with the reply that his wife did not wish to part with it, notwithstanding the fact that one had distinctly observed an intense desire on his part to possess the article proferred in exchange. In the same way, a Kaffir will readily desist from his intention to proceed somewhere, if his wife dissuades him from his purpose. ☐ 'No less do the women enjoy protection against brutal offences; the man will not lightly mix himself up in an altercation which his wife is engaged in but will certainly defend her should it develop into any action. When in time of war with other tribes, one wishes to negotiate with the enemy but does not feel certain of the safety of the emissaries, such negotiations are opened by women, because one is convinced that they will not be ill-treated and even much less so, be killed by the enemy.' (Alberti 1815: 59–60)

Bhaca married women. The headdress – a mop of thin twists arranged over a frame – is distinctive. (Shaw and Van Warmelo 1988)

into the nature of these ceremonies, and what follows is based largely on his work (Kuper 1982).

The essence of all Southern Bantu marriage, as we have seen, was the exchange of brides for cattle. But the Sotho-Tswana and Nguni approached this from rather different points of view. The Sotho-Tswana emphasised the bridewealth payment while, among Nguni, the important element was the transfer of the bride. This contrast affected other aspects of the ceremonies. Kuper expresses this contrast as follows:

> ... among Nguni the initiative lies with the bride and her party, and the main ceremonial acts are staged at the bride's home ... the transfer of the bride to her new home is elaborately celebrated, while the delivery of the bridewealth to her father, which often happens later, is by comparison a muted affair ... Among the Sotho-Tswana and the Venda, in contrast, a man or his father chooses a bride ... the bridewealth is paid at the bride's father's home with considerable ceremony, while the subsequent transfer of the bride to her new home is given little ritual emphasis. (Kuper 1982: 127–8)

Kuper states that 'the Tsonga appear to have developed an intermediate ceremonial structure'. He sees these major differences as affecting the detailed stages of the ceremonies: 'The divergences are striking and systematic: it is not too much to say that the Nguni and Sotho-Tswana marriage ceremonials represent systematic transformations of each other.' For instance, as far as the preliminaries to marriage were concerned, Nguni girls chose their lovers, visited the man for love-making at his home and it was the girl's group that pressed for the completion of the bridewealth payment; among Sotho-Tswana, on the other hand, it was the man who chose the girl and visited her for love-making, and his family that pressed for the transfer of the bride. Among Nguni the main ceremony was the delivery of the *bride* at the groom's home: this contrasted with the Sotho delivery of the *bridewealth* at the home of the girl. Among Nguni the groom's father made the main speech; among Sotho-Tswana this was done by the father of the bride. The contrast extended to the ritual sphere. The killing of an ox and the use of its gall to consecrate the marriage was the central religious rite. Among Nguni it was the groom's father who made the killing and the bride who was covered with gall and who wore the empty gallbladder. This was reversed among Sotho, where the bride's father sacrificed and the groom was covered with gall.

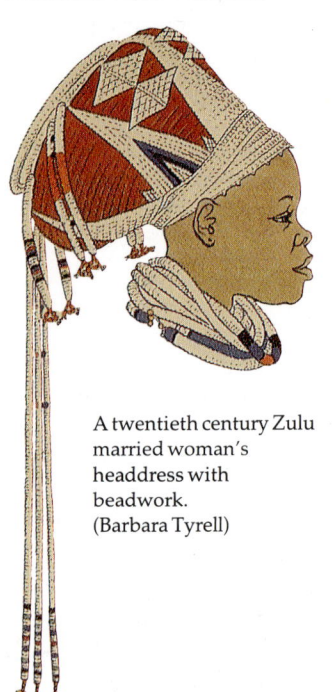

All this reflected the basic difference between Nguni and Sotho – the preferential cousin marriages of the former (and of the Venda) and the clan exogamy of the latter. The fact that the Sotho and Venda bride was a kinswoman, well-known since childhood, made a fundamental difference to the dynamics of the marriage relationship in these two systems. Among Nguni, as we have seen, the bride was a stranger, and therefore under a certain amount of suspicion. This was expressed in the strict avoidance that she had to observe towards her husband's parents, particularly towards her father-in-law, whom she had to *hlonipha*. She could not use any word that contained a syllable of his name, nor could she bare her breasts in his presence or be alone with him in the house. The whole emphasis in Nguni marriage was to bridge this gap. As a stranger, a Nguni bride could not drink sour milk at her husband's home, and this taboo had to be formally rescinded through the sacrifice of a special goat to the ancestors. This rite marked the beginning of the full incorporation of the Nguni wife into her husband's family so that, at her death, she was considered almost like an agnatic ancestor to her children.

The trauma of marriage was not nearly so great for the Sotho or Venda bride. She moved into a situation familiar to her from childhood and she was surrounded by well-disposed kin. There was indeed an expectation that her marriage would imply further marriages from the same family group, unlike the position among Nguni, among whom such marriages were unthinkable.

It seems that marriage in these societies was extremely stable. Stability does not appear to have been connected to the amount of bridewealth given, but rather to the way marriage was locked into the total structure. The procreation of children was so important for the survival of the group, and the involvement of both

A twentieth century Zulu married woman's headdress with beadwork. (Barbara Tyrell)

A Tswana homestead on the Vaal River, by Thomas Baines. (Africana Library)

The Lovedu Marriage 'Ring'

Marriage with the mother's brother's daughter (if continued over the generations) produces extensive links between groups. The Kriges, who described the Lovedu system in the 1930s, depict it as follows: ☐ 'In order to understand the Lovedu *munywalo* [marriage] ring ... we have to imagine a number of groups of people arranged in a circle ... Each group consists of patrilineal relatives and, in the very simplest configuration, each is doubly linked to two other groups. Thus A is linked to both B and F: to B it owes brides and from B it receives cattle; ☐ from F it receives brides and to F it owes cattle. B is cattle-obligated to A; A is bride-obligated to B. In the figure, brides pass clockwise round an outer circle and cattle move anti-clockwise along an inner concentric circle; the two circles cut through the groups A, B, C, D, E and F, which are all both cattle-linked and bride-linked. In real life there are no concentric circles and so simple an arrangement is never found; even the general configuration of the groups is obscured by a hundred complications. A polygynist – and about a third of the men have more than one wife – does not take all his wives from the same group. A man who uses his daughter's marriage cattle must return a daughter to be the daughter-in-law of the sister, or, in other words, the wife of the man's son; if he had used the cattle of two sisters whose husbands belong to different groups, his sons marry into these different groups. Endless new linkages and complications arise in this and in other ways. Essentially, however, the exchange pattern remains: one kind of valuable (cattle) travels in one direction, another (brides) in the opposite direction. Usually so many groups are involved that the circular reciprocity cannot be seen. But what is clear is that each man has a link (we may say a partner) in each direction; on the one hand, a cattle-linked sister, to whose son he must give his daughter if he is offered *munywalo*; on the other hand, his wife's cattle-linked brother, from whom his wife may demand a daughter-in law. (Krige and Krige 1943: 66–7)

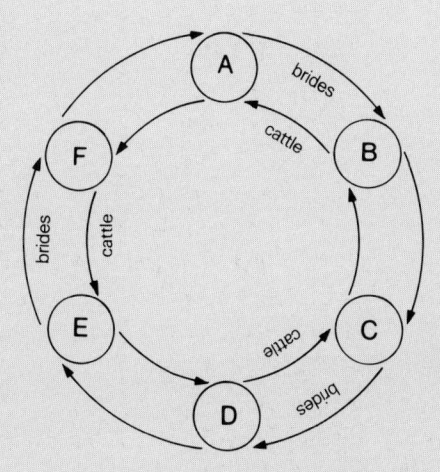

---

families in the marriage so great, that the emphasis was on the existence of the alliance, rather than on the happiness of the couple. Then, too, the passage of bridewealth, which had to be returned if the marriage was legally terminated (sometimes with some cattle retained for each child born of the union), acted to inhibit easy divorce. In the 'tight' system of the Sotho-Venda, especially, with its right of a sister to claim the daughter of her cattle-linked brother as a wife for her son, and the linking of family groups over the generations, the failure of a marriage could have serious consequences. In such a case, a husband might jeopardise the marriage of his wife's brother, and even more distant marriages, for the 'roots of the (same) cattle could be followed', and they could be demanded back.

It is clear that the frequent criticism of the bridewealth system as being the 'sale' of a wife, and an essentially economic transaction, is a crass distortion of its real nature. In the first place, it can be argued that the transfer of cattle was designed much more to legalise the children of the union than to establish rights over the wife (although this was extremely important) and thus secure the continuity of the group and the handing on of property. Then, too, the highly esteemed cattle provided a symbolic statement of the value of the bride to her husband's group – and this was further expressed by the elaborateness of the wedding ceremonies themselves. More practically, the fear of losing the cattle, if a wife left her husband for reasons of mistreatment and the court found that she was justified in so doing, acted as an important brake on the actions of a heavy-handed husband. The fact that divorce was so rare in these societies is ample proof of the effectiveness of the institution.

THE ROOTS OF BLACK SOUTH AFRICA

Chapter 7

Growing Up

MARRIAGE, in the nature of things, produces children – and children have to be socialised into society. Looked at from the broadest viewpoint this is, in fact, the chief function of the family. Every child is born with the human capacity to learn culture and, from the very beginning, is subjected to a constant barrage of sense impressions and other stimuli, not the least being language. Socialisation flows from social interaction and the initial social environment consists of mother, father and siblings, plus the doting relatives and neighbours who drop in to admire the new arrival. As time goes on the circle of contacts increases, each one adding its increment of experience to the developing child, both intellectually and emotionally. The process, as described, is essentially informal, but most societies find it necessary to supplement it by more formal methods of instruction. This is particularly so if the society is a complex one, with a well-developed division of labour, specialisation and technical demands that involve extensive and intensive training for professions and skilled trades. Southern Bantu society, however, had little in the way of specialisation (apart from traditional doctors and chiefs) so that the process of socialising the young was much simpler.

Children were much desired, and no marriage was considered complete without them. It was essential to have sons to ensure the continuity of the descent group, to look after one in old age and to sacrifice to one's spirit after death. They were also of more practical use. Little girls acted as nursemaids for the younger children and brought in cattle to the family on their marriages, while boys herded cattle and small stock. Barrenness was thus greatly feared and potent medicines were used to cure the condition. Special dolls to promote fertility were used by South Nguni and South Sotho.

A wife normally worked for most of her pregnancy and was subject to many taboos and avoidances, mainly to protect the unborn child and ease the birth. Typical of these were food taboos and limitations on outside activity, to avoid coming into contact with pollution or the medicines of sorcerers. For instance, Venda women had to avoid hot food, lest it scald the unborn child, and abstain from sweet foods and vegetables, while Zulu women avoided guinea fowl, hare and rock rabbit to prevent their babies having long, flat heads, long ears and long teeth respectively. Pregnant South Nguni women had a special association with a plant of the agapanthus family, which they planted in a pot and kept with them. They drank an infusion made from its leaves and confessed bad dreams, or adultery, to it.

A Lovedu *bogwêra* dancer dressed in characteristic grass regalia. The *bogwêra* is held a year or so after initiation and it is then that new regiments are formed. (Greg Marinovich)

South Sotho girl initiates wearing their reed costumes. (Department of Art History, University of the Witwatersrand)

Normally delivery took place in the woman's living hut and was attended by the older women, ritually free from the impurity of menstruation. The cord was cut, often with a blade of stout grass, and the afterbirth buried secretly to prevent witches from using it to harm the child. The baby was washed with protective and strengthening medicines, while some South Nguni and South Sotho held it in the smoke of a special fire on which herbs were burned.

Birth was considered polluting and a special ceremony, reminiscent of the Christian rite of the 'Churching of Women', was performed to reincorporate the mother into normal social life. This involved the killing of a goat among South Nguni, Tsonga and Sotho, provided by the father among Nguni and by the mother's brother among Tsonga and Sotho. The skin of the goat was used as a carrying sling for the child. Other protective rites were performed to ensure the health of the child. Some South Nguni, such as Bhaca and Xesibe, incised the child's face, while Xhosa and Thembu children had the top joint of the little finger of the left hand amputated, a custom borrowed from the San. Among Tsonga, Venda, Swazi (and some other Nguni), the child was ceremonially 'shown' to the moon – regarded as essential to its mental growth. During this period the child was also named, often being given a derogatory name to prevent the attention of witches. The Venda believed that a baby was the reincarnation of a dead relative, and great care was taken to identify the relative correctly, to avoid ancestral wrath.

The attitude to twins differed, but always they were considered unnatural (and therefore polluting) or in a potentially dangerous state. Generally they were killed as, especially among Sotho and Venda, it was believed that they caused countrywide drought. They were buried in damp earth to counteract the mystical 'heat' that they generated (see Chapter 9). On the other hand the Nguni, especially the

South Nguni, looked on twins as special. Among Xhosa and Bomvana two young euphorbia trees were planted next to their hut and watered with the babies' bath water. A mystical association was believed to exist between the twins and the trees, so that if one failed to flourish, so did the other. Among these people, if one twin died the other was symbolically 'buried' to prevent it following its twin.

Children were weaned at about three years of age and there was a taboo on sexual intercourse until this happened. The inconvenience of this for the husband was somewhat mitigated by the institution of polygyny. A common method of weaning was to apply aloe juice or pipe oil to the nipples. Among some groups, for example Zulu, Mpondo, Tsonga and South Sotho, this was reinforced by sending the child to live temporarily with grandparents (of either side). Weaning allowed the child to expand its social environment and to form wider relationships. As Virginia van der Vliet writes:

> For the next two to four years [the child] lives a relatively carefree, irresponsible life, with small jobs like chasing chickens and running errands being the only demands made on him. It is, however, a valuable period from the point of view of the child's socialisation. His circle of acquaintances increases and he ventures further afield in the exploration of his environment. Unlike Western children he is seldom lonely or lacking companions; the typical homestead has a number of women of similar age to his mother, who will themselves have children of about his age. This stage is important in that it lays the foundations for much of his future adult behaviour, which will require his co-operation within a group of contemporaries. His peer group, watched over by those just a little older, lay down rules for acceptable conduct and are in a strong position to see that they are obeyed. Sanctions such as mockery and ostracism enable them to deal effectively with displays of temper, selfishness and poor sportsmanship. (Van der Vliet 1974: 219–20)

Up to the age of six there was little difference between the day-to-day lives of boys and girls. Play groups included children of both sexes and they shared the same games and pastimes. But after that age differences became evident, signalling the marked social segregation of the sexes that was characteristic of adult life. Boys were employed in herding livestock, an occupation that, among Nguni, kept them out in the pastures for most of the day, and, among Sotho, involved lengthy stays at far-flung cattle posts. Here was a clear break from petticoat government and it played an important role in inculcating the masculine ethos so typical of these societies. Competitive duelling with sticks was an important way of passing the time, and it was here that qualities of leadership began to emerge. Younger boys performed menial tasks for older ones and bullying and teasing were common. Writers like Blacking have described the life of the herdboys as a 'micro-society'. It operated apart from the life in the settlements and, indeed, was a kind of adolescent counter-culture. Stealing, especially of food, and other petty pilfering was common, but adults tended to turn a blind eye to it.

In many ways this life had strong educational aspects. The frequent fighting between the boys, and also between gangs of different wards, fostered courage and resourcefulness, the interaction between boys of differing ages allowed for leadership and management of others (the 'gangs' had their own 'courts' which maintained discipline) and endless, halcyon days spent in the veld or bush meant that the boys developed an intimate and extensive knowledge of the veld and of wild life. The Kriges, writing of the Lovedu, state that 'A herdboy walking along

A young South Sotho nurse with her baby brother. Responsibilities began early! (Ashton 1952)

A Venda girl, after the *vhusha* puberty ritual, adopting the humble attitude expected of Venda women. Note the *thahu*, a funnel-shaped, tasseled, object made from the bark of the *mutanzwa* tree and plastered with ochre and fat, worn for six days after initiation.

South Sotho girls' initiation *(bale)*: girls returning from the river, led by the 'mother' of the school carrying a sleeping mat. (Ashton 1952)

with you will give you the name and uses of almost every tree or shrub you pass in that rich bushveld environment, and once a boy of fifteen astonished us by being able to name over 200 specimens of plants from that area.'

The life of girls was very different. Confined to the homestead, they assisted their mothers in caring for the smaller children, fetching firewood, collecting relishes, stamping, and so on. This meant that long before puberty they were competent little housewives.

It is clear that the socialisation of children was essentially informal. Children learned by doing, imitating the actions of their elders, and so were effortlessly moulded to the requirements of life in their society.

RITUALS OF PUBERTY

A major change occurred at puberty. Before this fundamental event children were regarded as essentially sexless and, as such, ritually pure. For this reason pre-pubertal children were frequently used in ritual, as among Venda and Sotho, who used immature boys and girls to sprinkle the country with rain-medicines or, as among some Nguni, where young girls played an important part in the agricultural ceremonies to ward against maize blight. But puberty signalled the onset of full sexuality, with all its sacred associations with fertility and adult accountability, and as such demanded the concentrated attention of the community. The vital change of status had to be 'managed' by ritual.

The physical change was formally recognised by all Southern Bantu. Among boys the first nocturnal emission was marked either by treating him with strengthening medicines to protect him, as among Sotho-Venda and Tsonga, or by

Mpondo Boys' Initiation in 1824

Henry Fynn travelled south from Port Natal to meet the Mpondo chief Faku, who introduced him to the Ntusi people of the Lusikisiki district. This is an extract from his diary: 'On returning to the amaNtusi, and during my somewhat lengthy stay there, I had an opportunity of observing the custom of circumcision. Boys of 13 and upwards who have not been circumcised are annually collected in each neighbourhood. The man whose business it is to perform the operation lives apart from everyone else, his hut being generally a short distance from those of the rest. He uses for the purpose an assegai which he sharpens on a rough stone. This is done that the blade may become more like a saw than otherwise, its roughness being supposed to facilitate the cure. After each boy has undergone the operation, the parts are washed with an infusion of roots of a cooling nature. Each now puts on a dress specially prepared for the occasion [this probably refers to the dancing regalia] and occupies a hut in which he and the others live apart from all relations and friends. In such locality the neophytes live from one to six months, food being brought them during that time from their respective homes. The dress is made of a kind of flaggy grass, tied in bunches and is intended to cover nearly the whole body, the face being painted with clay. The lads amuse themselves principally with dancing. At the end of their period of segregation they are deemed to have arrived at the state of manhood, hence entitled to engage in courtship, become married, etc.' (Stuart and Malcolm 1969: 114–5) Faku ultimately abolished circumcision among the Mpondo, but the pattern of local (not central) organisation and the age of the boys is typically South Nguni.

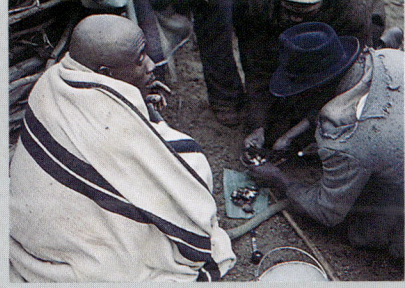

Scenes from Mpondomise male initiation. The central picture is of a boy during the period of licence immediately before the ritual. (H. Röntsch)

a specific ritual. The latter was only found among groups that did not have formal initiation ceremonies accompanied by circumcision. Thus, among Zulu, the boy was secluded in a special hut for a short period and given some sexual instruction. Thereafter a goat was killed for the ancestors and the boy ritually washed at the river. A Venda boy had to wait for the puberty ceremony (*vhutamba vhutuka*) until a number of local boys had reached the same stage. The rite involved six days of severe physical hardship (including daily immersion in icy river water), sexual instruction and introduction to etiquette and customs. In neither of these cases (Zulu and Venda) did the rite involve circumcision. The Venda did not have the custom and the Zulu abandoned it in the early nineteenth century under instructions from Shaka, who is said to have abolished it as it interfered unacceptably with the preparedness of his regiments. Venda and Zulu rituals, however, did mark the beginning of active sexual life and the courting of girls.

Pedi initiation figures used for instruction in the *kôma* (mysteries). Figurative carvings were only used in male initiation lodges and were carved by the 'fathers' of the initiates. They were burned at the end of the school. (Department of Art History, University of the Witwatersrand)

Puberty ceremonies for girls, like those for Venda and Zulu boys, usually occurred at the first clear signs of physical maturity, in their case at first menstruation. The ritual was broadly the same in all groups and consisted of the seclusion of the girl under a blanket in a special hut for about a week (a month among Tsonga), during which time she might not be seen by members of the community (although the girls of her neighbourhood spent the evenings with her in dancing and singing), and the observance of certain food taboos. At the end of the seclusion period she had to ritually wash at the river and was given new clothes to wear. This was the basic pattern, but there were minor differences between groups.

Among some, such as Tsonga, Venda and Sotho-Venda, the girl was subject to hardships such as being forced to sit in icy water for long periods, eating porridge without relishes (Lovedu), or being scratched, pinched and teased (Tsonga). Sotho and Venda girls were also given a certain amount of sex instruction at this time, mainly precautions against becoming pregnant. The Venda rite was called *vusha* and involved a six-day seclusion in a special hut, covered with a blanket. Associated activities were daily dancing to the drums, learning rules of etiquette and, perhaps most importantly, considerable sexual teaching. This latter was accompanied by a daily gathering at the river where the initiates were instructed in the technique of lengthening the labia and submerged for long periods in the cold river water. On the final day the initiates were taken to the river to wash, smeared with red ochre and each given a special funnel-shaped object *(thahu)* to wear tucked into her girdle at the back.

INITIATION INTO ADULTHOOD

In practically all groups the main ritual marking the attainment of adult status of males was circumcision, which took place during the winter months. Strictly speaking it was not a puberty ritual, for the age at which boys were subjected to it depended on custom and differed somewhat between groups. Broadly speaking, the Sotho organised their ceremonies on a chiefdom-wide scale, while South Nguni (and possibly North Nguni before Shaka's fiat) arranged local ceremonies on a more 'private' basis. We have no clear picture of the original Tsonga rite. Junod, the Tsonga authority, obtained his information from informants who had attended mixed Sotho-Tsonga schools in the Transvaal and it is quite clear that these had been heavily influenced by Sotho practice. As far as Venda were concerned, they originally had no circumcision but the custom was present among the Lemba, a small group of metal-workers and itinerant traders living among them and believed to be descended from east coast Arab traders originally from Oman (see Van Warmelo 1974: 83), and gained in popularity in the late nineteenth century. Yet, here again, there was strong Sotho influence. Stayt comments that 'much of the procedure [at the schools] was borrowed from the BaSutho, whose influence is reflected in many songs, of which the words are Sesutho and not Tshivenda'. We can only distinguish, then, two main forms of the ritual – one Nguni and one Sotho.

Among Nguni the age of circumcision was in the late teens. A father would decide that the time had come to circumcise his son and would typically arrange with other homestead heads in the sub-ward, with sons of about the same age, to establish a lodge and engage a specialist circumciser to perform the operation. Permission from the chief or headman always had to be obtained first. Perhaps from three to twenty boys might be circumcised together. The initiator of the initiation was termed the 'father of the lodge' and it was he who acted as master of ceremonies throughout the seclusion period. When sons of chiefs or headmen were initiated their fathers filled this role, and it was a great honour for a boy to be a member of a lodge at which a chief's son was initiated. Such a son always took precedence among initiates, who were otherwise regarded as equal.

For weeks before the ceremony beer was brewed by the boys' mothers and saplings were cut for the framework of the lodge. During this time the boys entered a period of licence, roaming the countryside in groups dressed in fantastical garb, pilfering, stealing chickens, and generally making a thorough nuisance of themselves. It was a sort of *mardi gras*, an exaggerated miming of the essential irresponsibility of childhood, soon to be replaced by the grave responsibilities of adult life.

The lodge (*isuthu*) was built by the boys' mothers, and was always sited a good distance away from the settlements, thereby symbolising spatially the special status of the initiates. It had a rough, bee-hive form and was thatched with grass or maize stalks.

On the day of the commencement of the rites the boys gathered at the home of the father of the lodge where a sacrifice was made of an uncastrated bull or ram, to inform the ancestors of what was taking place. The initiates were addressed by older men on how to conduct themselves while in the lodge and exhorted to put away all childish things. They must henceforth speak and act with the dignity of men. Their old clothes were taken from them and they went naked. They were then accompanied down to the river where they washed and the operation was performed by the *inchibi*. As each boy was cut he addressed the *inchibi* with the words, 'I am a man!', eliciting the response 'You are a man!', a ritual formula that signalled the moment of status change. The operation had to be endured with stoicism and to cry out was a great disgrace. The excised foreskin was buried in an anthill for the termites to destroy, to prevent it falling into the hands of witches, and the wound bound with the paper-like leaves of the *izichwe* plant, said to have styptic and pain-relieving properties. Finally the boys were smeared from head to foot with white clay, symbolically expressing their marginal status.

Initiation rituals among the Southern Bantu all exhibited the tripartite structure of rites of passage all over the world, defined by Arnold van Gennep many years ago. Van Gennep showed that so-called 'rites of passage', that is, those directed towards a change of social status (such as initiation, marriage and funerals), always fall into three parts: (a) *rites of segregation*, in which the person undergoing them is temporarily removed from normal social life; (b) *liminal rites*, referring to the period during which he or she is suspended, as it were, between the old status and the new, and (c) *rites of aggregation*, whereby the person is re-incorporated into the community. The act of circumcision, and the removal of the boys from their families to the isolation of the lodge, were obviously part of the ritual of segregation, as was the smearing with white clay to symbolise it.

The period of seclusion, which lasted for the three or four months of winter, was just as obviously a liminal one. No married woman could approach the initiates, who spent their time lounging around the lodge, hunting with the pack of dogs that lived with them or roaming the countryside in a group, visiting other lodges. Unlike the case in other groups, though, it seems that Nguni initiates were not bereft of contact with their girlfriends. Their food was brought to them by young boys from their homes, who fetched and carried for them and regarded them with awe. Salt had to be avoided until the wounds had healed, but there were no other food taboos. A daily chore was to renew the white clay that was the only covering

The 'mother' of a South Sotho initiation school bearing gifts. (Ashton 1952)

A South Sotho girl initiate holding a symbolic reed. (Ashton 1952)

for their nakedness (karosses were worn against the cold). The initiates were looked after by two or three men, called 'guardians', who visited them daily and checked their health, but there appears to have been little in the way of formal instruction (unlike the position among Sotho and Venda – see below). A feature of the seclusion period among some of the westernmost South Nguni (Xhosa, Bomvana) was the holding of special public dances by initiates dressed in elaborate costumes of reeds and palm leaf and vying with each other in the galvanic abandon of their performances. As we shall see, similar regalia were worn by initiates among lowveld Sotho-Venda, such as the Lovedu and Kgaga.

Finally, at the end of the seclusion period, there was a rite formally marking the full integration of the initiates into adult life. Here the symbolism was one of purification from the taint of childhood, expressed in the linked, but opposed, metaphors of water and fire. The white clay of childhood had to be washed off and replaced by the red clay of normality, and all things associated with the seclusion period had to be burned.

Early in the morning the initiates, encouraged by the shouts of their fathers and kinsmen, ran down to the river, where they carefully washed off the white clay, taking great care that no trace of it remained. They then proceeded slowly back to the lodge site, surrounded by the singing multitude, holding their hands before their eyes in a characteristic gesture that symbolised respect to the ancestors. On arrival at the lodge they smeared themselves with red ochre and were given new karosses and a special stick. At the same time they were exhorted to behave like men and instructed in their new responsibilities. While they were away the guardians had cleared out the lodge and placed all clothing and other appurtenances of the seclusion period on top of it. The lodge was now set alight, and the initiates moved off back to their homes. As it went up in a roar of flame they were adjured not to look back, as this would make them less than men.

The circumcision schools of the Sotho seem to have placed far more emphasis on the subjection of the initiates to various hardships and ordeals than those of the Nguni. They were organised on a chiefdom scale and were held at the capital. They were held every five to ten years and included all the boys of seven to about fourteen who had not yet been circumcised. Unlike the Nguni, then, whose initiates were not only members of the same little community, but were also in their

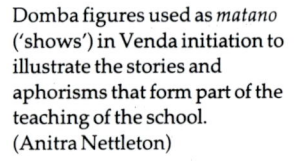

Domba figures used as *matano* ('shows') in Venda initiation to illustrate the stories and aphorisms that form part of the teaching of the school. (Anitra Nettleton)

Lovedu girl initiates, with drums, in symbolic attitude of respect. (Greg Marinovich)

late teens, Sotho initiates were, on average, younger and represented all the wards into which the chiefdom was divided. It appears that the average age of initiates among the Sotho-Tswana of the highveld was early or middle teens (old enough to be incorporated into the regimental system). Among the Sotho-Venda, on the other hand, who had a nominal regimental system but apparently no functional regiments, the age profile was much younger, ranging from six to about fourteen. Numbers attending the school were also much greater than among Nguni: as recently as the 1970s I visited a Kgaga (Sotho-Venda) circumcision school which consisted of over four hundred boys, of various ages (and this was held under the auspices of a headman, and not on a chiefdom scale). Sotho schools were also kept much more secret and there was a greater emphasis on formal instruction and the inparting of esoteric tribal lore.

Apart from the South Sotho, who did not have age regiments, the Sotho generally had initiation ceremonies that comprised two stages – a circumcision school (called *bodika*) and, after one or two years, a further school *(bogwêra)*, which completed the status change and marked the formation of a new age regiment. This was especially true of the Tswana and the North Sotho of the highveld, such as the Pedi. The *bogwêra* among the Sotho-Venda of the lowveld (Lovedu, Kgaga) does not seem to have been so clearly linked to regiments, but rather to initiation into the secrets of a mysterious being, called the Bird, among Lovedu, and *Senkônkôyi*, among Kgaga. The origins of this *kôma* (mystery) are unclear, but it may have come, via the Venda, from Zimbabwe.

The Tswana called their circumcision school the 'white *bogwêra*', from the lime with which the boys smeared their bodies. The boys were circumcised in order of precedence and then secluded in the lodge for about three months. Here they were taught a number of secret formulae and songs and instructed in the physiology of sexual relations, the dangers of intercourse with a woman in a state of pollution and in the absolute necessity for obedience to the political authorities. This was accompanied by ordeals, beatings and stringent food taboos, to drive the lessons home. This first initiation was completed, after the elapse of a year, by the *bogwêra bo bontsho* (the 'black' *bogwêra*), so called because of the ground charcoal, mixed with fat, with which the initiates smeared themselves. It was held in the great cattle-kraal adjoining the chief's *kgôtla* (place of assembly). The boys remained here for a few days only. They were made to go over the lessons learned at the previous school and given additional instruction, again reinforced by painful forms of discipline. The school ended with a military raid, or lion hunt, the initiates' first task as a new regiment.

Our knowledge of Sotho ritual is most extensive for the Pedi of Sekhukhuneland and the Kgaga of Tzaneen. In the former case the rites were closely associated with the formation of age regiments. Among Pedi the *bodika* was arranged by the chief and his councillors, who appointed a master of ceremonies and his deputy to oversee the school, and also a specialist circumciser *(thipane)* to perform the actual operation. A day was announced and boys from all over the chiefdom, accompanied by their mothers and with shaven heads and new loincloths, flocked to the capital. They were lined up in order of genealogical seniority and each was lashed twice with switches to impress upon them their relative rank within the political system.

JUNOD'S ACCOUNT OF THE FINAL CEREMONY OF THE INITIATES IN 1906

Junod gives a graphic account of the final ceremony of the Kgaga bogwêra/baale rites held in the presence of Chief Sepêkê Maake on 2 March 1906. ☐ 'After the ablution in the stream, they return to the lodge with their new garments, carrying in their hands a handsome stick prepared for the occasion ... turning their backs on the shed of the bagwêra *which is set on fire. The reeds and poles of the* baale *enclosure have also been carried there for general burning. The group starts to march very slowly. It is taboo, for all the initiates, to look back at the flames which consume all their past ...* ☐ *Suddenly Mawushe, the director of the school, arrives running, at the moment that the group of circumcised returns from the stream. He comes to look for a strange object, the standard of the tribe, a long pole carrying at its tip a kind of pommel, a hemisphere of ostrich plumes gathered in the middle ... "If we are vanquished in war"*, said Maake, *"this is the last object that the enemy will seize".* Mawushe holds it high and rejoins the group ... ☐ *Now the flames crackle and the group makes its entry, dominated by the Kgaga standard, which faintly recalls a Roman eagle. A veritable frenzy seizes all the people. Men rush around the initiates bounding like wild beasts: they come and go at a run, like madmen; they pass and repass in front of us, regarding us with the whites of their eyes, with a fixed look, besotted, as if hypnotized. Others adopt grotesque attitudes, brushing us in passing. Some make as if to strike us ... In the midst of all this tumult the initiates, very calm, advance slowly to the perimeter of the courtyard of the girls. They stop at the top of the reed enclosure, just underneath the pole surmounted by a carved antelope [the duiker, totem of the Kgaga chiefdom]. Certain furious young men dash themselves against the reeds, transfixing them with their sticks and climbing up with cries of triumph. What does this signify? Is it the symbol of the prize of possession of the female establishment by that of the male? Or perhaps these young men wish to show that they applaud the destruction of the infantile silliness of the girls, who give way gladly henceforth to their designs. I do not know ...* ☐ *To return: all the group of circumcized return to the side of the gate of the village, as if they were seized by panic. During this time the fire has increased in violence; and immense flame arises above the enclosure of the lodge.* ☐ [As for the baale *girls*] *They proceeded leisurely, the little ones, backs bent, making a right-angle with their arms, their eyes covered with their hands. The contrast with the circumcized, carrying upright and brandishing their new sticks, was striking ... They crossed the place in this manner, four or five abreast, and entered the court of the chief where they remained prostrate for about a quarter of an hour ...'* (Junod 1929: 142–44)

In the courtyard of the Kgaga *bodika* lodge. Note the extension of the ritual fireplace, the mat-covered table from which the initiates are fed, and the poles through which visitors must correctly thread their way on pain of being beaten (see plan). (W.D. Hammond-Tooke)

The shed-like enclosure in which the *bagwêra* sleep. (W.D. Hammond-Tooke)

They were then circumcised, again in order of rank, except that a boy of inferior rank would be circumcised first, in case of witchcraft. They were accommodated in a lodge, built in a remote mountain kloof, a large, temporary structure made of poles lashed together in a lattice-work and covered with grass and branches. It had two entrances, one (on the east) for the men and the other for the initiates. Down the length of the lodge was the fireplace, of great symbolic importance.

After the wounds were healed the initiates whitened their bodies with chalk and ash, they were taught a secret language, used only among themselves, and certain actions were performed in a peculiar manner. Water, for instance, was not fetched in the ordinary way: a large bundle of grass was immersed in a pool, rotated quickly to absorb as much water as possible, and shaken into the water pots. The special liminal state the initiates were in was symbolically expressed by these 'unnatural' acts. Food, a thick, unsalted maize meal porridge, was prepared by the mothers and brought to the lodge daily. The boys were not allowed to eat it from bowls, lest they touch an object handled by women. It was served on a mat of leaves and the initiates had to gulp it down in large chunks.

Most of the time in the lodge was taken up with hunting or making objects of

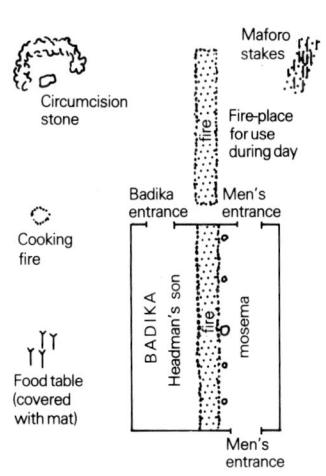

Plan of a *bodika* lodge. The initiates sleep on the left, while the right-hand side is occupied by their guardians. (W.D. Hammond-Tooke)

Lovedu *byale* girls at Mudjadji's capital. (Greg Marinovich)

wood or leather. The mornings and late afternoons and evenings were mainly devoted to instruction and singing the special songs of initiation. The instruction consisted of homilies on the qualities of manliness and responsibility and the necessity for obedience to elders and the political authorites, but there was little in the way of 'tribal lore', in the sense of a body of esoteric doctrine. Teaching consisted, rather, of the songs and traditional formulae of the lodge, which had to be word-perfect. The object of this was not so much the imparting of cognitive knowledge (many of the songs and liturgical formulae were recondite and sometimes couched in archaic language) but rather to provide proof, in later life, that one had indeed been initiated. Strangers claiming to be members of the chiefdom could be accosted and compelled to recite the formulae, and killed or beaten up if they failed to do so.

In addition to this instruction the boys were subjected to various tests of endurance. They were whipped daily to emphasise their rank and beaten by the guardians if they forgot the formulae. They were also sometimes forced to hop with a stick behind their knees or made to pick hot substances from the fire.

At the close of the seclusion period there was a public ceremony at which the white covering was washed off, the head shaven and red ochre applied. It ended, as among Nguni, with the burning of the lodge.

The emphasis in the *bodika* was on the separation of the boys from childhood and their acceptance as adults. The function of the *bogwêra*, on the other hand, was to incorporate them more specifically into the political and jural roles of adult men, for after going through it they were finally permitted to take full part in all the councils of the chiefdom. The school also stressed a very important aspect of their masculinity – their relationship *vis-à-vis* women, and this was reflected in the fre-

Venda *domba* girls with their drums. (Greg Marinovich)

quent pairing of the *bogwêra*, among these peoples, with a similar rite for girls, called *byale*.

The word *bogwêra* means 'friendship', and one of the purposes of the institution was to cement lifelong bonds between the members of the regiment. They were thought of as brothers, and were thus not allowed to marry one another's daughters. At the commencement of the school the boys washed at the river and then gathered in the mountains, where they discarded their old clothes and were dressed in a skirt made by their fathers, consisting of the leaves of a particular shrub. While they were away a special sleeping shelter was built for them at the capital as well as a lodge (with its long fireplace), in which they received instruction. Unlike the *bodika* lodge, with its secluded situation, the lodge of the *bogwêra* was in the capital, in full view of the women.

The routine of the *bogwêra* was largely a repetition of that of the *bodika*, although not so formal or strict. During the day the songs and formulae were practised and the boys hunted and collected firewood for the chief. During the first ten days, the boys had to race each morning to ensure their physical fitness. Finally, a pole was raised next to the lodge on which was placed the effigy of a flying bird, indicating that the school was over. A further ritual shaving of the head, and washing, as well as the burning of the lodge with everything in it, brought the activities to a close.

Among the lowveld Sotho the pattern of the initiation schools was similar to that of the Pedi, except for aspects of the *bogwêra*. As we have seen, among Lovedu and Kgaga (and perhaps all Sotho-Venda) regiments were not much in evidence and the emphasis in the school was more on what the Kriges call the 'mysteries of the Bird', and on the performance of masked dances in honour of it. Here Kgaga practice will be taken as an example.

A model hut used in the *domba* ceremonies for symbolic instruction in the responsibilities and dangers of adult life. (Anitra Nettleton)

The Kgaga *bogwêra* was held one year after the *bodika* circumcision school. Before it could be held the boys had to prepare their attire, which consisted of elaborate costumes of grass that took three months to prepare. Junod observed the procedure in 1905. He describes how the young men, circumcised the year before, were sent out by the chief to cut large quantities of a special grass and how, at a second calling together at the capital, the chief ordered the fathers of the boys to prepare twine from palm leaf. The whole month of June was spent by the boys in making the ritual masks and regalia, in the utmost secrecy, under the guidance of their fathers. The regalia consisted of a mask of grass, a stout flanged band that encircled the waist, bandoliers of grass and grass bracelets for arms and ankles. When all was in readiness, a large shed-like structure, without a roof, was built in the special enclosure at the capital.

But the crucial difference between Lovedu, Kgaga and Mamabola (and probably all Sotho-Venda) and other Sotho was the prominence given to the great *kôma* (mystery) of the 'Bird' or 'Beast', to whom the initiates, both boys and girls (for girls' initiation ran in parallel – see below) were presented. Among Kgaga it was called Senkôkôyi; among Lovedu 'the great Bird of Muhale', or of Zimbabwe, and was believed to come from a pool in the river on moonlight nights. It consisted of a light, semicircular framework about four feet high, over which were put strings of *muga* thorntree, which had been soaked in water to make them black. On top was an ostrich feather. 'It is seen only occasionally, when it comes dancing into the *byale* courtyard at night, and, in spite of the bright moonlight, its black colour makes it difficult to discern it clearly. It speaks and sings by whistling through an instrument ... made of the leg-bone of cattle' (Krige and Krige 1946: 135). The Bird was the controlling spirit of the lodge, and was especially associated with the girls'

JUNOD'S ACCOUNT OF THE KGAGA SENKÔKÔYI IN 1905

Senkôkôyi was the controlling 'spirit' of the Kgaga initiation lodges for boys and girls bogwêra and baale), and the chief of the kôma mysteries. Their missionary, Henri Junod, who came face to face with it in October 1905, describes his experience thus: ☐ 'During a beautiful night a few individuals take it [the hemispherical costume] in high secrecy and hide it in a thicket at the side of the stream. The next day all the men of the capital leave, amongst them the one chosen to play the role of Selwane, "the Beast", and who is named Musara. The strong men, long initiated and who know everything, go and fetch the terrifying animal ... who must now come and establish itself for a while in the little court that they have constructed for him very close to the lodge. The cortège returns, the Musara crouched under the little roof which is the carapace of "the Beast", advances slowly along the path that climbs from the stream to the capital ... He plays on a little flute of which the sound is known and to which all the subjects of the chief react and leave their villages to join the procession. "The Beast" arrives at the capital, enters and places himself in his small special court which is called siludu. The circumcised come one after another to contemplate it ... For the women, the children and the uncircumcised, "The Beast" will remain a dreadful object. It is the Bogey-man, the monster of the abyss.' (Junod 1929: 139–40) ☐ For the baale girls Senkôkôyi was a terrifying and mysterious being and the wailing of its flute was a summons for them to come out of their lodge and sing for it. The songs were answered through the flute (Sotho is a tonal language), as were the commands given by the 'Beast'. It 'spoke' in metaphorical formulae. Thus 'Bring me giraffe bones' meant firewood, 'teeth of the Tsonga' meant maize and 'marrow of the giraffe' indicated the sweet-tasting nuts of the nkanye tree (Sclerocarya caffra). They could not refuse to do its bidding. ☐ During the reign of Senkôkôyi certain taboos were in force. No undue noise could be made in the villages, no man might beat his wife, no one might get drunk, nor might the bottom of pots be scraped. Every now and again it made an appearance, especially on moonlit nights, and complained if these taboos were broken. People who did so were fined for 'cutting his heart'.

Venda women drummers with *domba* dancers. There are two types of drum, the hemispherical *ngoma* and the tall, conical *marimba*. Only the *ngoma* are decorated and each contains a stone said to be obtained from the stomach of a crocodile or of a deceased chief. (Anita Nettleton)

A group of South Sotho *bale* girls in traditional costume of sheepskin kilts and rolled grass hoops. (Levinsohn 1984)

byale school. The position among Kgaga was similar. For the girls, the Senkôkôyi was a terrifying and mysterious being and the wailing of its flute was a summons for them to come out and sing for it. During its reign (the period of the *bogwêra-baale*) certain taboos were in force. No undue noise might be made in the villages, no man might beat his wife, none might get drunk nor might the bottom of pots be scraped.

Baale (Lovedu, *byale*) was the initiation of young girls into a regiment which ran parallel to, and was linked with, that of the boys. Kgaga girls had already gone through the puberty ritual of *kgopa* at their first menstruation; now they were initiated as mature women. The two age sets were linked in a relationship that continued throughout life. *Baale*, like *bogwêra*, was held at the capital and the girls were accommodated in an enclosure made of reeds. They wore skirts of grass and left their breasts uncovered.

The complex ritual associated with the initiation involved the shaving of heads and a daily trip to the river where the girls were instructed on how to enlarge the labia (an interesting confirmation of Venda influence on these cultures), subjected to ordeals and made to sit in river water. There was a special *kôma* (mystery), the Fire-*Kôma,* in which both boys and girls combined in a ritual symbolising the importance of political authority, which involved lighting a fire by the drilling method on a floating raft of reeds. Last, the girls and boys were presented to the Senkôkôyi, followed by a final washing and annointing with red ochre.

Venda initiation was rather different. The *domba* was in fact a combined school for boys and girls, although more emphasis was placed on the compulsory attendance of girls than of boys. It was held by each chief at his capital, and lasted anything from three months to two years. The elaborate rites had, as their core, formal instruction in tribal lore, reinforced by the use of carved figurines. An important central event was the dancing of the sinuous 'Python Dance' of the female initiates. Shot through with symbolism, the *domba* was undoubtedly the most complex and colourful institution in southern Africa, after the Nguni first-fruits ceremonies.

THE MEANING OF INITIATION

Although an important aspect of the schools was undoubtedly instruction, what happened as the various stages of the ceremonies unfolded went far beyond the mere transmission of rules and values. They were, rather, co-operative attempts by

KGAGA INITIATION REGALIA

The making of elaborate dancing costumes was an important element in the Sotho-Venda initiation schools for boys, encouraged by the availability of suitable material in their lowveld environment. □ The whole of the month of July was spent at the capital making the ritual masks and costumes from lethokwa *stalks, under the guidance of their fathers, and the preparation took place in the utmost secrecy. To protect their work from what Junod calls 'profane eyes', the initiates roamed the countryside and chased away all who could not repeat the secret formulae of initiation. One such shibboleth, recorded by Junod in 1905, was 'The beast of the field, the porcupine, has transfixed me with his black and white spines, the spines that pierce the little ears', while another was 'Whose hyena are you?', with the response, 'I am the hyena of So-and-so', mentioning the name of a brother or sister.* □ *The regalia consisted of a mask of grass divided into two sections, the* mokuru *and the* sebetša, *topped by a bunch of feathers; a grass skirt (*mosôthô*), and a stout flanged band (*kgape*) that encircled the waist. Bandoliers of grass (*mefaka*) criss-crossed the chest, and wide grass bracelets (*maserêlêla*) were worn on upper arm, wrists and ankles.* □ *Two types of mask were made – a small light one, called* leswili, *and a grotesque heavy one (*naso*). The* leswili *was used for hunting and for when the initiates visited the surrounding villages, for their identities had to be kept secret. The* naso *is called by Junod 'Le typique costume de la Buhwira' and he describes it as follows: 'I say costume, rather than mask, for it also covers all the body ... The skirt, the belt and train are relatively easy to weave, but the making of the upper part, which encloses the head and chest, and which descends almost to the hips, is a lengthy task. There are two small openings by which the initiate can just manage to see his path ahead, but not to the right or left. The* naso *is very heavy and very uncomfortable. He can only don it and take it off with great difficulty with the help of another person. All the threads that sew the grass strands together are thick. It does not take long for them to cut into the skin. Also the wearing of the* naso *will soon cause real suffering. "It is the great goma [kôma]", the great test! But also, in this regalia the initiate is magnificent! He resembles a wild beast whose tail hangs behind and whose aspect is invulnerable. He is truly a superman.' (Junod 1929: 59)*

The leader of the Kgaga initiates in his dancing regalia. (A.G. Schutte)

The 'swooping' *matlakalana* dance of Kgaga *bodika* initiates. This is the penultimate ceremony, before the burning of the lodge and the 'coming out' of the boys. Early in the morning the initiates smear themselves with white clay and don special skirts *(metshabe)*. The special dancing sticks are also smeared white. Skirts and sticks are thrown on the roof of the lodge and burnt with it on the final day. (W.D. Hammond-Tooke)

the political authorities and the parents of the initiates to take boys and girls and transform them into responsible adults. This was achieved by the performance of the ritual, which in a mystical way, 'grew' the children into their new status.

The rites obviously conformed to the classic model for all rites of passage. Firstly, there was the strong spatial dimension. The initiates were removed from the normal life of their homes and located out in the veld, or in the forest ravines of mountains, far from prying eyes. The same statement of separation was made by nudity. The special status of the initiates was expressed in nakedness that recalled the nakedness of a new-born infant, for, in a very special sense, they were undergoing a rebirth. The use of white clay symbolised the liminal, dangerous, state of 'inbetweenness' in which they were involved, while the burning of the lodge and the ritual washing at the end of the school signalled their return to normal social life. The trials, ordeals and often harsh discipline served to impress on the minds of the initiates the solemn implications of the changes, especially the fact that they were from now on accountable to the political authorities for their actions. Especially in the case of males, there was indeed a great difference between the carefree attitudes of the herdboys, and the *gravitas* of mature men.

The Kgaga *Senkôkôyi* with the *bagwêra*. (A.G. Schutte)

It is clear from the above discussion that initiation among all Southern Bantu, with the possible exception of the Venda, conformed to a single basic pattern, involving, essentially, circumcision; seclusion in the lodge for the winter months; the donning of white clay; instruction in sex and in civic responsibilities; the burning of the lodge and reintegration into society of the initiates, expressed by red ochre. Even the terms for the schools (*bogwêra* and *ubukhwetha*) were the same for Sotho and Nguni. The differences we have observed are essentially relatable to the presence or absence of age regiments, or (possibly), in the case of the Venda and Sotho-Venda, to influences from Zimbabwe.

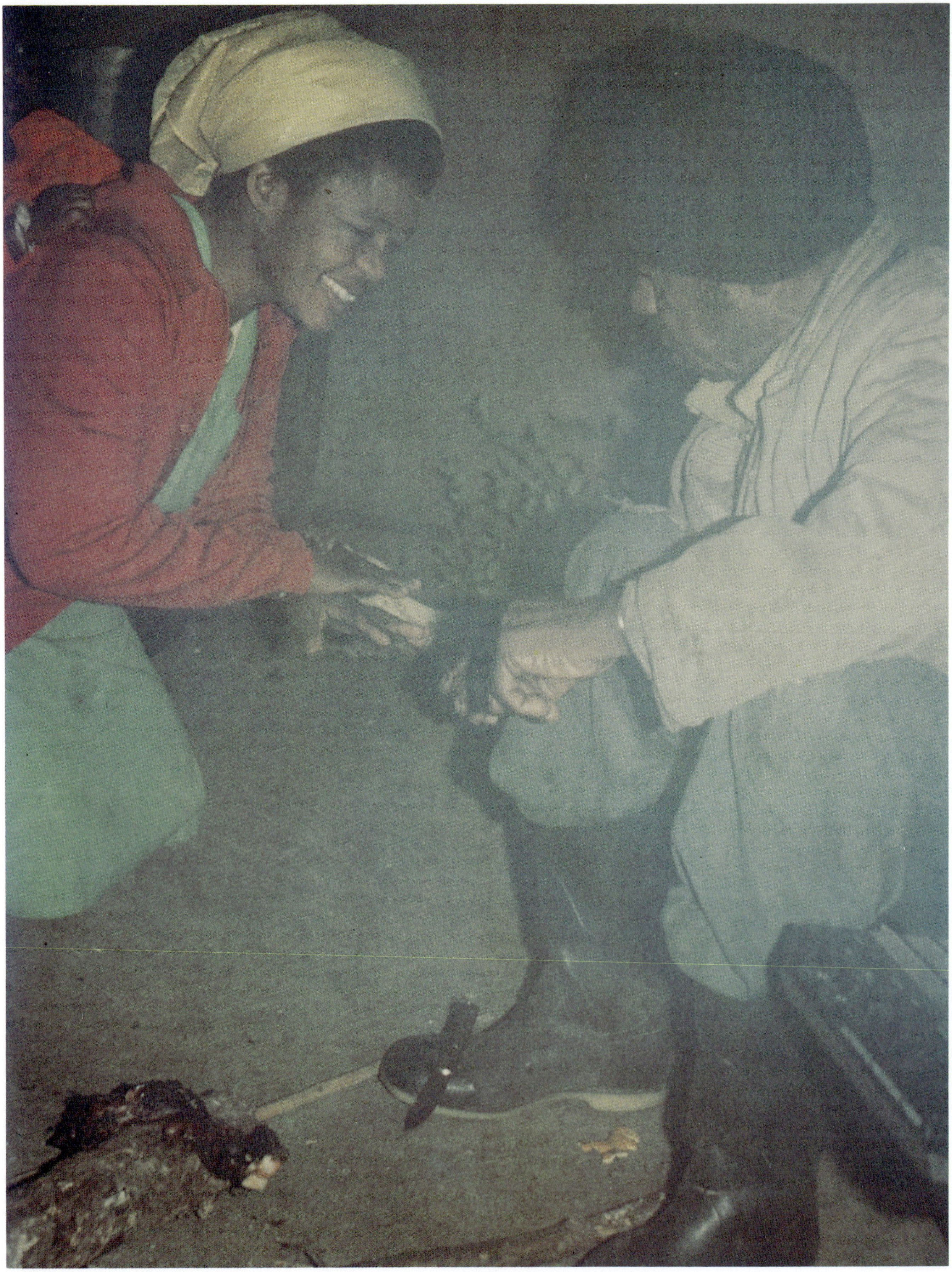

Chapter 8

In the Shadow of the Ancestors

ALL SOUTHERN Bantu believed in a life after death, although their ideas about it were vague. They made a distinction between the physical body, on the one hand, and aspects which somewhat resemble western concepts of the soul, on the other. These aspects were of two kinds. First there was the *moya*, a term that could also mean 'wind' or 'breath', which was used to refer to the essence that leaves the body at death. It thus seems to be best translated as 'life force', or simply 'life'. Writers on African religion often translate *moya* as 'soul' but it is doubtful whether this is justified. There was little or no speculation as to what happened to the *moya* at death, and no conception of rewards or punishments in an afterlife. Most importantly, the concept was not identical with that of ancestor spirit, which was accorded quite a different term, as we shall see. It seems that the term *moya* was not confined to the breath, but was thought of as suffused throughout the whole body, being especially associated with the lungs, liver, genitals, head and hair – organs believed to be especially susceptible to disease.

In addition to *moya* each individual had a 'shadow' (Nguni, *isithunzi*; Sotho, *seriti*). In one sense, *isithunzi* referred to the real shadow, an example of the almost universal belief in the importance of the shadow. The loss of one's shadow was a frightening possibility that could presage death. But shadow also had a more abstract meaning. The word was used in much the same way as we would use the term 'personality', the almost indefinable quality that determines the way we present ourselves to the world. Certain people, such as chiefs, diviners and great warriors, were said to have more, or greater, shadow than ordinary people. The concept had charismatic and slightly sinister overtones: *isithunzi* was something to fear.

These beliefs, in themselves, did not constitute any essentially religious system. As we have said, there was little of what might be called 'theological' speculation as to the fate of the generalised 'soul', if we can call it that. What *was* important was the belief that some people *also* became ancestral spirits at death and continued to take an active interest in their descendants. The belief in the spirits of the ancestors, then, lay at the very basis of traditional religion.

The concept of a Supreme Being, or High God, was not highly developed in traditional thought. All Southern Bantu believed in such a god, but he was a vague, distant, figure, taking little interest in his creatures. Each main group had its own name for God, which seems to indicate that he was thought of as a tribal god, rather like the God of the Hebrews. The Lovedu *Khuzwane*, the Kgaga *Kutšhaane*, the

The central point of the Mpondo ancestor ritual. The person troubled by the ancestors receives the ritual meat with crossed hands, while the dense clouds of acrid smoke symbolise the ancestors' presence. (H. Kuckertz)

Xhosa *Dali* or *Qamatha*, the Zulu *Nkulunkulu*, the Venda *Raluvhimba* and the Sotho *Modimo*, were all vaguely defined, with few myths relating to their doings and no regular rituals performed for them.

This comparative absence of myths is puzzling, and contrasts with the rich mythology of the San. Southern Bantu creation myths were of engaging simplicity. The Nguni and Tsonga believed that the creator 'broke off the nations' from a bed of reeds and the South Sotho, perhaps influenced by Nguni, taught that all true Sotho came from a reedbed at Ntsuanatsatsi in the Free State. An alternative story referred to the emergence of the first men from a hole in the ground. Xhosa told Alberti in 1801 that all people, stock and all forms of animal life came out of a cavern 'in a land in which the sun rises' and the Tswana, Tsonga and Lovedu pointed to certain places where the god's footprints could still be seen on the rocks. Another myth, significant for its wide distribution, was the explanation of death by the well-known story of the chameleon and the lizard. In the beginning the Creator sent the chameleon to tell mankind that it would live forever. Subsequently he changed his mind and dispatched the lizard with a message of mortality. The chameleon dawdled on the way and it was the lizard's message that reached its target.

There seems to have been little or no connection made between the creator god and the ancestral spirits, although the Sotho believed that *Modimo* could be approached through their good offices and one of the names of the Zulu *Nkulunkulu* was *Mvelangqangi*, meaning 'the First to Emerge', thus linking him with mankind.

There were differences in detail between the groups in the way in which they conceived the Supreme Being – the Venda believed that *Khuzwane* was 'another deity', in addition to *Raluvhimba*, and the Pedi maintained that *Modimo* (also called *Kgobe*), had a son, *Kgobeane*, who created man after his father had made the world – but generally the idea of a High God did not elicit much interest or speculation. It was, in fact, more in the nature of a First Cause, a *deus otiosus*, who created the world and everything in it and who left it to get on with its business without further interference. It is true that illness and misfortune were sometimes said to be caused by God, but this only occurred if a more specific cause could not be determined. The idea of 'God', therefore, was closer to our idea of 'chance' or 'luck' and was used to explain things otherwise unexplainable – rather as in our exasperated expression 'God only knows!'

Although they conceived of him essentially as a First Cause, some groups thought of the Supreme Being as responsible for the workings of nature, especially in its more majestic and dangerous aspects of storm, drought and flood. Thus, among Sotho, *Modimo* was manifested in thunder and lightning; indeed, the root *-dimo* is found in the word for 'sky' and *ledimo* means a whirlwind, hurricane or storm. The Venda *Raluvhimba* was believed to be connected with all astronomical and physical phenomena and was, in fact, identified with *Mwari*, the widely-revered Shona High God. Sometimes the two aspects, First Cause and Sky God, were split between two or more deities. Thus the Tsonga, who attributed the creation of the world to *Ntumbuluko*, also spoke of an impersonal power, *Tilo*, apparently a personification of the sky, who controlled life and death, sent storms and rain and afflicted children with convulsions. The Zulu, too, had a god, other than *Nkulunkulu*, called the 'Chief of the Sky', who brought storms and killed with lightning those who offended him.

But it was the ancestral spirits who formed the basis of Southern Bantu religion, and all groups had a special name to refer to these important beings – Zulu,

The father's sister pours a libation at a Kgaga shrine. The gourd is inverted after the mixture of meal and water has been poured from it. (W.D. Hammond-Tooke)

amadlozi or *amathongo*; South Nguni, *amathongo* or *iminyanya*; Tsonga, *swikwembu*; Sotho, *badimo* and Venda, *midzimu*. The ancestors were the spirits of the dead members of the clan among Nguni, of the family group among Sotho-Tswana, the bilateral kin group of Sotho-Venda and Venda, and the (shallow) patrilineal groupings of Tsonga, as discussed in Chapter 5. It is clear that descent rules and groupings determined the specific ancestors who were worshipped in the different groups so that it is necessary to discuss them here separately.

Perhaps the most important aspect of the Nguni clan was that it defined the group of ancestral spirits that a man worshipped, for this group was thought of as all the clan dead. This was obviously an enormous category, a kind of communion of saints, of all those who had gone before, the great majority of whom, of course, were unknown to the worshipper. It was an undifferentiated category, without a genealogical structure (it was impossible, without the aid of written records, to trace descent so far back into the past) and this was one of the reasons why the term for ancestral spirit was almost always used in the plural form. It was this great group of ancestors who were worshipped as a collectivity by Nguni, and who were believed to be present, also as a collectivity, at all rituals performed by their descendants. But there was another category of ancestors within this general group (and to some extent beyond it) who were also of importance. As we shall see, particular ancestors could affect the lives of their descendants and, in doing so, occasionally appeared in dreams to demand sacrifice. These ancestors tended to be those who had died recently, and so were recognisable (unlike the clan ancestors). They were typically grandparents, on both the father's and mother's side of the family. A deceased mother was frequently the one who was 'troubling'. There was thus a 'bilateral' dimension, within the overwhelming patrilineal emphasis, that resembled the bilateral system of Venda and Sotho-Venda.

One must imagine among Nguni, then, a great number of small worshipping groups, the agnatic clusters, meeting separately under the offices of their senior agnatic male representative, but all worshipping (a) the clan ancestors as a whole, and (b) the dead of their particular agnatic cluster (which differentiated them 'theologically' from the other agnatic clusters making up their particular clan). It is impossible, therefore, to speak of a 'tribal' religion. Each localised descent group acted as a little congregation, with its specific objects of worship. Only the chief's ancestors could be described as 'tribal'. They looked after the welfare of members of the royal lineage and, in so doing, ensured the safety of the chiefdom as a whole.

Among Sotho, Venda and Tsonga the ancestors formed a somewhat different group. Detailed evidence is lacking, especially for the Tswana, who had ceased to practise the ancestor rituals by the time anthropologists studied them. It is possible that, although they had no lineages, the patrilineal emphasis was strong among Sotho-Tswana. But among Venda and Sotho-Venda the category of ancestors included the dead on both sides of the family. Instead of stressing the patrilineal side only, as far back in time as it would go, these peoples gave equal stress to both paternal and maternal sides, but cut off recognition at the level of great-grandparents, including deceased mother's brothers and mother's fathers, both real and classificatory. Among Tsonga, too, both father's and mother's ancestors were of 'equal dignity'. They called their immediate ancestors on the mother's side *vakokwana* ('those of the grandparents') and their patrilineal ancestors *swikwembu swa la kaya* ('ancestral spirits of the home'). Only the immediate ancestors on both sides were recognised, limiting them to a single generation above the senior, still living, generation. The 'ancestor collective' among Tsonga was thus smaller than it was among Nguni. Theologically, the difference would appear to be that, whereas Nguni ancestral spirits were essentially unknown and (except for the recently dead) unknowable, most non-Nguni ancestors were known to their descendants.

There appears to have been a lack of clarity as to whether all deceased persons became ancestral spirits, especially the young and the unmarried. The Tsonga believed that every human being became a *shikwembu*, but the fate of children dying in infancy was uncertain: the Pedi believed that they 'went to their forefathers', but did not become ancestral spirits. All deceased persons, however, lived in the world of the dead, the only exception being those buried without the necessary funerary rites being performed.

The body itself was disposed of by burial, except among some Nguni who exposed it in the veld to be eaten by hyenas, although chiefs and headmen were always buried in the cattle byre. In most groups family heads and important people were interred in the cattle kraal or close to its fence, and less important men, women and children in a hut, or, more commonly, in some convenient place nearby. The bodies of Sotho-Venda chiefs were kept for a year on a raised platform in their hut before burial so that the sacred 'crocodile stone', swallowed on accession to chieftainship, could be recovered.

Variations occurred in the positioning of the body but a recess was commonly dug in the side of the grave and the corpse placed in a sitting position, often accom-

---

SOME TSONGA PRAYERS

'The most characteristic prayers ... are the family prayers. As a rule they are pronounced by the elder member of the family, his younger brothers have no right to approach the ancestral spirits, the law of precedence is sacred and it is taboo to transgress it. ☐ This is the formula used in the case of the marriage of a daughter. The father takes between the index finger and the thumb a small quantity of half-digested grass which has been extracted from the paunch of the slaughtered goat, touches his tongue with it and emits the sacramental "Tsu". Then standing behind the wedding pair he says: ☐ "My fathers, my grandfathers (he calls them by their names) ... look! Today my child is leaving me. She enters the wedded life. Look after her, accompany her where she will live. May she also found a village! May she have many children; may she be happy, good, just! May she be on good terms with those with whom she will be". ☐ He speaks with his eyes wide open, looking straight before him, as if the gods were really sitting near him. There is very little feeling of awe in the whole proceedings. Perhaps the brother of the bridegroom will interrupt him and say: "Yes, we will live peacefully with her if she does her duty and does not worry her husband," but the father will go on, taking no notice of the interruption, repeating the same words again and again. When the people think that he ought to stop, they send a young man to cut a piece of meat and put it into the old man's mouth. This is called "to cut the prayer", and then he keeps still. ☐ Prayer is also resorted to in the case of disease, when the divinatory bones have revealed that it has been caused by the ancestral spirits. Here is a sample of the prayer pronounced by the maternal uncle for his nephew ... ☐ "You, our gods, you [name] ... here is our offering. Bless this child and make him live and grow. Make him rich, so that when we visit him, he may be able to kill an ox for us ... You are useless, you gods! You only give us trouble! For although we give you offerings you do not listen to us! We are deprived of everything! You ... (naming the ancestor to which the offering must be addressed in accordance with the decree given by the bones) you are full of hatred! You do not enrich us! All who succeed do so by the help of their gods. Now we have made you this gift. Call your ancestors ... call also the gods of the sick boy's father, because his father's people did not steal his mother. These people [naming their clan] came in the daylight [to marry the mother]. So come to the altar! Eat and distribute amongst yourselves our ox [in fact, a hen] according to your wisdom." ☐ In this prayer the maternal uncle does not fear to address the gods with harsh words. To curse the spirits is a curious means to obtain their favour. Yet the reasoning is plain and convincing: If you kill us, you will also die, as nobody will remain on earth to remember you and to offer you sacrifices.' (Junod 1922:564–6)

panied by its more intimate personal belongings such as snuffbox, walking stick and spoon. Thus, among South Sotho, sorghum, gourds and pumpkin seeds (said to be the original food of the Sotho) were placed on or near the body, with wisps of *mohloa*, a grass symbolising family and community life because it grows near settlements, and *molile* grass, both plaited into miniature platters. Both Zulu and Sotho chiefs were interred, on occasion, with some of their councillors and body servants to accompany them, and, among Mpondomise, a number of chiefs were buried in rivers to prevent molestation by witches.

Among Nguni, the mere fact of death and burial did not necessarily make an ancestral spirit: a special ritual was necessary to effect the change of status from deceased person to ancestor. The symbolism of the Zulu ritual was especially striking. It was called *ukubuyisa idlozi* (to cause the ancestor to return) and took place a year or two after burial. The ritual was only performed for men, especially the homestead head, and its neglect could bring about misfortune. An ox was sacrificed and choice portions of its meat were placed on the special spot at the back of the great hut, sacred to the ancestors. At the ritual the name of the deceased was included in the praises of the ancestors for the first time after his death and he was specifically requested to return home and care for his descendants. Often, as a further measure to ensure his return, the officiator, his eldest son, took a branch and dragged it from the grave to the great hut, symbolically showing him the way.

Ideas about where the dead lived were vague, but the most generally accepted view was that it was underground. However there were alternative theories, often held by individuals. Among the Pedi, 'Some say it is underground, others say it is in the skies above, others again that it lies where the sun sets, in the west. The latter seems to be the largest consensus of opinion' (Mönnig 1967: 53). Life in the spirit world was believed to be much like that on earth but was idealised as taking place in a land of plenty.

The importance of the ancestors was that they continued to take a close interest in the affairs of their descendants. But their attitudes and actions tended to be unpredictable and this was reflected in a marked ambivalence towards them on the part of their worshippers. Generally speaking they were benevolent and deeply concerned with the wellbeing of their children. They protected one (up to a point) from witchcraft and were responsible for the fertility of the crops. Wilson comments on the Mpondo: 'On the whole the *amathongo* are propitious to their descendants. They see and hear everything that is done. They have the power to send health to man and beast, to increase property, to ensure good crops. Men returning from a fight praised their ancestors for having saved them ... If they were to desert a man, misfortune would befall him at once' (Hunter 1936: 234). Ancestors were believed to be always present with their descendants, wherever they might be, even when on a long journey and far from the ancestral graves.

But if the ancestors were merely benevolent they would not have played such a vital role in Southern Bantu religion. In fact, the ancestors were also considered to be capricious, jealous and easily offended, and their wrath was an important explanation of misfortune. South Sotho ancestors seem to have been particularly troublesome, for their ethnographer, Ashton, states that formerly *all* illness was attributed to them 'in the belief that they continually tried to compass the death of the living in order to secure their companionship'. If true, this was an extreme case. More usually ancestors complained of neglect, especially failure to perform the customary rituals associated with kinship. Among Nguni they also complained of being hungry, but this was not common in other groups. Lovedu ancestors, for

Venda sacred stones, representing the ancestors. The smaller stone represents the sacred black bull owned by noble lines and is called 'grandfather'. It is regarded as the embodiment of all the ancestors. The larger stone is called 'cow'. The ground around the stones is kept swept, and a yellow-flowered bulbous plant, *luhome*, is planted near them.

instance, never complained of hunger, but desired rather to be remembered: 'they want their beads worn, their name revived, a beast or goat dedicated or named after them' (Krige and Krige 1943: 233).

The ambivalent attitude of the living to the dead was reflected in religious behaviour. Some Pedi rituals were explicitly intended to prevent ancestors from interfering too much in the lives of their descendants. It is probably true to say that, generally, the attitude between worshipped and worshipper lacked the aura of reverence and adoration so striking in 'world' religions, although of course we have no real knowledge of this. Both Junod, for the Tsonga, and the Kriges, for the Lovedu, write of a seeming lack of humility on the part of worshippers, who 'pray to ancestors as man to man, scolding them to remind them of their duties to their children ... As the gods have human attributes, worship is not characterised by humility and formality' (Lovedu) and 'The attitude of the worshippers ... and the freedom they show in insulting their gods, indicates that they consider them as exactly on the same level as themselves' (Tsonga). But this was not always true. What we know of the Venda indicates a great reverence towards the spirits of the deceased, and this was certainly also true of Nguni. Berglund states that, among Zulu, 'A worthy invocation presupposes dignified language ... much care is given to the choice of words, expressions and gestures ... Very poetic and extremely beautiful Zulu is often heard at the invocation of the shades.' At a sacrifice he attended, 'The atmosphere in the hut was one of supreme reverence and dignified quiet', although people outside were talking and shouting. The officiant cut two strips off the *intsonyama* (a piece of meat cut from the top of the right foreleg, sacred to the ancestors) and gave them to his sick son to eat. The following graphic account is pregnant with reverence:

> When smoke rose from the strips on the coal, the officiant instructed his son to cross his arms, cut the strips in half, placed a piece of each strip into each hand and told him (the patient) in a whispering voice to eat them. He himself ate the remaining two bits and prior to putting the meat into his mouth said, whispering, yet fully audibly: *'Makhosi!'* ['Chiefs', i.e. 'ancestral spirits']. Both remained seated until they had completed eating the meat when the host, on his knees, fetched the vessel containing beer which had been placed on the skin by his sister. He handed it to his son who took a mouthful. Thereafter he took a mouthful himself, repeating *'Makhosi!'* The vessel was returned to its place. (Berglund 1976: 218)

Ancestors made their wishes known in two ways – either through dreams or through an illness that was subsequently divined as having been 'sent' by them. Dreams are reported from all groups, although apparently this was far less true for Lovedu than for Nguni. Among South Sotho, 'If the dead are only just glimpsed in a dream, it may not mean much more than that they are still interested and fond of one; but if they appear looking cross or loving, it is serious and means either that they are angry with one or longing for one to join them' (Ashton 1952: 114).

A further peculiarity among some groups was the belief that the ancestor could appear in the form of an animal. This was especially true for Venda, Zulu and some South Nguni. Among Venda it was principally a chiefly ancestor who returned, usually in the form of a lion. Zulu associated snakes with a visiting ancestral spirit. Chiefs and headmen returned as mambas but commoners did so in the form of a brown, non-poisonous snake. When such a snake visited a homestead the daughters-in-law of the deceased covered their heads in respect and a beast was

> **TSWANA BURIAL IN THE NINETEENTH CENTURY**
>
> The missionary, Robert Moffat, described mortuary customs among the southern Tswana as follows: □ 'When they see any indications of approaching dissolution, in fainting fits or convulsive throes, they throw a net over the body, and hold it in a sitting posture with the knees brought in contact with the chin, until life is gone. The grave, which is frequently made in the fence of the cattle-fold, or in the fold itself, is, for a man, about three feet in diameter and six feet deep. The interior is rubbed over with a large bulb. The body is not conveyed through the door of the fore yard or court connected with the house, but an opening made in the fence for that purpose. It is carried to the grave having the head covered with a skin, and is placed in a sitting posture. Much time is spent in order to fix the corpse exactly facing the north; and though they have no compass, they manage, after some consultation, to place it very nearly in the required position. Portions of an ant hill are placed about the feet, when the net which held the body is gradually withdrawn. As the grave is filled up, the earth is handed in with bowls, while two men stand in the hole to tread it down around the body: great care being taken to pick out everything like a root or pebble. When the earth reaches the height of the mouth, a small twig or branch of the acacia is thrown in, and on the top of the head a few roots of grass are placed; and when the grave is nearly filled, another root of grass is fixed immediately above the head, part of which stands above the ground. When finished, the men and women stoop, and with their hands scrape the loose soil around on to the little mound. A large bowl of water, with an infusion of bulbs, is then brought, when the men and women wash their hands and the upper part of their feet, shouting, 'Pula, pula, rain, rain'. An old woman, probably a relative, will then bring his weapons, bows, arrows, war axe and spears, also grain and garden seeds of various kinds, and even the bone of an old pack ox, with other things, and address the grave, saying, "These were all your articles". These are then taken away, and bowls of water are poured on the grave, when all retire; the women wailing, "Yo, yo, yo" with some doleful dirge, sorrowing without hope.' (Holden 1866: 381–2)

slaughtered to welcome it. The spirit-snake was recognisable as such from the resemblance it bore to the dead person, usually reflected in the marks of injuries acquired in life. Among South Nguni the ancestor responsible for the 'calling' of a diviner to her profession could take the shape of an *ityala*, a wild animal such as lion, leopard or elephant; she and her relatives would then honour it by not killing it, eating its flesh or mentioning its name.

Although no buildings were dedicated to the ancestors all groups had certain places associated specially with them. Among Nguni this was the cattle byre itself, in which all killings were made, and the raised niche built at the back of the great hut, above which the entrails of the sacrifice were hung. There is some evidence that this was also true of the Sotho-Tswana.

The Sotho-Venda, Venda and Tsonga, on the other hand, all had shrines specially dedicated to the ancestors. Lovedu, Kgaga and other lowveld Sotho made shrines of mud, shaped in a small mound, containing the bones of a sacrificial goat or fowl and sometimes other objects such as family heirlooms (old hoe- or assegai-heads (*thugula*) or a black river stone). A special plant, usually of the amaryllis family, was planted on shrines, and libations of beer or gruel poured over them. Venda shrines consisted of large river stones. They also possessed a number of ritual objects associated with the ancestors. Many important descent lines had a black bull, 'regarded as the embodiment of all the ancestral spirits', and those of lesser importance had large cylindrical river stones to represent the actual animal. Both bull and stones were addressed as *makhulu* (grandfather). Maternal ancestors were represented by a black female goat. There were other sacred objects, called collectively *zwitungulu*, such as axes, hoes, special cloth, old horns, copper ingots and beads, which had formerly belonged to the ancestors and which were jealously guarded and regarded with awe.

The Lovedu rain queen's ancestor shrine at which she pours a libation of beer to honour her royal predecessors. (Greg Marinovich)

The carved door of a Venda chief's dwelling. The geometric designs represent the crocodile, the primary emblem of Venda chieftainship. (Anitra Nettleton)

Tsonga had a shrine in the form of a sacred tree at the righthand side of the entrance to the village. The shrine, in the absence of a tree, could also consist merely of a forked branch planted in the ground, either inside the great hut or in the middle of the homestead area. Scraps of clothing were hung on the branches in honour of the ancestors.

The worship of the ancestors always involved a specific 'congregation' of worshippers. Each agnatic cluster among Nguni and Tsonga, or family group among Sotho-Tswana, Sotho-Venda and Venda, formed a separate and discrete cult group, worshipping its own particular set of ancestors, who only had influence over their own descendants. Membership of these groups depended on the accident of birth, although it could also be achieved by adoption and, sometimes, by marriage. Thus, among South Nguni, a married woman came under the influence of her husband's ancestors; at the other extreme, Tsonga women never did.

The group was led in worship by a ritual officiator, typically a senior kinsman, who played this role among a number of others. Perhaps the term 'priest' can be used for this office, but only if it is remembered that it did not involve a specially consecrated individual, set aside by training and with a special vocation to serve the gods.

Among Nguni, the priest was the head of that category of men whose names appeared on the (five-generation) lineage genealogy. He was called the *inkulu* (the 'big one'). He was also, in his capacity as 'head' (*intloko*), the leader of that part of the lineage (the agnatic clusters) whose members actually lived together in a defined area and who were descended from a common great-grandfather. As *intloko*, he convened and 'chaired' the agnatic cluster court. But it was as *inkulu* (which can perhaps best be translated as 'ritual elder') that he operated in the ancestor religion.

He presided over all the rituals performed by members of the wider lineage and the clan ancestors could only be approached through him, as the man genealogically closest to them. Ritual was essentially a homestead affair, called for by a homestead head when sickness struck the home, or when a member of his homestead was passing through some life crisis such as birth, initiation, marriage or death. On such occasions the actual calling on the clan ancestors to be present had to be done by the *inkulu*. The performance of this work often entailed much travelling. His homestead was not a special meeting place and rituals were held in widely dispersed homesteads. Dates of all sacrifices had to be arranged with him and he had to see to it that all lineage members were notified so that they could be present – for rituals to the ancestors concerned all members of the descent group. A similar system existed among Sotho-Tswana where the head of the family, as senior living representative of the ancestors, conducted the rites.

Among the other groups this strong patrilineal emphasis was not so marked. Among Tsonga, to whom the mother's family were of equal importance, the mother's brother played an extremely important role in the religious life of his sister's son, with whom there existed a joking relationship which included the 'snatching' of the meat of the beast sacrificed on his behalf by the mother's brother. Junod comments that 'Maternal relatives have a special religious duty towards their nephews. They act as priests, offerings being frequently made to the gods of the mother's family through the agency of the maternal uncle,' although, of course, the family was also under the paternal control of the senior male through whom all patrilineal offerings had to be made. Among the Venda:

> The sister of the head of the lineage [*makhadzi*] ... plays an equally important part in its religious affairs. She is the priestess of her lineage, and except on rare occasions paternal ancestor spirits may only be approached through her. Any person requiring her ministrations, in order to commune with an ancestor, must inform the head of the lineage, who summons his sister. If it is quite impossible for her to appear, her brother, the *ndumi*, may act in her place; failing him, the headman ... but in either of these two contingencies the substitute must use the name of his sister, the true priestess (Stayt 1931: 249).

The prominent role of the Venda father's sister was also found among Sotho-Venda, among whom she was termed *rakgadi*. She was ideally the person to perform the *phasa* rite of pouring a libation of beer on the family shrine of her brother; indeed, the family shrine should be made by the father's sister. A man could *phasa* for his family if the *rakgadi* was not available, but he did so in her name. Among Kgaga, in the absence of the father's sister the branch of a marula tree was used to asperse the beer on the shrine. It should be stressed that the role of the *rakgadi* was a purely ritual one and a man did not usually consult his sister on, for instance, economic matters. Among Lovedu, it was the *rakgadi* who officiated the annual harvest offering and she was considered 'the one best able to intercede with the spirits'. Any grievance on her part against her brother could cause the spirits to be 'stirred up' and bring illness to his children. However, the officiator at a *phasa* ritual could be either male or female, depending on the indication of the divining dice.

To sum up, it is clear that the role of priest was closely related to the social structure. Among the strongly patrilineal Nguni and Sotho-Tswana, it was always performed by the genealogically senior male; among Venda and Sotho-Venda (who stressed the cattle-linking of brother and sister) it was the father's sister who filled

Mpondo ancestor ritual. The afflicted person performs the dance and song of contrition, for the confession of anger in the heart towards kin is essential before the ritual can be effective. (H. Kuckertz)

this office. A Tsonga man's patrilineal ancestors were approached by his father and his mother's ancestors by his mother's brother: both were equally important.

The picture emerges, for all Southern Bantu, of a religious system in which a large number of discrete cult groups, each worshipping its own set of ancestors, existed. Religion among these people, then, was not a strong factor in promoting *chiefdom* integration: rather would it seem to have been divisive. But, for the worshipping descent group itself, participation in worship acted as a strong uniting force, for all members were expected to attend the rituals. There is also evidence that the rituals could only be effective if peace and harmony prevailed between kinsmen. As Brown records for the nineteenth century Tswana:

> the sacrifice itself is not considered sufficient. It must be accompanied by confession, and the confession usually, if not always, precedes the sacrifice ... In the case of a child on whose behalf the doctor [diviner] has been called in, the confession of possible strife between the parents, or their failure in any respect towards the customs of their tribe, is required. (Brown 1926: 151)

Schapera states that, among Tswana, a special ceremony of reconciliation was necessary if a person had quarrelled with his family head, before the latter could approach the ancestors on his behalf. Both Tsonga and Nguni also had such ceremonies. Intriguingly, in view of its widespread distribution across the world, confession of anger among Sotho, Venda and Tsonga was also accompanied by a ritual spitting, symbolising the expulsion of negative and disruptive emotions preparatory to approaching the gods. As in Christianity, effectiveness in rituals in southern Africa demanded a humble and a contrite heart.

Occasions of Ritual Action

The rituals associated with the ancestor religion can be divided into (a) life-cycle rituals, (b) piacular (or illness-related) rituals, and (c) contingent rituals (those made on *ad hoc* special occasions.

Among all the Southern Bantu the various changes in status, such as birth, initiation, marriage and death, were accompanied by certain symbolic actions and verbal formulae that not only called on the ancestors to be present to witness the event, but also mystically caused the status change. These were the rituals, usually involving the sacrifice of an animal or the making of a libation and accompanied by some invocation of the spirits, the neglect of which was a potent source of ancestral displeasure. Often a diviner's diagnosis of illness as being sent by the ancestors specified which ritual had been omitted so that the omission could be made good.

The life-cycle rituals were varied. Among South Nguni, for example, a white goat (for white was the ancestors' colour) was ritually slaughtered at the end of the seclusion period after the birth of a child; on the day before circumcision, to ensure healing of the wounds; at the end of the eight-day period of strict food taboos after circumcision; at girls' initiation; after a marriage ceremony, to permit the bride to drink sour milk at her husband's home; and at the two obligatory killings at a funeral. In the latter case, oxen were killed, one to 'accompany' the deceased on his way and the other, a year later, to bring him back as a fully incorporated shade. On none of these occasions were the ancestors specifically invoked, and the killings were referred to as 'merely customs'. A knife was used instead of the ritual spear to cut the throat of goats and sever the spinal cord of oxen. Although they did not involve formal invocation of the ancestors, they were always accompanied by some form of address – ostensibly to the person for whom the ritual was performed, or to those present, but in fact intended for the ears of the ancestors. An example of this is seen in a speech given by the master of ceremonies at a girls' initiation in the Ciskei: 'Today we are taking out these girls of the Zangwes, so that they will be healthy. We are fulfilling the custom so that they do not worry us in the future. You all know that by custom we are supposed to slaughter two oxen, but the Zangwes (i.e. ancestors of this particular clan) see we have nothing on account of the drought. They will excuse us.' Killings at the life-cycle rituals were thus rites of rogation and were intended to keep the ancestors informed of the doings of their descendants.

THE THEVHULA SACRIFICE TO VENDA ROYAL ANCESTORS

'The most important sacrificial rite of Venda royal families was thevhula, a form of first-fruits ceremony. It was confined to the royal descent group and took place in sacred groves where the ancestors lay buried. The whole group had to be present and a libation of eleusine was poured over the stones that represented departed ancestors. The informant here was a tshifhe (officiator) who had often performed the rites. ☐ On the day of the thevhula all the people assemble in the musanda [capital] and the beer is brought thither in great quantities. The order is given to bring the drums and horns. They are laid down according to size, ready for use. ☐ Then the members of the royal clan, both male and female, are told to get up. We all go through a small gate leading to the graves. The horns remain in the khoro [courtyard], ready for use, but are not yet blown. We of the royal clan and our wives all assemble at the graves. The heads of the clan muster us in a hushed silence and finally say, "Very well". Thereupon the makhadzi [father's sister] comes forward and lifts up the thungu [special calabash] while the girl designated by the divining dice takes up the vessel containing the beer. A great solemnity comes over us, we are all silent and serious. We leave the graves in solemn procession. The makhadzi goes in front and we follow, one behind the other. ☐ We pass through the khoro where all the people are assembled. The commoners don't say a word, they just stare at us. We go right through the middle of them. If there is no room to pass through, others say, "Make way for them". We ourselves say never a word, we are most serious. We go on, still in single file, with the makhadzi in front, the tshifhe behind her carrying the beer, and we all in their rear. The solemnity increases the more we approach the place of sacrifice, and there is none that speaks now. We go to the stones representing our dead fathers. We halt and the makhadzi puts down the thungu, while the tshifhe also puts down the beer calabash. The makhadzi sits down and we do likewise, forming a circle round the stones. The makhadzi says, "Let the tshifhe come and give his father of the crop of the new year". ☐ The tshifhe crawls towards the stone that represents our first ancestor, and says, "I thevhula [pour out] in the name of your descendant So-an-so [his own name], who was designated by the dice to be tshifhe". Then he crawls to the second stone and says, "You all in the domain of the dead, I sacrifice to you". ☐ Our prayer then is, "May the country resound with lamentation, may there be misfortune among the commoners, that we may grow rich thereby" [i.e. through the fines from the resulting court cases]... ☐ Then the makhadzi takes the thungu and drinks one mouthful out of it, the others do likewise. This is called eating the saliva of the ancestors [i.e. consuming what they have left over]. When she has done so, she utters a loud ululation of joy. Thereupon she puts it down and the khotsimunene, brother of the last deceased chief, takes it and takes a sip in his turn and also puts it down again. Then the one after the other of the rest who are of royal blood, also take a mouthful and put the thungu down. Only real clan members do this. Even very small infants, that are still carried about, have a little beer put into their mouths, but their mothers, in so far as they are not of our clan, are not allowed to partake of it, for this is solely the privilege of royal blood. When all this is over the khotsimunene utters loud shouts of joy. ☐ When the cry of the khotsimunene is heard, the men in the khoro get up and prepare to blow tshikona with horns and flutes. We return in buoyant spirits from the place of sacrifice. The tshikona music is in full swing. The makhadzi enters the circle of players and commands, "You all – silence! All you horns, be quiet and listen". In a moment all is quiet, the dancing men remain standing just where they happen to be. She then says, "We have given the people permission to hoe again. We have begun a new year for you. Our duty is done. You commoners may now each sacrifice to your own ancestors." ' (Van Warmelo 1930)

160

THE ROOTS OF BLACK SOUTH AFRICA

TSWANA
1. Beaded waist ornament.
2. Brass anklets.
3. Skin cloak (dikobo) of genet skins.
4. Hussif – needle case (molalathlale).
5. Horn snuff-box.
6. Bone snuff-box.
7. Bone snuff-box.
8. Spoon for porridge, with guinea-fowl carving.
9. Spoon with branded decoration on underside of bowl.
10. Pair of spoons.
11. Winnowing basket (leselo).
12. Wooden milkpail.
13. Calabash drinking vessel for beer (phafana).
14. Sweatscraper made by blacksmith of local iron.
15. Knife with ivory hilt and case. From Chief Sechele of Molepolole, late nineteenth century.
16. Bone waist ornament, possibly early nineteenth century.

IN THE SHADOW OF THE ANCESTORS

17. *Pot.*
18. *Garden basket* (tlatlana).
19. *Marula wood bowl* (mogopo) *used for porridge.*
20. *Calabash ladles* (sego).
21. *Small pot* (nkgwana).
22. *Head pad, for carrying loads such as pots.*
23. *Skin milk sack* (lekuka).

(South African Museum)

But the occasions where Nguni worshipper and ancestor come into closest and deepest contact were undoubtedly those termed 'piacular', a word meaning 'expiation' or 'atonement'. These were typically performed at times of sickness divined as having been sent by the ancestors for neglect of the (life-cycle) 'customs of the home', or for lack of respect to senior kin, thus underlining the importance of the descent groups. It is clear that such a diagnosis pointed squarely at the culpability of the sick person, who had thus brought the misfortune upon him or herself, hence the need for atonement.

The piacular ritual, called *idini* in Xhosa, was quite explicitly directed to the ancestors as such, for its main element was an invocation *(nqula)*, calling on them to be present and to intervene. There were other important elements. These included stabbing an ox in the cattle byre with the ritual spear kept in each home and passed down from father to son; dancing and singing clan songs; tasting *(shwama)* the *intsonyama* (the piece of meat sacred to the ancestors), not only by the sufferer but by all the lineage segment members present; drinking beer specially brewed for the ancestors; the use of special 'medicines of the home'; placing the sacrificial meat on the branches of special trees, and burning the bones of the sacrificial victim on the third day.

It was at an *idini* that the formal ritual calling on the ancestors took place. Among Xhosa-speakers the word used for this was *nqula*, referring to the reciting of the most important clan names of the sufferer, interspersed with the appropriate praises, such as *'Camagu!* (Blessings!) Cattle of Mondinga; Beast-that-does-not-give-birth: It-gives-birth-only-by-being-forced-to; Friends of Mnciwa' and *Camagu*! Cattle of Nxuba, of Mduma, of Lushoda; of-the-one-who-counts-stars-while-other-men-count-cattle; of Ngole-ka'. It should be noted that these names were all names of clan founders. No names of other ancestors, even the agnatic cluster dead, were included, except that the invocation might end with the name of the apical *lineage* founder, usually in the form: 'And you, people of So-and-so.' But even though not called by name, all the clan dead were included by implication in the invocation and were believed to be present. The invocation might be preceded

THE TSONGA 'SACRAMENTAL TSU'

Throughout South Africa rituals were preceded by a confession of anger, accompanied by spitting. Henri Junod refers to it as the 'sacramental tsu': here is his discussion of it among the Tsonga: ☐ *'Some features of this ritual are most interesting, especially the tsu so often mentioned, by which the offering is consecrated. What does it mean? The Natives themselves are unable to explain it, so we are reduced to mere supposition. It consists in an emission of saliva, generally mixed with something from the victim: some of the short feathers from the neck soiled with blood, in the case of a fowl, or a little psanyi [chyme: green stomach contents] also kneaded with blood, in that of a goat. But in the offering of bitterness there is merely saliva; this, however, is a true* 'hahla' [sacrifice] *and this fact shows that the saliva is a gift, the personal gift of the worshipper. He first gives his gods something emanating from himself, mingling it with the blood or psanyi of the victim, and only then does he approach them. So there seems to be a deep meaning underlying this sacramental act, though most of the worshippers are not aware of it (a circumstance which unhappily occurs in all religions); although unconscious, it exists and has given rise to the rite; the gift of oneself is necessary to obtain favour of the Divinity. – What is the intention of adding in the blood and the psanyi? Is there any meaning in the choice of the blood which is mixed with saliva in order to despatch the offering to the gods? Is the blood (ngati) regarded as containing the life of the animal, as was the case amongst the Jews, who used it 'to cover the soul' or the sins of the worshipper (hence the idea of atonement)? There is no sign of a similar conception among the Thongas ...' (Junod 1927: 415)*

by *bika*, that is, a report to the gathered assembly (and, of course, to the ancestors) of the nature of the illness and the identity of the sufferer.

Finally, if the ritual did not achieve its purpose, *ngxola* might be resorted to. The word can be translated as 'to make a noise', 'to utter words angrily', or 'to speak with deep feeling'. *Ngxola* was performed by a senior man of the homestead, or by the ritual elder. The officiant made two stations, in the cattle byre and in the space between it and the houses, and finally entered the hut where the sick person lay. He *ngxola'd* as follows: 'What can it be? Is it that this homestead has no people of its own (i.e. ancestors)? How is it that I am in difficulty when they are here?', or words to that effect. If the ancestors heard, the beast they wanted sacrificed to them became restive and dropped soft dung. A further killing was then made.

The form Nguni ritual took can perhaps best be described by an example, one admittedly taken from contemporary research among the Mpondo of the Transkei, studied by Henri Kuckertz (1990). Reports from early eighteenth and nineteenth century travellers among the South Nguni demonstrate a remarkable continuity in beliefs among these people from that time to the present, so the use of the example is perhaps justified.

Among Mpondo, illness divined as being caused by the ancestors was usually deemed to reflect an ancestor's demand for 'food'. The resulting ritual always had two parts, a public one and a private one in which the members of the agnatic cluster and their wives met on their own. The feast as a whole took place over two days, but the two parts were complementary.

The public feast took place in the morning, attended by members of the local area and others from further afield; in fact anyone could attend and many did, attracted by the beer that was an indispensable part of all feasts. The attendance of these people was important, for the ritual, essentially a family affair, had also to be made public so that the ancestors could be seen to be honoured and the homestead shown to be an important one. The public feast had three main elements: a formal announcement by the ritual elder explaining why it was being held; a thanksgiving and public statement by the homestead head; and a number of intercessions addressed to the ancestors on behalf of the afflicted person and various instructions directed to this person. The speakers were patrilineal kinsmen or kinswomen, or kinsmen's wives, and the speeches included reference to the necessity for compassionate concern for kin, good wishes for the patient's speedy recovery and expression of the hope that his or her recovery would benefit all the members of the homestead. These speeches were interspersed with singing, dancing and handclapping and could also include formal praise of the ancestors.

The climax of the public ceremony was the thanksgiving *(umbongo)* by the homestead head on behalf of the afflicted person. It was a public statement and therefore only the head could make it. He began by thanking all the kin, both living and dead, for their presence and concern and (in anticipation) for their help in curing the patient, but then focused on the specific relationship between the afflicted person and the ancestor who had been divined as being the cause of the trouble. Here there was a significant shift of emphasis. Now the ritual focus was on the culpability of the patient. In a ritual recorded by Kuckertz, the homestead head, having made the thanksgiving speech, commenced to dance towards the back of the hut, sacred to the ancestors, where the patient was sitting. Suddenly he turned to face the hearth and, in song, addressed the ancestral spirit, the patient's maternal grandmother, and identified the patient as the 'nuisance' *(ukunyakanyaka)* responsible for whatever anger had been aroused. At this point the people present burst into cheers and ululations of applause. As Kuckertz comments:

> With the thanksgiving and song, the ancestral public feast has accomplished its aim: it has made public the fact that the afflicted person is not sick on account of the malicious intentions of others [witchcraft], but because of the intervention of the ancestors. It is made public that, although the subsequent ritual will be taking place behind closed doors, this is not anti-social, for its participants are under the authority of the ancestors. (Kuckertz 1983: 124)

On the following day the members of the agnatic cluster gathered for the 'lineage' feast. The central episode in this ceremony was what Kuckertz calls the 'core ritual', aimed at supplying the troubling ancestor with the 'food' it had requested. This 'food' could either be a necklace made from the tail hairs of a certain cow, an animal killed ritually, or beer drunk in a particular way. The sacrificial victim should ideally be a head of cattle but, in practice, a goat was more often used; in any event it should not be a sheep, for a sheep does not cry out when stabbed. The crying of the victim was essential, for it carried the message from the living to the dead.

The main elements of the lineage feast were the invocation of the ancestors, informing them what was happening; the ritual in the main house, including the burning of meat for the troubling ancestor; the 'core-ritual', through which the afflicted person was healed and where he or she executed an act of reverence; and a common meal shared by all members of the agnatic cluster.

THE TSONGA RITE OF KIN RECONCILIATION

'When two brothers quarrel, when one has sworn that he will never see the other again, when there is disunion between their kraals, they may be brought to the hahla madjieta, not only by the fact that one of them must sacrifice for the other, but simply by the advice of the old men of the family. These old men will say to the divided brothers: "Our gods will punish you if you do not stop quarrelling! They do not like you to curse each other, being brothers. You must be reconciled to each other. Hahletelanan madjieta, viz,: Perform for each other the sacrifice for imprecation". The two brothers decide to follow the advice. The one who pronounced the imprecation prepares a decoction of a special herb called mudahomu, a word which means the grass which the ox eats, because cattle are fond of it. He pours it into a shikamba shansala, that is to say into a broken shell of a fruit called sala (Strychnos), as big as a large orange, and which is frequently used as a drinking vessel. Everybody meets on the hubo, the square of the village, and the two enemies sit in the midst, on the bare ground, and not on a mat. The offender lifts the shell to his lips, takes a sip of the decoction in his mouth, spits it out, making the noise of tsu. This tsu is the sacramental syllable by means of which the Ba-Ronga call their gods to the sacrifice. However, he does not pray to the spirits as is done in regular offerings. He only says: "This is our imprecation! We have pronounced it because our hearts were sore. Today it must come to an end. It is right that we make peace." The other brother, the offended one, then takes the shell in his hand, and having gone through the same rite of the tsu says: "I was justly angry because he offended me. I have been irritated myself also. But let it be ended today; let us eat out of the same spoon and drink out of the same pot and be friends again". Then he breaks the shell ... and they drink beer together. ☐ In this ... case a true sacrifice has been performed and the act of reconciliation bears a strong religious character. The gods have been more or less summoned as witnesses, and the enemies have become friends again because they feared to be punished by the spirits of their ancestors. ☐ But should a man pronounce an imprecation against a stranger, viz, against a man who has not the same ancestors, no such reconciliation would be possible. A man's gods have no reason whatever to interfere with people belonging to another family. The religion of the Ba-Ronga is strictly a family affair. The jusrisdiction of the gods does not extend further than their direct descendants ... and the moral influence is limited, therefore, to the narrow sphere of the family. (Junod 1910: 179–82)

The first part of the lineage feast took place in the cattle byre, especially sacred to the ancestors among Nguni. While the wives of the cluster and adult daughters of the homestead remained in the great hut, the men congregated in the byre where the sacrificial victim was waiting. The ritual began with the throwing of the victim on its right side. The senior man then took the ritual spear and passed it round the animal, between the forelegs, over the head and back and between the hindlegs, until it reached the spot on the stomach where the spear would enter – a symbolic act of consecration. Deep stabbing prevented the beast bleeding externally, for no blood should be spilt. As the animal was stabbed, the ritual elder *(inkulu)* called on the ancestors using the *nqula* praises discussed above, appealing to all the clan dead, wherever they might be, to be present.

The next stage in the ritual shifted emphasis away from the descent group members and ancestors in general to focus more narrowly on the afflicted person and the particular ancestor troubling him. The action now moved from the cattle byre to the main house of the homestead, where the women were waiting. Here the hearth became the centre of ritual action. The ritual elder took some fat, no bigger than a man's thumb, from the entrails and burnt it on the hearth fire. This was the 'food' of the troubling ancestor, belonging solely to it. The fat had to be totally consumed by the fire, thus symbolising the sacred gift to the gods.

The ritual up to this point was performed by the representatives of the group, but the afflicted person had now to become actively involved. For this a second piece of meat was necessary. This was the muscle below the armpit, called *intsonyama*, which was about the size of two hands joined together and of special ritual significance. The *intsonyama* was handed over to the ritual elder and roasted by him on the fire. At the same time the door of the hut was closed and it filled with acrid smoke, said to symbolise the presence of the ancestors. This was the most important moment in the ritual: it was no longer the affair of the agnatic kinsfolk as a group, but of the afflicted person, for the aim of this part of the ceremony was healing.

When the *intsonyama* was sufficiently roasted the ritual elder called the afflicted person to the central hearth. There he or she was made to kneel before him while he cut off a small piece of the ritual meat, about the size of a thumbnail. This the sufferer received on the back of the right hand, arms being held out, crossed, with palms towards the floor. The individual was instructed to 'suck' the meat (actually only touching it with the lips) and throw it over the shoulder towards the back of the house. The discarded meat symbolised the sickness which the person cast out *(ukujula)*.

The patient was then given another piece of the *intsonyama*, received in the same manner as before, but this time it was kept on the back of the hand, while the sufferer sat motionless. At this point the women present ridiculed the sufferer, criticising him or her for disrespect towards the ancestors and lineage members. The patient then ate the meat, whereupon all began a ritualised cheering and ululation, congratulating the individual for having 'eaten the ancestor' – and the door was flung open to let out the smoke. The ritual ended with the eating of the rest of the *intsonyama* by close family members.

The symbolism of the Mpondo ancestral feast has been brilliantly analysed by Kuckertz. The problem of all religions is to make statements about, and influence, the supernatural. Now, the nature of the gods is wholly other than that of this world and this fact must be expressed in metaphor: what more appropriate way of thinking about the sacred than to conceptualise it as the *opposite* of life on earth, as is done in the ritual symbolism we have described. The normal way to deal with meat is to receive it in cupped hands and to eat it. In the ancestor ritual, however, the sufferer takes the *intsonyama* meat on the back of his hands and throws it away. In other words, he 'eats' it, but does not eat it. The word used here means to 'suck', but can also mean to 'drink from dry breasts'. The meal is a sacred meal, in which the normal is symbolically reversed to express the special nature of the occasion. What is also expressed is the guilt that should be experienced by the afflicted persons. They are criticised for having behaved in such a way as to annoy the ancestors, and must express contrition. Parts of the ritual resemble a court case, in which culpability and blame is being allocated by the congregation, and accepted by the sufferer.

Contingent rituals, as their name implies, were *ad hoc* ceremonies for expressing gratitude to the ancestors for some benefit or to mark some special occasion. The main occasions for them among South Nguni were (a) the dedication of an ox to a named ancestor, (b) the killing of a goat to inaugurate a newly built homestead and ask blessings on it, and (c) the slaughtering of a goat or ox in thanksgiving for a safe return from a long journey.

People of the River

In both the extreme north of the country, among Venda, and the extreme south, among Xhosa-speakers, there were beliefs concerning subaquatic beings who lived in rivers or in deep pools. They do not seem to have been connected with the main religion of the ancestors, and were rather differently conceived of as between the two groups. Among Venda these beliefs were associated with the earliest inhabitants of the Soutpansberg, especially the Ngona. Near Sibasa there is a large pool beneath the Phiphidi Falls where the spirits of Ngona autochthones can still be heard dancing under the waters. As Stayt writes: ☐ *'A great many rivers and mountains are supposed to be inhabited by spirits not directly connected with any particular lineage ... There are mountain spirits (zwidhadyani) ... who are mostly of foreign origin, often BaSutho ... In addition to zwidhadyani, there are spirits living in streams and pools, a small war-like people with human form; they are always armed with bows and arrows and ... bring death to anyone who has the misfortune to encounter them.' (Stayt 1931: 238–9)* ☐ *The so-called 'People of the River' (abantu bomlambo) were believed in by all South Nguni. The River People lived in the deep pools of certain rivers, where they had beautifully built homesteads where they kept their herds of dark-coloured cattle. Some say they were fair, with long hair.* ☐ *There was a close association between the River People and human beings, an association which had both a positive and a negative side. On the good side they played an important part in the initiation of diviners (who dreamed of being called down into pools and rivers to meet them); the River People were also closely associated with rain. On the other hand, they were dangerous because they could send an illness, characterised by pains and swelling of the body. They could also cause drownings by calling a person to them: 'They do not really intend to kill him. They call a person because they love him.'* ☐ *A specific ritual, called* ukuhlwayela, *was required in the case of illness caused by the River People. It entailed sacrifice at a pool where the River People were known to live. Small grass baskets (iingobozi) containing small amounts of sorghum, rolled tobacco, pumpkin seeds, white beads and a calabash of beer were floated out onto the surface of the pool. These eventually filled with water and sank, having been taken by the River People. Mpondomise informants told me:* ☐ *'If they call a person into the water they keep him at their home for one or two days and, if those of his home do not bring an offering in the form of a dark beast, they kill him and let him float to the surface. Cattle should be driven into the water where he disappeared. One of the beasts sinks, and the victim comes to the surface alive. The victim may not be able to remember all that happened, but he will always talk of the kindness of the River People and their beautiful country where not a drop of water falls.' [An example of this ritual will be found on p. 186 in 'The Thwasa Dream of a Bhaca Diviner']* ☐ *The messengers of the River People were the crocodile and otter, half land, half water creatures who exhibited in their very being the ambiguous nature of the River People themselves.*

Unfortunately we do not have comparable detail of the ritual for other groups. As we have seen, the Tswana had effectively ceased to perform ancestor rituals when the first anthropologists arrived (this does not mean, of course, that they had stopped believing in them), and the only information we have on the Sotho-Tswana generally is Mönnig's account of the Pedi. Among them, the typical sacrifice was a libation of beer *(phasa)*, which links them to the Sotho-Venda and Venda rather than to the Nguni with their blood sacrifices. *Phasa* was accompanied by prayer, preceded by the saying of the praise-poem *(sereto)* of the particular ancestor. A goat was also killed and its bones placed on the grave.

There is more evidence for the Sotho-Venda. Krige states for the Lovedu:

> The order in which Lovedu ancestors are called upon varies according to the purpose of each occasion. At the annual harvest thank-offering of beer at the shrine of the group of descendants of a common male ancestor four to five generations back, it is the ancestor after whom the shrine is named that is first mentioned, followed by others, as they are remembered, and often including sisters. In a case of sickness, usually only the ancestor whose dissatisfaction has been diagnosed as the cause, is mentioned; in an offering for good luck, perhaps only a deceased parent, who will be asked to invite all the other gods to partake. The Lovedu officiator is usually a female, the father's sister or the sister of the family head or descending kindred; and the prayer is quietly spoken beside the shrine or animal representing an ancestor, *not*, as among the Zulu, shouted out loudly in the cattle kraal. (Krige 1974: 92)

Krige comments on the warmth of the prayers and general atmosphere at Lovedu rituals. Terms of endearment such as 'dear mother', 'dear *malume*' are used, except where there has been tension between worshipper and ancestor in life. As she puts it: 'The phraseology highlights the closeness, warmth and intimacy between the gods and the living.' A typical formula is 'I *approach* you with a head of cattle (or libation).' The word used here is *suma*: 'In the concept *ho suma* is reflected respect for age and authority, the relation of superordination and subordination between generations, as well as the principle of reciprocity' (p. 93).

Among Tsonga, Junod describes the sacrifice as having similar reverential aspects. After the consecration of the offering, with its ritual spitting to expel angry thoughts, the act of dedication of the offering began with the words *'Abusayi! Akhwari!'* ('Gently, smoothly'), 'pronounced with a gentle intonation as if to express deep feeling'. Then came the invocation. If the sacrifice was a piacular one, the responsible ancestor was asked to call all the other ancestors related to him to be present. Ancestors of the father's family could also be summoned, if the sacrifice was being made to those of the mother. The ancestors were entreated to bless the family, to prevent bad feeling or strife, and to effect a cure. As among Nguni, in cases where the misfortune was very great, or where the patient failed to recover, there was an explicit criticism of the gods.

Although the ancestor religion of the Southern Bantu differed somewhat from the so-called 'world religions' – notably in its emphasis on salvation in this life, rather than in the next, together with the fact that membership of worshipping groups was attained through birth, rather than by choice (the religion was, of course, non-proselytising) and the fact that the gods they worshipped were local, rather than universal – at the basis of all their beliefs and activities lay a poignant sense of *dependence* on the supernatural, surely the basis of all religions, everywhere.

THE ROOTS OF BLACK SOUTH AFRICA

CHAPTER 9

WITCHCRAFT, SORCERY AND POLLUTION

SOME ILLNESS and misfortune could be caused by the wrath of the ancestors, as we saw in Chapter 8. Among Southern Bantu there were two other causes of illness: witchcraft and ritual pollution. Although brought together in this chapter, they were very different in their nature. Witchcraft was caused by the machinations of people wishing, for various reasons, to harm others; pollution came from being involved, usually inadvertently, in a particular situation or state that was thought to be mystically contaminating, such as being in contact with a corpse or a menstruating woman. One aspect was common to both, however. Unlike misfortune caused by the ancestors, which, as we have seen, always pointed the blame at the sufferer (for neglect of religious duties) and was therefore merited, witchcraft attacks and pollution came from without so that, in a very definite sense, they were unmerited.

A Tswana diviner interprets his divining bones. The animal skin cap is traditional for all groups. The white bead headdress of Nguni diviners is a modern innovation. (Morris and Levitan 1986)

WITCHCRAFT AND SORCERY

Witchcraft, an all but universal phenomenon, is the (mystical) ability to cause harm to others which is believed to be possessed by certain individuals. Among Southern Bantu, it was believed that these people carried on their work either by changing shape or by becoming invisible, or by sending agents, called 'familiars' by anthropologists, to do their evil deeds. It was this ability which made the witch such a sinister figure, for these activities were beyond normal powers, making the witch highly ambiguous, both human and non-human at the same time.

But there were other individuals who, although not endowed with mystical powers, were also believed to act in an antisocial way. These were those who used medicines and other magical substances to kill or harm others. Unlike witches, who inherited their powers, these others were normal human beings who obtained the medicines from herbalists. Anthropologists have tended to use the term 'witchcraft' for the activities of the first group and 'sorcery' for those of the latter, although the distinction is not always clearly made by the people themselves, since to the victim the effects are the same.

The basic term for witchcraft/sorcery was *ubuthakathi* in Nguni and *boloyi* in Sotho, Venda and Tsonga. If pushed, Nguni distinguished between *ubuthakathi* 'with little animals' (witchcraft) and 'with medicines' (sorcery), while Sotho spoke of 'night *baloyi*' (witches) and 'day *baloyi*' (sorcerers). Generally speaking, witches were believed to be women and sorcerers men. This might have been because sorcery involved the actual buying of medicines from a herbalist, while witchcraft could be practised in secret, from within the demure confines of the domestic unit, and thus be more congenial to women. We shall consider later why women were so often cast in the role of witch.

Witchcraft was inherited, thus running in families, and it was believed that the witch-child was carefully trained in the techniques of her occult trade. To find out whether their child was a witch, Kgaga witch parents were said to throw a newborn baby aginst the hut wall and, if it clung to it like a bat, it was a sure sign that it had inherited the 'gift'. Witches had superhuman qualities. They could fly through the air in a flash of time, could enter a house through a crack in the door, and could plunge their victims into a sleep so deep that they could be sent out wandering into the night, perhaps to a secret rendezvous out in the bush or veld where they were made to dance, egged on by beatings, so that their bodies were bruised and swollen in the morning when they awoke. South Nguni witches were believed to fly through the air in a flying machine made from the ribcage of a dead man. Sotho witches were believed to insert millet and sand into the bodies of their victims, causing intense pain, and also destroyed the crops and fertility of men and stock.

Witches were believed to be gregarious and to seek each other out, often meeting naked at special places in the veld or bush, but, because of their evil and jealous natures, were said to often fight each other to the death with their magic. This propensity to meet together is reminiscent of the covens to which English witches were said to belong and at which the Devil, in the shape of a goat-headed man, was worshipped. Despite this macabre conviviality, however, the actual work of the witch was performed alone and in secret. Tsonga and Venda believed that a witch was unaware of her powers. They maintained that the witch was 'normal' during the day, while at night her witch spirit left her sleeping body and went out naked to perform her nefarious deeds. Nguni and Sotho, on the other hand, believed that the witch was fully conscious of her identity and activities, operating out of sheer malice and intrinsic evil.

Most commonly, the witch used a familiar to do her work. Among the Southern Bantu these tended to be small animals – wildcat, owl, snake, polecat – which were kept and fed by the witch. It is not certain whether these were conceived of as being real animals or not. Certainly they could go about invisible, so presumably they were not. The South Nguni were unique in their extreme elaboration of the idea of the familiar. Unlike the animal familiars of even their culturally closest relatives, the Zulu (who spoke of the wildcat and owl), they had a whole bestiary of mythical monsters. Perhaps the best known of these was the *thikoloshe* (which was later adopted by the South Sotho as *tokolose* (the *tokolosie* of Afrikaans folklore). *Thikoloshe* was a small hairy man, about the height of a person's knee, with exaggerated sexual features. It was kept in a store hut by female witches who used it as a sexual partner; sometimes frigidity in a woman was said to be caused by her harbouring it as a lover. *Thikoloshe* were regarded as fairly harmless and herdboys sometimes reported meeting them out in the veld, and even playing with them. They were particularly mischievous and had a penchant for stealing milk from cows.

Perhaps the most feared familiar among South Nguni was the *impundulu*, or lightning bird. It was associated with thunder, and lightning was the laying of its eggs. It could be sent to cause miscarriages, blindness and death to people and stock. It sucked blood from its victims, causing long, wasting illnesses, accompanied by coughing, stabbing pains and shortness of breath. It could turn into a beautiful young man with whom the witch had sexual intercourse. *Umamlambo* was a familiar owned by men. It was a charm, bought from a herbalist, but was also a snake that had the power to change shape, appearing as 'a baby, a beautiful woman, a variegated charm, a tin or a mirror'. *Ichanti* was also a snake that had the power to change shape. 'A man goes to the river and sees a tin dish. As he is looking it turns into a hat and then into a bullock chain', informants told Monica Wilson (Hunter 1936: 286). Any person who saw an *ichanti* fell ill and would die unless treated. Other South Nguni familiars were the baboon, on whose back witches were said to ride backwards (Venda witches used the hyena for this perpose), and the *impaka*, a small rodent sent by its owner to bite people's throats.

Among Sotho and Venda familiars were usually animals. Pedi witches used the baboon, polecat, wild cat, dog, snake, owl and bat, while Venda familiars were typically the hyena, weasel, crocodile and all snakes, except the python. The belief system of the (Sotho-Venda) Kgaga of the lowveld is fairly well documented. Apart from snakes and owls, the majority of their familiars were small carnivorous mammals: the small spotted genet (*Genetta felina pulchra*), the Cape polecat (*Ictonys striatus*), the banded mongoose (*Mungos mungo*) and the African snake weasel (*Poecilogale albinuca*). Of the larger animals, the hyena and the baboon were also sometimes used. What is striking about the smaller animals is that they are all characterised by dark stripes running longitudinally along the body, although, in the case of the genet, these are formed of dark brown reddish spots which tend to unite into stripes. The hyena, too, is spotted. A possible reason why these particular animals were selected to express the evil in witchcraft is that they are all highly ambiguous. Their two families – Viverridae (polecats, genets and mongooses) and Hyaenidae (hyenas) – have both cat-like and dog-like characteristics. The hyena, in addition, was believed, all through Africa, to be hermaphroditic because of the peniform clitoris and false scrotum of the female which made the sexes impossible to distinguish apart. Anthropologists have found that, all over the world, animals that do not fit into clear classificatory categories tend to be singled out to symbolise important religious concepts. What symbol more appropriate than these ferocious, ambiguous creatures – which, in addition, are strictly nocturnal, as are the witches themselves?

These familiars were not real animals, and they could change into human form in order to have sexual relations with their owners. But owning a familiar could be very dangerous, especially if one did not know how to feed it properly, for it could turn on one in anger. It should be fed on soft porridge, meat, milk, and, sometimes, human flesh. Some familiars demanded human blood, which could only be obtained by killing someone. The South Nguni *umamlambo* demanded the death of a close kinsman before it would work for its owner.

In addition to the belief in familiars, all Southern Bantu held that witches dig up corpses and use these zombies to work in their fields, as well as to harm intended victims. South Nguni called these creatures *izithunzela* and said that a witch would cut out the tongue and drive a wooden peg through their brains to make them tractable.

The belief in familiars seems to be common to many witch belief systems and was especially characteristic of seventeenth century English witchcraft.

As we have seen, the main differences between a witch and sorcerer were the latter's use of medicines and the fact that the sorcerer was an ordinary person, without the ability to change shape or become invisible. These medicines could include poisons, which were dropped in food, or substances placed on a path to be 'picked up' by passers-by. Sorcerers often used bodily exuviae, such as nail

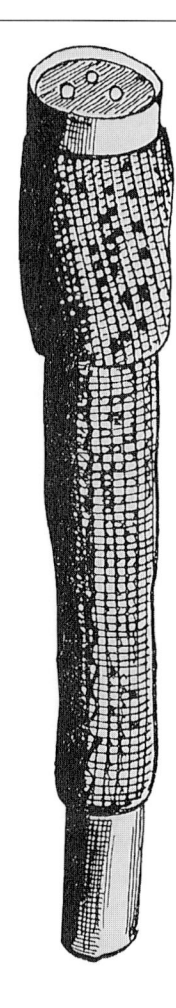

A Tsonga flute sounded to drive away thunderstorms. It is made of a five-inch hollow bone covered with leguaan skin and stopped at the wider end with a black wax-like substance, said to be obtained from the flesh of a lightning bird (*ndlati*), set with three seeds of the lucky bean.

parings and hair clippings, or even earth from footprints, to harm their victims. An elderly Kgaga told me: 'If I spit on the ground the *moloyi* might take my spittle, or my urine from behind the homestead [the usual place for urination]'. Among Mpondo, any hair cut off the body was carefully hidden in tufts of long grass and great care was taken by Xhosa and Thembu to hide the severed foreskins of circumcision initiates in ant heaps – all to prevent these body parts falling into the hands of sorcerers.

But sickness could also be caused by the sorcerer's medicines alone, even without the incorporation into them of parts of the victim. A common method of bewitchment involved chewing the medicines, then spitting them out and calling the victim's name. An Mpondo sorcerer took medicines and roasted them on the lid of a pot, then, dipping his spear in boiling water, put his fingers in the medicine and touched his lips, calling on the name of the person he wished to harm, and ending by hurling his spear through a rent in the wall, not through the door. It was believed that when the spear touched the ground the victim would begin to feel pain and that night would dream of being stabbed, and wake up the next morning coughing blood. Another method was to grind a dried chameleon into powder and mix it with a person's food or urine, causing him to waste away. Sometimes merely pointing with a finger in the direction of the victim was all that was required.

The only protection against witchcraft and sorcery was in the use of strong protective medicines, although, because witchcraft was believed to work only over short distances, it could be avoided by moving away to another area. The most basic precaution was to fence the homestead against attack, and for this the services of a herbalist were required.

Details of treatment vary, but among South Nguni, for example, *intelezi* (medicines to make things slippery) were mixed with water and sprinkled around the boundries of the homestead while other medicines were burnt in every hut and in the cattle byre. The inhabitants were also scarified and powdered medicines were rubbed in the cuts. Wooden pegs, rubbed with medicine and the fat of a black sheep, were driven into the ground in the spaces between the huts. Blood or fat was a necessary ingredient of protective medicines. On the day after the protective treatment, the people of the homestead washed and the huts were swept. Some of the medicine was left with the homestead head so that he might repeat the treatment from time to time. It was believed that the medicine placed between the huts acted like an invisible net to catch familiars or witches seeking to gain entry. Lightning, thought of as an attack by the *impundulu*, was greatly feared, and one of the most important precautions a man had to take was the protection of his homestead against it.

The Sotho also used medicines to protect their homes, but in addition made extensive use of urine. Witches were believed to have *fiša* (ritual heat) and cooling urine was believed to kill familiars if poured over them. Urine also weakened harmful medicines and, if sprinkled round a homestead, made it appear to an approaching witch or familiar that the area was surrounded by a sheet of water, and thus inaccessible. In addition to the general magical protection of homesteads, personal charms and medicines were used by individuals against witchcraft and sorcery.

The terrible thing about a witch was that it could be anyone. Typically there were no special signs or characteristics that could serve as a distinguishing mark. This was indeed disconcerting. The neighbour who greeted you in a friendly way at a beer-drink, the friend of your youth who had attended the same initiation school

A Zulu woman diviner *(isangoma)* preparing to dance.

(and thus called you 'brother'), the young wife in your homestead, married to your son – all these could be plotting your destruction. For the essential malignity of witchcraft and sorcery was that witches and sorcerers tended to harm people close to them, people like kin and neighbours, whom, in any normal society, one should love, cherish and co-operate with. What these evil-doers did was to overturn normal morality, and the basic values on which it was built. It is not surprising, then, that the image of the witch developed by these societies was grotesque and so often thought of in terms of inversions. South Nguni witches rode backwards on their baboon familiars, and it was widely believed that witches approached their victims' homes backwards. Witches worked at night, when all reasonable people are asleep; they went about naked, thus shamelessly flouting normal conventions of propriety; they killed babies and ate human flesh; they cohabited with animals. Worst of all, they harmed kinsmen and neighbours. All this was the reverse of normal human society: the very opposite of the 'good'; the upsetting of the essential balance of the universe.

The witch or sorcerer, then, was a feared and hated figure. He or she was the very image of the traitor within the gates, the quisling, the heretic. Witches as a category were a veritable fifth column in society. As such, they had to be identified and eradicated as soon as possible. Their identification was the task of the diviner, whose role in this important matter will be discussed in the next chapter.

The reaction to a discovered witch was violent. The culprit was put to death,

ALBERTI'S DESCRIPTION OF XHOSA WITCH-FINDING; 1807

'The whole tribe assembles and the female magician [diviner] proceeds alone to a hut in which she pretends to sleep, in order to see the malevolent magician [witch] in her dreams. During this period there is dancing, singing and clapping for about an hour. Thereupon the men advance to the front of the hut in which the magician is present, and beg her to come out, which she at first refuses to do, until a number of javelins [assegais] have been given to her as a present. ☐ She colours the periphery of her eye, the arm and the leg, white on the left side and black on the right. Only her hips are encircled with a covering when she emerges from the hut with the javelins which she received in her hand. Thereupon she is instantly covered with mantles and surrounded by the crowd. Somebody then demands that the name of the malevolent magician be made known, which demand the diviner apparently tries to elude, on the pretext of her slight skill. Finally she casts off the mantles with which she is covered, runs about amongst the horde, by throwing a javelin ahead of her to open the path, and then beats one or the other with the haft of such javelin, whereby she indicates the discovery of the witch. ☐ Now someone lays hold of the alleged witch. But before proceeding to his punishment, the diviner must establish her denunciation by indicating where the magical charms, which the person has used, are kept. She is, therefore, accompanied to the place which she has indicated, and where she then produces a human skull, a piece of meat, which she passes off as human flesh, or something else of the kind, and now the deed is irrefutably proved. Thereupon the chief of the tribe confers with his officials concerning the type of punishment to be meted out to the victim, which generally consists of placing him on his back, fastening his arms and legs to poles thrust in the ground, and then bringing a bag containing a mass of a type of large black ant. These are placed on the eyes, armpits, sides and stomach, which have been moistened with water, causing unbearable pain and the swelling of the whole body. Another punishment consists of laying stones heated in a fire against his sides and stomach. Both this and the previously-mentioned punishment often result in death. When this is not the case, the supposed witch is expelled from the tribe. At times the death sentence is imposed and carried out with knobkirries. In every case, the hut of such an unfortunate is burnt down and his cattle and other possessions become the property of the chief of the tribe ... For this reason it also happens that someone, who chances to be the owner of a goodly sized herd of cattle, is denounced as a witch, at the instigation of the chief or his officials.' (Alberti 1815: 49–50)

A Zulu diviner dancing to the clapping of members of the homestead who have called her in to diagnose an illness.

either by spearing, clubbing, strangulation, or, as among the Zulu, impaled on a stake. The South Nguni pegged a discovered witch to the ground and covered the culprit with water and honey: thereafter a nest of vicious black ants was broken over her so that she was bitten to death. In addition, the homesteads of Nguni witches were set alight and their whole families burnt to death, for, as we have seen, witchcraft was inherited and the evil should be eradicated root and branch. Tsonga witches were either impaled or drowned. The reaction to a witch was essentially a public execution, for among Southern Bantu witchcraft and treason were the chief capital crimes. A witch execution has been likened to a morality play. In it, the community as a whole rose up in righteous indignation against this attack on its integrity and symbolically (and literally) destroyed the evil element in its midst. In a very definite sense the witch-sorcerer was evil personified.

Not all the groups, though, reacted to a discovered witch or sorcerer in quite such a dramatic manner. The Kriges state that, among the Lovedu, 'only a small proportion of cases of witchcraft lead to an open accusation', but witchcraft was undoubtedly the major explanation for illness and misfortune among the Southern Bantu generally. According to Dudley Kidd, before annexation one person was put to death for witchcraft in Pondoland every day, and, even if this is a gross exaggeration, it gives some idea of the salience of the belief in traditional thought.

All over the world the logic behind beliefs in witchcraft and sorcery rests on the assumption that there is no such thing as chance in life. In southern Africa it was believed that all events were caused, and the prime cause of sickness and misfortune was the witch. Here we can usefully distinguish between an *immediate* cause and an *ultimate* cause. Suppose, to take a famous example from Evans-Pritchard's book on the Azande of the Sudan, a man is sitting under a granary and its supports collapse so that he is crushed to death. The Azande are perfectly aware that the immediate cause of the death was the collapse of the granary (or perhaps the activity of termites) – but they are not satisfied with this explanation. They ask further questions: Why was *this* man, and not another, sitting under the granary when it fell? Why did it fall *then*? After all, the shade cast by granaries makes them particularly congenial resting places, so that most people at some time or another are at risk. Western science has no answer to this question. It has to bring in the concept of 'chance' or 'luck' or 'fate' (in actual fact an admission of ignorance) which is not, psychologically, a very satisfactory response. Most people want to know, Why me? or Why now?; to impose *meaning* on things that happen to them. Witch beliefs not only provided a full explanation of the personal, the ultimate, cause, but also provided means for doing something about it.

Against this can be set the social disruption caused by witchcraft accusations. Anyone could be accused, and the paranoia engendered by the belief in invisible enemies who, at the same time, could be close associates, could degenerate into hysterical 'witchhunts' that could tear communities apart. The first question that came into the mind of people told that their troubles were being caused by witchcraft or sorcery was, in fact, not Why me? but 'Who'? Given the belief that major misfortune was caused by evilly disposed *people*, it was obviously imperative to discover who they were. They therefore scanned the range of their associates for the possible culprit – and the person their suspicions were likely to fall on was someone whom they believed had a grudge against them, or hated them for some reason or other. What is more probable, though, is that the person they suspected was someone *whom they themselves hated*, and on whom they projected their negative feelings.

The reason for this hatred was typically to be found in the competition over scarce resources. Harmonious social life was constantly being threatened by such negative emotions as envy, jealousy and pride, which are present in every community, however well integrated. After all, the good and desirable things in life are always in short supply. There are never enough fine cattle, fertile plots or beautiful women to go round so that competition is endemic to the human condition. This is the seedbed in which witchcraft and sorcery beliefs have their origin and in which they flourish. The Southern Bantu were aware of this and witches and sorcerers were believed to be motivated by envy and jealousy.

If this was so, we should expect to find that certain people were at risk of being accused of witchcraft. Such people would be those standing in a relationship to another that generated competition. But not only that. There should *also* be bonds uniting them in some way, resulting in an essentially ambivalent relationship of conflicting emotions. There is much evidence from southern Africa that this was indeed the case.

Among Nguni, with their strong exogamy rules, a daughter-in-law was the person most likely to be accused of witchcraft if a member of the homestead fell ill. The tense relations here were between the bride and her parents-in-law and between daughters-in-law and their sisters-in-law. As we have seen, among Nguni domestic and kinship life centred around the local cluster of agnatic kinsmen. This tight group was subjected to strong pressure to present a united front to the world, but, as Gluckman has shown (1955: 98–9), in practice there was rivalry and animosity between them, often over the apportionment of the family herd. Now it is clear that these conflicts could not be expressed openly by means of witchcraft

SOUTHERN NGUNI

1. Garden basket (ingobozi)
2. Watertight basket (isitya) for beer.
3. Foodmat (isithebe) used to catch ground meal from the grinding stones, or for serving food.
4. Oxhorn spoon (ukhezo) for eating sour milk.
5. Calabash flask (igula) for sour milk.
6. Foodmat, see no. 3.
7. Fringed apron worn by girls and women.
8. Beadwork necklet.
9. Necklet of scented tambuti wood (Spirostachys africana).
10. Tobacco pipe.
11. Tobacco pipe.
12. Long tobacco pipe smoked by women.
13. Pipe decorated with metal, inlaid.
14. Fighting stick (intongazana) with protective cloth, used by youths for stick fights.
15. Spear, for throwing.
16. Spear, for throwing.
17. Beaded gourd snuffbox.
18. Blue German-print cloth, sold in trading stores.
19. Snuff-box made of a paste of scrapings from the flesh-side of a newly flayed skin mixed with clay and blood. This was spread over a modelled clay figure and left to dry. An aperture was cut and the clay removed, leaving a hollow receptacle for snuff.
20. Snuff-box, see no. 19.
21. Bone snuff-spoon.
22. Ivory snuff-spoons.
23. Beaded pin used to decorate headdress, or as a pipe

Witchcraft, Sorcery and Pollution

cleaner.
24. Penis sheath of mongoose skin, worn by youths.
25. Ivory arm-bands (**umxhaka**) worn by distinguished men.
26. Necklet of bone carved to resemble claws, and glass beads.
27. Necklet of Nerita shells, which were prized.
28. Bag for pipe and tobacco.
29. Headband (**ingcaca**) of cowrie shells. This was a special ornament worn on important occasions.
30. Swallow-tail apron worn by women, probably early nineteenth century.
31. Arm ornament.
32. Arm ornament.
33. Women's anklets.

(South African Museum)

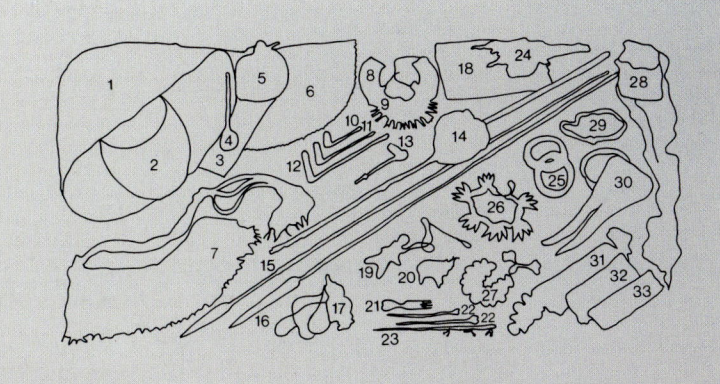

accusations without disrupting the group and damaging its good name in the eyes of the community (especially as witchcraft was believed to be inherited, so that if one was tainted by it, all were). A scapegoat had to be found. This is the reason why the stranger-wife was so often cast in the role of witch. Actually, as Gluckman has pointed out, these wives were, in truth, a disruptive influence, for it was through them and their children that men wanted to become independent of their fathers and brothers: '... the growth in numbers of the group through the women who bear its children both strengthens the group and introduces dissension into it; and the wives are the focus of the two conflicting processes'.

Accusations were also common between Nguni co-wives. In the polygynous family, the various wives and their children formed independent cells or 'houses', each with its own cattle and property, and there was frequent competition between houses for status and inheritance. Wives were ever on the lookout for husbandly favouritism either for another wife or for her children.

Among Sotho and Venda, as we should expect from their encouragement of cousin marriage, wives were not typically accused. After all, they came from well-known families which were also linked to one as maternal kin. Here conflict between co-wives seems to have been more common, followed by accusations between husband and wife. Unlike Nguni, among whom by far the majority of accused were women, Sotho-Venda, at least, thought that both men and women were equally liable to harm one. Sotho appear to have feared sorcery far more than they did witchcraft; this was reversed among Nguni.

It would seem that, generally speaking, these beliefs in witchcraft and sorcery served two major functions. Firstly, they provided an explanation for illness and misfortune that both clearly indicated a cause and also provided means of dealing with it. Secondly, the beliefs shifted the blame for misfortune from the shoulders of the ancestors to those of the witches. In other words, witchcraft beliefs had what theologians call a 'theodetical' function. Theodicy refers to the philosophical problem, especially urgent in monotheistic religions, of how an all-good, all-powerful god can allow evil to occur. There is, in fact no answer to this problem. Christianity and Judaism have attempted to solve it by postulating a powerful counter-force (the Devil) to explain evil, or by teaching that God's will and actions are so far above man's that they are unknowable and must be accepted with religious resignation. The Southern Bantu sought to protect their ancestors from this dilemma, and created the image of the witch to do so. Beliefs in witchcraft and sorcery, then, can be seen also as part of their religious system.

POLLUTION BELIEFS

Up to now, we have considered illness and misfortune caused by ancestors and witch-sorcerers and, to the very limited extent that this was so, by God. In all these cases the agency of causation was thought of in personal terms. Ancestors, witches and God were intelligent beings who *decided* to act in the way they did. But, among all Southern Bantu, there was a further cause of illness, this time operating independently of human or spiritual volition, that was the result of an individual's being in a specific dangerous state, often through no fault of his or her own. These states may be thought of as states of pollution. They are all 'mystical', and had to be removed as quickly as possible, by rituals or medicines.

Among Venda, purifications were performed at birth, after the birth of twins, after an abortion, after illness, after a crime and after a burial. There is evidence of a

Thembu diviners and their novitiates gathered at a ceremony to initiate new members. (Alice Mertens)

fear of 'heat', as when twins were put to death and buried in damp earth to 'cool' them, but generally the removal of pollution involved the use of medicines and rituals of washing, suggesting that pollution among Venda was thought of as *dirt*.

As far as the Tsonga are concerned, their ethnographer, Junod, lists the following as the five main causes of pollution: the menstrual flow, the lochia, sickness, death and the birth of twins. Of these, the last was the most serious as it affected the cosmic forces, especially rain. People contaminated by these states were regarded as temporarily marginal to society and were subjected to various taboos, particularly concerning sexual intercourse. The removal of the pollution state was accomplished by means of a ritual sexual act performed without seminal emission, or by 'exposure to the vapours and fumes emanating from cooked and burnt medicines, aspersions made with a decoction obtained from the same drugs, incisions with or without inoculation with medicinal powders, rubbing, the cutting of the hair and nails'.

Information on pollution beliefs is much fuller for Nguni and Sotho, especially the latter. Among Nguni it was the Zulu who seem to have developed the concept furthest, for the South Nguni had only the concept of *umlaza*. This was the ritual impurity associated with the sexual functions of women and with death. Among Mpondo, for instance, a woman had *umlaza* during her periods until she washed after the flow had ceased, after a miscarriage, for approximately one month after the death of husband or child, and after normal sexual intercourse until she washed. A man had *umlaza* for a month after the death of his wife or child, and after sex until he had washed. Contact with a polluted woman made a man 'soft' and easily defeated in combat. Meat of an animal which had died of disease, pork, and honey caused *umlaza* in those who ate them, until they had washed. *Umlaza* was dangerous to cattle, women and medicines (whose strength they nullified) and also to sick people. Thus a woman of child-bearing age avoided walking through the herd of her homestead and a man with *umlaza* could not enter the cattle byre. No one with *umlaza* could drink sour milk, neither could a polluted person touch medicines. South Nguni, like the Venda, thus thought of pollution as a form of dirt.

This was also so among Zulu. Zulu conceived of pollution in terms of 'darkness' (*umnyama, umswazi*) which seems to have had dirt-like qualities. As Harriet Ngubane writes: 'Among the Zulu pollution is essentially a happening associated with "birth" on the one hand and "death" on the other ... it is viewed as a marginal state between life and death ... *Umnyama* is conceptualized as a mystical force which diminishes resistance to disease, and creates conditions of poor luck, misfortune, "disagreeableness" and "repulsiveness" whereby people round the patient take a dislike to him ... in the worst form it is contagious' (Ngubane 1977: 77). *Umnyama* was typically associated with a woman who had recently given birth, a menstruating woman and with a girl who became pregnant before marriage. In all these cases the main danger was to men, whose virility suffered through contact. 'Blackness' could also be caused through contact with a corpse and a homicide was highly polluted. The darkness caused by the death of a homestead head was removed by the ceremony of 'washing the spears', which involved a ritual hunt; that of a widow by washing. But the technique mainly used by Zulu to expel pollution was through the use of enemas and emetics. There is some evidence that 'heat' was also a form of pollution among Zulu, but it was minor. It seems to have been mainly associated with the anger of men and the sexual act.

But it was perhaps among the Sotho-speaking peoples that the concept of pollution reached its greatest elaboration. Among them the metaphor used for thinking abour pollution was *heat*, usually referred to as *fiša*. There were slight differences of emphasis between groups. Here one representative example will be

---

HEAT AND COLD AS METAPHORS FOR EVIL

The use of the metaphor of heat, by Sotho, to express ideas of ritual pollution finds an echo in the Christian picture of hell as a place of eternal fire. ☐ The choice of this image would appear to be related, in both cases, to general ecological factors. What separates human beings from other members of the animal kingdom more than any other factor is their self-awareness. More specifically, only man is aware that he must die, a knowledge which is potentially psychologically destructive. It would seem that one of the main tasks of all religions is to provide some way of overcoming death. This is done, typically, by denying it, usually by postulating a fundamental opposition between the ordinary, everyday, secular world and another world (often referred to as the 'supernatural'), which is wholly other, set apart, holy. Death, then, is interpreted as a passage from one world to the next. From this derives the almost universal belief in the existence of an immortal 'soul', independent of the body. ☐ This other world is invisible and ultimately unknowable through direct experience. Yet it must be thought about, and mortals must enter into a relationship with it. To do this symbols are necessary, appropriate metaphors that express religious truths in evocative images. One such abstract idea is that of evil, misfortune, and (in the Christian worldview) damnation. How should this be conceptualised? ☐ It is striking that, among the pagan peoples of northern Europe, hell was thought of in terms of snow and ice. The Norse Niflheimr, also called Hel, was an underworld of cold and darkness, that vividly expressed the extreme discomforts of the long sub-Arctic winters. Those religions originating in the Middle East, on the other hand, all stress the torments of thirst and the tortures of extreme heat. In both cases, the symbol is poignantly appropriate.

discussed, that of the Kgaga, who live in the lowveld, near Tzaneen, and who belong to the category I have called Sotho-Venda.

Literally translated, *fiša* meant a state of hotness. This might be brought on by a number of factors, chief of which was contact with death or with a woman who was in an 'abnormal' sexual condition. Associated with *fiša* were certain other mystical states, each with its specific name, caused either by 'heat' or through contact with a sinister and contagious force known as 'shadow' (not the shadow of *isithunzi* or *seriti*, see Chapter 8). The term *go fiša* meant 'to be hot'. It could be used both in a literal sense, as when someone was suffering from a fever, or in a figurative one. Babies were also believed to suffer from heat, in the literal sense, precipitated by what was called 'fontanelle trouble', a depression of the fontanelle caused by dehydration. The usual cure for these types of *fiša* was medicinal, especially the leaves of an acid-tasting bush called *mokgalakane*, which were boiled in water and given to the patient to drink.

The *symbolic* meaning of *fiša*, however, was much more extensive. It seemed to have clustered round the following areas:

(a) The death of a close relative, especially of a spouse or child.

(b) Certain types of sexual contact, for instance, during menstruation and suckling, caused the husband to become *fiša*. Men who had sexual intercourse with such a woman became 'blocked' and were unable to pass water or defecate, a condition which could be fatal. A man in such a condition should not have contact with a young baby, nor should he slaughter an animal for a feast such as a wedding or funeral as the meat would cause those eating it to suffer stomach cramps and diarrhoea.

(c) A pregnant woman was *fiša*. She should not enter a room where there was a sick person, nor might she fondle small children.

(d) A miscarriage was perhaps the most dreaded cause of *fiša*, for, if a foetus was not properly buried, wide-ranging effects might be felt in the country as a whole. Junod, writing in 1910, describes how his informants told him that if a woman had had a miscarriage and concealed it, hot winds would blow and dry out the country, the hidden foetus preventing the rain clouds forming. As the Kgaga told him 'this woman has committed a great wrong. She has spoiled the country of the chief, for she has hidden blood which will never again come together to make a person' (Junod 1910: 140). Men were sent throughout the chiefdom to try and identify the culprit who was then arrested and forced to point out where the foetus was buried. Once found, the offending object had to be subjected to ritual purification. This took place at two levels. The place where it was buried was opened up and aspersed with a decoction made of two types of root. Some of the earth was thrown into a river, and river water was sprinkled over the place so that 'the country will be wet'. In addition, all the women of the chiefdom were summoned to the capital, each bearing a pellet of earth containing menstrual blood, which was then ground to powder and sprinkled onto the earth by young boys and girls of pre-pubertal age (and thus sexually pure), especially at river fords and on the approaches to Kgaga territory. As they did so they called out, 'Rain! Rain!'

A miscarriage caused both the mother and father to be *fiša*. The foetus had to be carefully disposed of in a small clay pot in a damp spot on the river bank. Some strands of river weed were tied round its arms, neck, wrists and ankles and the mother filled in the small grave with damp soil.

(e) Twins were *fiša*. The second to appear was put to death, and buried in the shade of the house eaves.

(f) Finally, people returning from a journey were *fiša*, caused by contagion arising from contact with strangers, and the friction caused by the travelling itself.

Fiša, as a state of hotness, had to be cooled. This was effected by using certain herbs, mixed with water; by administering *tšhidi* medicines burnt to a black soot, mixed with saliva; or performing rituals containing the elements of washing, aspersing or drinking infusions. The symbolism here concentrated on cooling water (including saliva) or soot (ash), a 'tamed' form of fire that was used against fire itself in a homeopathic way.

In addition to *fiša*, there were other states of ritual impurity which were equally dangerous. One of these was *makgoma* (from the word 'to touch'). It was caused by sexual contact with someone who had been bereaved or who had suffered a miscarriage or abortion, but it could also be caused by someone eating of the first-fruits before they were ritually 'bitten' by the chief. Symptoms of *makgoma* were fever, tiredness and irritability, lack of appetite and gastric disorders. Treatment was by smearing with *tšhidi* medicines and bathing the victim in water containing them. The most striking aspect of *makgoma* was its contagiousness.

A further pollution state was *magaba*, especially associated with newly born children and characterised by foaming at the mouth and feverishness. If not treated it could prove fatal. It was believed to be caused by the displeasure of the father's sister or the grandparents, often because of a failure to name the child after the relative concerned. Treatment consisted of drinking an infusion made from the roots of a certain tree, or a mixture of sorghum and pieces of white, crystalline stone called *magakabje*, often accompanied by a libation of water (not beer), made not at the family shrine but in the veld (for the troubling relatives were still living and not ancestors).

Finally, there was the concept of *sefifi* or *senyama* ('darkness'). This resulted from having contact with a widow or widower. The symptoms were loss of hair, coughing and swelling of the body. Victims withdrew from society and became introverted. *Sefifi* was said to be caused by the shadows of dead people that were picked up along the way as one travelled, causing 'heaviness'. The cure for *sefifi* was to steam the victim under a structure of poles covered with skins. An infusion of herbs was placed on the fire, with *magakabye* crystals, so that the vapours were inhaled.

The Sotho concept of pollution as 'heat' may have been due to the fact that they inhabited the interior plateau of South Africa in which drought was an ever-present possibility. 'Heat', then, would have been an appropriate way of thinking about, and dealing with, heat-caused illnesses. On the other hand, coolness, water, dampness, all could be used as potent metaphors for thinking about and counteracting the heat. It is not surprising that the medicines and rituals used to remove heat should all stress coolness and the use of cooling media. This was, in fact, a constant theme that infused the whole set of concepts, indeed also including ideas about ancestors and witches. The pouring of cool water on the ancestor shrine, and the variations on this theme, such as watered gruel, beer, and so on, all related at root to the cooling properties of water. As we have seen, protection from the attack of witches involved urine and *tšhidi* medicines, so that the themes of ancestors, witches and pollution were linked at this level.

In the anti-*fiša* rituals themselves the four dominant cooling substances appear to have been water, chyme (the green, undigested stomach contents), ash and soot. Water, perhaps the basic metaphor, formed a set with a series of other liquids including beer, gruel, saliva and urine. These liquids could be handled in a number

A Thembu diviner dressed in the beadwork typical of present-day Nguni custom. Before trade beads were introduced Nguni diviners were dressed like the diviner on page 172. (Alice Martens)

of ways: drunk in infusions, used in washing, poured on shrines, or the patient could be bathed in them or submerged in river water. By extension, objects could be buried in damp earth, as in the case of the aborted foetus and twins. Water was also associated with steaming procedures and the sprinkling of the sufferer with it and with medicines. Chyme, used in connection with certain funeral ceremonies, was valued for its cooling properties and was also used, mixed with mud and liquid dung, in the making of shrines (the ancestors must be kept 'cool') and smeared on branches to block the gateway of a homestead against a returning ghost. Perhaps the most interesting symbol of all was that of ash, denatured fire and thus the 'opposite' of heat.

The three sets of beliefs that have been discussed in this chapter were all part of indigenous ideas of illness and bad health. Which particular one was the cause in any particular instance had to be determined. This was the task of the healers, the diviners and herbalists, to a consideration of which we must now turn.

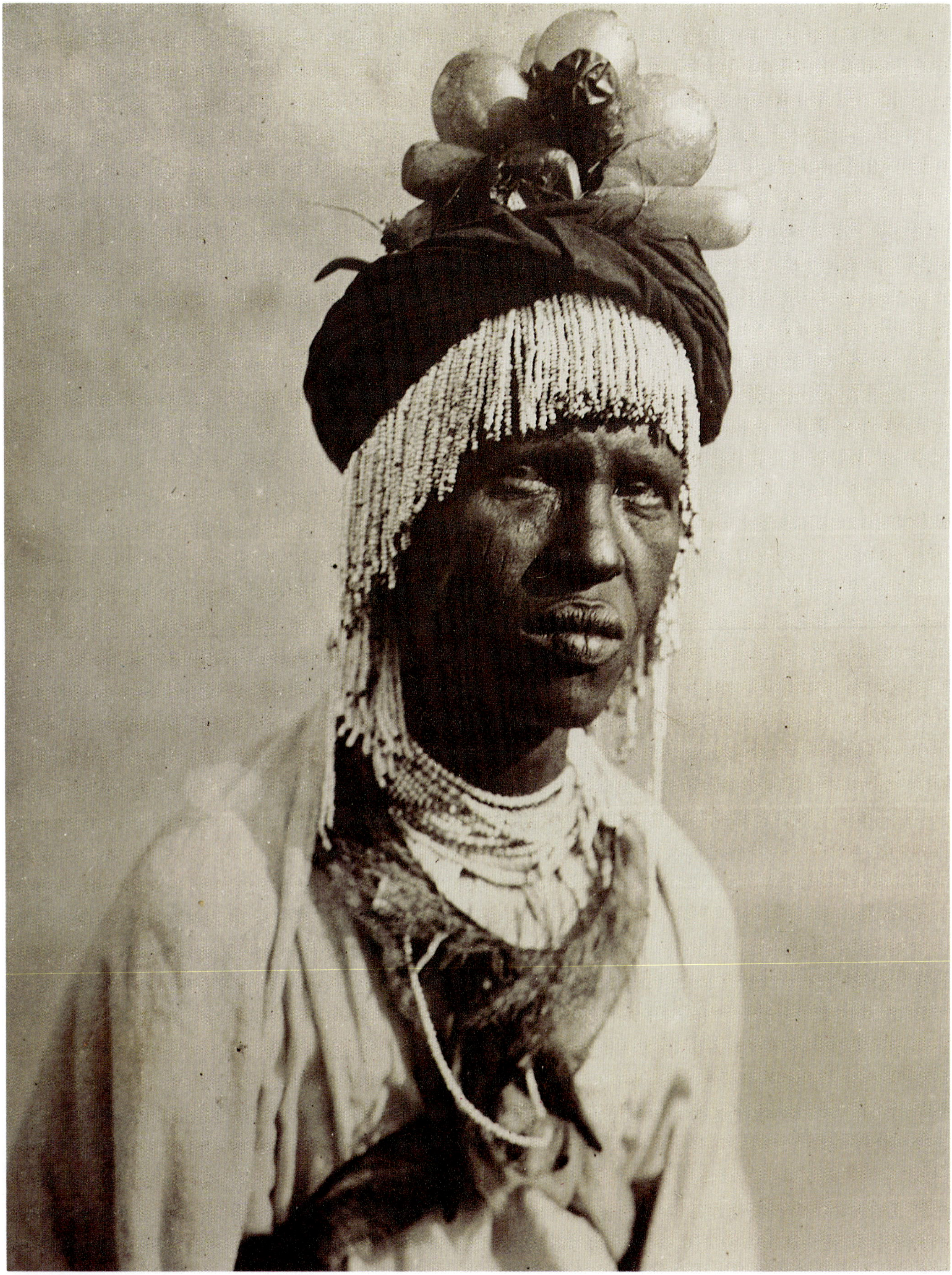

Chapter 10

The Search for Health

It is clear from the previous two chapters that health was a major preoccupation of the people of southern Africa. Although Alberti reported the apparent absence of serious diseases among Xhosa in 1801, this was certainly not true of groups living in the Transvaal lowveld, where malaria, sleeping sickness and other tropical diseases have always been endemic.

The great importance of health was reflected in the fact that healing was linked with the system of religion – which, as we have seen, included witchcraft beliefs as an explanation of evil. Pollution beliefs were not part of the religious system and, with their concept of contagion, indeed bore some resemblance to scientific concepts of infection, although the theory behind them was, of course, quite different.

Generally speaking, there is no doubt that indigenous knowledge of anatomy and physiology was very limited, and mainly gleaned from the slaughter of cattle and small stock. There were names for all the most important bodily organs, although people were not always sure of their location or physiological function. The Lovedu, for example, associated the stomach and intestines with digestion, the bladder with urine and the genitals with reproduction, but also believed in the existence of an internal snake which was closely associated with fertility and childbirth. Internal snakes were believed to inhabit the body of every individual, and stomach cramps and dysentery were explained by their movement or 'biting'. There was no knowledge of the circulation of the blood, although blood was an important concept in medical theory, in much the same way as the 'Humours' were in early western medical thinking. The state of the blood was believed to be the cause of most ills. Among Lovedu, rheumatism, stiffness, or a pain or swelling in any part of the body was attributed to blood that had collected there, or to blood that was 'boiling', thus making the body feverish. Swellings of all kinds were therefore cupped, and blood-letting as a cure for headaches was as popular among Lovedu as it was in nineteenth century Europe. Yet the beating of the heart was not thought to be continuous: it became apparent only in illness or after a sudden fright. The Lovedu used the same term for veins, sinews and muscles, and their different functions were not clearly perceived.

As far as psychological illnesses were concerned, these do not seem to have been clearly associated with the central nervous system. There was no idea of psychologically caused disease and manifestations of functional paralysis, hypertension, palpitations, tachycardia, hysteria, dizziness, and so on, were explained in terms of witchcraft or sorcery, pollution or ancestral visitation, and treated symptomatically. True psychotic states were usually explained as being caused by God, or the

A Bhaca healer-diviner (isangoma). Most Nguni diviners were female and were greatly revered as spirit mediums through whom the ancestral spirits spoke. The white clothes and beads have symbolic significance as white is the colour of the ancestors. The inflated gall bladders are from goats ritually killed at seances. (A.M. Duggan-Cronin)

ancestors, and were greatly feared. Pedi, for instance, identified four types of madness caused by the heart of the afflicted person being filled with blood, water or a white substance, or by a worm in the brain.

Given this unfamiliarity with the workings of the human body, people tended to confine themselves to the treatment of symptoms. This was by means of medicines, often combined with ritual. There was a range of illnesses that was believed to 'just occur', to be in the nature of things. Such were all minor ailments like coughs, colds and stomach disorders, and also more serious illnesses such as dysentery and malaria. On the other hand, most illness of any severity was believed to be intentionally caused, and the cause had to be diagnosed.

The essence of healing, then, was correct diagnosis (the establishment of the cause), and the Southern Bantu were effectively faced with three possible causes: ancestral displeasure, witchcraft-sorcery and pollution. The correct diagnosis of which of these three was responsible was crucial, especially because one possibility, that of witchcraft or sorcery, entailed dire consequences for the person accused and found guilty. The prospect of a public execution for witchcraft made it essential that the verdict of guilty be unequivocal and backed by the highest authority. This was the work of the diviner (Xhosa, *igqira*, Zulu, *isangoma*, Sotho, *ngaka*), and the reason why these healers played such an important role in the life

THE THWASA DREAM OF A BHACA DIVINER

The dreams of people called by the ancestors to be diviners were remarkably stereotyped. This account of the dream of a Bhaca initiate to the profession is typical of the experience of all Nguni diviners. ☐ Manyoni, a woman of about forty-five, became sick with pains in the body and dreamed about the recently deceased chief. Her husband was a member of the royal clan. The chief in her dream held in one hand an isiyaca, the fringed bead head-dress worn by diviners, and in the other a white stone (ikhubalo) also associated with divination. He placed the isiyaca on Manyoni's head, but told her that she would have to find the stone herself. All this happened in 'a very difficult and dangerous place in a pool in the river'. She then awoke. ☐ Early the next morning she went along to the pool indicated in her dream. She had wound a white cloth round her head. In it was a calabash with snuff. Still fully clothed she descended into the pool. She sank down until she reached the bottom, where she saw an old woman with one leg. The water above was making noise, but the old woman said: 'Don't look up, look down.' Manyoni followed the woman and found herself in a hut under the river bank; 'It seemed just like a homestead.' Spoons were hanging on the wall and she was told not to touch them. Then she saw a small, wizened little man carrying a milk pail and thongs 'just as if he were going milking', but he went out without speaking. The old woman beckoned to her and showed her a speckled black and white snake coiled up in a corner of the hut. Underneath it was the white stone. The old woman warned Manyoni that the snake would spit and asked for the snuff container. She put some snuff on the palm of her hand and threw it into the snake's eyes, blinding it. Quickly the old woman darted forward and snatched the stone. ☐ The old woman clasped Manyoni's hand around the stone and with it smeared her face so that it was covered with a chalky whiteness. This indicated that she was now a novice (umkhwetha). The old man with the pail reappeared but still said no word. The old woman explained that he was dumb. By this time the snake had recovered and Manyoni came out of the pool. ☐ When she regained the bank she found herself in the midst of a large herd of cattle. She learnt later that they had been driven to the river by her husband who thought that she had been taken by ichanti, a legendary river snake said to claim victims who can only be saved by driving cattle into the river. [This appears to be a Bhaca version of the Xhosa belief described in People of the River on p. 166: ichanti is in fact a witch familiar.] The men with the cattle threw stones to drive away the snake and a woman put a black, shiny stone on Manyoni's head to protect her from the cattle. She walked away from the river surrounded by the cattle and entered her husband's cattle byre. The beast that first passed water was earmarked for sacrifice at her eventual initiation ceremony.'
(Hammond-Tooke 1962: 313–4)

of the people. There were, in fact, two types of healer, the diviner and the herbalist. As we shall see, the diviner was one specially called to the profession by the ancestors and who worked with divine assistance. Divination was thus a vocation, and only certain types of people were called to it.

The herbalist (Zulu and Tsonga, *inyanga*, Xhosa, *ixhwele*; Sotho *ngaka*), on the other hand, was not called in this way. Some men (they were usually men, especially among Nguni) decided to take up this lucrative trade and apprenticed themselves to an established herbalist in order to learn his medicines. Everyone knew at least some medicines, and there were certain 'medicines of the home' that were handed down within families, but herbalists were masters of medicines and had a vast knowledge of plants, roots and other substances. They were rather like modern pharmacists, whereas diviners were analogous to medical doctors. To the extent that some of these medicines could be used to harm people and, indeed, sometimes consisted of human flesh, the position of the herbalist could be an ambiguous one. In unscrupulous hands this work could become anti-social.

A broad distinction can be made between the divinatory practices of the Nguni and those of the Sotho, Venda and Tsonga. Among Nguni the diviner was, in fact, a spirit medium who diagnosed the cause of illness, either through going into a trance and acting as a mouthpiece for the controlling ancestor, or by the exercise of what seem to be 'psychic' gifts of clairvoyance. Among the Sotho, Venda and Tsonga, on the other hand, divination by means of dice – a set of bone or ivory tablets, together with specially selected astragalus bones and other objects – was the preferred procedure. It would seem that the 'Sotho' method was more objective, in that the fall of the dice was governed by chance and was 'read off' according to specific rules, but there was also involvement with the ancestors, who were believed to direct their fall. The diviner would usually utter a short prayer to them and blow on the dice preparatory to throwing them, thus explicitly asking the *badimo* to assist these instruments to 'see' clearly.

An Mfengu diviner, by F. I'Ons. (Africana Library)

THE TRAINING AND INITIATION OF THE HEALERS

Among Nguni, a person (usually a woman) was called to be a diviner by the ancestors. This calling was made manifest by the onset of a series of persistent symptoms, indicating the state of *thwasa*. The symptoms of *thwasa* were vague and differed between individuals. Some suffered from stomach-ache, nervousness and 'throbbing'; others from severe pains in the back; others from pains in the joints, back, shoulder and neck, sometimes accompanied by periods of unconsciousness. Persons sick with *thwasa* became withdrawn and troubled by dreams; they continually yawned, twitched nervously and often suffered uncontrollable hiccups. Among Mpondo, for whom we have the most detailed information, the person suffering from *thwasa* saw constantly before her, whether awake or asleep, an ancestor spirit in the shape of a wild animal *(ityala)*, usually a lion, leopard or elephant, through which she was believed to communicate with the ancestors. Among Nguni *thwasa* could be caused by ancestors from either side of the family. It could be caused in a man, not only by his agnatic ancestors, but also by those of his mother or father's mother, and, in a woman, not only by the ancestors of her father, but also by those of her mother.

A diagnosis that one was suffering from *thwasa* was one not always greeted with enthusiasm by the patient herself. At the very least it demanded a radical change in one's lifestyle, for it made one a handmaiden of the ancestors. This could mean a lifetime of travelling round the country at the behest of patients. It also imposed irksome food taboos, especially during the period of the novitiate. A novice was in danger from ritual impurity (*umlaza*) and so had to live a secluded life at home. She could not attend beer-drinks and other social occasions, she could only shake hands with people much older than herself, no one's shadow might fall upon her and she must only eat from her own dish, using her own spoon. She had to avoid any sexual contact, for the *umlaza* flowing from it would both harm her and nullify her medicines. Yet, to refuse the call of the ancestors was dangerous: it could result in their sending madness, deformity and even death.

The only cure for *thwasa* was for the patient to submit to the inevitable and undergo formal initiation. To do this, she apprenticed herself to an established diviner and went to live with her, accompanying her on her travels through the community and on expeditions to collect and learn about roots, bark and other herbs for medicines. During this time, she also learned to dance the special *xhentsa* dance of the divining séance and how to enter a state of trance so that the ancestors could speak through her. During this two or three year period the novice wore short, unbraided skirts, no ochre and a skin bound low over her forehead (like a person in mourning or a young bride) and no ornaments except white beads round wrist, neck, ankle and forehead. Her head was shaved and she might not bare her breasts in public. Food taboos, which differed between individuals, were observed, the exact taboos being communicated through dreams of the ancestors. She also dreamed of a spear which, if necessary, had to be bought from its owner: its acquisition was essential 'for she might die if she did not get it'.

Because *thwasa* was ancestor-sent, and of such a special nature, its curing depended not on medicines, but on rituals. Special killings had to be made at various

---

NINETEENTH CENTURY DESCRIPTION OF THWASA

The following well-known description of thwasa was given to Bishop Henry Callaway by a Zulu informant in the mid-nineteenth century. □ 'The condition of a man who is about to be an inyanga [doctor] is this: At first he is apparently robust; but in process of time he begins to be delicate, not having any real disease, but being very delicate. He begins to be particular about food, and abstains from some kinds, and requests his friends not to give him that food, because it makes him ill ... he is continually complaining of pains in different parts of his body. And he tells them that he has dreamt that he was being carried away by a river. He dreams of many things, and his body is muddled and he becomes a house of dreams ... his body is dry and scurfy; and he does not like to anoint himself. People wonder at the progress of the disease. But his head begins to give signs of what is about to happen. He shows that he is about to be a diviner by yawning again and again, and by sneezing again and again. And men say, "No! Truly it seems as if this man was about to be possessed by a spirit". This is also apparent from his being very fond of snuff ... □ After that he is ill; he has slight convulsions, and has water poured on him, and they cease for a time. He habitually sheds tears, at first slight, and at last he weeps aloud, and in the middle of the night, when the people are asleep, he is heard making a noise, and wakes people by singing ... Perhaps he sings till the morning ... And then he leaps about the house like a frog ... and he goes out, leaping and singing, and shaking like a reed in the water, and dripping with perspiration. □ The people encourage his becoming an inyanga; they employ means for making the Ithongo (ancestral spirit troubling the man) white, that it may make his divination very clear ... At night while asleep he is commanded by the Ithongo, who says to him, "Go to So-and-so; go to him, and he will churn for you emetic ubulawo [a class of medicines used for cleansing and brightening], that you may become a fully-fledged inyanga". Then he is quiet for a few days, having gone to the inyanga to have ubulawo churned for him; and he comes back quite another man, being now cleansed and an inyanga indeed. (Callaway 1868–70)

occasions during the novitiate, the number depending on what the novice 'saw' in her dreams. In Pondoland a special beer feast was held once or twice during the period and there were at least two ritual killings, the *umvulo* ('the opening') and the *umgidi* ('the multitudes'), some months later. Ritual killings for a male novice were normally performed at his father's homestead, while for a woman, some were held at her husband's home and others at her father's.

Part of the treatment was the performance of the special *thwasa* dance *(xhentsa)*, and the confession of dreams. The dance could be performed at any time, but, because it had to be 'clapped for', the best times were when a crowd was present. The dance was always performed inside, except for the final day of the initiation, for one might not *xhentsa* in sunlight. The dance was usually performed solo, although other novices could on occasion join in. Here is Monica Wilson's description of it:

> The audience sit round the wall, and the performer gives them the time to clap, and possibly a phrase to chant. She stands in the centre of the hut, lifts her feet alternately in time to the clapping, comes lightly down on her toes, stamps her heels and quivers every muscle up her body to her cheeks and arms. The time gets faster and faster, the dancer lifts her feet higher and higher till after five minutes she stops abruptly, panting and dripping with perspiration. The clapping stops. After a bout of dancing the novice addresses the company, thanking them for their being present and confessing her dreams, and then addresses her ancestors, thanking them for recovery from sickness (partial if not complete). Then she dances again ... (Hunter 1936: 325).

Transvaal Ndebele diviner. Western materials have influenced the 'traditional' dress. (Levinsohn 1984)

The dancing always transported novices, as well as the attending diviners, into a trance-like state. Some began to tremble and weep, some fainted, others began hiccupping, but these occasions of dancing had no connection with divining or treating illness (although some Xhosa diviners always danced before divining). Rather were they important elements in the initiation process itself, in becoming a fully fledged diviner. The dances and confessions were essentially therapeutic for the novice herself, part of the cure for *thwasa*. The important part played by trance in Nguni (especially South Nguni) divination raises interesting historical questions. There is strong evidence of San influence. Among San, the trance dance was the central religious and healing rite; indeed, the very term for diviner in Xhosa *(igqira)*, and the name of the dance *(xhentsa)*, are clearly of Bushman origin.

Among Nguni the roles of diviner and herbalist were clearly differentiated terminologically; this was not the case among Sotho, Venda and Tsonga. Both types of healer were called by one term, *ngaka* (although among Lovedu the title was accorded only to initiated bone-throwers, or to herbalists who had achieved fame through their extensive knowledge of medicines). Unlike Nguni diviners, who were predominantly female, Sotho *dingaka* (plural form) were usually male. There was also a tendency for the profession to be passed on from father to son. This was partly because the training was so extensive and protracted that few adults could spare the time necessary to complete it. For those who entered the profession in maturity, apprenticeship could take up to three years or more. In such cases, an initiation fee of a beast was paid 'to loosen the bag of the initiation dice' and the apprentice was treated with medicines to enhance his abilities. At intervals he was tested. One method was for the instructor to throw the set of dice into a clay pot of beer, the initiate 'seeing' how they lay without actually being able to see them. Despite the rather 'technical' nature of reading the fall of the dice, Sotho diviners thought of themselves as being guided always by their ancestors. They would never, therefore, operate at noon (when the sun casts no shadow) since the ancestors were said to be resting then.

The final initiation of a Sotho doctor differed markedly from that of the Nguni *isangoma* or *igqira*. Mönnig describes Pedi practice as follows:

> This is done by throwing the divination set into a conically-shaped pot lid – *morufsi* – placed upside down, and covering the set with medicine extracted from the roots of a creeper *phelotheri (Helinus inegrifolius)*. This conical lid when placed upside down rests on a very small surface, which makes it extremely unstable. The initiate is then required, with his hands tied behind his back, and his ankles tied together, to approach the dish, hopping, it is said, like an eagle to drink off all the medicines and to throw the pieces of the set out with his mouth. He must then interpret them as they lie. The rite is said to give the initiate a very keen power of observation, and also to strengthen his memory, so that he will never forget any medicine or any combination of the divining set. (Mönnig 1967: 96)

Among lowveld Sotho, such as the Lovedu, the initiation of a diviner consisted of a ceremony called 'cooking the bones', for to really know the dice it was necessary to 'drink their soup'. The ceremony varied from doctor to doctor, but consisted in essence of three main elements. First, a goat was slaughtered, its flesh cooked with the dice and the broth drunk by the pupil. Second, the novice was given medicines containing, among other things, the heart and nose of the vulture and wild dog, so that he might see things from afar, and, third, the bones were buried at the crossroads overnight 'to gather the news', thus symbolically acquiring the qualities necessary for successful divination.

DIVINATION

As we have seen, methods of divination varied among the various groups. Among Nguni the most usual method was for three or four men, family members or neighbours of the afflicted person, to seek a diviner with a good reputation. If possible she should not reside too close, for they preferred one not conversant with local gossip. They sat down, with uncovered heads, in a hut, or in the areas between the huts and the cattle byre, the diviner squatting opposite them. The diviner's method was to make statements. After each statement the clients clapped their hands and shouted *'Siyavuma!'* ('We agree!'), the diviner judging from the heartiness of the response whether or not she was on the right track. If a point was established satisfactorily the clients would say *'Phosa ngemva'* ('Put it behind you'); if she were wrong they responded with *'Asiva'* ('We do not hear'). In diagnosing, no names were mentioned and the suspect was referred to only in terms of relationship or status. A diviner was not discredited if she made one or two wrong statements but, if she persisted in doing so, the inquirers would take up their money and go elsewhere. It is clear that the patient's representatives usually had decided in their own minds who was responsible for the sickness and that the diviner judged from the nature of their responses whether or not her diagnosis met with approval. It is also clear that the divination process among Nguni was essentially a co-operative one, a negotiation between diviner and the patient's support group.

An alternative method of divination was by ventriloquism. Instead of the statements coming from the mouth of the diviner, they were heard as emanating from

A Venda diviner interpreting the fall of the dice. The patient lies on a skin and is surrounded by a supportive group of close kin. The diviner carries his divining set and herbs in the skin bag. (N.J. van Warmelo. Reproduced under Government Printer's Copyright Authority 9612 dated 6 May 1993)

all round the hut and were believed to be the voices of the ancestors or (among Mpondo) of the diviner's mystical animals. The rarity of the gift gave this type of diviner much prestige. Among Zulu, ancestors also communicated by whistling: as all Bantu languages are tonal, meaning could be found in the tone pattern of the whistling.

Although Harriet Ngubane states that diviners had as extensive a knowledge of medicines as did herbalists, and sometimes prescribed medicines for their patients, more generally Nguni patients obtained these from a herbalist. Herbalists (Zulu, *inyanga*; Xhosa, *ixhwele*) had standardised charges depending on the nature of the cure or medicine required. Most of their work involved the dispensing of protective medicines.

Various techniques of divination were used by Sotho doctors, but by far the most common was that involving the divining dice *(ditaola)*, the so-called 'bones'. It was believed that the dice could answer any question put to them. Apart from indicating the cause of illness and misfortune, they could predict rain, the course of a war, the position of lost or stolen objects, and so on; they could also indicate what medicines should be used. A set of dice consisted of the astragalus bones of sheep, cattle, antelope, wild pig, baboon and antbear, but could also include such objects as sea shells and strangely shaped stones. An instrument made of reeds and with a set of small calabashes was sometimes also used. Basic to the whole set, however, was a group of four bone or ivory tablets, roughly triangular in shape and with one face incised with dots or lines, the other face being plain. These were given names: *legwame, selumi, thwagadima* and *thogwane*, representing adult male, young boy, adult female and young girl, respectively. They thus represented a complete family unit. When held in the cupped hands and thrown on the ground these four dice could fall into sixteen different combinations, or, if the direction of the pointed end was taken into account, thirty-two. If a dice fell with its marked side uppermost it represented a specific meaning; if showing the unmarked side, it was said to be 'silent'. As we have seen, a diviner's dice were consecrated at his initiation, and the throwing of the dice was always accompanied by an incantation to the ancestors.

It would be inappropriate to present here all the possible permutations of the dice and their interpretations. One (Tsonga) example, taken from Junod, must suf-

Zulu Divination in 1824

Henry Francis Fynn observed the following scene on his way to meet Shaka in 1824:

☐ 'One day we arrived at a large kraal containing 190 huts, the barracks of one of Shaka's regiments. We had not been there many minutes before our attention was drawn to a party of 150 natives sitting in a circle with a man opposite them, apparently interrogating them. In reply, they each beat the ground with a stick and said, He-sa-gee! [Yiswa nje! i.e. Listen!] After they had been answering with the same word about an hour, three of them were pointed out and killed on the spot. This man, whom they called an inyanga ... was dressed in an ape skin cap; a number of pieces of different roots were tied round his neck; and a small shield and assegai were in one hand, and the tail of a cow in the other. He was an interpreter of dreams and thought capable of telling what has happened in any other part of the country, also if one has injured another by poison or otherwise. His decision is fatal to the unfortunate individuals pointed out by him.' ☐ What Fynn had observed was a 'thumb-diviner' (inyanga yesithupha), who could not divine without assistance from his clients. This was given by their striking the ground with special sticks. When the diviner was deemed not to be correct they struck the ground gently with the izibulo (divining rods), but when they agreed with his statements they struck the ground violently, saying 'Hear' or 'True', and pointed to the diviner in a peculiar way with the thumb.

fice. The combination with all but the 'young girl' positive (face up) meant (a) dead things in the chief's village, (b) the heart is full of violent feelings and bitterness, (c) there is much disease and drought in the offing.

Venda divination was unique in South Africa, for a divining bowl was used in addition to the dice. It was carved in the piece, with symbolic forms depicted on the raised edge and on its shallow bottom, and it was used by filling it with water on which shells of certain fruits were floated. The positions in which the shells came to rest on the surface of the water, relative to the symbols, indicated the diagnosis.

Medicines

The importance of medicines in traditional healing has been noted. Great use was made of both medicines and charms, but with by far the greater emphasis on the former. Medicines were essentially of vegetable origin and the very term used to refer to them reflected this. In the Nguni languages this was *umuthi*, and in Sotho *dihlare*, from the words for 'tree'. As the Kriges report for the Lovedu: 'fully eighty per cent of medicines are of vegetable origin. There is hardly a plant in that rich lowveld vegetation which is not used in the pharmacopoeia of some herbalist or doctor and it is significant that new plants are constantly tried out.' Bryant compiled a list of some 240 medicinal plants used by Zulu, with their names and perceived properties, and estimated that about 500 more existed. Such trees as flat-crowns, wild plum, knobwood, forest mahogany, forest feverberry and pepper-bark provided leaves and bark for Zulu herbalists, and then there were the bulbs, roots and pods of innumerable shrubs and smaller plants. Unlike some other peoples, among whom the faultless uttering of a spell is essential for the effectiveness of the magical rite, Southern Bantu believed that having the right medicine was the all-important prerequisite. The spell, where present, was more in the nature of an informal exhortation for the medicine to do its work. Medicines, as we have seen, could also be put to anti-social use by sorcerers and, among Nguni, they were then referred to as *ubuthi* (destructive medicines) rather than *umuthi*.

At this point something should perhaps be said of the use of the term 'magical' to refer to these medicines and their use. The term 'magic' is so vague as to be almost meaningless. Generally it is used to refer to beliefs and practices not subscribed to by the labeller and dismissed as mere 'superstition' (itself a meaningless concept). A more helpful definition is 'those beliefs based on false assumptions of causation'. Thus a herbalist may include the eye of a vulture in medicines designed to help in divination, on the assumption that there is a causal connection between the acute vision of the bird and the diviner's ability to see into the future. This association made between things that are alike in some respects lies at the basis of all magical beliefs, wherever they are found.

Long ago the distinguished scholar Sir James Frazer laid out clearly the two broad principles that govern magical thought. He named these the Law of Similarity and the Law of Contagion (although they were not 'laws' in the scientific sense of the term). The Law of Similarity assumes that things that resemble one another in some way are linked together in such a way that they can influence one another, no matter how great the distance between them. This can be summed up in the axiom: 'Like produces like'. Thus, if a magician wishes to call up rain, one method would be to burn medicines on a fire so that thick clouds of black smoke rise into the air. The similarity between the clouds of smoke and the dark rain clouds is believed to represent, not only a similarity, but an actual causal connection between the two otherwise quite separate phenomena. The Law of Contagion states that once two things have been in contact with each other, they can continue to affect one another even if subsequently separated. An example of this is the belief that witches and sorcerers can harm one if they obtain pieces of one's body, such things as hair clippings and nail parings (even earth from one's footprints), and use them to do harm.

It is clear that such a theory of causation is not scientific. Science insists on proving the causal link in terms of established knowledge of how the universe works, expressed as scientific laws. There is a great gulf, then, between indigenous ideas of causation (which, as we have seen, also included ancestors and witches) and those of science.

This does not, of course, mean that traditional medicines were useless. Many of them were selected on the basis of the Law of Similarity (as when the Mpondo treated mumps with the bark of the milkwood, whose bulbous knobs resemble the swellings of mumps) but presumably at least some were retained because, over the centuries, they were found to work. The reason for their working may not have been that accorded to them by the doctor, but because they possessed pharmacological properties (some of which have subsequently been established by modern science). For instance, the Zulu used the roots of the bitter herb *ithethe* (*Polygala oppositifolia*) for scrofula, and an allied plant, *Polygala senega*, is listed in the British Pharmacopoeia as an expectorant for chronic chest ailments. Of course, this did not make these medicines 'scientific', for, in the eyes of the herbalist, their power derived from the very same principles as did his other medicines. It is also

INTERPRETING TSONGA DIVINING BONES

Unlike Sotho and Venda, among whom four bone or ivory tablets form the essential basis of a divining set, the Tsonga make use exclusively of bones, typically the astragalus (ball of ankle joint) bones of goats, sheep, antelopes, and, less commonly, of bushpig, baboons, antbears, hyenas and other carnivores. These animals are chosen for their symbolic associations. The secretive bushpig, which eats bones, is the medicine man; baboons, which are strongly territorial, represent the village; the lion is the chief; the ambiguous hyena, the witch; and the antbear, nocturnal and living underground, the ancestors. Bones of sheep and goats symbolise the ordinary inhabitants of the village, for whom the bones are being thrown. A set might also contain such objects as sea-shells (particularly those of the genus *Oliva*, representing the male attributes of courage, virility and weapon-bearing, and *Cypraea*, with female attributes such as baskets, pots, birth, bridewealth, and so on), kanye stones, of abnormal shape, and dark, so-called 'crocodile stones', said to come from the stomach of a crocodile. ☐ Junod lists the bones in the divining set of his informant Mankhelu, who worked with him at Shiluvane in the north-eastern Transvaal between the years 1899 and 1907:

In order for the bones to 'speak', the following aspects are scrutinised: the side on which they have fallen, the direction towards which they 'look', their position relative to each other and the mutual relationship of male and female. Each object can fall with either the convex or concave side uppermost. In the former case they are said to be 'full', 'to stand on their legs', 'to march forwards' – all positive (+) indicators. On the other hand, those falling with the convex side uppermost are 'empty', or 'supine', which is negative (−). In the first case, the person respresented by the bones is happy, at peace and strong; in the second, he is tired, ashamed, weak and dying. This does not mean that a convex position is always favourable. It depends on the bones. Astragali of goats and sheep with a convex presentation are always propitious, but a (positive) convex-lying astragalus of the antbear indicates that the 'digger is digging a grave', and that the ancestors are ready to punish. Some other examples of this are:

☐ baboon (+), 'the village is firm'; (−), 'the village is destroyed'
☐ kanye (+), 'the drugs will cure'; (−), 'the doctor will fail'
☐ crocodile stone (+), 'country at peace'; (−), 'starvation, death'
☐ tortoise shell (+), 'plenty'; (−), 'disorder'
☐ sea-shell (f) (+), 'rivers full', 'fertility'; (−) 'drought'
☐ sea-shell (m) (+), 'spears strong', 'success'; (−), 'broken spears', 'defeat'.
☐ Opposite is Junod's diagram of the fall of the bones in what he calls 'The Case of the Sick Mother', together with Mankhelu's description of how they should be interpreted (modified from Junod 1927: 560):
☐ In the centre we see the She-Goat (−); the mother is sick, on her back! Above, the Red Antelope (+), and

(Above) The actual fall of Tsonga divining bones, as drawn by Junod; (below) Sotho-type divination has spread to other groups. Here a contemporary Zulu diviner interprets the fall of the dice. (Morris and Levitan 1986)

Astragalus bones of goats (representing people of the village)

mbulwa	of old castrated he-goat	old man
mbulwana	castrated he-goat	elderly man
shivimbiri	whole he-goat	man in prime
shivimbidjana	whole young goat	young man
morisana	suckling kid	young boys

This is mirrored by a similar set for females, using bones from she-goats.

Astragalus bones of sheep (representing the royal family)

castrated ram	chief, old man of royal family
whole ram	sons of the royal family
old sheep	chief's widow
young sheep	girls of royal family

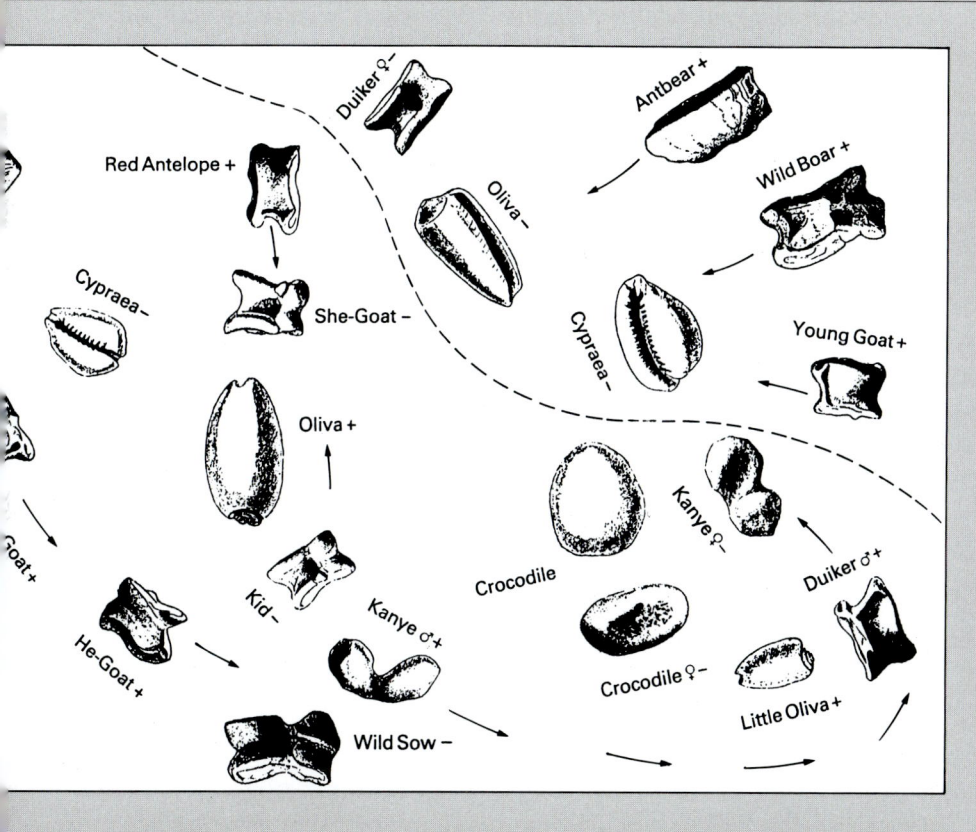

below, the shell Oliva (+), are looking towards her; these are the malignant influences that have caused her illness. The shell Cypraea (−), wide open on her left, shows that she is suffering from dysentry. On the extreme left we see Weaned Kid (+) and Young Goat (+), 'on their legs', walking; they are going towards He-Goat, who is also (+), not quite discouraged and pointing towards kanye (+), the medicines by which he hopes to cure his wife. By doing so he keeps in check Wild Sow (−), the ancestral spirit, who is thus prevented from adding his hostile influence. Near him is Kid (−), a young boy on his back, in despair, who keeps close to his mother. □

□ The He-Goat father, having spoken with his children, starts for the bush (follow the arrows at the bottom of the diagram). On the right is Duiker (+), walking. He carries the medicine that he has dug up [kanye (−)], but this stone is lying on its bad side: the roots were difficult to find. Moreover, two Crocodile Stones speak of death, and the small Oliva (+) looks at the father in a hostile manner. The bones on the right of the upper part of the diagram contain no encouragement whatever. Wild Boar (+) is accompanied by a girl, Young She-Goat (below him), who also goes towards the village with lamentations, shown by the open Cypraea in front of her. At the top, Antbear (+) comes to dig the grave! Near him, Duiker (−) is on its back, without strength, while Tortoise (−), in the left hand corner, is also lying on her back. No agreeable prospects, no peace, no happiness.

□ The bones here give a triple revelation; they depict the actual position, show its cause and indicate its course and the remedy. The disease is serious, but there is ground for hope if the father finds the right medicines. If the astragalus of the He-Goat had been on its back, and that of the Wild Sow on its legs, directed against the patient, the case would have been hopeless.

undoubtedly true that many traditional medicines were not effective; in fact some were downright harmful. Thus *impila (Callilepis euclea)* was sometimes used to get rid of tape-worm, but it is also poisonous and has proved fatal to human beings. Species of *Euclea* were also used for purgatives, but they are so strong that they often cause rectal bleeding. An analysis of a large number of traditional medicines, made in the 1920s, showed that only about five per cent of the ingredients had a pharmacologically specific reaction.

Not all ailments were treated with medicines and procedures that could be called 'magical'. Minor ailments were frequently dealt with in much the same way as in the west. Among Lovedu, for instance, sniffing up water was used for colds, the milk of certain euphorbias was applied to draw out deep-lying thorns, and splints made of strips of wood used for broken limbs or sprains. Teeth were levered out with a poker-like instrument. Blood-letting was common, as were enemas and emetics, especially among Zulu, among whom they were also used to remove ritual pollution. In some areas a homeopathic process, somewhat resembling vaccination, was resorted to. Among people as far apart as Pedi and Mpondo, parts of snakes and scorpions were used for treating snake-bite and scorpion stings.

But these 'non-mystical' treatments were in the minority and most ailments were treated with medicines involving the principles governing 'magic' analysed by Frazer. Thus, among Zulu,

> For spasms and the twitching of flesh, twitching animals are used ... If blood comes out of the body through the nose or mouth, it is necessary to take the bark of trees which have juice like blood ... To cure fear and nervousness, the heart, eyes, fat and flesh of lion, elephant and other powerful animals is mixed with the bark of many trees. (Krige 1936: 334)

Among Mpondo a key was tied around the neck of an ailing child to 'lock up the cough', and we have already noted the use of the *msenge* tree for mumps. And not only plants were used. Among substances that have been recorded were lion and elephant dung, powdered shark's fin, seawater, various animal fats (among Bhaca pig fat was particularly effective protective medicine, as pigs are impervious to snake-bite), *thikiloshe* fat, snake venom, to name only a few. These substances could be drunk in infusions, inhaled, rubbed into cuts, smeared on pegs and burried to protect homestead or fields, washed with or used as enemas.

HEALERS AND THEIR PATIENTS

As far as the relationship of healers and their patients was concerned, there is no doubt that healers were greatly respected as a profession. Diviners were not regarded as being superior to herbalists or vice versa. Diviners, with their close relationship to the ancestors, could in fact often be innovators. Thus a diviner might command that a traditional custom be modified in a certain way, or institute a new treatment of animals or crops, claiming as his authority inspiration from the ancestors. The influence of Xhosa diviners in the cattle killing of 1857 is a case in point.

But despite the authority and prestige accorded to healers generally, people's attitudes to individual practitioners were not uncritical. The verdict of just one diviner was not regarded as infallible and it was customary to consult more than one before a 'smelt out' witch was formally convicted and executed. Hunter gives some interesting examples of the sceptical comments of persons dissatisfied with a divining session in Pondoland in the 1930s: 'She put it there herself, weeks before'

Six sets of Venda divining tablets. Each set of four includes, from left to right, old male, young male, old female, young female.

> ### THE SCEPTICAL RAIN DOCTOR: 1853
>
> In the 1840s a famous debate took place between the missionary David Livingstone and a Tswana rain doctor on the relative merits of their different approaches. Livingstone recorded it in his private journals in 1853.
>
> ☐ Missionary: *I do wish rain most heartily, and I think your work tends to drive away rain and displeases God. He wishes us to feel our dependence on Him alone, and although you say you pray to him all the women in the town believe that you make the rain ...*
>
> ☐ Rain-doctor: *Well, if you wish rain and pray to God for it, why does it not come? You fail as well as we.*
>
> ☐ Missionary: *We pray for it but do not make it. We leave it to his good pleasure to give or withold it. You say you pray to him, but you believe you make it independent of him.*
>
> ☐ Rain-doctor: *And so we do. We make it, and if people – witches – did not hinder us by their witchcraft you would soon see it ... Whose rain was that which fell lately but mine? And by whom did the people eat corn for so many years? Who caught the clouds for them but me?*
>
> ☐ Missionary: *The rain was given by God, and would have fallen had you let your medicines alone.*
>
> ☐ Rain-doctor: *Of course, and it is so with all medicines, people get well though they use no medicines.*
>
> (Schapera 1960: 239)

(referring to a novice 'finding' white clay in a tree); 'What way is that to divine when the diviner just looks to see whom the people wish to hear accused'; 'Some diviners are just interested in money'. Yet most people believed that there did exist diviners whose divinations were true, usually those who lived at a distance, or in the past. Often foreign diviners were preferred.

For minor ailments patients tended to use their own medicines in an attempt to get relief. It was only in cases of grave or long-lasting illness that the formal step of consulting a healer was taken. This was because the illness now demanded drastic treatment which, in its turn, depended on correct diagnosis.

As we have seen, the divination process was a co-operative effort between patient, support group and diviner. The object of the exercise was to (a) impose meaning on the illness and (b) allocate responsibility for it. In other words, the social reality of the illness had to be constructed. The questions asked were: 'Does this illness mean that the afflicted person is suffering because of failure in good social relations with his or her kin (and, therefore, with the ancestors), or is the cause external, due to the envy of some ill-disposed individual (witchcraft-sorcery), or is it due to some adventitious circumstance (pollution)? If the diagnosis pointed to the ancestors, culpability rested squarely on the shoulders of the patient and the ritual, especially among Nguni, clearly expressed this in its court-like procedure in which the patient was accused of failing in filial duty. On the other hand, a diagnosis of witchcraft-sorcery pointed to a breakdown of relationships with others for which the victim was, presumably, not responsible. Only when meaning was imposed on the illness could it be properly comprehended and dealt with.

This labelling of the illness was essentially a social matter. The decision to consult a diviner or herbalist was taken by the immediate family group. It was as if divination (especially among Nguni) was a co-operative effort between all concerned in which the parties pooled, as it were, their knowlege of the patient and his or her social situation. Ultimately successful treatment meant coming to grips with fractured social relationships, either between kinsmen or between neighbours. In a very special sense, then, disease among the Southern Bantu was conceived of in terms of a breakdown in human relationships and the healing rituals and witch executions, in their different ways, were attempts to restore the disturbed balance and thus ensure harmonious social life.

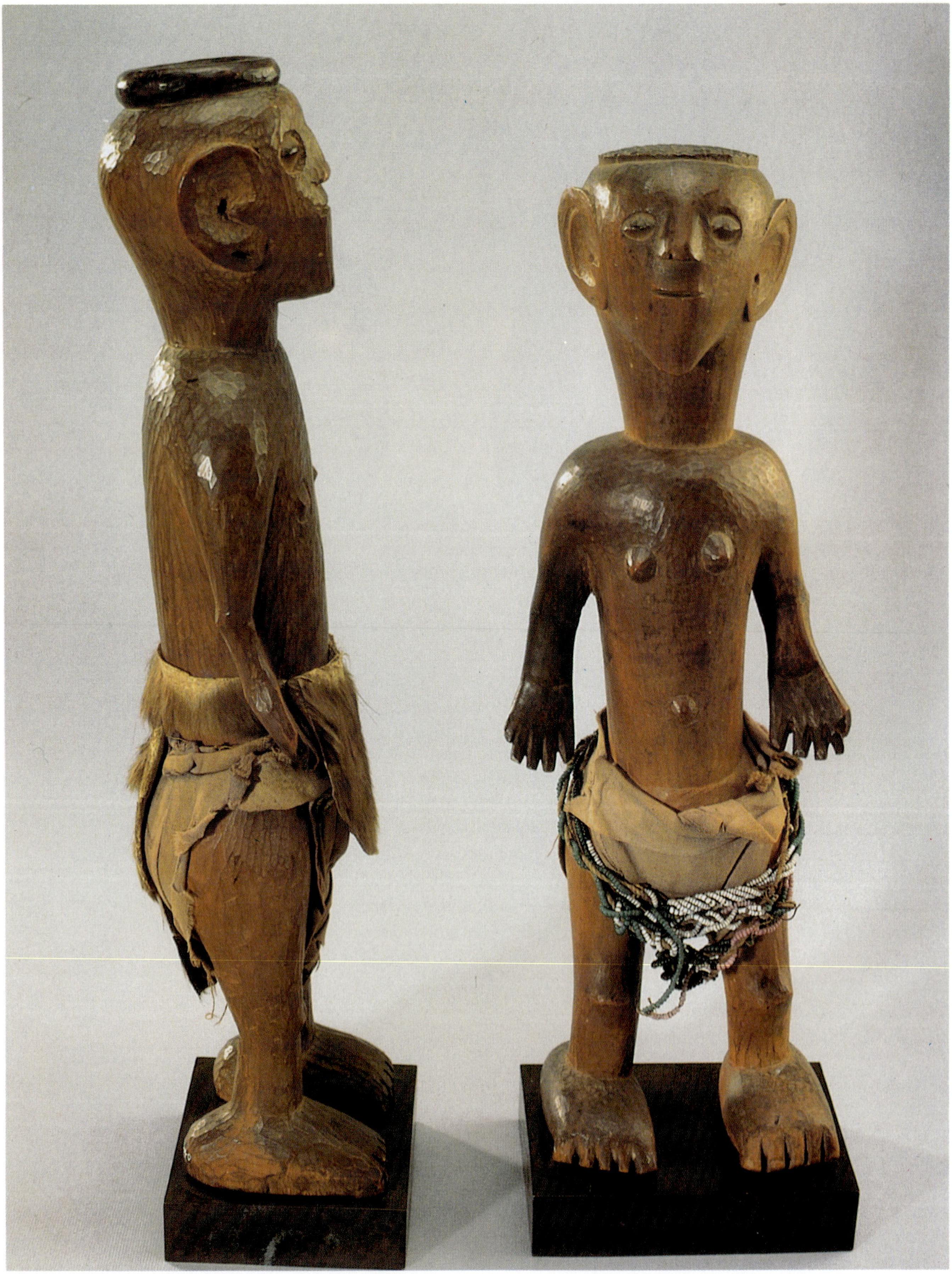

Chapter 11

Material Culture

U P TO now we have been discussing what might be called the social organisation of the Southern Bantu, the institutions and customs that governed the relationships between individuals caught up together in a complex web of kinship, marriage, political and religious rules and prescriptions. Our emphasis has been on the social structures of these peoples and the cosmological ideas that reflected them. But these structures did not exist in a vacuum. They were rooted in a specific environment which provided possibilities and limitations. We have already seen how the contrast between the bushveld and highveld ecosystems affected, not only settlement patterns, but even ideas about pollution.

But people do not live by rules alone. They are forced, by their physiological and psychological needs, to provide a 'cushioning' between themselves and nature in order to survive. Certain basic needs just have to be met. Chief of these are the provision of food and shelter, the covering of nakedness and the development of defence against attack from man and beast. All of this involves the manipulation of material objects. Food must be prepared to make it fit for human consumption so that cooking, with all its accompanying paraphernalia of pots and other utensils, becomes a central (and daily) preoccupation (indeed Lévi-Strauss sees cooking as one of the major metaphors that expresses our difference from the animals). The elaboration of shelter depends largely on climate and the type of material available, as does clothing, while the imperatives of defence (and hunting) make the development of weapons, unfortunately, essential.

But the mere meeting of these needs is not enough. Man has been called *Homo ludens* ('Man the Player'), referring to his propensity to elaborate on – or 'play with' – ideas and materials. It is not enough to cover one's nakedness; one should also use clothes to express social or ritual status. It is not enough to just cook; one should try to make food at least palatable, but also, if possible, attractive and 'special' – again to express status or hospitality. Baked beans on toast does not 'say' quite the same thing as Beef Wellington at a formal dinner! Utensils and functional objects, such as pots and headrests, are seldom allowed to remain unembellished, and much loving care is lavished on the best examples, raising the question as to whether they are to be classified as art, rather than as 'mere' crafts. Material objects need not be merely functional and mute: they are often elaborated beyond necessity and speak in symbols. The meaning of the spatial symbolism encoded in the relationship of cattle byre and houses in the Nguni homestead, discussed in Chapter 2, is a case in point.

Tsonga figures, probably used in initiation ceremonies. (Brenthurst Collection)

A North Nguni/Tsonga staff with unusual carvings. (Brenthurst Collection)

Zulu blacksmith, 1835, by C.D. Bell. (Africana Library)

Tsonga headrests. (Jaques Collection, Johannesburg Art Gallery)

Material culture, then, represents the intersection between an idea and the material in which it is objectified. The idea comes, usually, from a 'tradition', a template in the mind of a group that has been handed down from the past as to how an article of manufacture should look; the material is drawn from what is available, subject to its suitability to the job at hand. There are thus two types of constraint that produce the artefact. The material culture of the Southern Bantu of the eighteenth and nineteenth centuries was, as we have seen, a development from that of Later Iron Age populations that contained within itself three major 'streams', defined essentially by pottery types. The ideas as to form derived from these traditions. The material available was that associated with southern African grassland and savannah and not, typically, with high tropical forest. This meant that there was a comparative absence of really big trees suitable for building large rectangular houses or for elaborate woodcarving. On the other hand, the region was the home of perhaps the most diverse fauna on earth, so that a colourful range of skins, horns and feathers was available for clothing and ritual regalia. It is not surprising to find a strong emphasis on the weaving and plaiting of grass, the working of skins, the carving of horn, bone and wood and, of course, the making of pottery. Iron, copper and some gold were also present in the area and were considered so important that iron-workers formed a special caste in some groups. Our discussion of material culture must proceed with this background in mind.

The classification of objects of material culture is usually based on technology, under the headings of iron-working, woodcarving, grass-weaving, and so on. Here a more simplified classification will be adopted, based more on areas of social activity than those of technique. The following discussion is largely based on the pioneering work of Margaret Shaw (1974).

SHELTER

The comparative shortage of large forest trees meant that the only wood available for building came from the acacia, combretum and (in the north) mopane woodlands that constituted much of the savannah bushveld. On the almost treeless

Burchell Meets a Tlhaping Smith

The explorer William Burchell visited the southernmost Tswana chiefdom of the baTlhaping at Dithakong, also known to whites as 'Old Lattakoo'. The date was 1812 and the tribe was under the chief Mothibi. Dithakong was an extensive Tswana town, situated close to stone ruins that appear to have been built by people of Khoisan stock. Mothibi moved his capital to 'New Lattakoo', near to where Kuruman now stands, in 1817. ☐ Burchell's water colour of Old Dithakong is depicted on the dust-jacket of this book. ☐ 'Dithakong 29th July 1812 ☐ 'The Bachapins [baTlhaping] had but lately begun to practise the art of working in iron, and, as yet, there was but one motúri, or blacksmith, among them. This man obtained his knowledge from the north-eastern nations [probably other Tswana]; and though he was at this time but a beginner and an imperfect workman, he was, notwithstanding, overwhelmed with work from every side ... His work consisted generally in making hatchets, adzes, knives, hassegays, and hoes and mattocks for breaking up their corn-land. For this, he was paid either in unwrought iron obtained by barter from the north-eastern tribes, or in corn, oxen, cows, goats, tobacco, beads, koboes [blankets], leather and undressed skins. Even the Chief claimed no right to his labour, without paying him the same rate as any other person ... ☐ 'I this morning satisfied my curiosity by paying a visit to what my men had dignified with the name of "the blacksmith's shop". I found this industrious motúri at his work as usual; he was sitting in the open space on the outside of the fence which enclosed his dwelling, and having on one side of him a slight hedge of dry branches to screen his fire from the wind. This fire was made in the open air, and upon the bare ground, without any thing for retaining its heat. The fuel was charcoal: the art of making which he had also leant from the Nuakketsies [Ngwaketse, a Tswana chiefdom to the north of Dithakong]. ☐ 'The most ingenious contrivance was his múubo or bellows: this was formed of two leathern bags made from goat-skins taken off entire or without being cut open lengthwise. The neck was tightly bound to a straight piece of the horn of an antelope, which formed the nozzle of the bellows. These two nozzles lay flat upon the ground, and were held in their place firmly by a large stone laid upon them: they conveyed the wind to a short earthen tube, the end of which was placed immediately to the fire. The hinder part of the bag was left open, as a mouth to receive the air, and was kept distended by two straight sticks sewed along the lips or opposite edges, in a manner that permitted of opening the mouth to the width of about three inches ... These sticks are so held in the hand that they may be opened on raising the mouth, and closed on depressing it; by which means the wind is collected and forced through the tube. By taking a bag in each hand, and continuing this action of raising and depressing them alternately, a strong and constant stream of wind was produced, which presently raised a very small fire to a degree of heat equal to rendering a hatchet red-hot in two minutes. ☐ A stone for his anvil, a horn of water for cooling the iron, and two or three very small iron hammers, were the only apparatus, and all the tools, which he made use of. (Burchell 1824: 482–3)

---

highveld matters were worse, and it was here that the Later Iron Age groups made use of extensive stone walling to build their dwellings. The relatively short poles available imposed certain limitations on the forms the dwellings took. Among Nguni and South Sotho the huts were beehive shaped, made with a pole framework, roughly circular and thatched with grass. South Nguni dwellings were simply made and easily removable and were sometimes also covered with grass matting. It is tempting to suggest Khoikhoi ('Hottentot') influence here, for these close neighbours of the southernmost Xhosa-speakers were nomadic pastoralists and constantly on the move. South Nguni huts were built on the 'umbrella-shaped' plan. Thin poles were placed in a circle and bent over towards the centre, where they were securely fastened. North Nguni hut structures were different, consisting of two series of steadily increasing, then decreasing, 'arcs', set at right-angles to one another. North Nguni dwellings were generally more sturdily built than those of the South Nguni and were usually surrounded by a tall reed fence to provide privacy and shelter from the wind. Originally South Sotho huts were also of beehive shape, but with a long porch projecting at the front. This porch, and the

Uniforms of Zulu Regiments 1824

After the attempt on Shaka's life in 1824, four divisions, under Banziwana, were sent out to exact retribution. Henry Fynn described the scene. ☐ 'The force marched off in the following order: – The first division wore a turban of otter-skin, with a crane's feather, two feet long, erect on the forehead; ox-tails round the arms; a dress of cow-tails hanging over the shoulder and breast; petticoats of monkeys and genets, made to resemble the tails of those animals, and ox-tails round the legs. They carried white shields chequered at the centre with black skin. The shields were held by sticks attached to them, and at the top of each stick was the tail of a genet. They carried each a single assegai and a knobbed stick. ☐ The second division wore turbans of otter-skin, at the upper edge of which were two bits of hide resembling horns. From these hung black cow-tails. The dress around the breast and shoulders resembled that of the first division, a piece of hide cut so as to resemble three tails hanging at the back. They carried red-spotted shields. ☐ The third division wore a very large bunch of eagle-feathers on the head, fastened only by a string that passed under the chin, trappings of ox-tails over the breast and shoulders, and, as the second division, a piece of hide resembling three tails. The shields were gray. Each man carried an assegai and a knobbed stick. ☐ The fourth division wore trappings of ox-tails over the breast and shoulders, a band of ox-hide with white cow-tails round the head: and their shields were black. ☐ The force descended the hill in the direction of the enemy's country. They held their shields downwards at the left side – and at a distance very much resembled a body of cavalry. The first and third divisions marched making a shrill noise, while the second and fourth uttered a sound of dreadful howling.' (Bird 1888: 85)

Three members of the Zulu army, painted by G.F. Angas. (Africana Library)

---

fact that the inside walls were plastered with mud and cowdung, were probably adaptations to the intense cold of the Maluti winters.

Among all other groups dwellings were of the cone-and-cylinder type, with a circular wall made of closely planted stakes secured by interwoven withes, sometimes plastered both inside and out, and with a conical thatched roof that was put in place after the walls were constructed. North Sotho embedded the supporting poles in a clay wall of about one and half metres on which the roof rested, to form a veranda, while Tswana built two such walls, using the space in between for storage. In all groups the floors were made of a mixture of clay and cow-dung,

Swazi wooden vessel decorated with pokerwork.
(Brenthurst Collection)

stamped to a hard surface. Among Venda, North Sotho and some Tswana, this was extended to the floor and walls of the courtyard in front of the hut. Doors were made of wicker work and were detachable when not in use, but carved wooden doors were used for the main hut among Venda and Lovedu, especially by chiefs. Huts had no windows and smoke escaped through the thatch and the door. Huts and homesteads were fairly frequently renewed, often, in the Transvaal, because of the ravages of termites. Especially among Nguni and Tsonga, huts were burned or pulled down after the death of the occupant; on the death of the homestead head, the whole homestead would be destroyed or abandoned and a new one

A Lovedu salt filter made of mopane bark and branches. The salt-laden earth is filtered through large grass-lined filters, the filtrate is evaporated, and the crystals are moulded into small mounds for trading. (Davison 1984)

Venda granaries, raised above ground to prevent infestation (N.J. van Warmelo. Reproduced under Government Printer's Copyright Authority 9612 dated 6 May 1993)

built. The site of a new dwelling was always doctored with strong protective medicines against witchcraft or lightning and the occupation of a new hut was inaugurated by ritual intercourse between husband and wife.

Furnishing of dwellings was very simple. Nguni huts had two permanent built-in features, a circular hearth in the centre and a raised ledge at the back of the great hut which was sacred to the ancestors. All except Tswana used sleeping mats of sedge fastened by sewing or twining, which were neatly rolled and stacked against the wall when not in use. Tswana used animal skins, which hung in lines in the hut during the day, instead of mats. Wooden pillows or headrests were universally used. They varied from a simple block of wood or a forked branch to elaborately carved specimens among Zulu, Tsonga and Venda, all of whom had greater access to forest trees. Household utensils were fairly numerous, usually a variety of pots, bowls, platters, spoons, stamping blocks and milk pails. In the courtyards of Venda, North Sotho and Tswana clay seats were often built out from walls so that people could enjoy a sheltered place in the sun. Especially in the lowveld, with its mild winters and extremely hot summers, much of life was spent out of doors. Among the ancient mining community at Phalaborwa, with its barren and inhospitable climate, dwelling units were small and people slept by preference out in the open. In this connection, the strikingly small hut plans of the Later Iron Age settlements in the Magaliesberg and elsewhere seem to point to a similar outdoor orientation.

The furnishings of dwelling units, then, were typically made of grass, reed and wood, and something must be said of techniques of grass-weaving, basketry and woodcarving. There were two main techniques of basketry – weaving and sewing. Margaret Shaw describes the difference. 'In woven work two sets of elements are interlaced by crossing over and under each other to make a fabric. In sewn work one set of elements is sewn together by the other.' Very few tools were needed, a spear blade or knife for trimming and an awl or needle for the sewing itself. A great variety of materials was used. Grass stems were used for the delicate work, such as ornaments, and whole grass for the foundation of much coiled sewn work. Sedge stems, either whole or split, seem to have been the most common material, because of their sturdiness and durability, and were typically used for sleeping mats or baskets. Much depended on the local flora. Rush stems were used for sleeping mats; in coastal Natal palm leaves were made into flat pouches and a type of beer-strainer. Among some lowveld groups creepers were used for baskets; trimmed slivers of wood were used for weaving the winnowing baskets of the North Sotho and Tsonga and the characteristic lidded baskets of the Venda and Lovedu. Dyes, made mainly from plants, were used to decorate the basketwork. There is no doubt about the skill and artistic talent exhibited by these craftsmen and women, for both men and women practised the craft; who made what depended on the group.

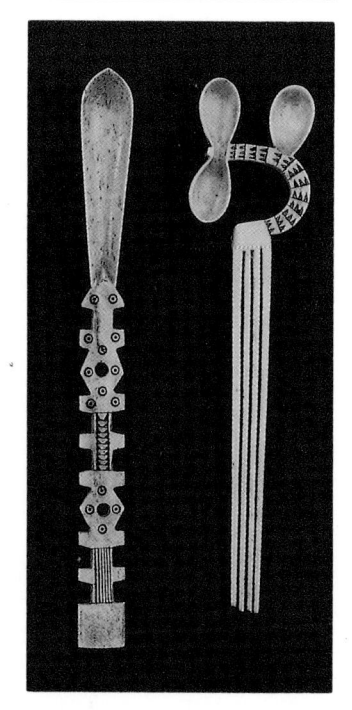

Generally speaking, woodcarving was not nearly as well developed in southern Africa as it was north of the Zambezi, mainly, as we have seen, because of the absence of suitable trees. There was thus little in the way of the free-standing figures, carved in the round, that are the popular hallmark of 'African Art'.

Wood-carving was for the most part a specialised craft and was confined to men. Traditionally there was no joinery and each object was cut out of the solid block. Axes were used for felling the tree and for rough hewing, and adzes for finishing the outside of an object and as much of the inside as possible. Thereafter a bent blade (used as a gouge) and a knife were used for finer work. Wood was allowed to season and might be rubbed with fat during the making to prevent splitting. Shaw states that 'Decoration was of two kinds – carved or branded. Carved decoration on utensils consisted of conventional designs in a series of grooves and ridges. Sticks, clubs, and pipes, however, might have naturalistic decoration – the head of a stick, for example, might be carved to the shape of a human or animal head ... Branding with a hot iron was used both to make conventional designs on woodwork, or to blacken the whole surface, after which it was greased and polished to a hard finish.'

Zulu snuff spoons. Tobacco was introduced to Africa from the Americas. Snuff-taking was widespread, but smoking was much favoured by both sexes among Xhosa and Thembu. (Brenthurst Collection)

> The objects made were troughs for feeding animals, mortars, pestles, drums, doors (Venda and Lovedu doors were elaborately carved), bowls and dishes, milk-pails, ladles, spoons, snuff-boxes, pipes, knife-sheaths, headrests, shafts for spears, hafts of axes and adzes, staffs, sticks and clubs, and in the Transkei ... spades. The Sotho and Venda used to carve figures of wood as puppets for use in initiation schools. (Shaw 1974: 120)

Household utensils were not only made of wood or sedge. Dried gourds or calabashes were used practically everywhere for a wide variety of purposes. Pear-shaped gourds, with a large bowl at the bottom and a smaller one on top, were typically used for sour milk, often having a small plugged hole at the bottom through which the whey could be let out. Long, thin gourds were split lengthwise for use as ladles or spoons. The smallest calabashes were used for snuff-boxes and other containers. The preparation of gourds was women's work and each provided them for her own family.

Food

The preparation of meals by cooking demanded, of course, suitable receptacles and all groups were accomplished potters. The makers of pots were the women and

South Nguni snuff boxes, made from a paste of blood, clay and tissue from the inside of a freshly killed skin. This was applied to a modelled clay core and a nap was picked up with an awl. It was then sun-dried and the core removed. (Brenthurst Collection)

(Below) A Zulu woman potter, by G.F. Angas. (Africana Library)

(Right) Finishing off a Zulu pot by rubbing the surface with gooseberry leaves. (Levinsohn 1984)

Lovedu women preparing strips of the creeper *lebibye*, used extensively for basketwork. (Davison 1984)

originally it was likely that each family made its own pots, although there seems to have been some tendency to specialise, leading to small-scale trade in pots. Most people had access to suitable clay, even if it was necessary to fetch it from some distance away. If the clay was inferior it was improved by the addition of crushed shards or sand to give it greater consistency. The potters' wheel was unknown and an old shard, or flat stone, was used as a working base on which the pot could be revolved. Shaw has identified four main techniques of pot-making in southern Africa: 'moulding from the lump, with the base completed at the beginning or the end (some Natal Nguni, Tsonga, some South Sotho, Hananwa and Venda (Lemba); building from the base with the addition of lumps or rings (some Cape Nguni, some Natal Nguni and some South Sotho); building from the base by continuous coiling (Mpondo, Swazi, Lovedu); and building upwards from the widest diameter or below it with the addition of flat pieces, after which the work is turned upside down and the base built on (Tswana, North Sotho)' (Shaw 1974: 116). It is intriguing that such differences in technique should be so widely distributed between groups, especially in view of the diagnostic importance given to pottery styles in archaeological circles.

Both the shape of the pot and its decoration varied from group to group. The Sotho preferred a single band of recurring triangles, black on the red of the pot, painted on and burned in, while Nguni pricked up the wet clay with a pointed stick to give the effect of patterns worked in raised keloids.

But cooking also involved storage, and all groups had means of conserving grain and crops not immediately required. Nguni and Venda generally buried it in pits dug in the cattle byre. These were often bell-shaped, and covered with flat stones, sealed with cow-dung and hidden under loose manure or soil. In other groups it was stored in a wicker cylinder, plastered with mud, perhaps raised on a wooden platform. Sotho, Tsonga and (unusual among South Nguni) the Xhosa-speaking Hlubi used enormous baskets of coiled weave for storage.

CLOTHING

All clothing was made of skins, of both domestic and wild animals. Working in skin was a man's craft and he was expected to make the clothing for his family himself, perhaps calling in the aid of a specialist for cutting, and for making sandals and shields. 'Skins were used for clothing, baby-slings, bedding, sandals, shields, quivers and a variety of bags for holding liquids, tobacco, or small personal belongings' (Shaw). After removal the skin was scraped clean and worked between the hands until dry and soft. For garments and blankets, skins were first pegged out and scraped and cleaned with an adze on the inside. If the hair was to be removed, it was shaved off and the skin subjected to rubbing between the hands and braying with sharp metal points or aloe thorns until soft. Fat or sour milk might be rubbed in and the skin was sometimes buried in the manure of the cattle byre for twenty-four hours to complete the softening. Sometimes tanning was resorted to, making use of the bark of various trees. Often karosses were made from the skins of small mammals, sewn together and worn with the hairy side inwards. This was particularly typical of Tswana.

The basic garments for women were one or more small aprons, possibly covered by a skirt, a cloak and, in some groups, a breast-covering. Married women always wore a skirt as an indication of their status. The shape of the skirt differed. Among South Nguni and South Sotho it was sometimes nothing more than a large apron covering the buttocks and a small apron in front; sometimes a full skirt, as among Zulu and Tsonga, and sometimes 'two separate skin panels, straight or cut to shape, hanging down back and front (as among North Sotho). Only the South Nguni seem to have worn a breast covering, and Shaw suspects that this might have been an early concession to missionary sensitivities.

The dress of men was exiguous. South Nguni and Tsonga men wore only a penis-sheath, although the Xhosa chiefdoms of the far west seem to have adopted the Khoikhoi apron of skin. North Nguni wore 'in addition to a prepuce covering (they did not circumcise), an apron of skin in front and, at the back, a kilt of animal tails or twisted strips of furred animal skin'. Sotho and Venda did not wear the penis-sheath, but a triangular skin loincloth, with one point taken through the legs and tied to the others at the back. All groups wore skin cloaks for warmth.

Normally the head was left bare, but Xhosa and Thembu women wore dressed skin caps, as did Tswana men. When Burchell visited them early in the nineteenth century, some Tswana were wearing basketry hats of a shallow conical shape; South Sotho also affected this style, but their hats were more sharply conical

There were also special costumes associated with certain professions or ceremonial occasions. At boys' initiations among South Nguni and North Sotho elaborate costumes, made of palm leaf, were used to conceal the identity of the wearers, especially when they were away from the lodge. Among Kgaga these costumes took three months to prepare, under the guidance of the boys' fathers and in extreme secrecy. The regalia consisted of a mask divided into two sections, topped by a bunch of feathers, a skirt and a stout flanged band that encircled the waist. Bandoliers of palm leaf criss-crossed the chest and wide grass anklets were worn on the upper arms and also on the ankles. The costume of Xhosa and Thembu in-

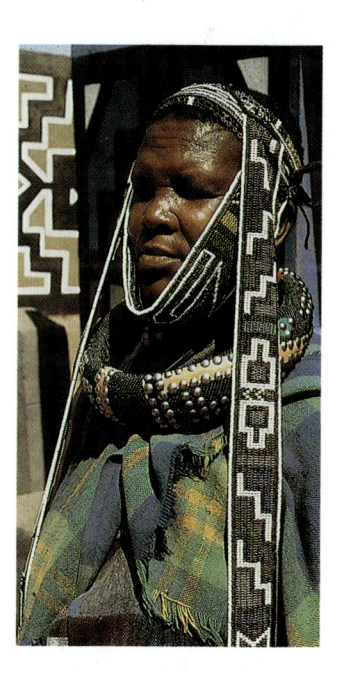

Modern Ndebele beadwork. The long strips apparently symbolise tears. (Levinsohn 1984)

Costume of a Tsonga Warrior

'The head was decorated with three plumes of long slender feathers, taken from the bird called sakaboinyi, the widow bird, which is only to be found in the mountains; sometimes the feathers of other birds are added ...; one of these plumes is worn in the centre, the others on each side, and all three are fixed to a conical helmet (shintlontlo) trimmed with ostrich feathers. The helmet is set on a kind of toque of another skin, which is held in place with a chin-strap. This style of head gear makes the head look about twice the natural size, and, to give it a still more ferocious appearance, is adorned here and there with porcupine quills. ☐ Round the neck he wore a necklace of plaited thongs of black calf skin (tinkocho). Armlets of long white ox hairs, carefully selected from the tail, ornamented his biceps, and garters of a similar make were on the calves of his legs. ☐ The belt round his loins was very rich, the beautiful skin of a civet cat, with its fine yellow stripes, hanging down in front to the middle of his thighs, and small antelope's skins behind. Finally, to complete the wild animal appearance, calves and ankles were covered with bracelets of large black seeds ... The size of the arms is thus considerably increased and conveys the idea of a pachyderm; when he jumped heavily or stamped his feet on the ground, it sounded like the tread of an elephant. ☐ The several component parts of the war-dress are kept in a little hut raised on poles, near the owner's dwelling, and are carefully looked after, being frequently dusted and exposed to the sun to preserve them from moths and weevils. (Junod 1927: 451)

itiates was remarkably similar, despite the great distance separating Sotho Nguni from North Sotho.

Warriors, too, wore special dress, designed to strike terror in their enemies. By far the most spectacular of these uniforms were those of the Zulu regiments founded by Shaka in the early nineteenth century. His crack regiments wore monkey and genet tails and each had its own peculiar head-dress. South Nguni warriors stripped for battle, but minor chiefs, officers and those who had distinguished themselves for bravery had the right to wear the feathers of the blue crane as a badge of honour. Sotho warriors wore ostrich feathers in the same way.

Diviners and herbalists wore costumes that indicated their status, often a baboon skin cap. After contact with the west Nguni diviners adopted white clothing as their special costume, symbolising their special relationship with the ancestors.

Chiefs, when in formal dress, wore the leopard skin cloak reserved for royalty. Among South Nguni, they also affected a necklace of special red beads and their capitals were distinguished by the royal insignia of an elephant's tail on a pole.

As is universal practice, the Southern Bantu adorned themselves with ornaments. Necklaces were made from pieces of reed, wood, shell or root and, for males, claws and teeth. Necklaces were also woven from shiny yellow grass, as were bangles for arms and legs. Xhosa men wore arm-bands made of ivory that were highly prized as they were gifts from the chief to show his favour. Iron, copper and brass bangles were common. The major preoccupation with beadwork of present day Nguni dates from white settlement, but east-coast glass beads, derived from Arab and, from the sixteenth century, Portuguese sources, were imported via the trade routes that transversed the Transvaal from at least the end of the first millennium. Originally beads of unbaked clay and of metal were made, and worn strung singly or in chains.

The most common cosmetic used was fat, to give the skin a shining, healthy appearance. Most South Nguni mixed it with red ochre to beautify young girls, but also to symbolise the re-entry of male initiates into society after the end of the initiation period. The latter was true also of all other groups, except that Tswana preferred yellow ochre. Margaret Shaw gives the variation in hair styles:

Various styles of hair-dressing utilize fat (or sour milk) and red ochre (e.g. Pedi girls, Zulu and Bhaca married women, Venda girl initiates, Tsonga nursing mothers), soot (Pedi women), powdered iron ore and fat (Tswana), charcoal (Venda and Tsonga young women), antimony (Tsonga young women), graphite (Pedi girls); while young Swazi men use fat and aloe leaf ash to bleach the hair.

Bhaca and some South Sotho cicatrised the face, while some South Nguni made limited use of tattooing, usually by women and on the cheeks. Zulu men pierced the ears and elongated the lobes to take decorated earplugs.

WEAPONS

The principal weapon used by all Southern Bantu except the Venda was the spear. Typically a bundle was carried. Soga gives a list of ten different types of assegai used by the Xhosa for war and hunting which includes a stabbing spear, for use at close quarters, and various throwing spears with blades differing in length and cross-section. Some were serrated, or barbed towards the base, and all had specific names. Hafts were on average five feet long. South Nguni battle tactics were to hurl the spears at the enemy when he came in range, but Alberti notes that the usual range achieved was only seventy to eighty feet. He also says that Xhosa spear-throwers were far from accurate. 'On several occasions I have had a coloured cloth hung up fully stretched and promised it to the one who could hit it from a distance of forty-five to fifty feet. However, in spite of zealous efforts to win this prize, they often took not less than twenty throws before they hit the target.' He goes on: 'From this it follows that a single javelin need not be greatly feared, and this the less so because one can see it coming and can side-step it, or deflect it with a knobkirrie or other cudgel. Javelins are only dangerous when a number of them arrive simultaneously at the spot one is occupying. This weapon is most dangerous in the hands of a determined person, who uses it to stab, and proceeds to implement his desire in the following manner. In such a case he holds his bundle,

Sotho knives. Note the typical wooden sheaths. (Brenthurst Collection)

How to Throw an Assegai

Before Shaka developed the stabbing spear, the throwing assegai (incusa) was the main weapon among all Nguni, together with the heavy knobbed kerrie. William Holden, a Wesleyan missionary in the Transkei; describes it, and its use: ☐ 'The blade is made of iron, ten or twelve inches long, admirably bevelled off on both sides to the sharpness of a knife, and gradually pointed to the end. It is thus like a sword with two edges, only being formed for entering the body rather than for amputation, and having a regular slope from the point upwards, and both edges sharp, there is no resisting part; so that when it enters the body only slightly, it makes a deep incision, or a frightful gash, inflicting often a deadly wound. The handle is a beautiful straight rod, about half an inch or a little more at the bottom, where the blade of the assegai is inserted, and neatly bound round with narrow strips of wet raw hide, or skin, and made perfectly secure; from this part it gradually tapers off to a diameter of a quarter of an inch or less, at the top or end. The execution is such as to make it quite worthy the appellation, "as straight as a dart". ☐ The spear is thrown in a manner very different to that which would be ordinarily supposed, not at all like throwing sticks and balls. The hand is raised to a level with the ear, the elbow forming an acute angle, the palm of the hand being turned upwards. The assegai, or dart, is then taken about the middle of the handle, and nicely balanced, being held between the thumb and fingers, and resting on the upper part of the palm of the hand; when about to be thrown, it is twisted round quickly, and moved backwards and forwards with rapidity, until the whole vibrates, and appears instinct with life, when it is thrown with great force, and flies quivering through the air, being directed with deadly aim, and thrown with fatal effect...' (Holden 1866: 248–9)

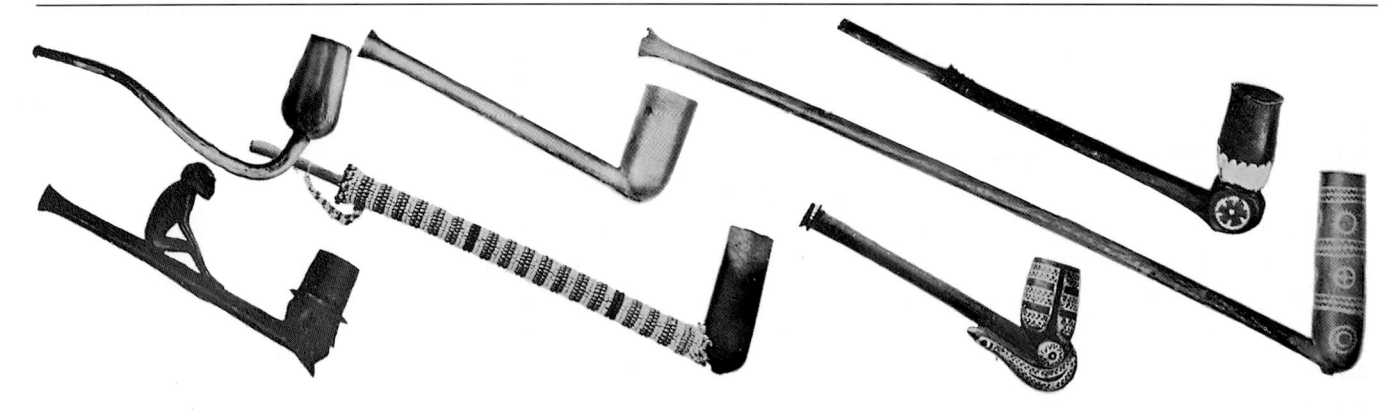

Xhosa pipes. Originally pipes consisted of a horn in the side of which a reed stem was inserted. Wooden pipes were modelled on the European clay pipe. Long stems and inlay were much favoured. (Shaw and Van Warmelo 1988)

consisting of ten to twelve pieces, in his left hand and throws them one by one at his opponent whilst running towards him, keeping, however, at least one of them back, so as to stab his enemy when he has finally reached him.' In battle, it was the custom for the South Nguni to pick up assegais thrown at them by the enemy and to throw them back. This rather ineffectual method of warfare was transformed by Shaka, who concentrated on the stabbing assegai, which he modified and improved. For a Zulu soldier to return without his assegai after an engagement was punishable by death.

All Nguni soldiers carried clubs and ox-hide shields to deflect spears. Nguni shields were oval in shape, those of the Zulu being by far the largest and covering most of the body. Sotho shields were smaller, the Tswana hourglass-shaped, the Pedi apron-shaped and the South Sotho winged. The Venda shield was round. Although the Venda carried shields and clubs, their main weapon was the bow, of the simple long type, about four and a half feet in length when strung. They were kept constantly strung. Arrows were unfeathered and tipped with iron heads, which were usually poisoned. Tsonga shields were of the Zulu pattern. Tsonga had both the stabbing and throwing assegai, and also clubs and battle-axes. Axes with crescent-shaped blades were made by Tsonga, Sotho and Venda, but there is not much evidence that they were used in battle. Nguni made no use of the battle-axe.

RITUAL OBJECTS

Generally speaking, the Southern Bantu had little in the way of what can be called 'ritual objects', if by that is meant objects *specifically* made for a religious or symbolic purpose. There were, of course, many occasions of ritual action that involved the use of material objects. We have already mentioned the sacrificial spear, dedicated to the ancestors, used in Nguni blood sacrifices, the shortened assegai carried by Nguni diviners and the sacred heirlooms buried in Sotho-Venda shrines. But these objects were not specifically made for these purposes. Rather were they ordinary, everyday objects (spear-heads, hoe-heads), selected for their associations with the past and consecrated to a particular use.

It seems that the only examples of objects made for ritual purposes (defined in the widest sense) were (a) the sets of divining dice, (b) certain figurines associated with Venda and Sotho-Venda initiation ceremonies, (c) the sacred Venda drums, and (d) the beautifully carved doors of Venda chiefs. Apart from the dice, it is perhaps significant that the elaboration of woodcarving seen here is associated with groups living in the densely wooded lowveld or on the forested southern slopes of the Soutpansberg, where suitable material for carving was freely available.

Divining dice were discussed in the previous chapter. Made of bone and incised with designs, they were simply constructed, although some specimens show careful workmanship. Their value was not aesthetic, but instrumental. Infused with the spirit of the ancestors, they achieved almost a life of their own.

The carved human figures of Venda, Pedi and (possibly) Tsonga were associated with the initiation schools and used essentially for didactic purposes. The most elaborate were those of the Venda *vhusha* and *domba* (see Chapter 7). They were used as *matano* ('shows') to illustrate the stories and aphorisms that were part of the instruction in the lodge, and the 'set' included figures of an 'ideal' Venda man and woman, a Venda renegade and his wife, a goat, a leopard and a number of snakes. These figures were sometimes made of clay, but wooden *matano* figures were used at the *dombas* of the Singo chiefs.

Venda drums were more clearly sacred, in the sense that some were believed to have intrinsic powers. There were two types of drums, the hemispherical *ngoma* and the *marimba*, tall and cone-shaped. The *ngoma* drums were reserved for use in the courts of chiefs and more prominent headmen, and they were the only ones decorated, with chevrons and concentric circles, symbolically expressing the two major metaphors of Venda chieftainship, the crocodile and the python. Inside the body of each *ngoma* was a pebble, said to have been obtained from the stomach of a crocodile and swallowed by a newly installed chief to magically confirm his sacred status. Chief and drum were thus symbolically identified with one another. The ritual powers of *ngoma* were also expressed in myth. In Venda traditions a drum of this type was said to have accompanied the original Singo royals from their home north of the Limpopo. It was called *thundundu*, an onomatopoeic name referring to thunder, and was said to have protected the invading chiefs like a latter day Ark of the Covenant.

This royal symbolism was taken up again in the highly decorated wooden doors, called *ngwena* ('crocodile'), which were reserved for use by chiefs on their personal dwellings and burial houses. Nettleton, to whom we are indebted for this analysis,

---

EARLY DESCRIPTION OF CHOPI ENTERTAINMENTS, 1562

In a letter to 'the Brothers and Fathers of the Society of Jesus in Portugal,' dated 5 December 1562, Fr André Fernandes wrote as follows about the people of Inhambane, still today famous for their xylophone orchestras and mimetic dancing: ☐ *'These people are much given to the pleasures of singing and playing. Their instruments are many gourds bound together with cords, and a piece of wood bent like a bow, some large and some small, and to the openings in which they fasten trumpets with the wax of wild-honey to improve the sound, and they have their treble and bass instruments, &c.* ☐ *At night they serenade the king and anyone who has made them a present, and he who makes the most noise is accounted the best musician.*

☐ *Their songs are generally in praise of him to whom they are singing, as "this is a good man, he gave me this or that, and will give me more"...*

☐ *Sometimes they have drinking feasts which last three or four days, during which they eat nothing. Their wine is made from the fruit of the thickets...* ☐ *Their dance represents all the actions of warfare, as surrounding the enemy, taking wood or water by force, and everything else that can occur in war, all very appropriately expressed.*

☐ *Their dress for this feast is finer than for any other for on this occasion they have skins of animals rather narrow with the tails attached, and these they tie round them so that when they twirl round on one foot, which they do with great lightness, the tails fly out in a large circle, and when one or two advance out of the ranks, they fly with marvellous lightness and throw the sand into the air with their feet to such a height that it is hardly credible by those who have not seen it. This they also do directly a great man dies.'* (Theal 1898: 142–3)

states that 'In effect these designs were largely composed of opposed chevrons and concentric circle motifs, the latter being called *mato a ngwena* (the eyes of the crocodile). In effect these designs constituted a kind of synthetic image of the crocodile which is very close to the image of the reptile which appears on Shona divining tablets *(hakata)* ... But the chevrons in the door's designs are also said by Venda informants to denote the python *(tharu)*. Both of these reptiles are associated by the Venda with Lake Fundudzi and smaller pools of water such as Manaledzi pool, on the Mutale River. The chief is associated with the crocodile through many metaphorical forms of speech ...' (Nettleton 1989: 3)

MUSICAL INSTRUMENTS

The musical instruments of the Southern Bantu can be divided into three main groups: percussion, wind and stringed.

The percussion instruments were rattles, drums, xylophones and the *mbira*, or hand-piano. All groups used dancing-rattles, either worn on the ankles or shaken in the hand. Ankle-rattles were usually made of cocoons filled with small stones or hard seeds; where cocoons were not available, tiny bags of goatskin (South Sotho), or receptacles of woven palm-leaf were substituted. Venda ankle-rattles were made of hollow fruit-pods filled with stones.

Drums were universal, except among Nguni, who used a rolled, dried ox-hide,

Drums being played by Lovedu women at a *gosha* dance. The men on the right are playing reed flutes. (Davison 1984)

An Impression of South Nguni Music

William Holden, the Wesleyan missionary to the Transkei peoples, records his reaction to their music:

'But I confess I am at a loss to describe the character of their vocal music; as for instrumental, they have none. The only attempt at an instrument that I have seen is the gubo. This consists of a calabash attached to a bow with a string of buck's skin: they beat the calabash with a rod, and it makes a monotonous, vibrating sound, without meaning or charm... □ In constructing their songs I think they have no rules whatever but the mere caprice of the song and tune maker; and, if the tune is not agreeable, the reply is at hand, "You do not understand it"; or, "Your taste is bad". □ The tone of the voice in general is low and sonorous, not well adapted to singing, according to European taste; but when well managed it has great power and surprising effect. Although they have no scientific rules by which to conduct their singing process, yet they are not ignorant of parts. □ I have often heard one lead off with a loud shrill whistle, and having proceeded though a few notes, a number of voices join in melodiously; and then comes the full force of the deep bass, with a rolling chorus of great power; the feet beating time, until the earth becomes vocal; and a scene of barbaric grandeur is presented to view surpassing all description. □ Their singing is also very monotonous, both in sound and time; but, when there are many together, this defect is somewhat compensated for by the strong effect produced, especially at the midnight hour... All nature then combines to give effect to the song... □ The songs for particular occasions are carefully taught to the different performers before the time of celebration arrives; and there is so much finesse about them, that if any one makes a blunder, he or she becomes the object of derision and the mark at which every pun is thrown.' (Holden 1866: 271–3)

---

beaten with sticks to provide percussive rhythm. Zulu, however, used a temporary 'drum', the *ingungu*, made by securing a goatskin over a clay beer-pot. It was not struck, but 'sounded by the friction produced by the wetted hands of the player being slid down a reed held vertically upon the centre of the skin' (Kirby 1937: 275). The Sotho had conical drums, with single heads of skin pegged in position, beaten by women with the bare hand. They were played at all the important agricultural rituals, such as the 'biting' of the termites and the tasting of the first-fruits. The Tsonga drum was made in the form of a tambourine, and struck with a stick: it was played by men and used mainly in rituals for the exorcism of spirits. We have already referred to the drums of the Venda.

Xylophones (*mbila*), consisting of tuned slabs of hardwood fitted on insulated frames over similarly tuned resonators of calabash, were found among Venda and played by men, in pairs. The *mbira*, which consisted of tuned tongues of tempered iron fixed to a wooden base and placed inside a large calabash resonator, was characteristic of the Lemba.

Wind instruments were mainly horns and whistles, used mainly for signalling. Antelope horns, especially those of kudu and sable, were typical of the Sotho-Venda and Venda and called *phalafala*, after the sable. Their sounding was a sign that the occasion they announced was being held under the auspices of the political authorities. The Tswana acquired the reed-flute at the beginning of the nineteenth century from the Koranna Khoikhoi, who also imparted the Koranna method of tuning them. Venda flutes were of fixed intonation. Kirby states that 'It is a curious fact that, with the exception of a secret instrument played by the Venda [initiation official], no wind instrument with a vibrating reed as a medium of sound production is found in South Africa' (Kirby 1937: 277).

Eight types of stringed instrument were used by the Southern Bantu. All were evolved from the hunting bow, and a resonator was used, either a calabash or the mouth itself.

Tsonga xylophones (*timbila*) showing calabash resonators on the underside. They were tuned to a ten note scale, and a number were often played together, producing complex counter-rhythms. Chiefs and headmen were honoured by the performances.

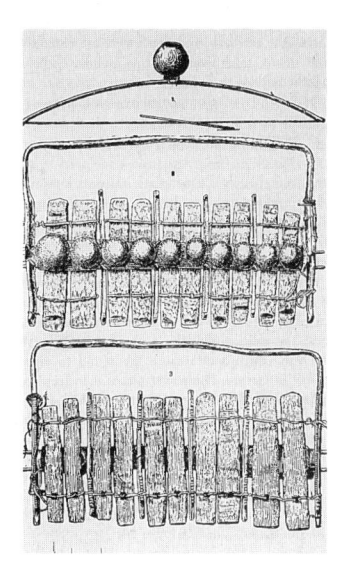

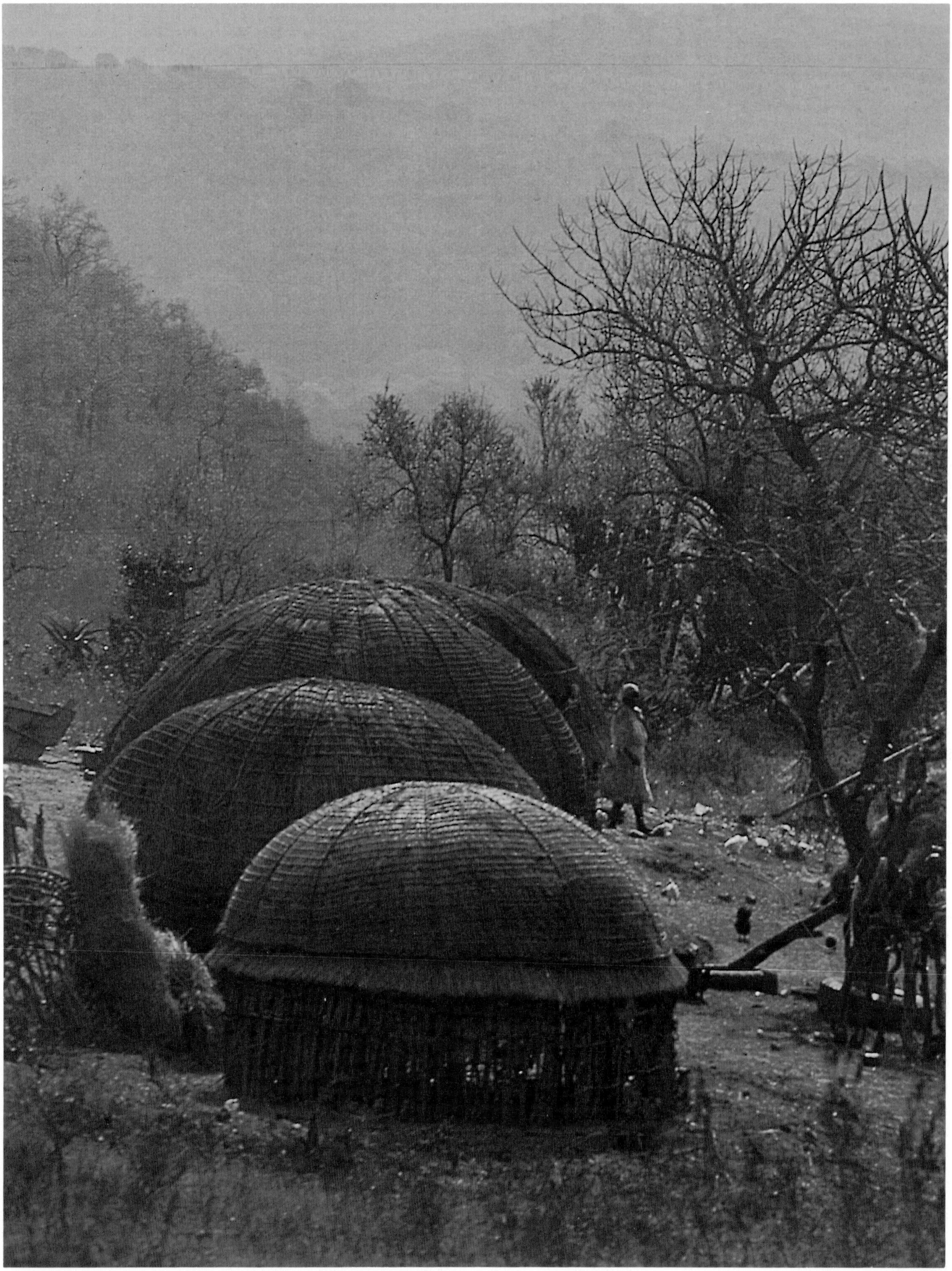

Epilogue

WE HAVE completed our survey of the main characteristics of Southern Bantu social and cultural life during the centuries before the white man established the victualling settlement at the southern tip of the African continent. We have seen that these societies were remarkably effective responses to a harsh, and often dangerous, environment in which human life was constantly being threatened by drought, disease and attack, from both man and beast. That they were basically successful is proved by their duration over two millennia and a steady, if slow, growth of population. Their extension over the southern sub-continent was only limited by climate: their form of subsistence economy, especially the cultivation of cereals, was not possible where the annual rainfall dropped below twenty inches (500 mm). Below this crucial figure, the land was conceded to other indigenous peoples – San hunters, with their lithic industries reminiscent of the Later Stone Age, and the pastoral, nomadic Khoikhoi. We have also seen that, despite differences in detail, all Southern Bantu had beliefs and institutions that were variations on a basic pattern: the differences were minor and essentially those of emphasis, deriving from both historical and environmental factors.

The coming of the white man destroyed this era forever. At the heart of the conflict between the two worlds of Europe and Africa were fundamentally different ideas of land ownership. The Southern Bantu saw land as being held by the chiefs in trusteeship for their subjects and the idea of selling it was totally foreign to them. Ownership of land, in the western sense, was unknown. A married man, by virtue of the fact of allegiance to his chief, had inalienable rights to a field for each of his wives, and enjoyed undisputed occupation of these fields (including the right of passing them on to his sons), provided that he continued to work them effectively. But there was no way in which he could alienate them to others for cattle, or any other consideration. Right from the start, the land-hungry settlers assumed ownership over a chiefdom's lands, through barter, sale and conquest. The westernmost South Nguni were the first Bantu-speakers to experience this (the Khoikhoi social systems had been destroyed and their carriers absorbed into the 'coloured' population by the end of the eighteenth century) and fought a series of Frontier wars (1777–1877) against the colonial forces to maintain their way of life. The territory of the last group of Xhosa-speakers to succumb, the Mpondo, was annexed to the Cape Colony in 1894.

But it was the movement eastward of Boer farmers out of the Colony and into the interior, in 1836, in the movement enshrined in South African history as the Great

Intimations of an era: dusk in the Mhlathuze valley, Natal. (Elliott 1978)

Trek, that began the real destruction of traditional societies. And, ironically, here history seemed to play into the Trekkers' hands. For the late 1820s and 30s was precisely the time of the Mfecane, and two decades or so of pillage and bloodshed characterised by the desperate flight of peoples from their traditional homes caused by the rapid expansion of the Zulu state under Shaka. When the Trekkers arrived in what is now the Free State and Transvaal, they found an apparently unoccupied territory. Admittedly there were the rumours of recent destruction and references to depopulation – even, on occasion, the mute bones of victims – but this did not appear to them to be sufficient grounds to prevent the staking of claims to extensive farms and the establishment of small towns and villages. On occasion, whites actually met some of the raiding groups. Thus the missionary, Robert Moffat, was present at the battle of Dithakong (1823), when the so-called 'Mantatees' were repulsed by the Tlhaping, assisted by Griqua freebooters, and the Trekkers themselves defeated the redoubtable Mzilikazi and his Ndebele warriors at the battle of Vegkop (1836), near where Heilbron now stands. By the mid-nineteenth century Boer settlements occupied most of the central plateau, their republics ringed by a 'horseshoe' of chiefdoms, stretching from the Tswana in the west, through the North Sotho and Venda in the north, the Tsonga in the lowveld, to the Transvaal Ndebele lying between the Pedi and Swazi in the east. Across the Drakensberg lay Zululand, under Shaka's successors, and, to the south, the solid block of South Nguni of the Transkei and Ciskei. Both the latter groups were soon to be incorporated into the British colonies of Natal and the Cape respectively. The pattern was set for the unequal distribution of land that was to lead, at Union in 1910, to only ten per cent (later thirteen per cent) of the total area of South Africa being left in African hands.

Alienation of land went hand in hand with loss of political independence. Although some chiefdoms, such as the Venda, Pedi and Zulu, put up fierce resistance, one by one all submitted, peacefully or otherwise, to white control. By the time of Union they had all become part of the newly formed South Africa, administered by the all-powerful Department of Native Affairs, through white magistrates, and under the austere and paternalist eye of the Governor-General, who was styled 'Supreme Chief'. Chiefs were retained as cogs in the administrative machinery, but their history of resistance made them suspect, and much use was made of government-appointed headmen to carry out the Department's wishes – until their resuscitation, in the 1950s, in the Bantu Authorities system that led to the establishment of the so-called 'Homelands'.

But changes were not only political. They were also economic, religious and social, all interlinked and reinforcing one another. Economically, the so-called 'Native Reserves' soon proved to be totally inadequate for the needs of an expanding population, and this was exacerbated by the imposition of a poll-tax that forced men out to earn money to pay it. Thus began the system of migrant labour that has had such baleful consequences for the lives of black South Africans. Pressure to engage in migrant labour came from a number of quarters. White farmers demanded labour, the mining industry that developed after the discovery of diamonds and gold in the 1890s acted like a magnet, and exposure to western goods made wage labour, for an increasing number, a necessity. The effects of the migrant labour system on the traditional societies was devastating. In some areas over half the able-bodied men would be away at any one time and this placed relationships within the family under enormous strain. And, as time went on, an increasing number of people moved permanently into the white towns and villages.

During and after World War II, with the rapid expansion of secondary industry, this movement to the towns became a flood, despite dedicated attempts at influx control. Large squatter settlements arose around the Reef towns, Cape Town, Durban, East London and Port Elizabeth, and an urbanised proletariat became more typical of black South Africa than were those still living in the rural areas. With urbanisation came education and the emergence of a considerable middle class of professionals and businessmen, and, in the homelands, politicians and civil servants. Today, the greater proportion of the black population is urbanised, and orientated towards western ideas of democracy, education and consumption patterns. The majority are adherents of Christian denominations. With the advent of the 'New South Africa' the shackles of the apartheid system are falling away, and black South Africans stand poised to take their rightful place in society.

In the light of this, the question arises: What is the relevance of the far-distant past to contemporary South Africa? What is the justification for presenting a book on this theme to a general public that is daily preoccupied with the problems of a multi-cultural, industrialised society, cursed with the legacy of centuries of injustice? Is there indeed a lesson to be learned from the past that speaks to the problems of the present, and future? An attempt must be made to answer these questions, for they are real and go to the very heart of the tensions in our civil society.

As author, it seemed to me that I had two choices in the matter – either to present the data without further comment, and leave it to the reader to draw his or her own conclusions, or to enter the arena and offer my own views. On consideration, the first route, although attractive, seemed an indefensible evasion of responsibility. It would mean that the book would function rather like one of those projective tests, so beloved of psychologists, that invite subjects to read into the material exactly what they wish. Thus, for some readers, a possible reaction to the precolonial past would be one of superiority, or perhaps repugnance, at what is perceived as barbarism and the excesses of 'primitive' behaviour. For others, in contrast, what I have described in these pages could be pictured as a Golden Age, a time of peace and plenty, when all men were brothers, performing a stately hieratic dance governed by respect for rank and seniority and choreographed by the comforting constraints of immemorial custom. It is conceivable, of course, that this knee-jerk reaction will occur anyway. If so, it is probably unavoidable: any information can be used to bolster preconceived ideas.

In the event, I have chosen the second of the two courses. It seemed to me that to present my own conclusions as honestly as I can was unavoidable. Apart from the matter of intellectual integrity, it is a debt I owe to those who have had the interest and patience to read this book.

Here again, there are two possible approaches: one can adopt a cultural relativist position or one can reject this in favour of rather more definitive value judgements. The route of cultural relativism is an old and honourable one. Briefly put, it is the belief that all cultures, everywhere, are of equal worth. Each culture is perceived as a perfectly valid 'design for living' which suits its bearers perfectly. This is because it is the result of centuries of successful adaptation to local circumstances. A nice adjustment has been made, a delicate balance achieved, leading to a state of (more or less) homeostasis. This is in accord with the organic model of the functionalist anthropology of the first half of the twentieth century, with its stress on well-integrated societies in which all the parts were assumed to be interlocked and smoothly functioning for the good of the whole. It will be noted that this is an essentially conservative viewpoint, which tends to see change as disruptive and somehow pathological. It tends to overlook the conflict that is endemic in all societies.

Cultural relativism, in its philosophical form, became prominent in the 1930s as a reaction to the rise in Europe of Fascist regimes, especially those espousing arrogant *Herrenvolk* ideas of racial superiority. It was also a reaction against Social Darwinist theories of society, influenced by evolutionary doctrine, with their belief in levels of cultural development through which all societies had to pass – until they reached the apparently incontrovertibly superior civilisation of the west. As such the influence of cultural relativism was wholly benign. It was an attempt to eliminate western cultural arrogance.

But there are problems in taking an extreme relativist position. In effect, it means that one cannot pass value judgements on other cultures. All are equally valid, and thus cannot be criticised. More particularly, one cannot allocate blame. Such institutions as cannibalism, head-hunting, infanticide and suttee are explained (or explained away) as being 'functional' (useful) in the maintenance of the societies that practise them, and are thus tacitly approved of. Anthropologists are particularly guilty of this. It would also seem to make it impossible to condemn the excesses of Hitler's Germany, on the grounds that they were caused by the culture of the German people of the period. Nearer home, it could equally be used to explain away segregation, and apartheid, in South Africa. *Tout comprendre, c'est tout pardonner*. In this connection, it is clear that the apartheid policy itself contained elements of cultural relativism. Its official justification was that it allowed for the expression of black cultural values and held out the promise of separate, but independent, institutions based on 'building up from one's own foundations' *(Bou van eie bodem uit)*. Finally, cultural relativism can lead to a subtle form of racism, as in the (patronising) expectation and acceptance, often implicit and perhaps unconscious, of different, 'lower', standards of behaviour from people of other cultures. Despite its laudable intentions, cultural relativism has its undoubted pitfalls.

It seems to me to be possible, in fact, to avoid an all-or-nothing approach in this matter. What is needed is a clear sense of history, and an empathetic understanding of the differing perceptions and resources available, both in the past and the present, to people coming from very different positions on the world stage. One must not fall into the trap, as many historians do, of judging the past in the light of present-day standards of morality and knowledge. It is clear that these cultures we have been examining were excellently suited to their time and place; they obviously provided full and meaningful lives for those that lived them. With this granted, the question arises: to what extent are these cultures of the past useful today? Are there indeed lessons to be learned from them, and perhaps structures to be adopted from them, that could contribute to a more humane society? Should one welcome a new syncretism in which, in the words of Paul Kruger, the best is taken from the past?

In some areas, of course, this has already happened, especially in the fields of religion and health. Both, significantly, involve cosmological beliefs that claim to provide answers to fundamental questions regarding existence. The rise of the African Independent Church Movement, and the use by many blacks of both indigenous and western medicine, are cases in point. There are also differences in black expressions of westernisation, among even the most urbanised, resulting often in distinct sub-cultures. But, in other areas of social life, syncretism is absent. Thus, in the workplace especially, traditional values and ways of doing things, particularly concepts of time and the dislike of exercising authority over others, have to be drastically modified – and all blacks are subject to the same legal and judicial system. Formal schooling is unambiguously western in orientation.

It seems to me quite clear that the gap between the precolonial past and the realities of contemporary South Africa is so great that there is in fact little in traditional cultures that can be used. The institutions created in the past were designed to solve quite different problems, and frankly, are not appropriate to the expectations of the modern world. The belief that they presented a 'socialist' system is a myth. It is clear that traditional economies were not 'communal', in that private ownership of property existed and wealth was not equally distributed; the societies were not 'classless', nor was the political process 'democratic' in the modern sense of multi-party systems and an institutionalised opposition. The comparative slowness of change, and the resulting lack of urgent 'issues', made it acceptable in the past that traditional leaders achieved their office by birth. Innovative planning and administrative competence were not essential in rulers, and problems tended to be solved with reference to custom and precedent. (There were, of course, notable exceptions.) Extreme respect for seniority made for muted expression of dissent. It is significant that the attempt by the apartheid architects to base local government on chiefs ran into complex problems that are still with us. Finally, the position of women as perpetual minors, although of course not unique to the Southern Bantu, is becoming increasingly unacceptable in the modern world. On the other hand, there were elements in past societies that were wholly admirable, and offer a model for our consideration. I am thinking of the respect for family authority, the compassionate care of the aged and the involvement of the extended family in the nurturing of children. Unfortunately the individualism of modern society works mightily against these humane institutions: their retention (if it were possible) would be of inestimable value in the South Africa of the future.

Be this as it may, the question still remains: What is the value of a knowledge of the past for present-day black South Africans? The answer would seem to lie in the problem of identity. There is striking evidence that a full acceptance of oneself depends on knowing who one is – and the link with the past, both genetic and cultural, seems to be an essential prerequisite in this knowing. Even if one rejects the past and one's cultural roots, this would be at least a conscious choice, the taking of intellectual and emotional control of one's life – an act of mature responsibility. It should lead to the liberating self-confidence that comes from full understanding.

REFERENCES

ALBERTI, L. 1815.	*De Kaffers aan de Zuidkust van Afrika*, Amsterdam. English translation by W. Fehr, 1968. *Alberti's Account of the Xhosa in 1807*, Cape Town: A.A. Balkema.
BERGLUND, A-I. 1976.	*Zulu Thought-patterns and Symbolism*, Uppsala.
BIRD, J. 1888.	*Annals of Natal*, London.
BROWN, J.T. 1926.	*Among the Bantu Nomads*, London: Seeley Service.
BRYANT, A.T. 1949.	*The Zulu People*. Pietermaritzburg: Shuter and Shooter.
BURCHELL, W. 1824.	*Travels in the Interior of Southern Africa*, London.
CALLAWAY, H. 1868–70.	*The Religious System of the Amazulu*, Springvale, Natal: J.A. Blair.
DELEGORGUE, A. 1847.	*Voyage dans l'Afrique Australe*, Paris. English translation by Fleur Webb 1990. *Travels in Southern Africa*, Pietermaritzburg: University of Natal Press.
GLUCKMAN, M. 1938.	Social aspects of first fruits ceremonies among the South-Eastern Bantu. *Africa* 11, London.
GLUCKMAN, M. 1955.	*Custom and Conflict in Africa*, Oxford: Blackwell.
GLUCKMAN, M. 1963.	*Order and Rebellion in Tribal Africa*, London: Cohen and West.
HAMMOND-TOOKE, W.D. (ed.). 1974	*The Bantu-speaking Peoples of Southern Africa*, London: Routledge and Kegan Paul.
HAMMOND-TOOKE, W.D. 1981.	*Patrolling the Herms: Social Structure, Cosmology and Pollution Concepts in South Africa.* Raymond Dart Lecture 18, Johannesburg: Witwatersrand University Press.
HAMMOND-TOOKE, W.D. 1992.	Twins, incest and mediators: The structure of four Zulu folktales. *Africa* 62:2, London.
HOLDEN, W.C. 1866.	*The Past and future of the Kaffir Races*, London: Richards, Glenville.
HOLLEMAN, J.F. 1986.	The structure of the Zulu ward. *African Studies* 45:2, Johannesburg.
HUFFMAN, T. 1982.	Archaeology and ethnohistory of the African Iron Age. *Annual Review of Archaeology* 11.
HUFFMAN, T. 1986.	Archaeological evidence and conventional explanations of Southern Bantu settlement patterns. *Africa* 56:3, London.
HUFFMAN, T. 1989.	Ceramics, settlements and Late Iron Age migrations. *The African Archaeological Review* 7.
HUNTER, M. 1936.	*Reaction to Conquest*, London: Oxford University Press.
INSKEEP, R.R. 1978.	*The Peopling of Southern Africa*, Cape Town: David Philip.
JUNOD, H-A. 1910.	Les conceptions physiologiques des Bantous sud-africains et leur tabous. *Rev. Ethnogr. Sociol. Paris* 1.
JUNOD, H-A. 1910.	The sacrifice of reconciliation amongst the Ba-Ronga, *South African Journal of Science*.
JUNOD, H-A. 1922.	Bantu heathen prayers. *Internat. Review Missions* 11.
JUNOD, H-A. 1927 (1913).	*The Life of a South African Tribe*, London: Macmillan.
JUNOD, H-A. 1929.	La seconde école de circoncision chez les Ba-Khaha du Nord de Transvaal. *J. Roy. Anthrop. Institute* 59, London.
KIRBY, R. 1937.	The Musical Practices of the Native Races of South Africa. In I. Schapera (ed.) *The Bantu-speaking Tribes of South Africa*. London: Routledge and Kegan Paul.
KRIGE, E.J. 1936.	*The Social System of the Zulu*, Pietermaritzburg: Shuter and Shooter.
KRIGE, E.J. 1974.	A Lovedu prayer. *African Studies* 33:2, Johannesburg.
KRIGE, E.J. and J.D. 1943.	*The Realm of a Rain-Queen*, London: Oxford University Press.
KUPER, A. 1982.	*Wives for Cattle*, London: Routledge and Kegan Paul.
KUPER, H. 1947.	*An African Aristocracy*, London: Oxford University Press.
KUCKERTZ, H. 1983.	Symbol and authority in Mpondo ancestor religion. *African Studies* 42: 2, Johannesburg.
KUCKERTZ, H. 1990.	*Creating Order: The Image of the Homestead in Mpondo Social Life*, Johannesburg: Witwatersrand, University Press.

REFERENCES

MACLEAN, C.R. 1992.	*The Natal Papers of 'John Ross'*, Pietermaritzburg: University of Natal Press.
MAGGS, T. 1986.	The Early History of the Black People in Southern Africa. In T. Cameron and S.B. Spies (eds) *An Illustrated History of South Africa*, Johannesburg: Jonathan Ball.
MOFFAT, R. 1945.	*The Matabele Journals of Robert Moffat* (ed. J.P.R. Wallis), London.
MÖNNIG, H.O. 1987.	*The Pedi*, Pretoria: Van Schaik.
NETTLETON, A. 1989.	Venda Art. In D. Hammond-Tooke and A. Nettleton, *Catalogue: Ten Years of Collecting* (1979–1989), University of the Witwatersrand, Johannesburg.
NGUBANE, H. 1977.	*Body and Mind in Zulu Medicine*, London: Academic Press.
OLIVER, R. and J.D. FAGE. 1962	*A Short History of Africa*, Harmondsworth: Penguin.
PRESTON-WHYTE, E. 1974.	Kinship and Marriage. In Hammond-Tooke 1974.
SANSOM, B.L. 1974.	Traditional Economic Systems and Traditional Rulers and their Realms. In Hammond-Tooke 1974.
SCHAPERA, I. 1935.	The social structure of the Tswana ward. *Bantu Studies* 9, Johannesburg.
SCHAPERA, I. 1936.	*The Bantu-speaking Tribes of South Africa*, London: Routledge and Kegan Paul.
SCHAPERA, I. 1938.	*Handbook of Tswana Law and Custom*, London: Oxford University Press.
SCHAPERA, I. 1956.	*Government and Politics in Tribal Society*, London: Watts.
SCHAPERA, I. 1960 (ed.).	*Livingstone's Private Journals*: 1851–1853.
SCHAPERA, I. 1965.	*Praise Poems of Tswana Chiefs*, London: Oxford University Press.
SHAW, M. 1974.	Material Culture. In Hammond-Tooke 1974.
SMITH, M.G. 1956.	On segmentary lineage systems. *J. Roy. Anthrop. Inst.* 86, London.
STAYT, H.A. 1931.	*The BaVenda*, London: Oxford University Press.
STUART, J. and D. McK. MALCOLM, (eds) 1969.	*The Diary of Henry Francis Fynn*, Pietermaritzburg: Shuter and Shooter.
THEAL, G.M. 1898.	*Records of South-Eastern Africa*, vol. 2, London: Government of the Cape Colony.
THOMPSON, G. 1827.	*Travels and Adventures in Southern Africa* (VRS edition, 1967).
VAN DER VLIET, V. 1974.	Growing Up in Traditional Society. In Hammond-Tooke 1974.
VAN WARMELO, N.J. 1930.	*Contributions to Venda History, Religion and Tribal Ritual*, Pretoria: Government Printer.
VAN WARMELO, N.J. 1935.	*Preliminary Survey of the Bantu Tribes of South Africa*, Pretoria.
VAN WARMELO, N.J. 1974.	The Nature of Cultural Groups. In Hammond-Tooke 1974.
VAN WARMELO, N.J. 1977.	*Anthropology of Southern Africa in Periodicals to 1950*, Johannesburg: Witwatersrand University Press.
VAN WARMELO, N.J. and W.M.D. PHOPI, 1948.	*Venda Law, Part 1*, Pretoria: Government Printer.
WALTER, E.V. 1969.	*Terror and Resistance*, London: Oxford University Press.
WEBB, C. de B. and J.B. WRIGHT (eds) 1976.	*The James Stuart Archive*, vol. 1, Pietermaritzburg: University of Natal Press.
WEBSTER, D.J. 1991.	*Abafazi baThonga befihlekala:* Ethnicity and Gender in a KwaZulu Border Community. In A.D. Spiegel and P.A. McAllister (eds) *Tradition and Transition in Southern Africa*. Johannesburg. (*African Studies* Special Number 50:1 and 2).
WILSON, M. and L.M. THOMPSON, 1969.	*The Oxford History of South Africa*, Vol. 1, London: Oxford University Press.

Suggestions for Further Reading

Readers interested in pursuing these matters further are directed to the following sources. They are all of a general nature: much of the important literature is to be found in (often inaccessible) journals.

GENERAL

W.D. Hammond-Tooke (ed.) *The Bantu-speaking Peoples of Southern Africa* (London, 1974); I. Schapera, *Government and Politics in Tribal Society* (London, 1956); M. Wilson and L.M. Thompson (eds) *The Oxford History of South Africa*, Vol. 1 (London, 1969); A.T. Bryant, *The Zulu People* (Pietermaritzburg, 1967); L. Thompson (ed.) *African Societies in Southern Africa* (London, 1969); S.M. Molema, *The Bantu Past and Present* (Edinburgh, 1920); J.H. Soga, *The South-Eastern Bantu* (Johannesburg, 1930).

THE MAIN ETHNOGRAPHIES OF SPECIFIC GROUPS ARE:

NORTH NGUNI

E.J. Krige, *The Social System of the Zulu* (Pietermaritzburg, 1936); B.W. Vilakazi, *Zulu Transformations* (Pietermaritzburg, 1965); D.H. Reader, *Zulu Tribe in Transition* (Manchester, 1966); A.I. Berglund, *Zulu Thought-patterns and Symbolism* (Uppsala, 1976); H. Ngubane, *Body and Mind in Zulu Medicine* (London, 1977); B.A. Marwick, *The Swazi* (Cambridge, 1940); H. Kuper, *An African Aristocracy* (London, 1947); H. Kuper, *The Swazi* (New York, 1963).

SOUTH NGUNI

J.H. Soga, *The Ama-Xosa: Life and Customs* (Lovedale, 1932); M. Hunter, *Reaction to Conquest* (Mpondo) (London, 1936); P.A.W. Cook, *The Social Organization and Ceremonial Institutions of the Bomvana* (Cape Town, 1931); W.D. Hammond-Tooke, *Bhaca Society* (Cape Town, 1962); J Peires, *The House of Phalo* (Xhosa) (Johannesburg, 1981); H. Kuckertz, *Creating Order: The Image of the Homestead in Mpondo Social Life* (Johannesburg, 1990).

TSWANA

I. Schapera, *A Handbook of Tswana Law and Custom* (London, 1938); I. Schapera, *Married Life in an African Tribe* (London, 1940); I. Schapera, *The Tswana* (London, 1953); W. Lye and C. Murray, *Transformations on the Highveld: The Tswana and Southern Sotho* (Cape Town, 1980).

SOUTH SOTHO

E.H. Ashton, *The Basuto* (London, 1952).

NORTH SOTHO

H.O. Mönnig, *The Pedi* (Pretoria, 1967); E.J. Krige and J.D. Krige, *The Realm of a Rain-Queen* (Lovedu) (London, 1943); W.D. Hammond-Tooke, *Boundaries and Belief: The Structure of a Sotho Worldview* (Kgaga) (Johannesburg, 1981).

VENDA

H. Stayt, *The BaVenda* (London, 1931); N.J. van Warmelo, *Contributions Towards Venda History, Religion and Tribal Ritual* (Pretoria, 1932).

TSONGA

H.A. Junod, *The Life of a South African Tribe* (London, 1927); E.J. Krige and W. Felgate, *The Tembe-Thonga of Natal and Mozambique* (Durban, 1982).

INDEX

Number references in bold italic refer to illustration material.

aged persons, respect for 105
agnatic clusters 109–111, 118–119, 151
anatomy, knowledge of 185–6
ancestor worship 19, 57, 110, **148**, 150–167
animals, association with rituals 154–155, 170–171
army regiments 79–80, 83

Bantu Authorities 216
basketry 53, 204–205
beadwork 208
Bhaca
– childbirth 132
– dialect 39
– diviner **184**, 186
– ethnographic classification 21
– facial decoration 209
– first fruits ritual 82
– hairdressing 209
– married woman **103**, **127**
– medical treatment 196
blacksmithing 200–201
bodika (cricumcision school) 139–143
bogwèra (circumcision school) 139–140, 142–144
Bomvana 53, 57
bows and arrows 210
boys
– initiation rituals 136–147, 207–208
– puberty rituals 134–135
– rearing and training 133–134
bridewealth 17–18, 53, 56, 117, 119, 122–126, 127–129
burial ceremonies 152–153
– purification rituals 178
Bushmen *see* San

calabashes, used as utensils 205
cattle byres 55–57, 63, 152, 155
cattle
– bridewealth 17, 56, 58, 122–126
– contracts 96
– early Iron-Age culture 27
– importance in Nguni culture 12, 39, 48–50, 52–53, 58
– pollution beliefs 180
chief induna, functions 79
chiefdoms 27–28, 40
– central government 66–67, 70–75
– communal rituals 80–83
– dispute settlements 67
– local government 78–79
– political subordination 69–70
– rival expansion claims 67
– role of women 75–78
– rules of succession 67
– splitting up of 67–69
– subdivisions 48, 50, 62–63, 66
– territorial basis 66, 69–70
chiefs
– burial customs 152–153
– dress 208
– executive duties 79, 216
– judicial duties 91
– limitations of power 71–75
– mystical nature 65, 75
– powers and privileges 70–71
– praises 73
– religious rituals 81–83
– ritual ceremonies 81–83
– sacred objects 56, 71, 211–212
– status 65–66
chief's messenger 79–91
childbirth
– procedures 132
– purification rituals 178–179, 182
child rearing 133–134

children, relations with parents and older siblings 98
circumcision 134–141
civil law 95–96
clans
– definition 107–108
– exogamy 118–119
– functions 110
– role in ancestor worship 151
class distinctions 69–70
clothing 207–208
cold, use as metaphor 180
colonialism, effect on Southern Bantu culture 215–216
contracts, forms of 96
coolness (anti-pollution ritual) 182–183
corpses, pollution beliefs 180
– use in witchcraft 171
cosmetics 208–209
councils 71–73
cousins, relations with 107
see marriage rules
creation myths 150
criminal law offences 96–97
crops, protective rituals 81

defamation 96
Delagoa Bay 12, 28, 86
descent, definition of 101–103
see Kinship
dice, use in divination 187, 189–195, 196, 210–211
Difaqane (Mfecane) 32
Dithakong 35–**37**, 201, 216
divination 190–192
diviners **172**–**174**, **179**, **183**, 186–192, 196–197, 208
domba (initiation school) **138**, **143–145**, 146
doors, carved 205, 211–212
drums **145**, 211–213
dwellings, design and furnishing 55, 201–205

enemas and emetics 180, 196

familiars (witchcraft) 170–171
family courts 91–92
family relationships 103, 110–111
farming communities 50–53
father, physical and social connotations 103–105, 125–126
fees 96
first-fruits rituals 81–83

girls
– initiation 143, 145–146
– puberty ceremonies 136
– rearing and training 133–134
God, belief in 149–150
gold artefacts 33–**34**
grain storage 51–**53**, 207
grandparents, relations with 105
grass-weaving 204–205
Great Trek 215–216
Great Zimbabwe 33

headmen 59, 62, 71–72, 79, 216
– judicial functions 91–92
healers, training and initiation 187–190
healing, links with religion 185–187
heat, pollution beliefs 179–182
herbalists 79, 81, 96, 191–193, 196–197
– apprenticeship 187
– dress 208
– *inyanga* 187
Hlubi 32
– grain storage 52, 207
hoes 51
homesteads 54–59
– political importance of 69
homicide 97, 99

Hottentots *see* Khoikhoi
hunting methods 53–54
husbands, rights and duties 125–126

illness, diviners' interpretation 98, 185–187
– religious rituals 162–166
Imbongi (praise singer) **80**
incest 97
inheritance rules 55–56
initiation ceremonies 15–16, 135–146
– meaning of the ceremonies 147
Iron Age culture 12–13, **22**, 24, 45–46, 200–201
isangoma (diviner) 186

Kgaga
– circumcision 140–**141**
– cultural grouping 41
– early settlement 13
– ethnographic classification 21
– female chiefs 78
– initiation 16, 139, **141**, 144–**147**, 207
– kinship 112
– Kutshaane (god) 149
– marriage 119, 122
– pollution beliefs 181–183
– shrines **150**, 155, 157
– totem groups 113
– Venda influence 40, 76
– witchcraft 170–172
Kgalagadi 69
Kgatla 21, 80
Khoikhoi (Hottentots) 23, 215
– influence on Nguni language 12, 215
– reed flute 213
Khoisan settlements 23, 25
kinship
– classification 107
– definition 101–103
– importance in moral values 98–99
– Iroquis system 103–107
– relation to neighbours 114–115
Kuruman 35–36
Kwena 21, 68

land alienation 216
land allocation 66
land ownership, rules governing 51, 215
law courts 90–97
law enforcement 90–91, 99
Lemba 136, 206, 213
Leopard's Kopje 31, 33
levirate 125–126
life cycle rituals 158–159
lineage 107–108
Lovedu
– anatomical beliefs 185
– ancestor worship 154, 167
– circumcision 139
– diviners 190
– door carvings 205–**206**
– drums **212**
– early settlements 12, 13
– ethnographic classification 21
– everyday life 60–61
– huts 203
– initiation 143–144
– kinship relations 112
– law courts 99
– marriage ring 129
– marriages 119, 122–123
– medicine 192, 196
– pole figures **79**
– pottery 206
– rain queen 65–66, 76–78, 126
– rain rituals 81
– sacred drums **81**
– sacred objects 155
– salt filter **204**
– shrines 155
– village life 60–61

– witchcraft beliefs 21, 174
lowveld Iron-Age settlements 40–47

Mapungubwe kingdom **31**, 33, **34**, 85
marriage rules 16–18, 59, 87, 117, 126
– Nguni 118
– Sotho-Venda 118–119, 122–123
– Tswana 119, 122
– Xhosa 120
maternal kin 103–105, 113–114
medicines 171–173, 187–188, 191–193, 196
Mfecane (Difaqane) 32
Mfengu
– diviner 187
– ethnographic classification 21
– headmen **99**
– homestead **89**, **125**
milk, sour, symbolic importance 53, 56–57, 128, 180
miscarriages, pollution beliefs 179, 181
misfortune, interpretation of 98
morality 97–99
mother, physical and social connotation 105
Mpondo
– ancestor worship **148**, 153, **157**
– army doctoring **82**
– assembly of men **92**, **93**
– descent groups 109–110
– ethnographic classification 21
– homestead **44**, 54
– husband 124
– illness rituals 163–166
– initiation ceremony 135
– medical treatment 196
– pollution beliefs 179–180
– pottery 206
– rain rituals 81
– witchcraft 172
Mpondomise
– burial customs 153
– clans 110
– descent groups 109–110
– dialect 39
– ethnographic classification 21
– initiation 16
– rain ceremonies 81
Mudjadji (Lovedu queen) 65–66, 76–78, 81, **90**

Ndebele
– beadwork **207**
– class distinctions 69–70
– conquest of Southern Zimbabwe 70
– diviner **180**
– ethnographic classification 21
– expansion of power 67
– first fruits ritual 82
– secession from Zulu 86
neighbours, co-operation with 99, 114–115
New Lattakoo *see* Kuruman
Ngona 12, 69, 166
Nguni
– agriculture 51–52
– ancestor worship 19, 151–152, 159
– bride, social position 128
– bridewealth 126
– burial customs 152–153
– cattle 12, 39, 49, 52–53, 55, 155
– chiefdom splitting 68–69
– chiefdoms 48, 67
– civil courts 96–97
– clans 109
– crop protection 81
– dialects 39
– divination 187, 189, 190–192
– early migrations 21, 29
– ethnographic classification 21
– first fruits ritual 82
– geographical regions 14
– grouping 41

– house property 58, 203–104
– initiation 15–16, 136–138
– *inkulu* (ritual elder) 156–157
– kinship relations 105, 114
– language 39, 43
– local government 79
– marriage relationships 16–18, 57–58, 118
– patrilineal descent 18–19
– political system 15, 31
– pollution 19–20, 179
– pottery 206
– settlements 35, 39, 47, 50
– siblings 105, 107
– storage 206–207
– succession rules 67–68
– weapons 209–210
– wedding ceremonies 127–128
– witchcraft 19, 170–171, 175, 178
– wives 55–57
North Nguni 14, *21*, 41, 80, 85–86, 113–114, 199, 201, 207
North Sotho 14, 21, 40–41, 79, 81, 83, 96–97, 139, 202–206

ornaments 208–209

patients, relations with healers 196–197
patrilineal descent 18–19, 57, 63, 98, 101–102
patrilineal kin 101–103
Pedi
– agriculture 51
– ancestor worship 153–154, 167
– bridewealth 126
– circumcision 139–143
– diviners 190
– ethnographic grouping 21
– federation 66, 85–86
– initiation 136
– rain rituals 81
– witchcraft 21, 171
– wives 57
– wooden figures 211
piacular rituals 162–165
political hierarchy 98–99
political system 66–73, 79, 83–87, 90
pollution beliefs 19–20, 178–183
polygyny 55–59, 117–118
popular assembly 73
pottery 26–29, 205–206
praise singers 70–71, 73, 80
pregnancy, pollution beliefs 181
– taboos 131
'priests' 156–158
property damage, punishments for 96
puberty rituals 134–136

rain doctors 81
rain rituals 80–81

San (Bushmen) 12, 23, *25*, 69, 81, 189
seduction 96, 98
serfs, political status 70
settlement patterns 21, 45–64
– patrilineal influence 18–19
sexual morality 98
Shona groups 12, *14*, 70
Shona language, influence on Venda 43
siblings, age difference 98, 105–107
snuff-boxes and spoons 205
sons, married, inclusion in homesteads 57–58
sororate custom 124
Sotho
– agriculture 49
– ancestor worship 19, 151
– chiefdoms 48–50, 72
– childbirth 132
– diviners 187, 189–191
– dress 207
– drums 213
– dwellings *20*
– ethnographic classification 21
– geographic regions 14, 39
– grain storage 52
– hunting 54
– initiation 15–16, 138–141
– kinship 105, 111–112
– knives *209*
– language 12, 40–43
– local government 79
– maternal kin 114
– marriage 16–18, 118–119, 122–123
– medicines 172
– origins 29
– political system 15, 31
– pollution beliefs 180–183
– pottery 206
– ritual pollution 19–20
– settlements 33–35, 48–49
– siblings 105, 107
– storage 207
– totem groups 113
– village life 62–63

– warriors 208
– weapons 210
– witchcraft 21, 170
– women's role 208
Sotho-Tswana 41
– ancestor worship 151
– descent groups 110–112
– initiation ceremonies 139
– wards 62
– wedding ceremonies 127–129
– wives' ranking 57
Sotho-Venda 13, 41
– ancestor worship 151, 167
– brides 128
– burial ceremonies 152
– descent groupings 110
– initiation 139
– kinship 105, 112
– 'priests' 157
– puberty rituals 134, 136
– shrines 155
– women as chiefs 58
South Nguni 14
– ancestor worship 151
– army organisation 16
– childbirth 132
– clans 110
– dress 207
– ethnographic classification 21
– hunting 54
– Khoisan influence 25
– life-cycle rituals 158–159
– medicines 172
– music 213
– neighbours 115
– political system 69, 71–72
– pollution beliefs 179–180
– pregnancy taboos 131
– red ochre, use of 108–209
– snuff boxes *205*
– tattooing 209
– utensils 176–177
– warriors 208
– witchcraft 170–171
– wives' ranking 55
South Sotho *14*
– agriculture 51
– ancestor worship 153–154
– army organisation 80
– bridewealth 126
– burial customs 153
– court actions 96–97
– dialect 40
– dress 207
– facial decoration 209
– initiation *132, 134, 137*
– pottery 206
– rain rituals 81
– war chiefs *69*
– war dances *67*
Southern Bantu 12, 17–19
spears 209–210
stock theft 96
stone structures 29–30, 49, 201
sub-chiefs, administrative functions 79, *92*
sub-wards 79
Swazi 14
– childbirth 132
– cultural grouping 41
– ethnographic classification 21
– fire-making 42
– first-fruits ritual *79*, 82
– hair dressing 209
– political system 15
– pottery 206
– reed dance *76*
– role of queen mother 75, *76*
– wives ranking *55*, 57
Swazi kingdom 66, 85

Tembe-Thonga 86
theft 96
Thembu *139, 179, 183*
– chiefdoms 68
– childbirth 132
– dialect 39
– diviners *179, 183*
– dress 207
– ethnographic classification 21
– initiation regalia 208
– Mfecane 32
– witchcraft 172
thwasa 186–188
totem groups 113
trade 27, 31–33
Tsonga
– agriculture 51
– ancestor worship 19, 151–152, 154, 158, 167
– cattle 49, 55
– chiefs 48, 71–72
– childbirth 132
– court actions 97
– descent grouping 110

– divination 187, 191–195
– drums 213
– dwellings *28*
– ethnographic classification 21
– fishing 54
– geographical regions 14, 39
– hairdressing 209
– headrests *200*, 204
– homesteads 28, 58
– initiation figures *199*
– kinship 103, 112–113, 164
– local government 79
– marriage rules 16–18
– maternal kin 173–174
– musical instruments 171
– pollution beliefs 179
– pottery 206
– prayers 152
– 'priests' 158
– proverbs and riddles 112
– puberty 134, 136
– rain rituals 81
– rite of kin reconciliation 164
– sacramental *Tsu* 162
– shrines 155–156
– storage 207
– village *27*
– warriors 208
– weapons 210
– witchcraft 170
– wooden carvings *199*–200, 211
– xylophones *213*
Tswana (West Sotho)
– advisory council 71
– agriculture 49, 51
– ancestor worship 158
– bridewealth 126
– burials 155
– cattle 49
– chiefs 72–73
– circumcision 139–140
– class distinctions 69
– corporal punishment 96
– cosmetics 205–209
– courts 96–97
– dialects 40
– diviners *169*
– dress 160–161, 207
– ethnographic classification 21, 30, 34–35
– grain storage *53*
– homestead *128*, 202–203
– kinship 105
– local government 79
– marriage rules 118–119, 122–123
– polygyny 117
– pottery 206
– rain doctor 197
– tribal splitting 68
– towns 30, 34–35
– utensils 160–161
– villages 62–63
– warriors *86*
twins 132–133, 178–179, 181

ukusisa (patron-client relationship) 96
urbanisation 217
utensils 204–205

Venda
– ancestor worship 19, 151, 154, 159
– chiefdoms 48–49
– chiefs 65, 67, 71–72, *156*
– childbirth 132
– class distinctions 69
– connections with Zimbabwe 33
– courtyards *40*, 204
– descent groupings 110
– divination 187, *191*, 192, 197
– door carving *156*, 205, 211
– dress 207
– drums 145, 211
– ethnographic classification 21
– first fruits ritual 82
– geographical regions 14, 39
– granaries *51*–52, *204*, 206–207
– headrests 39
– homesteads 58, *115*
– hunting 54
– influence of Sotho 40
– initiation 15–18, *138*, 143–146
– iron smelting *39*
– kinship 105, 112
– language 43
– law and customs 89, *94*, 97
– local government 62, 79
– marriage 16–18, 118–119, 122–123
– maternal kin 114
– musical instruments 213
– pregnancy 131
– political system 15
– pottery 206
– rain ritual 81
– ritual of puberty *133–136*
– River People 166

– rules of succession 67–68
– sacred stones *153*
– sacrifices 159
– settlements 48–49
– shrines 155
– storage 206–207
– totem groups 113
– tribal relations 69
– villages 58, **111**, *113*
– weapons 210
– women, status 58, 75, 105
– wooden figures 211
– worship 150
villages 58, 62–63, 79

wards 59–63, 71–72, 79, 99
warriors' weapons 210–211
weapons 209–210
wedding ceremonies 126–129
wind instruments 213
witchcraft and sorcery 19, 21, 97, 99, 169–178, 186
witchcraft executions 174–175, 177
wives, ranking 55–56, 58–59
– conflict situations 175, 178
– pregnancy taboos 131
– relationship with husband 98–99, 122–126, 127–129
women
– agricultural role 51
– clothing 207
– marriage ranking 55–57, 128–129
– political role 75–78
– pollution beliefs 179–181
– social role 98, 122–126
– status in Xhosa society 126
woman-to-woman marriage 126
women's courts 92
wood carving 205, 210–212

Xhosa 66
– army 80
– cattle 48, 50
– childbirth 132
– clans 110
– councillors 72
– courts 95
– Dali (belief in God) 150
– dialects 39–40, 43
– dress 207
– ethnographic classification 21
– *idini* ritual 162–163
– initiation 207–208
– Khoisan influence 25, 43
– marriages 120–121, 126
– pipes *210*
– politics 69
– spear throwing 209–210
– women's status *100*, 126
– witchcraft 172–173
– xylophones 211–213

Zimbabwe Empire 31–33, 85
– iron-age sites 27
– political conquest by Mzilikazi 70
Zulu
– ancestor worship 151, 154
– army 16, *202*
– blacksmith *200*
– burial customs 153
– cattle 53
– chiefs 71
– clans 110
– dialect 40, 43
– divination *172, 174*, 192
– dress 207
– ear piercing 209
– ethnographic classification 21
– folk tales 108
– hairdressing 209
– headrests 204
– homesteads *15, 50, 59*
– local government 62, 79
– marriages *123*, 127
– medicines 192–193, 196
– Nomkhubulwana 78
– political expansion 66–67
– political system 15, 85–87
– pollution beliefs 42, 180
– pottery *206*
– praise singers *80*
– pregnancy taboos 131
– puberty rituals 135–136
– rain ceremonies 81
– shields 210
– snuff spoons *205*
– *umkhosi* rite 82–83
– utensils *122*
– villages 62
– wards 62
– warriors *84*, 208
– women *128*